W9-CEZ-645

D. 38

HANDICRAFTS OF NEW ENGLAND

HANDICRAFTS OF NEW ENGLAND

Authentic Handicrafts from Maine, New Hampshire, Vermont, Massachusetts, Connecticut, and Rhode Island; All Are Referred to in the Text. The Shop Is Imaginary.

HANDICRAFTS
OF
NEW ENGLAND

by
ALLEN H. EATON

AUTHOR OF
HANDICRAFTS OF THE SOUTHERN HIGHLANDS

ILLUSTRATED

HARPER & BROTHERS PUBLISHERS
NEW YORK

HANDICRAFTS OF NEW ENGLAND

COPYRIGHT, 1949, BY HARPER & BROTHERS. PRINTED IN THE UNITED STATES OF AMERICA. ALL RIGHTS IN THIS BOOK ARE RESERVED. NO PART OF THE BOOK MAY BE REPRODUCED IN ANY MANNER WHATSOEVER WITHOUT WRITTEN PERMISSION EXCEPT IN THE CASE OF BRIEF QUOTATIONS EMBODIED IN CRITICAL ARTICLES AND REVIEWS. FOR INFORMATION ADDRESS HARPER & BROTHERS

FIRST EDITION

I-Y

To the Memory of My Father
JOHN BURNHAM EATON, Jr.
Once of Conway, Fryeburg, Hanover, and Boston, who, with his four brothers, carried to the Oregon country New England's way of right making and right doing, thus helping to make the western communities to which they moved better places to work in and to live in

337024

*Art when really understood is the province of every human being.
It is simply a question of doing things, anything well. It is not an
outside extra thing . . . He does not have to be a painter or a sculptor
to be an artist. He can work in any medium. He simply has to find
the gain in the work itself, not outside it.*
ROBERT HENRI

*We have lately become convinced that accurate work with carpen-
ter's tools, or lathe, or hammer and anvil, or violin, or piano, or
pencil, or crayon, or camel's hair brush, trains well the same nerves
and ganglia with which we do what is ordinarily called thinking.*
CHARLES ELIOT

*The pleasure which ought to go with the making of every piece of
handicraft has for its basis the keen interest which every healthy man
takes in healthy life, and is compounded chiefly of three elements:
variety, hope of creation, and the self-respect which comes of a sense
of usefulness, to which must be added that mysterious bodily pleasure which goes with the deft exercise of bodily powers.*
WILLIAM MORRIS

*We of the United States are amazingly rich in the elements from
which we weave a culture. We have the best of man's past on which
to draw, brought to us by our native folk and folk from all parts of
the world. In binding these elements into a national fabric of beauty
and strength, let us keep the original fibres so intact that the fine-
ness of each will show in the completed handiwork.*
FRANKLIN D. ROOSEVELT

*The things which men have made . . . are inevitably the best witness.
They cannot lie, and what they say is of supreme importance. For
they speak of man's soul and they show who are his gods.*
ERIC GILL

*There is no wealth but life. Life, including all its powers of love, of
joy, and of admiration. That country is richest which nourishes the
greatest number of noble and happy human beings.*
JOHN RUSKIN

CONTENTS

PART III

SIGNIFICANT INFLUENCES IN THE HANDICRAFT MOVEMENT

PART IV

VALUES OF HANDICRAFTS

ILLUSTRATIONS

PREFACE

Faced with the opportunity, the challenge, to say something in a couple of pages about Allen Eaton's incomparably valuable service to the cause of handicraft in the modern world, I hold my pen poised a long time over the paper. There is too much to say. His book combines detailed, accurate, factual statements about the present, a luminous historical treatment of the past, and a remarkably fine philosophical and psychological analysis of the underlying bases of hand skills. With which of these diverse values should the preface concern itself?

In the end, paradoxically, I believe the most emphatic, perhaps the most essential, comment to make is a negative one, to wit, that there is no nonsense about Mr. Eaton's attitude toward handwork. It is important, I feel, to get this said plainly because a great deal of nonsense has been written and spoken on this subject.

The prevalence of unsound, sentimental, and insincere talk about the value of making things by hand (in a world crammed with marvelously productive machines) has created—such is my observation—a prejudice against the whole idea in the minds of many of the people who might casually pick up this book, attracted perhaps by its fine illustrations.

They are often the very men and women who, although they don't realize it, are starved and pining for a vitamin essential to their personalities. Without it, they can no more thrive and grow strong than a person fed on devitalized, dried, ready-prepared food can thrive and grow strong without the saving daily salad. Many of them turn away from the florid ignorance and pretentiousness of the claims often made for hand skills. In so doing they turn their backs on a door open to health-restoring homely beauty, grace, and psychological equilibrium. They need Allen Eaton's fine book more than others.

So it is well to assure them that he is a fully intelligent, perfectly reasonable, modern intellectual, whose claim for the human values of creating things by hand—as set forth in his admirable last chapter of Summary and Conclusion—will convince any reader. Any reader, that is, who will take the trouble to open the inner door of his mind and push his prejudices aside for long enough to let his brains move freely.

In this last chapter the author sums up the meaning and vital importance of non-mechanical production in the twentieth century. He gives the reasons for this importance, reasons both temporary and eternal, for some stem from the special state of our contemporary society and its economics, and some are permanent elements in our human nature. His statement is written with such lucid and persuasive skill that the Preface can do no better than serve as signpost for those last pages.

Allen Eaton serves, patriotically, civic and national health and vigor as part of his campaign for more personal contentment. In giving many years of his life to the defense of this good cause, he has deserved well of the Republic. The theory of democracy has always recognized the need for political and economic freedom for each individual human being. The final paragraph of this book makes as fine a plea as was ever written for the added recognition by our democracy of the potential artistic dignity and value of every man and woman alive.

DOROTHY CANFIELD FISHER

Arlington, Vermont

INTRODUCTION

A STUDY of the handicrafts of New England might well be considered an inquiry into the place of handicrafts in our present civilization, for within her boundaries are combined all the elements which make what we call modern civilization.

Notwithstanding the great industrial and commercial developments of this region today, there is practiced within the states of Maine, New Hampshire, Vermont, Massachusetts, Connecticut, and Rhode Island perhaps the widest variety of handicrafts in any country. The spread of motivation ranges from those whose handicrafts must provide the necessities of life to others who, although free from economic pressure, still make objects with their hands because of man's natural urge to convert materials of his environment into useful and beautiful forms.

The word "handicraft," as used in this book, is a broad term including all those things which are shaped by hand either for the maker's own use or for others. The article may be fashioned entirely by hand, including the preparation of all the materials as in basketmaking; or it may be in part machine made, as in the preparation of woods for fine cabinetwork, and the machine spinning of thread and yarn to be woven on a hand loom. But if the final product, the character of the thing itself, is shaped by hand, it is an object of handicraft. Thus the old word "handicraft," as defined by Webster, is a good word for it says exactly what it means.

It seems unnecessary to say that the motive of this study is not to advocate substituting handmade for machine-made products, except in a few instances, nor the abandonment or curtailment of mass production, which has brought so many comforts to the people of America. It is an inquiry into the place of handicrafts in the economy and culture of the people of New England. An attempt is made to report ways in which they are recovering values that were lost in the change from a handicraft to a highly mechanized economy; and to suggest advantages and compensations which the new handicraft movement is bringing to individuals, to families, and to communities in all the New England states.

Both machine and hand production are essential to our economy and our culture; indeed, each is now amazingly dependent upon the other, but the hand comes first.

All that we owe or ever shall owe to tools and machines we owe first to the forming hand; there is no tool or instrument comparable to it. No paw of mammal or foot of bird, no teeth, horns, beak, tusk, trunk, tail, or fin can perform more than a fraction of the functions of the human hand with its thumb and articulating fingers. Some scientists attribute man's evolution and ascent mainly to this articulation of thumb and fingers. They claim that through his ability to pick up, to hold or drop, to pinch or push, to pull and twist, to thrust and throw, together with every conceivable kind of physical manipulation, man has arrived at his position of highest control in the animal kingdom.

The tools which man has discovered, invented, and used are extensions of his hand; every machine increasing and multiplying his output had first to be built by hand. When the machine stalls or breaks down, the only way to bring it into use again is through adjustments made primarily by the hand. It is not only the most nearly perfect instrument for manipulation that we know; it is also the center of the indispensable sense of touch. The human hand is a subject for deep contemplation, and the correlation of hand and mind must have high consideration in any plans for a happy and an enduring future.

With all deference to this superb instrument, there is much to be said for the ways in which its power has been increased. Although tools and machines are extensions of the hand, they are much more than that—they are multiplications of power, and it is largely through these multiplications that humanity has been reaching out toward that "era of abundance," which can be realized when man's moral concepts and ethical practices catch up with his techniques. An era of abundance, in our type of economy and culture, could never come through hand production alone; machine production is indispensable.

Yet necessary as mass production is to the solution of immediate problems, it alone will not save our world. There is desperate need to recapture values that have been lost in the transition from a handicraft to a highly industrialized economy and culture, and in a too heedless race for power, both personal and mass power. We must remind ourselves again and again of our relatedness to the earth which war in our time has so desecrated; we must regain the sense of respect, yes, of reverence for all life on the earth. We must recover; we must rebuild. Much of the rebuilding will be done by individuals, and slowly—by hand. Many of the processes of rehabilitation will be largely personal, a matter of individual adaptation and of growth, often from modest beginnings. This will be true of both simple and sophisticated people. All plans for such reconstruction must be referred back to the question: Will this course help the people to help themselves—not only to a better economic level, but to a better spiritual state—to more useful, more purposeful, and happier ways of life?

How then can more natural ways be found to supplant superficial ways, more cooperative ways to displace selfish ways? For one thing mass production should yield a margin of time for man's activities to become more creative. We can expect handicrafts to exert a restorative and healthful influence, leading those who pursue them to become more and more aware of their own relatedness to the natural world, and to find in cooperation with nature and with their fellows a better way of life. Essential self-reliance will come to many in the future as it is coming to an increasing number today, through related efforts of head and hand and heart.

The time is not far off, let us hope, when every kind of work will be judged by two measurements: one, of the product itself, how it appeals to us, how it conforms to our taste, how it seems to fit our needs; the other, of what making the object or doing the work means to the producer. When that time comes, handicrafts will be given a much more important place in our plan of living than they now have, for unquestionably they possess values which are not generally recognized. In New England many people are discovering these values; indeed, individuals and government are cooperating closely to encourage and to strengthen the handicraft movement.

GENERAL SCOPE AND PURPOSE OF THIS BOOK

On remote New England farms men make tools and equipment for agriculture which they cannot afford to buy—hoes, rakes, forks, grain scoops, beehives, wheelbarrows, hay racks, stone sleds, sleighs, ox-yokes, and numerous other articles; and fishermen along the seacoast build their dories and lobster boats, weave and repair their fishnets, make lobster traps, and whittle claw pins. In countryside and villages women, and sometimes men, card and spin wool from their own sheep or have it converted at a small mill into yarn from which they knit or crochet mittens, gloves, mufflers, sweaters; or they weave on hand looms for family use or for sale a great variety of garments and objects, such as rugs, curtains, towels, tablecloths, napkins, blankets, and bed coverings.

This work includes observations on all the handicrafts practiced in

New England as far as it has been possible to discover and study them. As to the craftsmen themselves, it will be understood that specific reference can be made to comparatively few of the many persons with whom contact has been established in the course of the study. Even thus restricted, many hundreds are referred to by name, and those who are mentioned will in a way be symbols of all.

The suggestion that a study of handicrafts in the New England states would be of benefit not only to the people of that area but to the handicraft movement throughout America was made by Mrs. J. Randolph Coolidge and Miss Jessie Doe of the League of New Hampshire Arts and Crafts. This proposal was supplemented by requests from several groups of craftsmen, and the study was begun in the Department of Arts and Social Work of Russell Sage Foundation in 1941 and was continued with interruptions during seven following years.

Persons who make useful and beautiful things by hand are coming to know that the work has satisfactions for both maker and user which society in the pursuit of happiness for its members must find ways to encourage and conserve. This truth, of which the writer has long been convinced, has once again become strikingly apparent while gathering materials for the present book. Parallel to this is the conviction that one of the most remarkable facts in the field of aesthetic experience is the ability of the untrained frequently to deal skillfully and movingly with the elements of material, design, and color. Reluctance to act in unaccustomed ways often restrains this faculty, but when it is forced out by external pressure (for example, the dire need to earn), or by some subjective experience, or even by a word of encouragement at the right moment, it sometimes appears in forms which are a challenge to the most highly trained and sophisticated.

In addition to gains that are accruing to New England as a region through the increasing support which she is giving to handicrafts, there is also the working out of patterns and forms of cooperation which, once established, can be extended to other parts of the country. New England in a sense belongs to all of us; New England is home, and what she is doing for herself in these economic and social experiments she is doing as well for other states of the Union, and for other countries of the world.

The purpose of the book is to present facts and to interpret them. On the factual side the objective has been to discover and describe, sometimes as individuals, at other times in relation to their organizations, what is probably the largest number of workers in handicrafts to be found in any area of equal size in our country. The attempt is made to bring out the wide range of objects made in this area and often to indicate their high standard of design and craftsmanship; it has also placed considerable emphasis upon the variety of taste displayed by producers and by users.

On the interpretative side the effort has been made to discover the values experienced by the craftsmen themselves, both the direct and indirect values connected with hand production. Every man labors either for the satisfaction which the work brings to him, that is, the direct return, or for the money he receives, the use of which brings him other satisfactions. In the latter case, economic reward is the main purpose, and how much he can earn, regardless of how he earns it, may be his chief interest.

The direct satisfactions in the work itself include social, educational, recreational, aesthetic, therapeutic, and ethical values. The most important fact to note here is that the direct and the indirect returns are not necessarily opposed to each other but are supplemental; that is to say, one who practices a handicraft chiefly for the money it brings will often experience the other satisfactions as well. Values to the consumer have also been indicated and some reasons given as to why the public is concerned with the handicraft movement and its encouragement.

Hundreds of calls upon individual craftsmen in their shops, studios, or homes were made in all the counties of the six New England states; craftsmen's fairs, sales, institutes, and exhibitions were visited and group meetings attended. In addition visits were paid to many museums, galleries, libraries, and private collections related to handicrafts, as well as to New England citizens who are not craftsmen but are interested in the movement.

Correspondence marked the study from the beginning. Many informing and helpful letters came from craftsmen who could not be reached personally. Visits were often followed by letters, and fuller data thus gathered. Correspondence was also carried on with a large number of organizations in this highly populated area which are actively engaged in handicrafts or in some way interested in them. Considerable study was made of the handicraft literature of New England—books, public and private documents, including early diaries and town records, magazine articles, newspaper reports, and an occasional thesis.

DIVISIONS OF THE BOOK

The book is divided into four parts: Part One, Backgrounds of New England Handicrafts, is intended to suggest early influences exerted on the evolution of our handicrafts by the first permanent English settlements on this continent. Reference is made to the appearance in America, late in the nineteenth century, of the Arts and Crafts Movement, which had its origin in England, and also to the contemporary handicraft movement. It is hoped that reference to these developments, even though treated briefly, will help the readers to feel the relatedness of the present movement to what has gone before.

Part Two, New England Handicrafts Today, comprising fourteen chapters, is the heart of the study and justification for it. An account is given of contemporary handicrafts from every state in the area, with separate chapters devoted to the main divisions of the subject. Here will be found the personal records of individual workers which give authenticity and life to the story of handicrafts in present-day New England.

Part Three, Significant Influences in the Handicraft Movement, is also an integral part of the story of contemporary handicrafts, but the emphasis in this part is shifted from the individual craftsman and his product to the contribution made by important private and state-supported organizations. The brief accounts given of some of these agencies outline their rise and function, their encouragement of good standards, and their ways of promoting production and suitable marketing facilities.

Part Four, Values of Handicrafts, is composed of two chapters. The first discusses briefly the growing therapeutic use of handicrafts since World War I. Occupational therapy is such an influence in spreading knowledge of handicraft values, and New England has been so eminent a pioneer in this field, that it seemed to justify a separate chapter, even though it had to be a brief one. The final chapter of the book gathers up the evidence of what has been stressed throughout, namely, the influence of handicrafts on individuals and on community life, suggesting once again their values to both maker and user.

The handicraft movement is bringing to an increasing number of people in New England and in every corner of America the satisfactions that come with freedom to choose what things they shall make, and the high privilege of making them well.

The writer cannot begin to acknowledge here his indebtedness to the persons in New England and out, whose cooperation has made this report possible; he hopes all who have helped will accept this general statement of his gratitude. He must, however, record the names of a few who have given indispensable collaboration in the course of the study. He is especially under obligation to Mrs. James

Shirley Eaton, Mrs. Edith D. Minor, and Miss Margaret R. Dunne, all of the professional staff of Russell Sage Foundation, without whose aid in the preparation of the manuscript the book could not have been completed; also to his former secretaries, Mrs. Matilda W. Heidtmann and Miss Sylvia C. Stone; to Mrs. Olive Johnson for assistance generously given since the retirement of the writer from the staff of the Foundation; and finally to his daughters, Betty Eaton for editorial suggestions and attention to countless details in manuscript and illustrations, and to Martha Eaton for designing and drawing the frontispiece and end papers.

Acknowledgment is also made to *School Arts Magazine* for permission to include in this book material from the article by the writer on Handicrafts in New England Today which appeared in its issue of April, 1945.

Part I

BACKGROUNDS OF
NEW ENGLAND HANDICRAFTS

CHAPTER 1

PILGRIM HANDICRAFTS AND SOME
EARLY INDUSTRIES

IF A history of handicrafts in New England were to be written, a
logical starting place would be that fateful December day in the
year 1620 at Plymouth, Massachusetts, when the Pilgrims from old
England began building their first house. It was Christmas Day, when
having come "to a conclusion by most voices to settle on the mainland," work was begun in earnest—about seven weeks after the
Mayflower with its company of 102 harassed and ailing but courageous
souls had first sighted land off Cape Cod. They had coasted outside and
inside the Cape, had sent small exploring parties up and down, and
had finally sailed from the little harbor under the northern tip of Cape
Cod directly across the bay to the more protected harbor of Plymouth.

All able-bodied men, and no doubt the older boys, went ashore that
Christmas morning with axes and saws "some to fell timber, some to
saw, some to rive, and some to carry, so no man rested all that day."
They cut the trees into dimensions and laid the foundation of their
first substantial dwelling. "Some made mortar and some gathered
thatch, so that in four days half of it was thatched." Each night they
returned perilously in their shallop or in their long boat to sleep on
board the *Mayflower*, except the men left on guard, and for them
rough, temporary shelters were thrown together. Into their Common
House, recorded to have been about twenty feet square, went such
skills and materials as the Pilgrim Fathers could muster. Here they
kindled the first fire for religious and economic freedom in America,
and here they planted the seeds of European culture which were to
grow into a new world.[1]

---

[1] Among our first-hand sources of information about the Plymouth Colony are
notes by Governor Bradford and others printed in England as early as 1622 and
now reissued in a popular edition as *Homes in the Wilderness: A Pilgrim's Journal
of Plymouth Plantation in 1620* by William Bradford and others of the Mayflower
Company. (New York, William R. Scott, Inc., 1939.) It is from this text that
phrases quoted above have been taken.

Thus, in response to urgent need, began the handicrafts of a transplanted people—a people whose progress in the use of metal and metal tools had already outdistanced the original inhabitants of America by thousands of years. The Indians of whom the Pilgrim settlers caught glimpses, half frightening, half reassuring, were still living in the stone age. If an Indian wanted to cut down a tree, he would build a fire around it and hack the charred wood away with his stone hatchet, burning and hacking again and again until the tree was severed. With what amazement he must have first watched these white men felling and cutting trees with their metal axes and saws; and wonder of wonders must have seemed to him the broadax in the hands of a skilled craftsman as he shaped a log into timber for house or barn or ship.

The mastery of metal marks for the anthropologist a spread of thousands of years in the relative progress of the white man over the "red savage" of America, as the Indian was called. But we have slowly come to understand that in broad ethical concepts the two races were not so widely divergent. In the matter of their material progress, however, there were differences even more striking than the mastery of metal by the white man indicates. The invention and development of the wheel and the domestication of animals are both gifts of the people of the Old World. They are monumental milestones in the cultural advance of the human race; and both are intimately related to the handicrafts with which this book is concerned.

The wheel as a mechanical contrivance, so the scientists tell us, as we rub our eyes in wonderment, was not known to the inhabitants of this continent until the white man brought it. There were no potter's wheels, no carts or wagons, no spinning wheels, no clocks known to the Indians, nor indeed any of those tools or contrivances which have wheels on, in, or under them. A few American Indians had learned of the wheel about a century and a quarter before the coming of the Pilgrims, when Columbus and his immediate followers landed; but it is certain that until the Pilgrims came the Indians of the northeastern coast of America knew little or nothing about it. In Chapter 5 we shall be reminded of how the Spanish of the Southwest and the Indians and their descendants today use not the wheel but the hand spindle for making beautiful thread and yarn.

Some appreciation of the importance of the wheel to our civilization may come to us if we try to think of a single creature comfort that does not owe its origin in some degree to the wheel. This will explain the excitement with which both specialists and laymen follow attempts to discover whence came the first potter's wheel to be used in America, or when the first spinning wheel or wagon was brought to New England or made there.

A like fascination attaches to domestic animals and their appearance on this continent. The principal domestic animals of Europe were introduced by the Spaniards into the South and Southwest of what is now our country. There was not a horse, a cow, a domestic sheep, a tame goat, or a donkey in America until the coming of the Spaniards. What they and other Europeans did in the South and West, the English did a century later for the New England area.

Every student of handicrafts will realize the importance of domestic animals in the development of craftsmanship not only in New England but in every part of the United States. The textile industry in this country began, one might say, with the fleece of the first sheep brought to New England in 1629. In this study our minds will travel onward to our own day when spinning and weaving of wool by hand, sometimes from the weaver's own sheep, have again come into the home, not as the primary and principal means of providing clothing, but as supplementary means.

It is difficult to realize the tremendous contrast between the two cultures which met in New England when the Pilgrims settled at Plymouth and came in contact with the Indians three and a quarter centuries ago. But striking as was this contrast, there were certain common denominators; the one with which we are chiefly concerned is that each civilization supported and was supported by a handicraft culture. At that time everywhere the human race was dependent chiefly upon agriculture and handicrafts, supplemented by hunting and fishing, themselves handicrafts in the broad sense of being unmechanized. Among European countries, of course, there was relatively much commerce, but people on the American frontier then, and for long after, depended for subsistence largely upon the work of their own hands. In the early years in America man was usually both his own powerhouse and engine; later he gained more power from his domestic animals and still more through the harnessing of air by the windmill and water from streams and tides by the water wheel. One of the earliest windmills to grind grain in New England still remains in good working condition on the island of Nantucket.

Agriculturally, the Indians, although their methods were primitive, laid the new settlers from Europe under very great obligations. From them the Pilgrims learned how to grow corn and other food plants which the Indians had not only "tamed" but developed. Even today more than 50 per cent of all the agricultural products of the United States is obtained from plants discovered or developed by natives of this country before the white man came. Among these are corn, potatoes, tomatoes, beans, squashes, and peppers, foods now raised in many countries of the world, but unknown, it is believed, outside of America until after the return of Columbus and other explorers to Europe. To this list of native plants should be added cotton and tobacco. In hunting and fishing the skills of the Indian were obviously of great help to the settlers.

the Indians

As for their native handicrafts, we are beginning to recognize, however tardily, the Indians' extraordinary gifts in the creative designing and skillful execution of their objects of utility and of ceremony. One of the fine chapters in the history of human culture is that relating to the arts and crafts of the American Indians.

Both white and red men in this interchange of culture profited by the past experiences and the achievements of the other. This blending of cultures and mutual cooperation which we note in colonial New England marked many areas where white men and Indians came together and is an element too frequently ignored in our history.

CLUES TO EARLY HANDICRAFT

The written record of craftsmen and their achievements in the earliest days at Plymouth is exceedingly scanty. It appears from a book written by Captain John Smith, *A Description of New England,* published in London in 1616, that he had prepared maps of the Massachusetts territory already explored by him, had recommended that it be named New England, and had advised how to provide for the fourfold task of planting, housing, trading with the Indians, and defense against them. He had advocated for colonization in New England the inclusion of "Carpenters, Masons, Fishers, Fowlers, Gardiners, Husbandmen, Sawyers, Smiths, Spinsters, Taylors, Weavers, and such like." The Pilgrims had studied the maps and read Captain Smith's observations, and therefore were equipped with a considerable fund of information. He had offered, as he records in a later book, to conduct the expedition of the Pilgrims to New England country, but they declined his services because, as he explained, "my books and maps were much better cheape to teach them, than myselfe." This was possibly one of the reasons, but by no means the only one, for declining his offer.

The passenger list of the *Mayflower* bore only a slight resemblance to the list of master craftsmen prepared by Captain Smith. Much research has been attempted to discover the origin and occupations of the first arrivals, and not without some success.² Not all the designations quoted by authorities are identical, but there is little doubt that among the ship's company were a sawyer, one or two carpenters, a "smith," and a cooper, young John Alden, who was taken for a year's service as a hired man and set to care, according to the law, for the ship's hogsheads of water, beer, and "strong water." All these occupations could be turned to good use in the building of shelters, which at first was the people's chief concern.

During that terrible first winter, when fire destroyed the thatched roof of their first building, and before March 21 when the entire Mayflower Company were finally assembled to live ashore on "ye firme and stable earth, their proper elemente," they had managed to erect individual houses. These were not the log cabins fondly remembered by most of us from the illustrations in our history primers. The few "small cottages" were probably of "wattle and daub construction with steep thatched roofs, typically English in design."³ But these first shelters did not determine the later pattern of the houses and buildings that have given New England the architecture of distinction admired and cherished throughout our country and the world. Death and sickness had left at one time only six or seven able-bodied men to do the work of the colony, the clearing, building, and planting. Still Governor Bradford could write reassuringly of the first return of autumn, nine months after the fire: "They begane now to gather in ye small harvest they had, and to fitte up their houses and dwellings against winter, being all well recovered in health and strength, and had all things in good plenty."

A few important hints concerning handicrafts are to be found in the usually cryptic reports on the cargoes of the ships returning to England during the first year or two of Plymouth settlement. In November, 1621, the second contingent of colonists, thirty-five in number, "most of them lusty yonge men and many of them wild enough," as described by Governor Bradford, came on the *Fortune*. The ship "was speedily dispatcht away, being laden with good clapboard as full as she could stowe, and 2 hoggsheads of beaver and otter skins."⁴ The skins were probably traded from the Indians. With all the building, planting, and

² Ames, Azel, *The May-flower and Her Log*, July 15, 1620—May 6, 1621, Boston, Houghton Mifflin and Co., 1907; Willison, George F., *Saints and Strangers*, New York, Reynal and Hitchcock, 1945.

³ Willison, *op. cit.*, pp. 165–166.

⁴ Bradford, William, *History of Plymouth Plantation*. Collections of the Massachusetts Historical Society, Fourth Series, vol. 3, Boston, Little, Brown and Co., 1856, pp. 105, 106, 108.

other activities engaging the first settlers it was unlikely that they could so quickly have found time for serious trapping. As to the clapboards, however, there can be no possible doubt that they were prepared by the Pilgrims.

These clapboards offer the first substantial clue in our search for facts about early craftsmanship in the colony. But the word "clapboard" had at that time, and has even now, two meanings: one, a narrow board used in cooperage; the other, a long board used for houses and barns and often called siding. Because there was a demand in England for both kinds of clapboard, we are uncertain as to which kind made up the cargo. The fact that John Alden was a cooper and undoubtedly had with him the tools for his work might suggest that the boards he would have made were cooperage boards. But there is another more reasonable explanation. The clapboard, in the sense of siding, was used at that time in the southeastern counties of England from which most of the original Pilgrims came. So the clapboards that were shipped back to England may have been for house building.

The question arises as to how these clapboards were made, whether they were split or "rived" by hand, as is still done in the Southern Highlands of the United States, or were sawed out. They may, of course, have been sawed lengthwise by hand, for the pit saw and other saws for converting logs into lumber had long been used in Europe. If sawed, some contrivance then used in England would undoubtedly have been employed, and such may have been brought over by John Alden the cooper, or by the carpenters, who would probably have had with them the best apparatus they could command. "Clapboards" as used to describe cargoes of returning ships may have meant any type of board or timber, split or sawed, even including small logs which could be loaded onto the ships; for such forms of timber were being worked up in England at that time into various kinds of lumber for building and other purposes.

In the spring of 1622, following the *Fortune*, a shallop bringing seven persons to the colony came from a third ship, the *Sparrow*, a fishing vessel then off the coast of Maine. A letter to the Governor from the owner of the *Sparrow* begged the colonists to "goe in hand to fell trees and cleave them to ye end lading may be ready, and our ship stay not." To one who works in lumbering today the word "cleave" would mean to split or rive, that is, to cut the long way of the grain, which would indicate that the lumber was made by splitting. But for centuries "cleave" has also meant to "sever" or "cut up," so we do not know whether instructions were given simply to fell the trees and cut them into logs, or to split them. In this case, we do not even know if they were intended for "clapboards." However, we do know from the cargo records that before the end of the first year the colonists were already engaged in the logging and lumbering industry. It is recorded of a later arrival, the *Anne*, that she returned to England in the early autumn of 1623 laden with clapboards.

These several references to clapboard are not without purpose. In the first place, "clapboards" are integral parts of the typical New England house of today. The clapboard house was almost inevitably the kind of house in its structural and related elements that the Pilgrims would build after their first need for any kind of temporary shelter had been met. It was of timber because that was most abundant. In the second place, it is the clapboards and the type of timber frame for their support which have made it possible to trace the New England house back to its prototype in the southeastern counties of England.

The origin of the houses which established the general pattern of what came to be known as "New England architecture" was long a mystery, but it is no longer so. In *The Homes of the Pilgrim Fathers* Martin S. Briggs connects the seventeenth century New England wooden houses with their "predecessors, contemporaries, and counterparts in the districts of England from which the colonists came." He has also given consideration to the question "whether Holland, the refuge of the exiles before they became Pilgrims to the New World, had any share in dictating the form and construction of this rustic architecture." The investigation begins with the study of the Separatists in England, and of the religious movement which caused them to seek refuge in Holland; a study of the architecture follows, especially the timber-framed houses of these English counties; then an extensive examination and recording of the houses in America built by the Pilgrims from 1635 to 1685, of which a considerable number still stand —Briggs lists sixty-five. These houses in both England and America, including barns and other structures, are compared in their methods of construction, and are presented in drawings and photographs in addition to the text. A description is also given of the comparatively few timber-framed houses at this time in Holland.

The result of the inquiry, it seems clear, is the establishment of the fact that the American houses, timber framed with exteriors of clapboards, are definite reflections of the timber-framed houses of southeastern England. The inquiry also made clear that such influence as Dutch timber-framed houses exerted, of which there is some evidence, was quite likely to have been from Holland directly on the domestic architecture of the English counties rather than on English refugees who had lived in Holland just previous to sailing on the *Mayflower* for America. It is in the southeastern counties that practically all the timber-framed and weather-boarded houses are to be found in England today. In fact only there, according to Briggs, had houses of such type been developed by 1620. Thus it appears that New England architecture was largely derived from this area.

Twenty years after the landing of the Pilgrims we find a population of about 25,000 in the Massachusetts colony, of whom it has been estimated that close to two-thirds still traced their origin to southeastern England. Religious persecution no longer constituted the motive for emigration—new settlers were coming from other parts. But those who came in the first years had set their indelible stamp on the culture of New England.

LATER COLONIAL HANDICRAFTS

Although no attempt will be made in this book to trace in detail the development of handicrafts from their beginning, certain changes have taken place which help to give a thread of continuity from the earliest days to our present mechanized economy.

It was a handicraft culture carried on mainly in colonial farm and village homes, which brought this nation to its birth and gave it the needed strength to take its place among the great governments of the world. Handicrafts and the small industries growing out of them formed the economic base which made victory and survival possible. For those who fought and for those at home who helped to sustain the ragged little army and the small improvised navy, it was the homely crafts of field and fireside that made the difference between hard-won success and desperate failure. The same was true of the War of 1812 when the people girded themselves once again to maintain the liberty of the young nation.

The part they played in the War for Independence is best understood by remembering two facts: first, it was the almost continuous policy of England to regard the colonies as subjects whose function was to promote the industrial development of the mother country; and second, when commerce was cut off from England the colonies had no way of supplying most of their needs except through their handicrafts, or "household manufactures," as they were accurately called. To encourage these the colonists passed ordinances and laws, imposed fines and punishments, and provided rewards to prevent waste and to induce thrift and production.

Among the expressions of the growing national spirit were spinning bees and contests in which "young ladies of good reputation," as well as older women of the community, would come together in a neighbor's home, and with hand carders and spinning wheels demonstrate their desire for independence and their ability to attain it by spinning strenuously the whole day through.

It is amazing to consider the number and variety of industries that were carried on in the home, from the making of many types of textiles to the making of iron nails. The household manufactures enumerated in Hamilton's famous *Report on Manufactures* in 1791 was to the people of his time a prosaic list of handicrafts made at home; to us it is an eloquent explanation of why and how the colonists were able to achieve and maintain their freedom. It is not to be understood that New England was alone in this; indeed, other colonies met the problems in the same way.

FROM HANDICRAFTS TO FACTORY

Following the War for Independence a tendency to transfer manufacture from farm to factory appeared. For two hundred years, from 1620 to 1820, New England was largely in the handicraft stage, but then small factories sprang up along rivers and streams capable of developing water power. Such modest enterprises included weaving and spinning mills, tanneries, forges, grist- and sawmills.

The restoration of George Washington's home in Mount Vernon gives a vivid and reminiscent picture of how nearly everything needful for the support of life was produced in his day around the great estate. Here were all the facilities for making fabrics of cotton, linen, or wool, and until after the American Revolution the cloth for much of the clothing for Washington and his family and all of it for his workers was made on the home place. Broadly speaking, this was true of the Virginia colony and the other colonies as well. But it was a proud day for industrial America, says Ella Shannon Bowles in *Homespun Handicrafts*, when, on delivering his first address to Congress in 1790, President Washington wore a suit made of broadcloth from the woolen factory of Colonel Jeremiah Wadsworth of Hartford, Connecticut, where all the processes had been performed in the factory except the spinning. Spinning was done in the homes on single wheels. Soon even spinning was done in mills. New England was the leader in the movement that resulted first in factory-made cloth being supplied to people to be made up at home, later in its being converted into factory-made clothing and other marketable articles. Ultimately New England became one of the most highly industrialized sections of our country.

In the collections of old tools and machinery in which New England is rich one may see much evidence of inventiveness. From the earliest settlements everything that could be changed into a better tool or machine was worked on. In scores of instances the hand product of some countryman or villager was of such worth that a small business was built around it and in time, through Yankee ingenuity and organization, this handicraft beginning developed into a great industry. In the early days of the United States Patent Office, in proportion to population, more patents were issued to inventors in New England than in any other part of our country.

The increase in factory-made goods became especially marked at the turn of the nineteenth century, and after the Civil War the corresponding decline in handicrafts was pronounced. The "back country," however, was an exception for here many thrifty New Englanders have always made, and still make, tools, implements, and farming and fishing equipment in order to save a little or to get something better than they can afford to buy. Changes from water power to steam, and toward the end of the century to electric power, and the invention of many new machines, together with abundant labor, much of it from Europe, brought on a period of great industrial expansion, accompanied by the appearance on the market of many poorly designed and cheaply made goods. At this point a reaction set in against these often inferior articles of mass production.

It was in the closing years of the nineteenth century and early in the twentieth century that a new voice was heard, at first in tones of inquiry and then of protest, coming across the sea from England—a voice which, as has been stated, ushered in what was know there, and later here, as the Arts and Crafts Movement. This was the first effective challenge to mechanized and mass production in our country. It raised the question with which this book is primarily concerned: Is mechanized and mass production to be accepted as the sole method of meeting man's wants and needs; or is there to be a place in our economy and in our culture for hand production or handicrafts? The beginning of the answer to this question will be found in the following chapter.

CHAPTER 2

THE ARTS AND CRAFTS MOVEMENT AND HANDICRAFTS TODAY

A STUDENT of handicrafts observing their history from its beginning with the Pilgrims in New England will find himself, for several reasons, viewing their development from a point of exceptional vantage. He will be standing on a high bridge, so to speak, from which he can see clearly both backward and forward.

Looking backward, he will see the Pilgrims as a connecting link with the Old World whose artifacts reach as far as the memory and intelligence of man can carry us. Looking forward, he will see on this continent a handicraft and agricultural economy, including the important American Indian element, prevailing for about two hundred years, followed in turn by the unprecedented development of mechanized and mass production, to which we have referred, and with which we are so familiar today.

Looking more intently from this vantage point, bridging two worlds, the student will also discern, at the close of the nineteenth century, that new influence, the arts and crafts movement starting in England then extending to the United States, an influence which encouraged a partial return to the practice of handicrafts. Looking still farther ahead he will see, in our own day and in our own country, a return to a far wider practice of work with the hands in what is now known as the handicraft movement.

THE ARTS AND CRAFTS MOVEMENT IN ENGLAND

Toward the end of the nineteenth century the prevalence in England of cheap, badly designed, factory-made goods resulted not only in protest, but in the encouragement of the application of beauty to useful objects. The leader of this movement was the English artist, writer, and reformer, William Morris. But the basic ideas from which it was derived had been impressed upon the conscience of England

13

by Thomas Carlyle, whose doctrine of work and whose sincerity had influenced John Ruskin, and he in turn with his new sociological, political, and aesthetic concepts was the determining influence upon the thought of William Morris.

In his book, *Chapters in the History of the Arts and Crafts Movement*, Oscar Lovell Triggs brings out these relationships. Ruskin, he says, was the first to include the arts as an integral part of our modern economic system. The economy that concerned itself with merely objective wealth Ruskin called the science of avarice. In this connection he posed his famous and still unresolved question, "How can society consciously order the lives of its members so as to maintain the largest number of noble and happy human beings?"

As one step toward this end Ruskin believed that each man "should learn to do something finely and thoroughly with the hand, so as to let him know what *touch* meant; and what stout craftsmanship meant; and to inform him of many things besides, which no man can learn but by some severely accurate discipline in doing." At about the time that Morris was entering Oxford University Ruskin's *Stones of Venice* was published. Morris maintained that in this book was first to be found the doctrine that art is the expression of man's pleasure in work. "It seemed," he said in after years, "to point out a new road on which the world should travel."

Mr. Triggs remarks that where Ruskin theorized, Morris demonstrated, devoting himself to the problems of the worker and his relation to art. In one of his appeals to bring the element of personal satisfaction and even pleasure into the daily task, Morris once said, "If I were to work ten hours a day at work I despised and hated, I should spend my leisure I hope in political agitation, but I fear in drinking." To the end of his days he was to protest against "the reckless waste of life in the pursuit of the means of life."

What may well be called the mission of Morris and his associates— to mention only a few of the most distinguished, Edward Burne-Jones, T. J. Cobden-Sanderson, C. R. Ashbee, Walter Crane, Emery Walker, and W. R. Lethaby—began with exhibitions of handicrafts selected for the quality of their design and their fine workmanship and especially for their fitness for use. They were held under the auspices of the Arts and Crafts Exhibition Society, which the group had organized in London in 1888. Attention was focused upon the qualities that articles of home and everyday life might have, representing them to be as worthy of the consideration of artists as are the traditionally fine arts of painting and sculpture. No one had done so much as Morris to make such objects important, and his advice to all homemakers, often quoted today, was: "Have nothing in your houses which you do not know to be useful or believe to be beautiful."

These exhibitions created so great a demand for objects of beauty in the home that Morris and his associates engaged in the making of furniture, textiles, wallpaper, and perhaps most important of all, in the printing and making of books. The flow of fine handwork, the frequent exhibitions, lectures, and articles, accompanied by inspired teaching, resulted in raising the level of taste and sensitivity to new heights throughout England, and set a standard for other countries of the world. Among those to respond best to the stimulus from England were Norway, Sweden, and Denmark, but every nation of Europe was touched to some extent, and England found herself a leader in the arts of the common people. Of all the lands coming under its influence probably none owes the movement so much as the United States.

THE ARTS AND CRAFTS MOVEMENT IN THE UNITED STATES

A talented young craftsman in the art of printing, Henry Lewis Johnson of Boston, had followed the progress of the handicraft revival in England through the public exhibitions held between 1888 and 1896. At a meeting of prominent citizens in the Museum of Fine Arts in Boston, on January 4, 1897, Mr. Johnson presented his belief that a similar movement in this country would have a wholesome influence on popular taste and would create a desire for more beautiful objects made under better standards of workmanship. Such an exhibition was arranged and opened at Copley Hall in Boston on April 3, 1897, where it continued for two weeks and was attended by visitors from New York, Philadelphia, Baltimore, Chicago, and San Francisco. Newspaper accounts of the exhibition were published in both the large and small cities of this country.

The result in America of this ferment was the incorporation in Boston of the Society of Arts and Crafts, described in some detail in Chapter 17. In the Middle West a similar development was being followed, which resulted in the formation at Hull House of the Chicago Arts and Crafts Society, antedating the one in Boston by a few months. Many other handicraft societies sprang up, but the Boston Society is the oldest of those still active. This organization did more than plant the seeds of the Old World in the soil of New England; it helped to scatter them throughout the land, transmitting to other towns and cities ideas inherent in the arts and crafts movement. Ten years after its inception the Society became the center of a national group of twenty-four member societies known as the National League of Handicraft Societies (organized in February, 1907). The number of constituent societies soon increased to thirty-three, of which thirteen were in New England. They reached from Portland, Maine, to Portland, Oregon, and from Minneapolis to New Orleans.

With due credit to all who had a part in these far-flung organizations, the National League of Handicraft Societies was primarily the result of stimulation from New England. By this time the Society of Arts and Crafts, through the influence of its salesroom and its educational program, had begun to make a definite impression upon the taste of this country. Its magazine, *Handicraft*, first published in Boston in 1902, was also a strong influence in the development of the movement. The best record of activities of the many contemporary handicraft groups is to be found in various issues of this magazine. *The Craftsman*, published from 1901 until 1916 and edited by Gustav Stickley, was another influence in popularizing and advancing the movement. It was "an illustrated monthly magazine in the interest of better art, better work, and a better and more reasonable way of living."

The pioneers who took part in the arts and crafts movement not only served their day well but in many instances became links with the later movement which this book records. Among those who were thus active, Frederic Allen Whiting, the first secretary of the Society of Arts and Crafts, should be mentioned not only for his pioneer work but for his long-continued efforts in the interest of handicrafts. He later became president and director of the American Federation of Arts—an organization that zealously promoted the principles and traditions of sound handwork. During his administration the Federation circulated, in 1933, an exhibition of the Southern Highland Handicraft Guild, which went as far west as Omaha and was received hospitably by several art museums, including the Corcoran Art Gallery, in Washington, D. C., and the Brooklyn Museum of Art.

Robert W. de Forest, for many years president of the American Federation of Arts, was an untiring advocate of the arts for all people. In addition to leadership ably exercised through his presidency of the Metropolitan Museum of Art in New York, he gave invaluable support to handicrafts through other organizations with which he was identified. Here should be noted the interest in handicrafts and the cooperation of Miss Leila Mechlin during her long service as secretary of the Federation; also the special work of Horace H. F. Jayne as its director. Mr. Jayne assembled and sent an exhibition of handicrafts to the International Exposition held in Paris in 1937, the first of its kind to go abroad from the United States. The author was the first field secretary, and later an adviser to the American Federation of Arts, who originated and directed the Arts and Crafts of the Homelands Exhibitions in New York State, projects in Americanization. He also assembled the first traveling exhibition of Southern Highland Handicrafts for the Federation, and with its cooperation and that of Russell Sage Foundation he organized and directed for the seventy-fifth anniversary of the United States Department of Agriculture the first national Rural Arts Exhibition ever held in our country. These three exhibitions were predominantly handicrafts.

Outside of the New England area handicrafts have received helpful encouragement from New Englanders who, going into other sections, have themselves become leaders of projects and programs, or have cooperated with local leaders in the advancement of their work. This has been especially true in the Southern Highlands. Here a considerable number of New Englanders have worked and influenced some of the trends in this vast mountain region, where a continuous handicraft culture has existed longer than in any other part of our country. Among these pioneer workers in Highland handicrafts must be noted Miss Frances L. Goodrich of Asheville, North Carolina, who was born and reared in New England, and Mrs. Olive Dame Campbell, a native of Massachusetts, a founder and for many years director of the John C. Campbell Folk School at Brasstown, North Carolina, where the handicraft program is one of the vital factors in the economy and culture of the community.

THE HANDICRAFT MOVEMENT TODAY

The handicraft movement of today, although it differs in many respects from the earlier arts and crafts movement, owes much to it in point of traditions and leadership. Here, however, it seems appropriate to indicate some of the divergencies. The influence of the former movement was felt mainly in the cities and towns where the societies were functioning. The objects made were usually good in design, in materials, and excellent in execution, but they were comparatively expensive, and for this reason their influence failed to reach many persons, especially those living in villages and on farms. In contrast, many of the objects now being made are within reach of a modest purse. Hence they represent a more democratic trend in the sense that they provide for wider participation. The fact that large numbers of the population of a rural area may participate in the rural handicraft movement gives tremendous impetus to it. Many who formerly felt excluded from creative artistic work are now associated with it. Certainly the movement today is more general, with prospects of unlimited growth. Its strength comes largely from rural areas, but often the urban centers with their teachers, craftsmen, libraries, museums, and interested citizens give invaluable cooperation. In addition assistance has been provided by a few state-supported handicraft services.

In the country people are continuously compelled to use their heads and hands in devising and inventing for everyday needs. This condition has led to the making of original objects, as well as those of traditional character, which often deserve recognition as rural arts. Country life holds two great gifts for most of its inhabitants: space and time. Elbow room is a common possession, and most rural people have intervals of leisure, seasonal or otherwise, for pursuits which are not easily fitted into urban schedules. Although few country people can gain a livelihood entirely from making and selling handicrafts, many supplement their income in this way. Important as the economic objective is, however, it does not by any means comprise all the values inherent in rural handicraft practices. Reference is made to these other values throughout this book and they are briefly summarized in the concluding chapter.

The present-day handicraft movement in New England is much wider in its implication than the making of things by hand for personal and home use. It is in reality a new and an inevitable movement growing out of a number of influences, past and present, which, taken together, distinguish it as something unique in the development and progress of our civilization.

Among the influences which have shaped and are shaping this revival in New England, at least the following five should be noted: First is the long, persistent influence of pride of workmanship in both sea and land trades, which, ingrained in early New England craftsmen, is partly an inheritance from the apprenticeship system of Europe. This pride of craftsmanship is still active in descendants of the artisans of earlier days. The second factor, the early arts and crafts movement of English origin, not only protested against machine products and processes; but advocated original design and hand execution, and its artists and craftsmen produced superior objects of use and beauty. Third, and more recently, certain private and state forms of encouragement were given the handicraft movement. Fourth was the depression of the 1930's during which countless unemployed persons, having been separated from the factory and mill tools and machines of production, turned to whatever they could make with their hands and home tools.

Fifth is the recent and unprecedented use of handicrafts in occupational therapy.

Fortunately there is considerable evidence of the part played by each of these influences. Of the pride in work and excellent craftsmanship in colonial years and in the early days of the Republic, many records survive in houses, barns, churches, schools, town halls, state capitols, and in the almost unlimited examples of special handicrafts. No other area of our country has done so much as New England to preserve the cultural record of the white race on this continent. From the earliest days New Englanders have carefully recorded contemporary events and preserved the fragments of her heritage—achievements which, both in number and in quality, are not easily matched. One can live New England's history over and over again in her literature and in her relics, for in the preservation of each she has been provident; and many of the best traditions of early New England are still to be found among today's carpenters, blacksmiths, housewives, and the various other craftsmen and artists, who are now the transmitters of old cultural values and the inventors of new ones.

The influence of New England's craftsmen and of their skills has spread in some form to every part of the Union, mainly through the migration of her sons and daughters. This has been especially true in the northern states extending from New England's western borderline to the Pacific Ocean. One of the best records of this influence is in architecture, in which so many of the handicrafts are combined. In several western states houses of the New England type followed the early log cabins and sod houses of the pioneers, and in the Far West there were villages almost as "New England" as those of the old homeland. The little town of Union, Oregon, where the writer was born, was in frontier days one of these instances. A book by I. T. Frary, *Early Homes of Ohio*, gives excellent illustrations of this westward trend of the New England influence in architecture.

No more need be said at this point of the second factor in the development of New England handicrafts, namely, the arts and crafts movement, because a discussion of its influence on the growth of handicrafts in our own country appears both in the early part of this chapter and in Chapter 17.

Of the third influence, that of recent private organizational, and state efforts, there is much evidence. It is in part an extension of the arts and crafts movement of earlier years and has made itself felt in the various means taken to encourage local centers of work and to record and stimulate progress by exhibitions and permanent collections. Among such efforts to encourage a wider practice of handicrafts

in New England, were the exhibitions of 1927 and 1928 known as
Craftsmen at Work, fostered by the Women's Educational and Industrial Union of Boston, under the direction of Miss Ethel Browne.
These had a very definite influence on the newly forming handicraft
revival in New England. New Hampshire was the first state in the
country to offer governmental assistance to the handicraft movement.
The late John G. Winant, when governor of New Hampshire, appointed a commission in 1931 to promote a program for the state, and
Mrs. J. Randolph Coolidge, who had already shown vision and leadership in the field in connection with Center Sandwich Home Industries,
was asked to serve as chairman. The League of New Hampshire Arts
and Crafts, the story of which is told in Chapter 18, was founded with
Mrs. Coolidge as president. Later Vermont and Maine for a period
formed their handicraft services supported by state funds.

Fourth   The fourth influence, the great depression of the 1930's, affected
the handicraft movement and was affected by it in two ways: first,
when people found their jobs gone and sometimes their life savings,
they began, as has been said, to work with their hands at whatever
they could to produce life's necessities, to barter or sell their handwork.
The result was that many handicraft projects were developed in New
England, as elsewhere in the country, some of which still continue.

Another effect of the depression and its accompanying unemployment was the establishment by the federal government of work
programs for unemployment relief among which handicraft projects
were prominent. Brief mention should be made here of two of the
outstanding achievements: One is the Index of American Design which
records by photographs, drawings, and paintings the handicraft subjects dating from colonial days to near the end of the nineteenth
century. These are now preserved in the National Gallery in Washington. The second is the Connecticut Work Projects Administration
Crafts Project, one of the most successful of the national work-relief
programs in the field of the arts.

Fifth   The fifth and most recent influence on the handicraft movement
in New England has been the greatly expanded application of occupational therapy in connection with treatment of the sick and wounded
in our armed forces. Hundreds of young men and many women are
being helped by handicraft therapy back to health, and not infrequently to a new and permanent life interest. Also must be noted the
unprecedented use made of handicrafts in recreational programs for
men and women through the Arts and Skills Corps of the American
National Red Cross.

It has not been possible to make a study of handwork in present-day New England without being conscious of the old English strain in her population. One is likely to think of that first and last because it is the positive element, the persistent and permanent strain which sets the character of the region. But positive and pronounced as it is, the English stock is not all of New England. There are now many newer strains that have come to our shores from various countries, especially in the past fifty or sixty years, representing origins as mixed as can be found in any section of America. In the fishing villages along the coast, on the inland farms, and in the industrial cities people have come from everywhere, and have made, and are making, many important contributions to the handicrafts of the area. An indication of this variety was suggested in the Exhibition of Contemporary New England Handicrafts held at the Worcester Art Museum in the winter of 1943 and recorded in its catalogue as follows:

> The student of this exhibition will find names and patterns and objects that . . . bring to mind the English Colonists and still others that recall immigrant ships and modern ocean steamers and lands across our borders both north and south. It is this combination of people that is contemporary New England. . . . Among the craftsmen of this exhibition he will find a few American Indians. He will see the names Alden, Adams, Wentworth and many others reminiscent of early New England. Finally he will meet with such names as Dufresne and Marcoux from French Canada; Miettinen from Finland; Anderson, Malmstrom, and Ingles from Sweden; Kunberger from Germany; Czarnecki from Poland; Royko and Rehorka from Czechoslovakia; Krumin and Namaka from Russia; Pellegrini, Conti, and Stellato from Italy; and many from other homelands.

Nearly all of these names and others equally significant appear in the present study. Thus in New England handicrafts today one often discovers traditional symbols and Old World techniques, from the homelands of Europe, which have strengthened and enriched all of America.

In New England, as we might expect, the old, the middle-aged, and the young are all benefiting in some way from the revival of handicrafts. When a resurgence of interest came about in the late 1920's in several New England communities, it reached some who had in times past been spinners, weavers, knitters, basketmakers, quilters, wood or metalworkers, and who were eager to take up work again. In many communities these older craftsmen are active today, doing not always the same type of work as in earlier days but executing patterns for whatever is now in demand.

Several old basketmakers and a number of netmakers work along the coast of Maine. A former expert machinist makes wooden clocks by hand and spends his summer vacation shooting woodchucks for the farmers of Vermont. An elderly couple have a shop in a New Hampshire village, where they sell their own handiwork made from wood and metal. The wife reads to her husband while he shapes a violin from wood, but when he hammers out metal bowls so hard he cannot hear her voice, she knits. In Connecticut a man who has made baskets for fishermen and clam dealers for sixty-five years now sells all his output in his home shop. Some of the old knitters who one time plied their needles turning a perfect heel for a soft gray sock are now using their skill to knit intricate patterns in colorful yarns for stockings, mittens, and sweaters to be worn by skaters and skiers in the long-winter states of Vermont, New Hampshire, and Maine. Some of the best patchwork and quilting throughout New England, as well as much hooking and braiding and weaving of rugs is carried on by older folk. When retirement from active duty occurs, one can turn to handicraft to keep up morale, to fill time constructively, and often to help replenish the pocketbook. If in this study the work of old people may seem overstressed, this has been due to a serious recognition of the fact that our future population is certain to have an increasingly larger percentage of the aged. Whatever makes them happy contributors to life is indeed worth heeding.

However, the great majority of persons participating in the handicrafts of New England, as in other regions, are not the elderly but the middle-aged still in their most productive years. They are either trained craftsmen who are working for their livelihood, or the much larger number of village and country folk who have acquired some special skill with their hands in addition to the vocation by which they provide for most of the needs of home and family. In some localities there is hardly a household without at least one skilled worker, and often there are several members who can join in the making of handicrafts for home use or for sale. There are instances in which all members of the family make some type of handicraft.

The younger folk are active too, making boat models and airplane models and unlimited miniatures of army and navy equipment, and even hooking rugs if the designs catch their interest. A father and son are carving all the land and water birds of New Hampshire; another father and son are whittling the animals of Maine. In Vermont children are raising rabbits and spinning their fur into fine yarn; in Massachusetts a youth has built a kick wheel on which he makes pottery; and girls and boys throughout New England are flytying, making pottery and jewelry, knitting, stenciling, linoleum block-printing, dyeing, weaving, and making furniture.

A heartening fact resulting from the wide participation in the handicraft movement is the extent of original work. Handicraft workers are not to be thought of as large groups engaged in making somewhat the same kind of object, nor must the processes through which they create be thought of as the result of one worker copying another. More than sixty different types of handicraft came to the writer's attention in visiting communities and studying exhibitions in New England.

The factor of design is one of the most important in handicraft production. Design has been defined as an arrangement of forms or colors, or both, intended to be wrought out for use or ornament in or on various materials; a pattern; a preliminary sketch; coordination of details.

There are two attitudes toward design in handicrafts: one school would have the design prepared by one person and carried out by another or by several other craftsmen; the second would have the craftsman both design and make the object under consideration. In the latter case he is sometimes called the designer-craftsman or the artist-craftsman.

One is always glad to find a craftsman making his own designs, even if they are crude, because this is the creative way and it usually means growth. But there is much to be said for those who choose a design which another has made when that choice is discriminating. Often more thought is expended in the search for a design and more taste exercised in carrying it out than in the hasty scribbling or devising of something original.

Every faithful reproduction of a fine example of furniture or copy of a worthy old piece of silversmithing, or even the selection of an appropriate stencil pattern for a wall or tray, and its thoughtful arrangement thereon, comes within the category of creative work. One of the choice things which that distinguished silversmith George C. Gebelein did for his clients was to copy with exactness some of Paul Revere's creations. There is a great world of beauty for the modern craftsman to bring to light in reproducing as well as he is able the best designs that have been made by others; but it should be realized that this process alone will not vitalize the handicraft movement or give it the ongoing spark it must have to endure.

Let us turn briefly to a few of the many instances of originality of design which give pleasure either for their beauty or charm, or of equal import to the writer, because of the happiness that doing the creative thing has given the maker.

In Maine the writer recalls the satisfaction which Robert P. Tristram

Coffin took in thinking out his verses, then writing them down in his best round hand and drawing delightful illustrations of his own invention, thus getting as much as possible out of the subjects recorded in his homemade volume.

In New Hampshire one remembers the lovely needlework of the Saffron and Indigo Society celebrating in stitchery the plants of garden and countryside—the wild strawberries, for instance, in silk on natural gray linen, and especially a village street showing every human habitation. Remembered, too, are the beautifully wrought silver pins and earrings by Thomas Gotshall with snow crystal designs from the microphotographs which the farmer-artist William A. Bentley had captured with his camera from many a winter storm at Jericho, Vermont. At the World's Fair at Tunbridge, Vermont, was a quilt for which the maker had pieced more than a hundred "favorite scenes and objects" of family life in the country near Chelsea.

In Massachusetts probably more and better designs have been worked out by silversmiths than in any other state. Remembered are the newly created forms in jewelry too, and a needlepoint tapestry in which are recorded the best remembered things of a trip around the world. On the Cape near South Orleans is the little Church of the Holy Spirit, in which all the furniture and many of the furnishings were designed and made by people in the neighborhood, or by those visiting from a distance who wanted to make their contribution. The crucifix in wood was carved by Francisco Peviri, a blind, self-taught craftsman.

On a Connecticut farm, far in the country, Swedish-born Mrs. Margareta Ohberg "dyes in the wool" her handspun yarn and weaves it into colorful tapestries. In Rhode Island in the little fishing village of Point Judith, between Jerusalem and Galilee, Mrs. Patrick Dillon, a fisherman's wife, works into the hundreds of mittens each winter the prettiest colors and figures that she can "make up."

These are a few of many hundreds of craftsmen in the New England states whose work reflects their personalities and often their environments and gives to the handicraft movement in varied measure its most precious quality—creative craftsmanship.

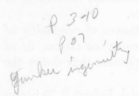

Part II

NEW ENGLAND HANDICRAFTS TODAY

CHAPTER 3

CRAFTSMEN IN WOOD

"FOR Wood there is no better in the World I thinke," wrote the Reverend Francis Higginson of the new colony at Plymouth in his book, *New-Englands Plantation* (published in London in 1630), "here being foure sorts of Oke differing in the Leafe, Timber, and Colour, all excellent good. There is also good Ash, Elme, Willow, Birch, Beech, Saxafras, Juniper, Cipres, Cedar, Spruce, Pines, Firre, that will yeeld abundance of Turpentine, Pitch, Tarre, Masts and other materials for building both of Ships and Houses." Higginson also throws light on the tools then used for woodworking when he sets down as essential to the equipment for the colonists: "1 Broad Axe, 1 Felling Axe, 1 Steele Handsawe, 1 Whipsawe, 1 Hammer, 1 Shovell, 1 Spade, 2 Augres, 4 Chissels, 2 Percers stocked, 1 Gimlet, 1 Hatchet, 2 Frowes, 1 Hand-mill, 1 Grindstone, 1 Pickaxe, Nayles of all sorts."

From the days of the earliest settlement New Englanders began their long record of craftsmanship in wood, with agriculture a first industry to be followed by white men on the eastern part of our continent. Thousands of objects of bygone days have been preserved in public or private collections, many of them copies from articles used in the various homelands of Europe, where wood had been for centuries a chief factor in home industries. The subject, early American woodenware, has received admirable treatment by Mary Earle Gould of Worcester, Massachusetts, in her book of that name. Indeed, the period from the landing of the Pilgrims through the American Revolution deserves to be known as the American wooden age. Almost everything that was made was either entirely or partly of wood: houses, ships, bridges, plows, harrows, wagons, carts, sleds, other farming and fishing tools, furniture, household utensils, looms, spinning wheels, dishes, and novelties.

Any observation of New England hand craftsmanship in wood suggests at once a separation of these activities into several divisions. They are so important that several chapters concern them: Basketry;

Carving and Whittling; Toys, Dolls, and Miniature Objects; Nautical Handicrafts; Puppets and Marionettes. The products to be considered in the present chapter range all the way from woodpiles to ball bearings and as arbitrarily classified include: (1) objects used for sports in which wood is largely if not wholly the material employed; (2) furniture, cabinetwork, and also articles for farm and household use; and (3) a division that has recently assumed new importance among New England craftsmen, though a very old one, namely, woodturning.

"From woodpiles to ball bearings" is not merely a figure of speech, but rather a true indication of the wide range in the art of woodshaping to be found in New England. An ingenious potter, referred to elsewhere, unable to buy ball bearings needed to make his kick wheel run smoothly, made them from hard close-grained wood. If there were time to dwell fully upon the rural arts of New England, woodpiles would be given an important place, for the common woodpile is often an aesthetic expression which is a symbol of man's quest for beauty in everyday life.

The piling of hard wood for winter fires as done by Elmer Watson at the Coolidge farm at Center Sandwich, New Hampshire, has particularly appealed to the writer. Never two years alike, for yearly the pile of firewood changes both in size and variety, maple, birch, or beech, sawed squarely and split skillfully, often with single strokes of the ax. Arranged closely and evenly with no spaces lost, Mr. Watson's tiers of new clean wood present a picture of peace, plenty, and comfort.

FOR SPORTS AND SPORTSMEN

Starting in Maine, we will make a tour among some of the workshops where craftsmen are pursuing their woodworking crafts, visit them occasionally in their homes, discover their interests, and in conversation learn what we can of their techniques, their markets, their ambitions, their difficulties. We shall begin by visiting a few men engaged in making articles for use in winter sports.

In Aroostook, the most northerly county of eastern United States, is a small but unique rural community known as New Sweden. It was settled by immigrants from Sweden in the 1860's and is still occupied mainly by persons of Swedish birth or descent. There are five small settlements—Sweden, New Sweden, Jemtland, Westmanland, and Stockholm—with their churches and schools and hundreds of acres of fine farmland. A very interesting local museum makes it possible to trace readily much of the development of this "culture island."

Henry Anderson, who farms and also keeps the local garage, is of Swedish stock. He is an expert skier and makes skis for both adults and children, which he sells not only in the community but throughout the country. Each pair is stamped by burning his "trade name" into the wood with a well-designed metal die which he made himself. He spoke with enthusiasm of the craftsmanship of Herman Ek, one of the first really fine ski-makers of Maine, examples of whose work he thinks should be in the village museum, with the exhibit of skis the pioneers used long before skiing became a popular sport in this country. Mr. Anderson has time for ski-making only in the winter, when he averages about two pairs a week.

Farther down the state in Cumberland Center lives Clifford G. Anderson, also an expert in the making of skis and snowshoes. He has made hundreds of pairs of snowshoes, some for the smallest children able to use them, some for the heaviest adults. He is a thorough student of snowshoemaking and carries on the fine traditions of his craft. His own statement indicates the care used in materials and craftsmanship: "I make my snowshoe frames from clear, straight-grained white ash, free from knots and flaws, using only the butt cut logs [the cut nearest the ground]. They are fastened at the heel with copper rivets which will not rust. They are filled with cowhide lacings . . . thoroughly stretched and guaranteed not to sag. The finished shoe is coated with high-grade spar varnish. Each operation is performed by hand, each shoe is sold under the guarantee that if . . . not absolutely satisfactory, money will be refunded."

Clifford Anderson makes a surprising number of styles of shoes, each adapted to some special use, as for instance "Alaska," good for fast travel in deep, loose snow, but not for hill climbing or hard-packed snow; and "Beaver tail," good on crusty or hard-packed snow, because it is made without fine mesh in the toe and heel so that pieces of crust falling on the toe go through. Clearly there are a number of considerations in selecting snowshoes for man or woman; if the country is rough, a short broad pair is advisable; if the country is hilly, flat shoes take a better grip; if there are few hills to climb most people prefer a turned-up toe.

Robert L. Smallidge of Northeast Harbor also makes snowshoes, usually for his own use and for members of his family, although occasionally he makes a pair to sell. No man in New England has greater skill in both land and sea handicrafts than Mr. Smallidge. He makes a fine archer's bow, with arrows, and nearly all his own hunting equipment. A beautiful piece of craftsmanship is the walnut gun barrel of his hunting rifle, which he has made to suit his size. After finishing it carefully, he laid in a number of figures in brass, which are polished off to the surface of the stock. He also contrived for himself a leather belt for carrying cartridges, decorating it with a simple design of pine cones. His hunting knives are made of steel, wood, and leather. A compact linen cord smaller than his little finger, braided by himself, can be slipped into a pocket of his hunting belt, but it is strong enough to haul the largest buck over the snows of Maine. An illustration of some of his work is shown.

At North Berwick the writer was directed to the shop of Alton Weymouth, a specialist in racing sulkies. On the way there he talked with Alton's cousin, Woodbury Weymouth, an old-time woodworker who has a combined carpenter shop and forge. In his younger days Woodbury Weymouth was a carriage maker, but in recent years he has done general repair work in wood and iron and had just finished restoring a wagon wheel which had come in with only the hub and a few spokes. He had made new spokes and the felly, and had shaped and shrunk on the tire. In Mr. Weymouth's shop were also objects of general utility for home and country use, and furniture, including chairs of a popular pattern that he had made of local pine, and benches and tables of similar material. He did not put a high valuation on his work, but with a pine shaving in his mouth gave a dissertation on good craftsmanship, and finally took the writer to his storeroom beneath the shop where he had some beautiful sleighs of his own design and construction.

In Alton Weymouth's commodious shop and great barn there were several racing sulkies, and parts of others, that had been sent in for repair from all over the New England states; one had been shipped from Ohio. He was probably the only man at that time in Maine who specialized in the repair of sulkies, but he was far from the only one interested in horse racing. From his childhood, like many another from Maine, he followed with fascination the trotting and pacing races. All about his shop were photographs, drawings, and lithographs of famous horses. Often these subjects turn up in hooked rugs, patchwork quilts, embroideries, and carvings, reflecting the indelible impression the racing horse has made in Maine.

Among the finest examples of craftsmanship in wood to be found in New England are the fishing rods made by Leon J. Thomas of Bangor and known to sportsmen throughout the world. They have been made here by hand for many years, a small industry having been started by Mr. Thomas' father.

At Round Pond, Lincoln County, Miss Ada Wentworth makes walking sticks from roots and branches of native trees. She has a special interest in imaginative shapes and growths, which she features usually at the top or handle of the cane. The wood is peeled of its bark, scraped carefully, cut to practical length, and dried thoroughly.

The most unusual canes and walking sticks which the writer has seen in New England were those derived from sapling roots collected by Mr. and Mrs. John Visscher of Waterbury, Connecticut, who see in these natural forms suggestions of an elephant head, a giraffe, a fish, an eagle, the head of an Indian chief, or some other figure. With pocketknife and carving tools Mr. Visscher makes each one unmistakable. He does other carvings in various materials, including ivory, talc, and wood. One of his best pieces is an elephant from mastodon ivory.

CARPENTRY, FURNITURE, AND CABINETMAKING

If the person who scans this chapter has ever lived in any of the six New England states he may read between the lines the name and accomplishments of a local carpenter he has known and would wish to see included in this record, for New England is a land of handymen in which carpentry, cabinetwork, agriculture, and other trades are often joined in happy combinations unknown to city dwellers.

Maine. Charles A. E. Long has for years been the carpenter for Matinicus Isle, one of a group of islands which might be described as Maine's outermost seacoast. In his *Matinicus Isle: Its Story and Its People* Mr. Long writes:

> Situated sixty miles east of Portland, eighteen miles south by east from Owl's Head, and twenty miles out of Rockland by boat, Matinicus is the largest of a small cluster of islands which guard the entrance to Penobscot Bay. Besides Matinicus the group consists of Criehaven, Wooden Ball Island, Matinicus Rock, Seal Island, Ten Pound Island, No Mans Land, Two Bush Island, and numerous smaller ledges and rocks.

Mr. Long was born on the mainland, in Lincolnville, and worked at carpentry in various parts of New England but long cherished the plan of going to Matinicus to live. When he finally settled there he continued to work as a carpenter, and although he had never prepared himself to write a book, he began to gather information, dating from the time of the first white settlement, which he ultimately put into his history. He says:

> Matinicus is approximately two miles long, and of varying width, nowhere more than a mile wide, with an area of about seven hun-

dred and twenty acres. The shores are mostly rocky; in some places very precipitous. In other places there are long reaches of massive boulders worn to a smooth roundness by ages of pounding by the relentless ocean. There are three small sand beaches which form ideal bathing spots, and furnish a favorite habitat for sand-loving plants. The general surface of the island is well elevated, but there are numerous bogs and marshes, and two or three extensive deposits of peat, the edges of which are exposed at the shore. In several places the ocean is slowly encroaching upon the land. . . . Each particularly furious storm claims its few inches from those localities where the soil itself is exposed to the action of the sea.

Such, briefly described, is the very definite kingdom of this New England carpenter, who, in addition to his interest as historian in Matinicus and its people, has made a special study of its flora. In his home and workshop he has built cabinets for specimens of 640 plants which he has personally collected, including what he believes to be all the native grasses and ferns of the island, a beautifully mounted and preserved exhibit, fascinating to botanist or layman.

These small islands are centers of culture which the man on the "continent" little suspects. For example, Mrs. Arthur A. Philbrook and her husband, a fisherman, both self-taught naturalists, have made a complete bird census of Matinicus, identifying 122 varieties. On the neighboring island of Criehaven, Miss Dorothy Simpson has listed ninety-six birds and Mrs. Ava C. Simpson, covering a wider area of the Penobscot Bay region, 128.

In the southeastern tip of Maine Mr. and Mrs. Horace Newey of Kittery are enthusiastic workers in wood. Mrs. Newey specializes in carving and her husband in fine cabinetwork and inlay. She carves trays, boxes, chests, buttons, pins, but especially animals. She creates her own designs, often working them out as she carves. One of her principal satisfactions is discovering and encouraging talent among both children and adults who rarely dream they have such gifts.

Edson W. Fletcher of Searsport, listed under miniature furniture makers in Chapter 12, should also be mentioned here for his work in inlays. One of his prized objects is a cribbage board inlaid with 361 pieces of wood, which required 310 hours to complete. The board is made of white, pink, and brown mahogany, ebony, white pine, weather-stained pine, beechwood, apple wood, walnut, teak, basswood, and oak. The white mahogany came from furniture taken from the cabin of a royal yacht; the teakwood from an old sea chest; other pieces were from old vessels, relics of shipbuilding days, and from old beech and apple trees; the ebony was given by the president of the

Sheridan Transportation Company; the brown mahogany came from a letter file in the office of the John Hancock Life Insurance Company in Searsport.

New Hampshire. Crossing the state line into New Hampshire near Bedford, the traveler will find a farm with a saw- and a gristmill run by George Woodbury, who was assisted at the time of the writer's visit by John H. Burrowes. Mr. Woodbury was formerly an archaeologist in the Peabody Museum at Harvard University. Bedford, however, was his native soil, and in the early 1930's he returned, with his young wife, to the site where, in 1744, his great-great-great-great-grandfather, John Goffe, built the first saw- and gristmill on Bowman's Brook. The land on which the mill stands has been in the hands of Mr. Goffe's descendants ever since his death. The original building was burned in 1845 but was rebuilt within a year with "new and improved mechanical devices." Years later, together with the tanbark mill and the fulling mill once near neighbors on the same stream, Goffe's Mill was abandoned and tumbled into ruins. After the hurricane of 1938, Mr. Woodbury tells us in a leaflet published by him in 1946, "the long rusted machinery was dredged up from the slime and broken rum jugs of oblivion. A new building arose on the breast of the great stone dam. Once more the water wheel turned with a groan on its wooden thrust pin, and John Goffe's Mill with a seventh generation at the massive water gate came alive again. The present lumber and grist mill serves even a wider area than did its predecessor, logs coming from seventy miles away and corn from a far-flung neighborhood. The story of the mill and its evolution into a furniture factory is told by Mr. Woodbury in *John Goffe's Mill*, published in 1948.

The Woodbury farm was a busy place on the day of the writer's visit in the summer of 1943. The children and their sheepdog were driving Abelard, the huge white pig, into his pen in the barnyard, and Mrs. Woodbury served the visitors cakes made from their water-ground cornmeal with maple syrup.

On the previous day the Woodbury family had exhibited at the Craftsman's Fair at Manchester, where the large variety of water-ground meals and flour from the gristmill and the white pine farm furniture, some of it in the Shaker tradition, excited much interest. But the object which drew most attention was a hobbyhorse, made by Mr. Woodbury for his children, which looked as though it might have come out of New England three hundred years ago. Arrangements were soon made to exhibit it at the Exhibition of Contemporary New England Handicrafts, then about to be held at the Worcester

Art Museum, where its fame spread. The hobbyhorse may be seen in the frontispiece.

Mr. Woodbury grinds all the grain for flour and cereals between two old millstones which he found in the neighborhood and which he sharpens every two or three weeks of the grinding season with a special stone chisel. It takes about half a day to sharpen them. He likes the "clatter, groan, rumble, and whine" of the sawmill, the whine being the protest of the circular saw as it is forced through the long oak log that it cuts into usable timber. Most of the sawing is done in spring and summer, while the grinding of the grist comes in fall and early winter.

Mr. Woodbury told the writer that "the mill is much as it has always been, an individual enterprise. The only marked difference is that it now combines some of the conveniences of the 20th century with the basic simplicity of the 18th. . . . In addition to a circular saw of modern design, it also has an 'Up & Down' saw for sawing broad boards of exceptional width. We think it is probably the only one of its kind still running in the state. . . . We select and fell our own trees in our own woods, haul them to the mill and saw them to furniture stock. It is seasoned in the high temperature kiln that we designed and built. Finally it is worked into furniture of our own design. The entire process from the stump to the finished product takes place in a five hundred yard radius."

Albert B. Hoag of Sandwich, near Squam Lake, took up cabinet-making as a hobby and now is a teacher of woodwork. He became interested in the Tappan chairs that had been made in Sandwich for more than a century. These were a sturdy type, much resembling chairs made also in the Southern Highlands.

The small chairmill set up by an English cabinetmaker named Abraham Tappan, and which was part of a family enterprise, had been flooded in 1882 and work had stopped. Fifty years later the League of New Hampshire Arts and Crafts encouraged Walter Tappan to make a few samples of the chairs for which his forebears had been noted. With the help of Mr. Hoag some of the very old patterns salvaged from the flood were reproduced and the worthy quality of the original in materials and workmanship maintained.

Under a spreading elm tree at the Craftsman's Fair at Holderness School, Plymouth, in 1942, Arthur L. Cunningham of Antrim had set up his workbench and was making his popular three-legged stool. Visitors watched him shape the pine lumber into one of the objects he had chosen as his contribution to the League of New Hampshire Arts and Crafts. At its first annual Craftsman's Fair held at Crawford Notch in 1934 he had been a demonstrator.

Describing his experience with the League, Mr. Cunningham wrote as follows: "Here is my story—I was a toolmaker by trade but had to give it up on account of the break in my health, so it was in 1931 when I read in the paper that Governor Winant had appointed a committee to try to do something that would give employment to some of our rural people, I applied for information. Mrs. Coolidge and Mr. Staples[1] came to see me and I began working on a three-legged half-moon fireplace stool, then I started a three-legged banjo stool, and then I worked on a three-legged stool with a rush woven seat. I have made hundreds of these stools and have sold them through the League of New Hampshire Arts and Crafts. I also made a hardwood bread and cold meat cutting-board in the forms of a small and a large maple leaf. And I made bunches of wooden window wedges, designed to keep windows up and to keep them from rattling in the wind."

Other craftsmen closely associated with the League live in the city of Concord and its neighborhood, where much diversified work in wood is carried on, some craftsmen specializing in small articles, such as trays, boxes, mirror frames; others devoting themselves to making fine furniture. Harry P. Hammond is a skilled cabinetmaker whose interest in furniture began as a boy when he purchased a fine old piece at an auction. Later in life he turned seriously to the restoring and making of fine furniture, and is now a student of furniture styles. His tea table and mirror were displayed at the Worcester Exhibition. Two Concord craftsmen, who have died since this study was begun, are George Chandler, a woodworker for fifty years, who reproduced early American furniture and repaired antiques; and Ernest Kunberger, a stairbuilder in his early days. Later in life, when stairbuilding came to be a machine rather than a hand trade, Mr. Kunberger opened a shop well equipped with small machines for shaping wood. His best-known product, which he sold through the League, was cutlery mounted with apple-wood handles.

Outside the Concord area Rodney D. Woodard of North Conway has been interested in doing creative woodwork since he was a small boy, but made no attempt to follow it for a living until 1937. Then he and his wife set up The Artisan Shop.

Clifford Goss of Canaan writes that he has been working with tools ever since he was a boy of ten or twelve years, when he used to "figure out" with his father's square many kinds of framework for

[1] Frank Staples was the League's first director, and Mrs. J. Randolph Coolidge was a prime mover in its organization and activities described in Chapter 18.

model barns and houses. His father considered his son "a queer chick," but the boy's mother thought him just like his Irish great-grandfather, who was a shipwright. Mr. Goss, who says he "learns every day," does delicate inlays.

Although it is not possible to describe the work of schools and instructors, the writer wishes to make a brief reference here to Virgil Poling, of Hanover, director of the Student Workshop at Dartmouth College, who is not only a very skillful designer and worker in wood but a teacher and writer of wide influence, and an authority in the properties and uses of the most widely employed handicraft material in New England. Mr. Poling has helped many craftsmen outside the Dartmouth campus through his page in *Craft Horizons*, "The Woodworker Suggests," and his other writings.

Massachusetts. E. Laurence White of Beverly Farms had always wanted to work in wood. He was never able to realize his ambition, however, until he was convalescing in a hospital as a result of overwork. There his food was brought to him on a tray which served the purpose well but did not satisfy Mr. White's idea of what a tray should be. Encouraged by the thought that his mother could do anything with her hands, he decided to make a tray himself; and before he left the hospital he had done so. In a short time he received orders for others. His work in wood includes inlay.

"Learning to use woodworking tools is the most important thing that ever happened to me," said Mr. White. He learned how to hold his chisel and how to get the best results in woodturning from an old neighbor; and from a Polish-American neighbor, "Mike," otherwise Ignace Skornik, he learned that tools could be given a cutting edge of such perfection that a chisel would cut accurately and with almost no pressure. Mr. White reported that Mr. Skornik has the most beautiful chest of carving tools he had ever seen, the handles of the tools having been made by the owner.

Ignace Skornik makes accordions by hand—an art rare in New England. He was born in Poland, one of a family of craftsmen in wood that had served for several generations in the royal household. While a boy he learned to use woodworking tools. Coming to America in 1915, he settled in Salem, Massachusetts, where he still works steadily as a skilled cabinetmaker and woodcarver. About his work with accordions, which he calls his hobby, he writes: "I have been fond of the accordion from the very day that I first began to play the instrument as a young man. One day I took the accordion apart to see what it looked like inside and found it to be very intricate. It was then that I decided if other men could make accordions so could I."

A year of Mr. Skornik's spare time is required to complete an instrument. He makes all the parts and carves and inlays the case. He also makes the dies for punching holes in the steel, a special steel implement for cutting reeds, and other tools of his own invention. So far four instruments have been made: one four-row chromatic accordion and three piano accordions. They are not made for sale. His daughter, Pauline, is an expert performer, and she also gives instruction in accordion playing.

Lincoln J. Ceely, a native of Nantucket, is a cabinetmaker, a woodcarver, a toymaker, an easel painter, and maker of other things as he takes a notion. While perhaps best known to visitors as an expert cabinetmaker, a trade learned from his father, to the children of the island he is "the toymaker," his specialty being wind toys; to these children he is both wonderworker and friend. On a sunny day a charming feature of his yard and shop, just off Maine Street, is the array of wind-powered toys, such as sailing ships, sailors, traffic cops, wood sawyers, whales, and dozens of birds and animals perched on the pickets of the fence and whirling in the summer breeze. He also designs, carves, and paints full-sized weathervanes in the form of ships, windmills, and other subjects suggestive of life on Nantucket. When the writer bought a gull carved by this old craftsman, his comment was, "That fellow has got a bill that hooks down as it ought to. I think you'll like him."

Mr. Ceely began to teach himself painting several years ago while repairing old clocks, which often had painted scenes on the glass doors. At first he undertook to restore only the sky in these sometimes elaborate scenes, but, compelled by necessity to go a little farther, he found that he could put into the picture houses, trees, animals, and human figures. He had watched artists at work and almost before he knew it he was painting the whole scene. Then he made up pictures of his own, some of which are on glass, and copied paintings of others. His best work, he thinks, is a Nantucket street scene painted on canvas directly from life. He did not wish his neighbors to see him experimenting, so he went to work very early one morning and made an outline drawing of the scene below his shop. Later, again alone at his window, he painted in the details.

Wallace Long, director of the Whaling Museum at Nantucket, is an all-round craftsman of wide experience. Besides making many pieces of fine furniture, including drop-leaf tables and notable mirror frames, he has done a great deal of work on clocks, repairing the works, building some very fine cases, and stenciling and painting decorations on them. A banjo clock with gilt acorn doors and shelf was one of his finest pieces. He has also made miniature furniture, ship models, and half-models.

In Quincy, Arvid R. Tisell and his son, Thure C., members of the Society of Arts and Crafts, make a variety of furniture, including Sheraton sideboards, pedestal dining-room tables, serpentine bow-front chests of drawers, Pembroke tables, desks, and other pieces to order. They are among the best cabinetmakers in New England. Their work is done in mahogany imported from Cuba and Honduras, and in walnut, cherry, maple, and oak. Arvid Tisell was born in Sweden, where as a boy he began to learn his trade, then continued in the schools of Germany. The son learned from his father, and they have worked together in their own shop since 1932.

Almost any weekday in spring or summer, David Lunt may be seen climbing the hill from his workshop near Millbury, with a piece or two of his rustic furniture tied to his wheelbarrow to deliver to some customer. Mr. Lunt, well over three score years and ten, makes a lot of serviceable things for country use, chairs, benches, and tables of native materials, sleds for children with braces of the natural crooks of limbs. He made for the writer a special ax handle and a folding sawbuck, and showed him how to make a bowed handle from a limb so that one man could use a six-foot crosscut saw without its buckling. During a recent winter, just to keep his hand in, Mr. Lunt cut twenty-two cords of wood. "Of course, I have long since outlived my useful-ness," he explained to an admiring neighbor. "Now I am just living for spite."

Connecticut. John Royko came to America in 1910 from Czecho-slovakia. From his wages in a sugar factory, he and his young wife managed to make the first payment on a stony farm in Connecticut, not far from the village of Burlington. In his homeland Mr. Royko's father used to make woodenware utensils for family use and for the people of the countryside, and there John learned this practical supplementary trade, which helped him pay for his house in America and to rear his family. He soon rigged up a little sawmill and workshop across the road from the farmhouse, using the engine of a discarded Ford car to run his circular saw. With this he cuts the blanks, which he works up into farm and household utensils of various kinds— about thirty-five different articles. He said that in Czechoslovakia woodenware was usually not so well finished as that which he makes for people here, who are willing to pay for nicely shaped and finished articles. Preferably he uses hard maple but sometimes other local woods. Many of his things are made from stumps and large sections of trees, which he shapes with ax, adz, and handsaw. These he later finishes with special cutting tools he has made himself from files, old saw blades, and other pieces of good steel.

When the Royko children, three girls and four boys, were little, they would help their mother smooth and polish the woodenware, and Mr. Royko, alone or with one of the children, would peddle it around the countryside. This enterprise, together with careful farming of the land, increased the year's cash income, and made it possible to meet payments on the farm during the depression years. Mr. Royko also makes straw seats for his chairs, binds his fence pickets together with wild grapevines, makes his own beehives of straw, and perpetuates many other rural practices of the Old World.

A rural industry established early in the Connecticut countryside is The Old Bow and Hoop Shop belonging to George W. Smith of Canterbury. Mr. Smith lives near Chick Brook and his shop is near Mudhole Brook. All the work is done by hand, the principal products at present being oxbows and hoops for ship spars, the last-named produced for the government during World War II. The manufacturing process is a very simple one. The hoops are made of native oak; the material is first roughed out on a circular saw, then worked with a drawing knife on a shaving horse until the wood is pliable enough to bend into shape. These hoops are then drawn together, fastened, and piled up to dry. After a short period of seasoning they are ready to ship.

Richard Perry, a farmer-craftsman living at South Windham, died before this book was finished. He had what his wife appropriately called an "affection for wood," which he expressed in some fine examples of craftsmanship, notably Windsor chairs. He was a member of the Society of Connecticut Craftsmen and showed his work in its exhibits. Looking out from the door of his workshop on the edge of his apple orchard across the Shetucket River to the Lebanon and Windham hills, he remarked in response to the writer's comment, "Yes, it is beautiful, especially in summer: the North is way out there, and in winter it comes down here with nothing to stop it; nothing can stop the North."

After teaching manual training in Connecticut schools for several years, Thomas M. Belden, who lives in Danbury, decided in 1929 to establish a shop for repairing, restoring, and reproducing antique furniture. Among Mr. Belden's assignments was a memorial for the Congregational Church of Ridgefield, a table and two chairs, work which he enjoyed because he was allowed time to do it as he thought it should be done. The work included a good deal of handcarving. The chairs are copies of the Governor Winthrop chair, the original of which is at Wesleyan University, Middletown, Connecticut. The table is a copy of the famous Salisbury Communion table.

F. E. Banning of Hadlyme is a fine chairmaker. He exhibited a secretary chair with writing arm at the Worcester Exhibition, which is a typical example of his artistry and craftsmanship. The chair was finished in a thin yellow stain; it is shown in the frontispiece. Mr. Banning has a large shop with modern equipment in which it is possible to turn out almost any kind of job in woodwork. However, when it comes to the making of special pieces of furniture, particularly chairs, the work is carried on as it would have been in an old-time hand shop.

Among other Connecticut craftsmen skilled in wood who should be mentioned are: J. Medwick of East Hartford, who brings to his work the best traditions of his native Lithuania, rich in timber and wood and good craftsmanship, and who has made many copies of early American furniture; and Leon Lewis of Bakersville, a farmer, a naturalist, and "a craftsman on the side," who finds time each year to make Windsor chairs and other pieces of furniture for his home. Many other craftsmen in wood, now working in the Nutmeg State, deserve mention which space limits will not allow.

Women Who Make Fine Furniture

Three women cabinetmakers who do notable work have become known to the writer. Miss Louise Taylor operated her own shop in Hartford, from 1933 to 1942. It was a fully equipped Delta shop, with circular saw, drill press, band saw, lathe, bench, and hand tools. Here she did her own designing and drafting and made both traditional and modern furniture. A wine cabinet designed and built by Miss Taylor is shown. She writes as follows: "I have always been a designer and craftsman at heart . . . and it seemed that furniture provided the best medium to express that wish, but this does not exclude my pleasure in room planning, display work, toys, and objects of other kinds besides wood manufacture."

Miss Aletha Macy, a native of Nantucket, served an apprenticeship of twelve years with Lincoln Ceely. She built her small house largely from old lumber found on the island; the ridge pole was a beam from a barn where she had played as a child. Among her choice pieces of furniture is a tambour desk of mahogany, holly, ebony, and other special woods which she copied from one of Mr. Ceely's. "He can do anything!" exclaimed Miss Macy, "but he never likes to make more than one specimen of a kind."

Furniture making and woodworking have been traditional in the family of Miss Barbara Marshall, who directs The Sawhorse Studio in Rockport, Massachusetts. She cannot remember when she did not work in wood, but she took formal training at the University of New Hampshire and served an apprenticeship of one year in Taos, New Mexico.

WOODTURNING

Woodturning by hand is an old craft that has been greatly diminished by automatic machinery and modern lathes. However, there are now throughout the New England states a number of turners who work with native woods and some who specialize in woods from other lands. The examples given will at least suggest the character and quality of the recent revival of woodturning.

Vermont. Among the first to develop woodturning of the modern type in New England were the Kennedy brothers, John and Paul, formerly of Charlotte, Vermont. They began by making small bowls from native woods, turning and finishing them carefully. Their success in this small Vermont community, and the favorable publicity concerning it, was an encouragement to others. The Kennedys now have a well-established wood industry under the name, Green Mountain Woodcrafters, in Bristol, Vermont. John Kennedy has recently developed a type of pottery known as Mountain Kiln Pottery, which is also marketed at the shop in Bristol.

H. C. Dubuke of Florence did woodturning as a hobby, and was one of the earliest craftsmen in New England to revive the making of plates, bowls, and other pieces for the table. These were of native maple wood. Through Mr. Dubuke's example other craftsmen became interested in turnery.

The Craft Shop on Putney Road, Brattleboro, comes into this account through the woodwork of Ralph E. Carpenter, one of a family of craftsmen, who prepares many of the articles sold in the shop. He uses mainly Vermont maple and makes bowls of all sizes, always of carefully selected wood and attractively finished.

His mother, four sisters, and a niece knit sweaters and mittens, make braided and hooked rugs, cloth toys, preserves and jellies, the last named mostly for home consumption though a few glasses of prized wild strawberry jam are for sale. The father, who is not living, made a specialty of raising corn which he braided very skillfully, a craft still practiced by several New England farmers, notably by Martin Hidu of Fairfield, Connecticut, whose long strands of golden seed corn— twelve to fifty ears in a trace—supplied appropriate decoration for the national Exhibition of Rural Arts, which took place in Washington in

1937. Other skilled corn braiders of New England are Edward Harris of Laconia, New Hampshire, who calls his braidings "traces of corn," and Mrs. Addie M. Eastman, also of Laconia, who when last heard from was braiding at the age of ninety-one.

Arthur W. Laughton of West Brattleboro, Vermont, is an all-round carpenter and woodturner, good at repairing and restoring anything from a small wooden trinket to a large country house. Among his highest achievements in woodworking are bowls, plates, and boxes, which he turns on an old-fashioned foot-power lathe. He said: "My first bowls were small and made from rather thin stock. They didn't have the right 'look' or 'feel' and my wife kept urging me to make them deeper. I kept on using thicker wood and making the sides not quite so abrupt until I got them to look and feel about right. I made no attempt to copy anything I had seen but in time developed that black cherry bowl pattern. Just the same way with other pieces I have done. I try to work out an idea as well as I can and then we develop it until it seems better, about as good as we can make it."

Mr. Laughton makes small turned boxes of apple or other favorite woods, in which the fitting of the lid to the box is done with such precision that it is a pleasure for anyone, sighted or blind, to experience the feel of putting the cover on and taking it off. Mrs. Laughton is an expert knitter, and her work is often shown with the woodturning of her husband in exhibits of Vermont craftsmanship.

New Hampshire. Three May brothers, John, the originator of the team, Richard T., and Willard R., design and make fine pieces of furniture and do woodturning in their shop at Jackson, New Hampshire. Most of their furniture is made to sell, but their turning, much of it from choice, and sometimes rare, imported woods, is what the wood itself and the treatment and the skill of the craftsmen make it. In many instances the pieces are exceptionally beautiful, for they are products of much thought from the time the wood is selected in the rough to the finished product. The woodworking shop, near the end of a ski towline operated by the May brothers, is in a sense an outgrowth of their original work in making and repairing skis.

Willard does most of the designing but the judgment of all is brought to bear upon any problem in turning or furniture making. He said: "An object in wood is not like one in silver in which the result is constant; with wood it often takes years before it reaches its permanent stage and we must try to visualize what it will be when thoroughly seasoned and matured. In this inconstant material the careful designer and craftsman must do much advance calculating."

Fred E. Brown of Concord, New Hampshire, and William Ward of

Nashua, make wooden tableware—plates, bowls, and cutlery. Mr. Brown uses maple principally, although occasionally he employs birch, pine, beech, walnut, and butternut. His pieces are turned skillfully in many sizes. Mr. Ward uses maple exclusively. He selects his material carefully and separates the bird's-eye, the fiddleback, and the curly maple from the less striking grain, so that his pieces represent every characteristic of the wood. His turning is sturdy and graceful in type. Since 1938 he has utilized much of the "hurricane wood" from maple trees that were uprooted in the storm.

Massachusetts and Connecticut. In Massachusetts mention should be made of Hans Gaidies of Huntington, an economist trained in German universities, who showed an unusual collection of turned bowls, tobacco jars, plates, and trays at the Handicraft Fair at Northampton in 1943. He also exhibited at the Worcester Exhibition. Among his best articles were a wooden bowl of maple, finished in black, and a sandwich plate turned from a single plank more than two feet across.

Some remarkable woodturning has been done by Alvan L. Davis of Waterbury, Connecticut, a good mechanic and a careful student of woods and their properties. Most of his turned pieces are from the trunks of young trees or the straight limbs of older trees, often preserving the rings which register the year's growth. Mr. Davis has developed a formula for cutting and curing his wood so that he often turns his boxes with the bark on and it remains a permanent part of the finished piece. With its turned and well-fitted cover, a box of hickory or oak so treated is attractive.

Alfred Rossiter, proprietor of Poverty Hollow Workshop, Redding Ridge, Connecticut, is one of the most particular craftsmen in the handling of wood from lumber to finished product known to the writer. He uses a wide selection of woods including imported timber from the West Indies, South America, and elsewhere.

Mr. Rossiter does all his own turning and shaping of bowls, salad forks, and spoons in magnolia, walnut, apple, maple, and mahogany. His skill, as well as his facilities for curing the wood, is kept at the highest point of efficiency. The kiln and workshop are now under one roof, making the plant a model for convenience. It is also popular with native birds. A wren has a nest only a few feet from where Mr. Rossiter works, and she never seems to be disturbed by the whirr of his lathe. No craftsman could have a pleasanter location, for every window in the shop commands an outlook on flower garden, vegetable garden, or orchard. No wonder the birds have the impression that the shop was built for them.

MAKERS OF MUSICAL INSTRUMENTS

One of the finest uses to which wood has ever been put is the making of musical instruments for the pleasure, the inspiration, and the solace of man. Among these instruments the fiddle, or violin, has long held high place; convincing evidence of its hold on mind and heart is the making of an instrument for oneself. In this study a surprising number of such instances were discovered and a chapter on Musical Instruments was prepared, but the limitation of space requires that it be omitted. Hence a brief reference to a few of these skilled and often inspired craftsmen is appended here.

More than thirty fiddle, or violin, makers were discovered in New England; according to their own records, they had made a total of more than 2,000 instruments. About half of these craftsmen were native sons of New England; others are American citizens from other homelands where the fiddle was a traditional instrument.

Among those who brought the love of music and the skill of instrument making to their adopted land the following may be mentioned: Alexander Thoma of Dorchester, Massachusetts, learned his trade in his father's shop in Vienna; both father and son came to America and became the violin repairers for the Boston Symphony Orchestra. Alexander has made about fifty violins and several violas and cellos. From Karlstad, Sweden, came Anton Olson to Worcester, Massachusetts. Trained as a cabinetmaker in his homeland, he came to the United States when still a young man. Seeing a fellow workman make a fiddle, he started making violins as a hobby, then professionally, completing sixty-seven. From Germany Reinhardt Meyer, now of Worcester, came first to Lawrence, Massachusetts, at eight years of age. He became a violinist, then leader of an orchestra. Learning thoroughly the technique of violin structure, he has made about one hundred instruments, his most famous group of five were finished in 1936 and dedicated to Cecile, Emilie, Yvonne, Marie, and Annette Dionne.

From Frankfurt, Germany, the late Fred L. Dautrich came to Torrington, Connecticut. First a violinist, then an instrument maker, his unique contribution was a family of violins which began with a violin; then were added a new alto called a vilonia, a new tenor called a vilon, and a new small bass called a vilona. With these and the bass viol his quintet often played in concerts, giving a close harmony of tone unachieved heretofore. In a booklet, *Bridging the Gaps in the Violin Family*, Mr. Dautrich explained the need in chamber or orchestral music for the instruments he invented.

From Moravia came Ladislav Kaplan now of South Norwalk. Mr.

Kaplan started to play at six years old and at twelve played first violin in a small orchestra "on a $4.00 violin, getting only squeaks and scratches out of it." "So," he said, "I determined to be a violin maker to make a better violin for myself." After many experiments he developed a process which would give him a good instrument and has since made more than seventy-five violins. Mr. Kaplan is now manufacturing violin strings.

From Italy came Michael Gozzo, who had served an apprenticeship under his grandfather, Michael Gozzo I. By 1946 Mr. Gozzo had made himself 198 violins and with the aid of his pupils more than 250. On all his instruments, which are often Stradivari or Guarneri models, he uses the same reddish brown colors and varnish employed for generations by his family in Italy.

There are other musical instrument makers in New England ranging from an amateur organ maker in Maine to a boy in Connecticut who makes snare drums of good playing quality. But perhaps the best-known musical instrument maker in New England today is William Koch of Haverhill, New Hampshire, who makes recorders of cocobolo wood, an ancient type of woodwind instrument resembling a primitive flute. For a time Mr. Koch combined the designing of hooked rugs with the making of recorders, but the demand for the musical instruments by amateurs later took all his time, and now he sells all he can make to music stores.

CHAPTER 4

BASKETRY

BASKETRY is one of the most ancient arts of man. Scholars seem justified in believing that baskets were made long before pottery, but because of their perishable nature the earliest evidence of their existence is not so definite nor so widespread as pottery, which acquires, when the clay is hardened by fire, an almost everlasting quality. It has, however, been established beyond doubt that some of the earliest forms of pottery were molded in and around baskets before the clay was hardened by the sun or made permanent by fire. In most of the ancient civilizations there are records of basketry, but it has remained for Egypt, with its dry atmosphere and preserving sand, to save for us predynastic baskets, found in the Fayum, that were made and used for storing grain at least as early as 4000 B.C.

Basketry is still a lively handicraft in our own land and in many other countries. It should have a special interest for every American because the Indians, particularly of North America and that section comprising the United States, have developed the art to a perfection never reached elsewhere.

George Wharton James in his book, *Indian Basketry,* quotes Mrs. Jeanne C. Carr as saying, "Among primitive arts, basketry . . . furnishes the most striking illustration of the inventive genius, fertility of resource, and almost incredible patience of the Indian woman." The Office of Indian Affairs now gives encouragement to Indian crafts, one result of which is that very fine baskets are being made by the Indians of today.

Basketry, which has always been a rural handicraft, is carried on by people not generally known outside their own communities. In rural areas baskets are still made in considerable quantities, loaded on trucks, and taken to a shopping center or roadside stand where they are picked up by travelers. Of the hundreds of baskets in New England museums little is known; they are "just baskets that have been here a very long time." In pursuing this subject an attempt has been made to follow back some of the clues which still exist.

In terms of basket shapes and of materials used no area in our country produces a greater variety than New England. Classified according to materials are the following: (1) ash splint baskets; (2) willow baskets from native willows or osiers; (3) baskets of roots and branches of trees; (4) sturdy baskets woven of birch bark especially prepared by Finnish-Americans; (5) the Shaker workbasket made from very fine splints of native poplar trees; (6) the Lightship basket made only on the island of Nantucket, partly of native woods and partly of imported cane materials; (7) baskets of various materials including reeds from China, raffia from Madagascar, palm leaves from Cuba and Florida; (8) modern Indian baskets; (9) a Vermont porcupine quill basket.

ASH SPLINT BASKETS

Of all baskets made in New England the ash splint basket is the best known and most widely used; it is possibly the oldest kind of any now being made there. In some form it has been produced by both Indians and whites farther back than anyone now living can remember. It resembles the oak and hickory splint baskets of the Southern Highlands, the Ozarks, and other parts of the country where an occasional basketmaker still plies his craft. In New England the brown or black ash is the favorite basket wood; it differs from all other trees in one important respect, namely, that by a pounding process each annual growth may be separated from the adjoining layers so that the splints are readily peeled off rather than split off or rived. This natural splint, the thickness of which nature has determined by the year's growth, is the right thickness for sturdy utility baskets in medium and large sizes. But in delicately made baskets the ash splints are divided and subdivided until some are almost as thin as paper. They can be bent at sharp angles without breaking and can also be twisted and curled.

The ash splint is the most practical basket in use today in New England. Similar baskets have been made in rural England, Holland, Germany, and other European countries for centuries, and hence this type is traditional in the homelands from which most of our people have come. The Indians may have made ash splint baskets before Europeans came to New England, although not much evidence has been uncovered on this point. In *Seneca Splint Basketry* Marjory Lismer deals extensively with the subject in New England and in other areas of the country, but does not attempt to give even an approximate date for the earliest splint basketmaking among the Indians or to describe the earliest forms. There are, however, fragments of evidence available.

The Essex Institute in Salem, Massachusetts, has some Indian ash splint baskets made probably in the eighteenth century; and in Longfellow's home in Portland, Maine, there are a few splint baskets of Indian make, known to be more than a hundred years old. Others included in permanent collections have been given a quality of decoration not achieved by the white basketmaker. This was usually done by blockprinting on the outside of the basket a simple design cut either on the end of a piece of wood or possibly into a section of a potato. Whatever the means used, the effect was pleasing, and the perfection attained would indicate a craft that had long been followed.

It would be a fascinating bit of information could we know precisely what kind of Indian baskets the Pilgrims dug out of the sand on their earliest explorations on Cape Cod. Bradford's record, *Homes in the Wilderness,* gives us only a few hints: "We . . . found a fine great new basket full of very fair corn. . . . The basket was round and narrow at the top and was very handsomely and cunningly made. It held about three or four bushels." In addition to "well-wrought mats" of flags and bulrushes used to reinforce the Indian shelters and for other purposes, the Pilgrims found in the unoccupied shelters made of boughs other "baskets of sundry sorts, some bigger and some lesser, some finer and some coarser, and some curiously wrought with black and white in pretty works." In our own day splint baskets, which these may have been, are made by the Indians of Oldtown, Maine, by the Passamaquoddy Indians of eastern Maine, and possibly by a few Indians in other New England states.

Making a Splint Basket

The process of making an ash splint basket begins with finding a tree that will yield a good quality of splints. There is some difference of opinion among basketmakers as to the best size, but the tree chosen will have a trunk at least four inches in diameter, although six to ten inches is preferable. It is possible to use wood from larger trees, those with a greater number of rings, but they are difficult to handle. The trunk is cut into logs from five to eight feet long. One log is then laid across another and pounded in order to loosen the layers. This pounding is begun at the upper end, the log being moved along and around until each year's growth is actually separated from the other. After this, all that is needed is to cut down the full length of the log and peel off the growth in strips of the widths desired.

The usual procedure in making splint baskets is to form the bottom and side pieces, or ribs, from the same splints and then to weave in smaller splints. The best craftsmen make their baskets in the traditional way without nails or metal and finish them at the top with one or two hoops around which smaller thongs are woven. Either handles or bails of the wood are notched into the rim in such a way that they are held firmly. Some makers give their baskets a perfectly flat bottom, whereas others bend the splints slightly so that the bottom will be concave, leaving most of the structural parts of the base off the ground. This throws the weight of the basket when filled to the outer rim of the base. A basket so made will last longer but only a careful craftsman will take the pains to follow this method.

In most factory-made baskets the log, instead of being pounded, is ripped into strips of approximately the width desired by methods injurious to the grain, often cutting across it and fracturing and weakening the surface. Also nails and other metal fasteners are generally used, in violation of the better and older tradition calling for wood alone in handles and for binding parts together.

The Black or "Brown" Ash Tree

A word should be said as to the tree itself from which these splint baskets are made. The "brown ash," as New Hampshire basketmakers call it, is undoubtedly the black ash described by Charles S. Sargent in his *Manual of the Trees of North America*; by Romeyn B. Hough in *Handbooks of Trees*; by Charles H. Snow in *The Principal Species of Wood*; and Julia E. Rogers in *The Tree Book*. All give to the black ash the qualities for basketmaking that we have described. None of them lists a "brown ash" tree, although white, blue, green, red, and other varieties are mentioned. Snow says the black ash is called "brown" in New Hampshire and Tennessee and "swamp ash" in Vermont and Rhode Island. This nomenclature reveals that "brown" is a localism for the black ash tree known botanically as *fraxinus nigra*. It is widely distributed from Quebec to Virginia and west to Assiniboia and the Dakotas, but is more extensively used for baskets in New England than elsewhere. With the exception of the heart of the tree which is white, the wood of the black ash is a beautiful light brown. Sometimes a basketmaker will combine the white splints with brown.

Splint Basketmakers

New Hampshire. The Sandwich Home Industries of Carroll County, one of the earliest community groups in New Hampshire to revive handicrafts, published a small illustrated catalogue picturing some of the baskets made and sold in the village of Center Sandwich. Fourteen types of the ash splint basket were illustrated, including large market baskets, clothes hampers, wastepaper baskets, mail baskets, one- or two-bushel apple baskets, egg baskets, garden and flower baskets, sandwich baskets, pie baskets, sewing baskets, and even a set of small coasters. The publication stated that the community had long been the home of basketmakers, "in fact a road leading toward the north part of the town was commonly known as Basket Street because of the number of baskets made there."

At the first annual Craftsman's Fair of the League of New Hampshire Arts and Crafts, Hiram Corliss of Tamworth demonstrated for visitors how splints were separated from ash logs and shaped into baskets. Mr. Corliss was an excellent craftsman and a valuable demonstrator who did much to popularize ash splint basketmaking. After his death Ernest L. Parsons, who lives near Concord, was persuaded by the League to pick up the work where Mr. Corliss left off. He, too, became a successful basketmaker and demonstrator.

In 1937 when the national Rural Arts Exhibition was held in Washington, D.C., the League sent a section of a black ash log showing how the splints were separated by pounding. This was a revelation to basketmakers outside of New England because most splint baskets are made from other trees which do not separate into natural layers but require splitting and shaping.

Among other basketmakers of New Hampshire who should be mentioned more fully than space will allow are the following: Charles A. Sprague of Center Effingham makes baskets ranging from three-bushel to the size of a teacup. Eugene Fogg of Concord, one of the early members of the League, lived formerly at Sandwich. His baskets were of native materials worked out of the log with tools which he made himself. Jonathan Moses of Orford is a first-rate basketmaker of the old splint ash tradition; no better baskets of their kind are made, according to Cornelius Weygandt, who has a collection of them from all the eastern states. Mr. Moses is over seventy years of age and is one of the few ballad singers of New England.

Massachusetts and Vermont. Benjamin G. Higgins is proprietor of the basket shop in Chesterfield, Massachusetts. His father was a basketmaker and with Benjamin had made many baskets by hand before the latter returned from World War I and decided to develop an industry of his own. He shaped so many tools and contrivances in finding short cuts that a visitor to his shop, who had great appreciation of the inventive power of New England craftsmen, said, "Here is all of Yankee ingenuity gathered under one roof!" Instead of pounding the ash log with a maul or axhead, Mr. Higgins has fashioned a heavy triphammer under which he places the log and moves it along, giving it as thorough a pounding as could be achieved by hand. He has also devised a way of shaping the splints more accurately and more quickly than he could by hand, and has made a special shaving mechanism that saves time and reduces the thickness of the wood without injuring its grain. The short cuts devised by Mr. Higgins are not of the kind used in most factories. He is very particular to get the splints off by year's growth. Although the basket in which he uses some metal and nails does not equal the best that he can make by hand, it is a superior product and will probably last as long as the average completely handmade basket.

The separate parts of a black ash splint basket prepared by Arthur M. Sweetser of Waterbury, Vermont, and illustrated here, give an idea of the anatomy of this type. Mr. Sweetser seems to be the last in a zigzag line of basketmakers, having learned from his father, who was taught by Arthur Sweetser's maternal grandmother. Mr. Sweetser reports of her that she learned the skill from her neighbors, the Indians. He said to Arnold Nicholson when the latter was preparing an article on Vermont handicrafts for the *Saturday Evening Post* of January 1, 1944:

> I've heard father tell many times how his father—granddad—once took grandmother . . . by oxcart across the Connecticut River to a New Hampshire town where he was accustomed to trade. When she went into a store with him, bringing her baskets, he introduced her as "my squaw." Grandmother was so mad she didn't make any baskets for a couple of years.

Maine—The Basket at Abbott's Farm. The most extensive bit of research in connection with splint baskets that we were able to carry on resulted in securing a number of first-hand accounts from several old-time basketmakers. In the old barn on the Abbott farm in South Berwick, York County, we saw an ash splint two-bushel basket with all the requirements of a first-rate specimen of its kind. The bottom of heavy splints had been so woven that exposure to wear was on the outside rim; no nails or metal had been used; and the handles had been carefully shaped. The Charles E. Abbotts said the basket had come into their possession as part of the barn furnishings. The work of Mr. and Mrs. Abbott in their favorite crafts is described in Chapter 9.

From older settlers we learned that the neighborhood had once been a center for making baskets which were peddled throughout that part of the country, but the makers themselves had died. As we went along, we inquired about basketmakers, having always in mind the basket at Abbott's farm. One of these was Ira Spriggs, living at Spriggs City, with whom we had a long talk. Ira was celebrating his seventy-seventh birthday. He brought out a couple of partly finished bushel baskets he was making to sell for seventy-five cents apiece. He said he had made baskets of "brown ash," which he had cut in the swamp from trees about six inches through. He always liked to work his baskets while the wood was green, then set them aside to dry out.

Ira's father, Levi Spriggs, had taught him how to make baskets, and Levi had in turn learned the craft from his father. Ira thought that basketmaking might have gone even farther back in his family. When enough baskets had been made to peddle, the Spriggs men would take a big wagonload to Portland or to Old Orchard or "down Biddeford way." Once Ira's father made a large special basket for Lorenzo Pease's father "up to Parsonfield." This basket, said one of Ira's visitors, he never would forget. It held six bushels and Pease put it in his cart to peddle apples from. It fit exactly into the bottom of the light market wagon. The elder Pease thought it was the means of selling twice as many apples as any container he had ever had. When the Portland housewives saw that wagonload of apples all glistening in the sun they would gather around and pick out all they wanted.

Several days later we saw on a fish pier near Ogunquit a two-bushel basket resembling the one we were trying to trace. We asked a fisherman where the basket had come from, and he replied without hesitation that Alexander Moulton had made many such baskets ten or more years ago at South Berwick, Maine, and he was confident this was one of them.

Mr. Moulton, then eighty-five years old, was in a hospital, but his daughter, Mrs. Ray Seavey, representing a fourth generation of basketmakers, had saved several examples of her father's craftsmanship. Here at last were baskets with characteristics of the one at Abbott's farm. Mrs. Seavey was very obliging in telling how the Moulton baskets were made. Her father did not use black ash or employ the process of separating his splints by pounding. He used a white ash about six inches through, which he peeled and quartered, "splitting it right through the heart."

Mrs. Seavey said: "You take these quarter sticks and with a shaving horse split them into different thicknesses, then place a leather pad on your knee and ross [free of bark or roughness] these into smooth lengths of varying widths. With sixteen of these thickest and widest splints start laying your basket stakes across each other and bend them up in the center so that the bottom of the basket won't touch the ground. Then take the narrow filling and weave it over and under these while holding them in place. When you have finished the bottom and have bent the uprights into a deep crown, you put in a thick strip of wood about eight inches long, bending it outside the stakes, so the basket sets even and firm.

How to

"One time I was talking with a basketmaker up on Great Hill, and I said, 'Here is my basket, you show me yours, and I'll let you jump on mine upside down, but if I just stand on yours it will fall in.' Well, he wouldn't let me do it—just goes to show. You take a basket made our way and put it between your knees and you can't budge it no matter how hard you squeeze. Most any other basket will squeeze flat and not come out again. So that is how the best basketmakers made their baskets; in all sizes, mostly two-bushel or four-bushel, always good measure for the woolen mills, or the farmers, or the fishermen of York County."

So we had found not only the maker of the Abbott farm basket but also a champion of the best old-time methods for making baskets. According to Mrs. Seavey's calculations her father's grandfather made splint baskets in Maine about 1830. This does not mean that the first splint baskets were made in the 1830's; indeed, it is quite certain that they were made much earlier. It happens to be one of a few instances in which we have been able to trace basketmaking back for more than a hundred years—in this case, in a direct family line.

Connecticut. A. G. "Bert" Stevens of Route 1, Guilford, Connecticut, has probably made more splint baskets than any other man in New England and possibly in the United States. He began making baskets of white oak splints when he was eight years old and has continued doing so for about seventy-five years. During forty of those years he averaged at least three baskets a day. He supplied one firm with about two dozen baskets a week over a seven-year period. The writer believes that 50,000 is a conservative estimate of the total number of baskets Mr. Stevens has made.

Back of Mr. Stevens' workshop is a stream three or four feet deep, where he keeps his white oak logs immersed until ready to work them up into splints. He cuts his own logs twelve feet long, then splits them approximately into quarters before putting them in the water. His tools are an ax, saw, maul, three wedges, and a frow, a drawing knife and hand knives, one of the last named over a hundred years old with a "new" handle which he made about fifty years ago from grapefruit wood. Mr. Stevens sells his baskets at a roadside stand. "It was in the past one of the poorest paying trades," said Mr.

Stevens. "Baskets which bring $3.50 each now, I used to make for $2.75 a dozen, and my $3.00 baskets I once made for 16 cents each."

BASKETS OF WILLOWS

Willows are still widely used in different parts of Europe and America for basketmaking and sometimes on an extensive commercial scale, but they are not commonly used in New England. However, basketmakers in Maine and in Connecticut have had success with them.

I. S. Skillin of Freeport, Maine, relates that during the depression of the 1930's his own local business of box manufacturing was practically destroyed. His neighbors being generally discouraged, he tried to think of ways in which they might employ themselves pleasantly and constructively. Since his health was frail, it occurred to him that a form of concentrated handwork with some easily available material might provide the answer. He began making baskets of willows, native to that part of the country. He soon interested some of his neighbors, with the result that several of them became expert, and in meeting with regularity to follow their handicrafts they discovered in the work social values which they all prized. The local doctor took great satisfaction in gathering willows for the special type of baskets he liked, and in time he came to be regarded as one of the best of the group.

Most of the baskets were finished with the bark on the willows, and by selecting the wands for their color much variety in pattern was attained. The group worked out a plan to cure the willows so that they retained for a long time much of their natural color. One of the pleasures which comes from baskets woven with the bark on the wands is that for years with returning rains and fogs the fragrance of the willow comes back again. Not many of these baskets were marketed outside of Freeport, but the local people found many uses for them in their homes.

William Rozensky, born in Czechoslovakia but now a citizen of the United States, makes pussy willow baskets on his farm near East Haddam, Connecticut. They are of several sizes and shapes, some of them serving for farm measuring baskets. The bottoms are reinforced, which makes them practical for hard rural service in all kinds of weather.

This type of basket is one that Mr. Rozensky's family used to make in large numbers in their old home in Bohemia. When he bought the Connecticut farm for his family he found the same kind of willow trees as those native to his former home. In late fall he cuts the switches, leaves them in a damp place outside to cure slowly, weaves them during the winter months, and in the spring pussy willows often appear. Mrs. Rozensky says that this is just one of the nice things that can happen on a farm.

BASKETS OF ROOTS AND BRANCHES

Two basketmakers, born in Poland and now living in New England, have adapted the materials they have found in their respective neighborhoods to traditional patterns of their homeland.

August Keen of Stowe, Vermont, digs roots of the pine tree and makes baskets usually round or elliptical in form. Most of them are in small and medium sizes and are sold locally.

Ignacy Czarnecki, whose home is near Amherst, Massachusetts, weaves his baskets in much the same way Mr. Keen weaves his, using the roots of pine trees and occasionally the tough branches of the pine, maple, elm, and other trees. Because of irregularities in roots and branches and the generally intractable character of the materials, these baskets are among the most difficult to make, but when handled by expert craftsmen they take good form and will stand almost any strain.

WOVEN BIRCH BARK BASKETS

The many baskets, boxes, and other receptacles made from birch bark are so generally known that no description of them need be given here. Strictly speaking, they do not come within the category of basketry in the sense of being woven; they are containers of countless forms made to show the very attractive birch bark itself. However, there is a type of birch bark basket that is carefully woven. It introduces into the circle of American basketry a traditional handicraft of the Scandinavian people, who have for generations used birch bark for baskets, for shoes, and other useful objects. A considerable number of people born in Finland or of Finnish extraction, who live in the New England states, make these baskets, but the work of Mrs. Anna Miettinen of Bethel, Vermont, has been selected for illustration. A portrait study of her is shown with some of her baskets and a roll of the birch bark as it is prepared from the native tree. These baskets are practical, attractive, and have to a marked extent the quality of endurance; all of the Miettinen family weave them.

English is not so easy for Mrs. Miettinen to speak as for her children, so she dictated the following in Finnish to Lempi, her eldest daughter, who excels at whittling: "As a young girl in Finland the art was taught to me by my mother, who made birch bark baskets for a livelihood. She had to walk many miles to the railroad station and then ride 35 miles on the train to the city to sell her baskets from house to house, which is so different from the way we can sell our articles today.

"The bark is stripped from the trees in the early summer months by a process which does not damage the trees, as only a very small gash is cut into the outer bark to start a strip. When I was asked to send articles to a gift shop near here and was wondering what else to send besides my hand-woven rugs, the children suggested the baskets, which we had been making only for our own use. Since then we have been sending them to different shops all over the New England states.

"I have taught my children to make baskets so that the art will not die. It is fascinating and they love to make them and are thinking up new designs to use instead of the plain baskets that my mother taught me to make."

SHAKER BASKETS

Of quite a different character are the Shaker baskets made from the very fine splints of the native poplar tree or basswood. They are among the most delicate examples of craftsmanship to be found in the basketry of our country, excepting, of course, the extraordinarily fine work of certain American Indians. The Shakers (of whom there are still groups in Sabbathday Lake, Maine; Canterbury, New Hampshire; and Hancock, Massachusetts) are noted for handicrafts wrought from materials either wild or cultivated by the Shakers themselves. For instance, they still use wheat and rye straw for weaving and plaiting but their special contribution to the basketry of New England is the use of the delicate poplar splints which they prepare with knives and scissors. Using a fine strong white thread as warp, they weave the woody filler on a special loom designed for that purpose. The splints are very carefully laid in, and when once woven into a web, a kind of grass cloth is produced, which can be used to cover a box or basket frame.

Not too far removed from basket weaving are the traditional straw bonnets made by the New Hampshire Shakers. They are among the finest examples of craftsmanship in straw that rural America affords.

The Shakers in their houses, barns, shops, and other buildings, their built-in cabinets and furniture, their strong, graceful but suitable tools for agriculture, and their handicrafts generally have contributed fine elements of invention, artistry, and craftsmanship to our cultural heritage. And New England is one of the areas in which the Shaker influence has been most pronounced. For authentic studies of the Shakers see *The Community Industries of the Shakers* by Edward Deming Andrews, *Shaker Furniture* by Edward Deming and Faith Andrews, and *The Shaker Adventure* by Marguerite Fellows Melcher.

THE LIGHTSHIP BASKET

On the island of Nantucket is made the Lightship basket, so named because for a long time it was made exclusively by the men on lightships off Nantucket. In time the government objected to the men working at this craft; since then the basket, one of the most interesting, beautiful, and so far as the writer knows, original American baskets to be made by white men, has been produced only on shore.

The Lightship basket is made over a special wooden block resembling the kind used by hat blockers and cleaners. Most of these forms are circular or oval in shape, and they come in many sizes, sometimes graduated so that the baskets can be fitted in nests. Among the exhibits of the Nantucket Historical Society there is such a nest of eight.

Charles G. Coffin of Nantucket has made a special study of the Lightship baskets, of which Mrs. Coffin has a large and choice collection. The following notes are taken from a statement prepared by Mr. Coffin for a *Loan Exhibition of Heirlooms and Many Other Old-fashioned Things from Homes on Nantucket Island,* published in 1935 by the Nantucket Cottage Hospital:

> The Nantucket Lightship Basket is so called because, for many years, it was made aboard the South Shoal lightship, by successive captains, mates and crews. Presumably some baskets were made on the Cross Rip ship which was established in 1828. The first South Shoal ship was established in November, 1853. . . .
>
> This type of basket may have originated with the Indians but we incline to the opinion it came into being during the first quarter of the 19th century when the people of this Island were particularly influenced by whaling and by Quakerism. . . . A similar basket has been made for generations by a colony of Quakers on the "continent" who could have exchanged ideas about baskets as well as religion with the Quakers of this Island.
>
> Each whale ship carried a cooper. To this day the vertical splints of the basket are called "staves," the circular top binding finish "hoops," the boards "bottoms." . . .
>
> This type of basket consists of a bottom board with deep-grooved edge into which the staves are thrust. In some early examples the

bottom was of two boards nailed together. The wood of bottoms was pine, later sycamore from old plug tobacco boxes, then black walnut, mahogany and other woods. They were turned out by hand and later by lathe. There was a lathe on the South Shoal ship.

The staves were mostly ash, then white oak and hickory, now usually white oak. They were split out of cord wood, much of it from Mattapoisett and elsewhere on the continent. In old times old wood binding ties on baled hay were much used. Some old baskets used rattan staves. [The filler is a half round of Chinese rattan.]

Ears (2) to hold swinging bale (handle) were set in top of sides extending through hoops on line with grain of wood in bottoms. They often extended into bottoms, and were apt to be of same hard wood as staves. Brass ears, easier to handle and smaller, were introduced about 40 to 50 years ago.

Handles were of straight green wood bent, tied, and "stood" to set, not steamed. Rarely were they set rigidly into sides of basket even extending to bottoms, without use of ears. Handles were attached to ears by copper, later brass, gudgeon pin with head on one end and brass burr on other. Two small wood bow handles with ears a part of bow were occasionally used, one at each end, especially on elliptically shaped baskets. . . .

Nests of baskets were much prized; such baskets were of round or oval shape, usually 8 in number, with the smallest one pint size, the largest 12 quarts. Flat covers of same construction were occasionally made and attached by line, rivet or hinge.

These baskets were very strong and durable. . . . They were used for everything from gathering potatoes, fire wood, and carrying fish to holding knitting. . . . Some have lasted in good condition well onto one hundred years.

There are now a few men who continue to make Lightship baskets, among them Sherwin Boyer, who devotes part of his time to basketmaking. Mitchell Ray and Ferdinand Sylvaro give practically their full time to it. Mitchell, better known as "Mitchey" Ray, carries on in his shop, a long low building open to every passerby, at the end of Starbuck Court, Nantucket. His grandfather, Captain Charles B. Ray, and his father were both skilled in the same craft. Mitchey still uses a crude little shaving horse or bench which once belonged to his grandfather and nearly the same tools, namely, a drawing knife and a jackknife. In November, 1886, Captain Ray informed the *Inquirer* and *Mirror* newspapers that he had just completed his two hundredth rattan Lightship basket, 140 of which he had sold.

We found that the basket materials in Mitchey Ray's shop followed closely the items in Mr. Coffin's article, except that the large number of assorted handles and beautifully bent bails hanging on walls and from rafters were not of white oak but of red oak from the "continent." This variety of oak, Mr. Ray explained, most of which comes from Cape Cod, possesses bending qualities comparable to hickory. It keeps its shape better and for complicated bends is even more pliable when green. The most extraordinary feature of this shop was the collection of solid wood basket forms inherited in part from Captain Ray. They were strewn all about the shop, on the floor, piled on shelves, and in the open loft, perhaps a hundred all told, looking like weathered tops of giant mushrooms. Most of the baskets are in sizes for measuring products sold to and bought from local stores. Similar measures are still used today by the old colored man who peddles "Bless the Lord vegetables" to the homes on Nantucket.

In response to the question as to how the staves were fastened into the grooved wooden base so that they would not break out when the basket was heavily loaded, Mitchey Ray demonstrated the surprising trick by sharpening a thin oak stave, driving it into the groove of the wooden base by tapping it with his knife-handle and inviting us to pull it out. It looked easy but it was very hard, requiring a twist to dislodge it. He had sharpened the stave so thin and the oak was so pliable that driving it in had the effect of turning the tough end over in a kind of inverted plug; pulling on it made it hold all the tighter. It is clever of the craftsman to utilize the natural qualities of wood to make this strong joint.

Pride of craftsmanship is strong in Mitchey, and he is irked when baskets are poorly made. He thinks people should be helped to know what a good basket is. "Poor work spoils the trade," he remarked, but he would not name the poor workers. He avoids misunderstandings about orders by never taking money in advance. Once when a customer insisted that she had already paid for her basket, he asked if she always paid in advance. She admitted that sometimes she did and sometimes she did not. "Well," said Mitchey, "I have just one rule, never to take anyone's money in advance and I always keep that rule." The woman thought it over and paid the amount with satisfaction. Usually Mr. Ray encloses this little verse with the baskets he sends out:

> I was made in Nantucket
> I'm strong and I'm stout.
> Don't lose me or burn me,
> And I'll never wear out.

Ferdinand Sylvaro, a native of Nantucket of Portuguese descent whose orderly workshop on Orange Street adjoins his home, can depend on his wife to guard him from chance intruders. But those really interested in basketry find him always ready to explain it. He is a careful student of the craft and a good workman. In his possession are some of the old basket forms once belonging to David Hull, who made baskets on the South Shoal lightship. The governmental objection which caused basketmaking to be transferred to the island was made, Mr. Sylvaro says, when he was a young man.

The writer does not know of any place besides Nantucket where this type of basket is now made. In a collection of old handicrafts attributed to the Shakers in the New York State Museum at Albany, he has seen a basket of the Lightship type and the form over which it was made.

BASKETS OF VARIOUS MATERIALS

Reeds from the tall palm trees of China and the Philippine Islands and raffia from Madagascar are the materials for basketmaking used most commonly in schools and urban centers throughout our country. Little of distinction in the product usually results, although many people learn something of processes. There have been in New England exceptions to this rule of mediocre reed and raffia basketry. Any report on basketry must take into account the baskets of a Deerfield woman, Mrs. Gertrude Ashley, who, with her two daughters, Mildred and Natalie, began to make baskets about 1910. They worked out techniques and set new patterns that are followed by craftsmen in New England and elsewhere today. Mrs. Ashley and Mildred wrote a book entitled *Raffia Basketry as a Fine Art*, containing an account of their work. It is largely to this book and to Natalie Ashley Stebbins, to whom it was dedicated, that acknowledgment is made for material in this brief sketch. Mrs. Ashley was an outstanding leader in crafts and at one time president of the Society of Deerfield Industries, to be mentioned in Chapter 11.

Deerfield women demonstrated that skillful hands could make raffia baskets in many forms, that raffia is a fiber susceptible of beautiful coloring, and that decorations of great detail and charm could be achieved by those who were willing to try hard enough. At the Society of Arts and Crafts in Boston and at the Worcester Art Museum raffia baskets stemming from the pioneer work of these earlier craftsmen have recently been shown.

Mrs. John T. Timlin of Reading, Massachusetts, was one of the prime movers in the organization of the Reading Society of Craftsmen, the first meeting of which was held in her home in 1929. Her unusually attractive baskets are of reed and raffia, and she has been making them for about forty years. She is much interested in their history and use, and has written about them and about the value of a handicraft society to a community.

Miss Mildred Hanks of Wellesley, Massachusetts, became interested in a magazine article on Indian basketry more than twenty-five years ago. She immediately set about teaching herself how to make baskets of reeds and raffia and for many years sold them through the Society of Arts and Crafts and through the Women's Educational and Industrial Union. In recent years she has been using designs from Yugoslavia.

There is one contemporary craftsman in Massachusetts, Mrs. Mary F. Vaughan of New Salem, who makes baskets, woven mats, and a large variety of other articles from palm leaves. These are of such good quality both in design and in workmanship that they were shown at the Worcester Exhibition. Mrs. Vaughan wrote in 1944 as follows about her use of palm leaves:

> The palm leaf was brought from Cuba probably in the eighteenth century. The large leaves, being shut up like a fan and dried, were sold to hat shops which had them split into different sizes and sent out to families to be woven into webs on a loom right in their own houses. When returned to the shop these webs were made into what were called Shaker bonnets. They also made palm leaf fans. Soon afterward men's and boys' hats were braided by hand, finally being pressed and finished in the shop. When a child in the country, this was the only way we had of earning.
>
> Somewhere between 1895 and 1900, my aunt, Mrs. Merriam King, became interested in the Deerfield Arts and Crafts and with a few others began to make baskets and boxes of the palm leaf, obtaining the leaf from the hat shops. Soon she began to get so many orders from gift shops in Michigan, Minnesota, Missouri, Oregon, and other places that she asked me to help her as I had always braided hats.
>
> We made glove boxes, lunch boxes, stationery and handkerchief cases, knitting bags, cases for knitting needles, round and square boxes of all sizes. People called for different things for different uses, and we had to use our ingenuity. All the articles had to be pressed on blocks or other object to bring the desired result. About 1915 this work was mostly given up, it being hard to obtain the palm.
>
> Recently a cousin, who is interested in the Hampshire Hills Handicraft Association in Northampton, asked me if it was possible to revive this work. Not knowing of anyone else to do it and as I had some palm kept over, I began basketmaking again with the result that you see.

Mrs. Sophia Cooper of Somerville, Massachusetts, comes from a long line of basketmakers, including her parents and grandparents. Since her husband died Mrs. Cooper and the older children have been able from their basketry to support the family of eight. They make ash splint and also sweet grass baskets, gathering the sweet grass each season in the marshes near Wells Beach, Maine, where they market their work. They also make horsehair and birch bark baskets.

Sweet grass, to be referred to later, is used in many homes along the coast of Maine. Many housewives make workbaskets and trinkets of it for the family as does Mrs. Susie Thompson on Cape Split near Addison.

MODERN INDIAN BASKETS

Indians, who were the first basketmakers of New England, are still among the most important today, especially in the state of Maine where at the Penobscot Indian reservation, Oldtown, there is a considerable output of baskets and other handicrafts. Some Indian baskets are sold directly by the makers or through their shops on the island and elsewhere.

Splint baskets of black ash in a variety of types are made on the reservation. Many of them have been designed and shaped to meet some present need of the population in New England and elsewhere, such as bicycle baskets, lunch and pie baskets for automobiles; but in more demand than any others are the traditional Indian types of New England, known generally as the Penobscot baskets.

These are made of ribbonlike splints of ash, some thick, some medium, and some very thin according to the size of the basket. In recent years an oriental vine or ropelike plant imported from Asia has often been mixed with the splints in building up the filler of the basket, and also native sweet grass is worked into the sides and covers. The splints take dyes readily; some of the baskets are brilliant in color, others are subdued.

Sweet grass native to the swamps of New England, and especially in the Penobscot Bay area, is one of the most satisfactory basket materials to be found. The stems are tough though pliant, which makes it possible to do very fine weaving and braiding with it, and its various green shades hold their colors well. Sweet grass baskets are great favorites with the Indians themselves, especially the women.

No detailed description of Indian baskets can be given here, but there are two sources of information available to the student in New England—the collections in the Abbe Museum, a part of the LaFayette National Park Museum located in Acadia National Park near Bar Harbor, Maine; and the book, *The Handicrafts of the Modern Indians of Maine* by Fannie Hardy Eckstrom, illustrating especially the Mary Cabot Wheelwright collection in the Abbe Museum.

There are two kinds of baskets which the women of Oldtown especially like to make: one, the curlicue, sometimes called porcupine basket, because of its bristling exterior; the other, the tiny horsehair basket. The former, which is also small, for this clever weaving is usually limited to small things, is achieved by curling the paper-thin ash splints as the weaving of the filler progresses. This type, also called birthday basket, is used as a work- or trinket-basket. It has nothing in common with the true porcupine quill boxes and baskets.

The tiny horsehair basket, the largest the size of a thimble, is now made, as far as the writer knows, by only one elderly Indian woman, who lives on the Oldtown reservation. She is past eighty but makes miniature baskets in considerable number. They are used for decorations and favors, and are objects of wonder and admiration to Indian children. The horsehair is dyed in bright colors and usually two or more shades are worked into a basket. They are not, of course, important from a utilitarian point of view, but besides the pleasure they give the maker, which is registered in the face of the old Indian as she works, the enthusiasm of her family and neighbors for her skill and artistry gives the craft both a social and aesthetic value.

A VERMONT PORCUPINE QUILL BASKET

On a visit to one of the early handicraft exhibitions in Vermont, the writer was asked to speak to a group of exhibitors. He said, "I will begin by selecting some of the things which have interested me most; here is one of them." He held up to his audience a small, neatly made birch bark box decorated with natural-colored porcupine quills, explaining that he knew something about the quill work of the Indians but knew of no Indians in that part of Vermont. "Could anyone tell us about this basket?" Mrs. H. A. Foster of Stowe, who made the basket, was in the rear of the hall, and after considerable urging told an interesting story.

A good many years ago she had seen some Indians using quills to decorate birch bark, and she wanted to do it. "I could get plenty of birch bark, but I could not get hold of a hedgehog. At last one came into our woodshed; I saw my chance, and I killed it with a stick. I would not have had the courage to do it if I hadn't had need of those quills."

She had plucked the quills and counted them, fifteen hundred in all. Then she made a basket. Later she used a few quills for other purposes, but she never threw a single one away, and when word came that there was to be an exhibition of Vermont arts and crafts, she decided to make a new basket. When it was finished she thought the old one, made thirty-two years earlier, was the prettier of the two because it had aged to such an attractive color, but maybe in thirty-two years this one would do the same. Mrs. Foster's story was the feature of that meeting.

PRODUCTION AND MARKETING

Handmade baskets seem to be increasing in popularity in New England; the best basketmakers are selling a good portion of their products annually. The factory-made basket is sometimes cheaper in price. Factories use shapes originated by the craftsmen, spend less time on the preparation of materials, and take short cuts in manufacture. So they are coming to be more and more serious competitors of the individual basketmaker. It is generally conceded that basketry is one of the crafts in which the handmade product is superior in appearance and serviceability. A handmade basket can be produced quite economically, often with very little overhead.

One of the most serious difficulties facing splint basketmakers, who far outnumber others of the craft, is the decline of the black ash tree in some of the regions where baskets are made. Both white men and Indians suffer from this shortage; Indians especially now have to go so far for the trees that they cannot usually make the journey, cut their logs, and return to the reservation the same day. Few of them have motor trucks. Steps should be taken to reforest the black ash so that this important material may be assured in the future. If even a small plan for reforestation of the black ash were put into operation now, it might save an age-old handicraft of real economic and social value. An ash tree of from fifteen to fifty years of age is worth several times as much for basketry as for lumber or rough building materials.

CHAPTER 5

SPINNING AND WEAVING BY HAND

PART I. SPINNING

THE great abundance of textiles of every grade and unlimited patterns to be seen in American stores—a wealth beyond the dreams of ancient kings and queens—naturally raises the question why anyone today should spin or weave by hand. Understanding why people still do by hand what is so efficiently and extensively done by machinery may be helped by a recognition of how basic spinning and weaving have always been to man's economy and culture. Those who spin and weave by hand today, and their numbers are rapidly increasing, find themselves a part of the continuity of history, the textile processes being among the proudest, most important, and most beautiful inventions of ancient man. To this continuous record New England has made a lasting contribution.

Hand spinning is the process of converting fibers into the form of yarn, thread, or string. The best-known animal fibers in New England are sheep wool and rabbit fur. Practically the only vegetable fiber raised there is flax; but other interesting fibers, both animal and vegetable, are used somewhat sparingly.

The word "yarn" will be used to describe a loosely spun fiber, while "thread" will designate a fiber that is more tightly spun and twisted; the product of man's earliest attempts to make thread, however, would be more accurately described as "string," which resulted from separating fibers with the fingers and twisting them into the strength or thickness needed without the use of even the hand spindle. Unquestionably string of this kind was made long before anyone conceived the idea of weaving thread into a textile, and undoubtedly it had many obvious uses for primitive man.

During a long conversation with the great American scientist, George Washington Carver, at Tuskegee, Alabama, in 1941, the writer saw string made much as primitive man must have made it. Dr. Carver separated with his amazingly skillful fingers the fibers of a plant with

65

which he was then experimenting, pulling the strands from the main stem, intertwining and twisting them without interrupting the flow of his talk, until he had effectively illustrated this prehistoric process. A similar experiment was made by a New England woman who found, while working with the raw silk of the pierced cocoon which she desired to convert into a thread for rough weaving, that it was easier for her to separate the fibers in about the sizes needed by pulling them out by hand than by using cards as she would do for wool. In both of these instances the fingers alone secured suitable thread or string. In Egypt the craftsman, after separating the fibers of the flax plant, would twist them by rolling them with the palm of his hand over his leg above the knee. In this way strong string could be made, but it was a slow process, which in time was improved and refined by the hand spindle.

THE HAND SPINDLE

The hand spindle was the first known tool invented to help man make yarn and thread, and it was used for thousands of years before the spinning wheel was developed. Many spindle whorls of stone, bone, or baked clay used in spinning thread have been found in European excavations among lake dwellings, in one instance, according to Professor James Henry Breasted, with a spool of flaxen thread attached. In our own country Massachusetts enacted a law in 1642 under which "In every towne the chosen men . . . are to take care that such as are set to keep cattle bee set to some other impliment [employment] withall as spinning upon the rock,"[1] that is, with hand spindle and whorl. A herdsman could not, of course, carry a spinning wheel to pasture; he must have used the primitive hand spindle, which peasants of old had carried with them while tending their flocks.

CARDING

The carding process as practiced today consists of combing the material out into the form of tossed rolls, after which the fibers can be reunited in the size desired by twisting them on the spindle. In the

[1] Quoted by C. J. H. Woodbury in *Textile Education Among the Puritans*, pp. 16–17. (A paper read before the Bostonian Society, Boston, Mass., April, 1911.)
   "This 'spinning upon the rock' is a unique reference not known to occur contemporaneously elsewhere. . . . The rock was a whorl of stone or dried clay in the form of a torus or a round doughnut in which the hole was small enough to prevent from passing through the large end of the wood spindle forming the distaff and . . . also [by its weight] keeps it in a vertical position."

case of flax the combed mass is placed on a distaff from which the spinner can pull a few fibers at a time through her fingers either to the hand spindle, or to the spinnerette of the wheel where it is twisted into thread.

THE SPINNING WHEEL

The spinning wheel, a much later invention, was brought to America by the early settlers from Europe, probably being carried to New England on one of the vessels following the *Mayflower* early in the seventeenth century. Surprising as it may seem in a group coming to the New World from such a clothmaking center as Leyden, no spinning wheels or looms appear in the earliest inventories, although there were linen weavers and wool carders among those who came on the *Mayflower*. Even today there are a number of Spanish-American and Indian wool yarn spinners in New Mexico, Arizona, and Colorado who use only the primitive hand spindle. Our southwestern states probably first acquired the spinning wheel when immigrants from the East carried it across the continent.

Both the high wheel and the low wheel were in use in early New England. The high wheel was also called the "walking wheel" because the spinner walked back and forth while manipulating the fiber with one hand and the wheel with the other. The low wheel, propelled by the foot, although probably first used in the colonies for the spinning of flax, can be used for spinning any fiber. In addition to early handmade wheels patterned after English models, others have been brought to America from many homelands in Europe.

The revival of interest in spinning in New England recently has been much advanced by the formation of the American Angora Wool Spinning Association, several of whose members live in Connecticut. A member of the board of directors, F. D. Reeves of Thomaston, and Mr. and Mrs. Ted Raymond of Winsted, enthusiastic spinners and collectors, have given valuable information about spinning wheels. The Raymonds have discovered six or seven low wheels, which they have reconditioned. One, somewhat larger than the usual English wheel, has a French name carved in the block and may be of Canadian origin; another, having the wheel in the center, is Dutch; still another is Scandinavian and resembles the Dutch but has two wheels in the center, one over the other, and two "wish bones." The English wheel is of the chair type with double treadle and two small wheels in the center. This collection of spinning wheels has been discovered largely by inquiry among descendants of early settlers in Connecticut and Massachusetts.

SPINNING IN COLONIAL TIMES

We know that the early laws of Massachusetts required of the colonists the raising of flax and the training of children and others in its use. Even Britain encouraged the growth and use of flax, while sternly repressing the wool industry wherever it threatened to compete with English sheep and English cotton.

An outstanding event in connection with flax spinning was the coming to America of a group of Scots-Irish from Londonderry, religious refugees and members of the North Ireland community of trained spinners of flax. On August 4, 1718, five ships bearing a company of 319 Scots-Irish sailed into Boston harbor. A considerable number of them formed a colony in Nutfield, New Hampshire, a neighborhood known today as Amoskeag Falls, Derry, and Londonderry. In an article for *The Chronicle of the Early American Industries Association* of May, 1941, Miss Ruth Gaines of New Hampshire, whose spinning and whose research into the art are both noteworthy, reports that this colony "brought with them the newest ideas in flax culture and the up-to-the-minute treadle wheel." There is some question, as Miss Gaines indicates, as to whether the Scots-Irish were the first to bring over this low-type linen wheel operated by the foot, but the important fact to be noted is that they came ready and equipped to establish a rural linen industry in New England.

Between 1718 and the War for Independence several thousand spinners and weavers came to America, and schools for spinning and weaving were established in several communities. Enthusiasm for the production of linen cloth ran high, especially in Boston, where according to an early authority quoted in *The History and Antiquities of Boston* by Samuel G. Drake, "The females of the Town, rich and poor, appeared on the Common with their wheels and vied with each other in the dexterity of using them. A larger concourse of people was perhaps never drawn together." This demonstration can be traced directly to the influence of the Londonderry group.

In Revolutionary days, it is said, one New Hampshire woman fitted out her brother for military service with a suit of wool which she had sheared from the sheep's back, washed, carded, spun, and woven in twenty-four hours. Spinning continued to be carried on in the homes of the New England colonists long after the weaving of cloth was transferred to the factory. Gradually it was superseded in New England by machine spinning, and by the middle of the nineteenth century little of it remained.

THREE TYPES OF HAND SPINNING

In October, 1937, three spinners took part in an interesting demonstration of old and new methods of hand spinning. This was sponsored by the Universal School of Handicrafts at the New York Museum of Science and Industry.

Mrs. Helen B. Cunningham, of Bridgeport, Connecticut, a native of Fifeshire, Scotland, showed the spinning of yard on a new contrivance that utilized a modern electric motor attached to a spindle similar to the type used on spinning wheels. The process of feeding the new spindle was the same as that used in feeding the spinning wheel, but the motor gave it greater and more continuous speed and left the operator better use of her hands in feeding the fiber to the spindle. This, it was said, could be done at a rate twice as fast as was possible on the foot-driven wheel.

At the same time Mrs. Catherine Maietto, also from Bridgeport but a Neapolitan by birth, was making yarn on a primitive spindle (in Italian a *fuso*) in the form of a slender, round, tapering stick with a torus at the lower end. This, the oldest method of making yarn which employs a tool, has been in use for thousands of years on both the eastern and western continents. Mrs. Maietto used for a distaff the trunk of a small tree about three inches in diameter, quite straight, and as tall as she. With it placed against the wall she hung the carded wool near its top on nails in the tree. Pulling the fibers from the mass with skillful fingers, she attached them to the *fuso*, to which she gave a whirling motion as the fibers were twisted into yarn and later wound onto a paper spool. This method repeated many times made a yarn of good quality.

Mrs. Maietto explained that as a young child in Italy she was able to earn four cents a day spinning wool in this fashion. It was a skill she prized and was happy to demonstrate; she had taught it to her four daughters, "because I have to keep the art alive in our family."

The third spinner demonstrated the familiar process employed by our colonial ancestors and in widest use for hand spinning today. The high and low wheels were both used.

Mrs. Cunningham showed, as she said, "how wide a gap stretches between the old days and the present," for the electric motor enabled her to spin as much as two pounds in an eight-hour day as against the one pound that Mrs. Maietto could achieve if she worked from early morning until late at night. She expressed pride in the fact that she and her husband between them can take the raw wool from the sheep and through hand processes make it into finished cloth. During the depression of the 1930's the Cunninghams turned to spinning and weaving as a means of livelihood. When better times returned they did not lose their adeptness. "It takes the worry away," as Mr. Cunningham put it, "to have something you can turn to." Both husband and wife weave a variety of articles for their own use and for sale. Their daughter has a coat for which the wool was carded and the cloth woven by her father. Mrs. Cunningham spun the thread and made the coat.

NEW ENGLAND MILLS

With the application of power—first water, then steam, then electric—some of the finest spinning mills in the world were developed in New England; in some instances machines are so perfectly built and adjusted that should the operator, who attends hundreds of spindles, leave the building they would continue their work without interruption for hours. If there should be a break or an irregularity of thread, the mechanisms are so delicate that the spindles momentarily affected would stop and the others continue. The student of handicrafts might well visit one of the few remaining older and simpler mills where a transition phase from early to modern spinning is to be seen. At the Thomas J. Sheehy Mill, for example, in Phillips, Maine, is machinery reminiscent of the early development of American mills. Here is a spinning mule with twenty to fifty spindles which one man can attend: sometimes Frank Bennett runs the whole mill from cleaning the wool, washing and carding it, to the making of yarn. A similar service is performed by the H. A. Bartlett Mills of Harmony, Maine, and by the Caribou Woolen Mills of Caribou, Maine.

ADVANTAGES OF HAND SPINNING

There are certain definite gains in spinning thread or yarn by hand, among which are the following:

1. Hand spinning provides the opportunity to make yarn or thread as fine or as coarse as is desired. Also the weight and quantity of the yarn or thread may be changed at any moment. In contrast to this, in a spinning mill where elaborate preparations are made to spin one type of yarn, no changes can take place from beginning the run until the batch of yarn or thread is completed. In working up some flax two

New Hampshire spinners spun three or four different thicknesses of thread from the same handful of flax; then by spinning the tow into rough yarn they gained added variety and utilized what might otherwise have been a waste product. These several weights gave beautiful texture to their weaving.

2. Hand spinning makes yarn available when it is difficult or impossible to buy. During World War I the scarcity of yarn became so acute throughout the nation that at one time the American Red Cross was forced to hold up deliveries and thousands of hands were kept idle. In the Dakotas, however, where there are a large number of Icelandic immigrants, the men went into the field and sheared the sheep while the women brought out their cards and spinning wheels, prepared yarn on the spot, and continued their knitting of sweaters and socks for the boys in service.

3. By hand spinning the fleece of his own sheep, or the fur of his own rabbits, the owner can realize a greater return than by selling the raw material. There are many examples to be drawn from New England to illustrate this point. On a Vermont farm known to the writer a flock of sheep is cared for by a craftswoman and her family. This mother, whose story is told more fully in the following chapter, helps to shear the sheep, and when the wool is cleaned she cards it and spins it into the weight she desires for sweaters, socks, and other useful garments, which she knits for her boys or for sale. She could sell the spun yarn at a fair price in these times, but she finds greater gain and personal satisfaction in carrying the whole operation through from the sheep to the finished product.

4. Spinning one's own wool or other fiber makes it possible to get colors and color combinations in yarn not otherwise to be had. Control over color is appreciated particularly by tapestry weavers, who need great variety of color in their textiles. There are three ways of coloring wool: (a) to dye the finished garment; (b) to dye the yarn or thread that goes into the garment; (c) to dye the wool after it is carded but before it is spun. This last method interests us most at this point. Dyeing the wool is exceedingly pleasant and the color thus attained can again be modified to almost any extent desired by mixing the differently colored wools in the carding process. The craftsman working in this way has as much freedom in the selection of his colors as the painter in oils who combines and recombines colors on his palette. The separate yarns of various colors can also be twisted on the spinning wheel with interesting results.

5. To spin wool or other fibers gives one a sense of accomplishment and of control of material, which is one of the greatest human satisfactions.

SHEEP-RAISING IN NEW ENGLAND

Sheep-raising, which with shearing and carding is intimately related to spinning and weaving, is on the increase in some sections of New England, especially among small farmers and craftsmen who may have from one sheep to a dozen or more and who have practical ways of utilizing a part of the annual clip.

On an island off the coast of Massachusetts, No Mans Land, owned by the Alexander Crane family, sheep have been raised for several generations. Something about the location, and possibly the food, gives the wool a particularly fine quality, and it brings a good price in the market. Mr. Crane converts some of the wool of his flock annually into yarn, partly through hand spinning and partly through the small spinning mills. Like several other craftsmen he keeps a few black sheep in his flock. In New England, probably more than in any other place in our country (unless it be in the Southwest where the Indians have for generations followed the same practice), the black or the dark sheep are prized highly because their naturally colored wool is always ready for the special uses of the craftsman. Another large flock owned by Edward Waldo Forbes, a grandson of Ralph Waldo Emerson and until recently director of the Fogg Museum of Art at Cambridge, is kept on Nashawena, one of the Elizabeth Islands outlining Buzzard's Bay.

Many farmers shear their own sheep, but the majority depend upon the itinerant shearer, just as spinners of one hundred years ago relied upon the itinerant weaver to visit them once a year and weave up the yarn the family had spun. One such shearer should be mentioned. William Dickinson of Whately, Massachusetts, has perhaps sheared more sheep than any living man. He has gone up and down and across New England for more than fifty years, shearing a single sheep on a remote farm or camping for a week to shear a large flock. He estimates that he has sheared about a quarter of a million sheep. He has won several contests and received awards. When competition has been close it has been the superb skill, as well as the speed with which he removes the fleece (usually in one piece) without a scratch on the exposed skin of the often struggling animal, that has given him the admiring decision of the judges.

FIBERS OTHER THAN SHEEP WOOL

A small number of spinners, knitters, and weavers use animal fibers other than sheep wool, including rabbit fur, the fur or hair of various dogs, and occasionally the fur of a cat. Of plant fibers only flax for linen is used to any great extent.

Fortunately one can now get almost any fiber spun by hand in New England, from that of the silkworm to the almost silky fur of the famous Siberian dog known as the Samoyed, or the beautiful silk carrier of the milkweed seed; examples of each have been made by New England hand spinners for this book. Miss Martha E. Humphriss of Westerly, Rhode Island, is a breeder of the Samoyed dog, which produces a white wool of fine quality that she has had spun into yarn and woven into many textiles from simple scarfs to evening coats. Much of this yarn she knits and crochets into various articles. Of all American bred dogs the Samoyed has perhaps produced the finest fiber for handspun yarn for either knitting or weaving. An illustration is shown.

THE ANGORA RABBIT

The Angora rabbit industry includes the breeding of the animals and the shearing and plucking of fur, or wool as it is commercially called, for sale; the spinning of it into yarn by hand or in selected mills; the distribution of the yarn; and its use in knitting, crocheting, and weaving.

Angora rabbits can be bred at seven months and about four litters a year obtained with five or six offspring to a litter, the average being about twenty-two to each doe. They live from five to ten and sometimes fifteen years. The young rabbits are weaned at about eight weeks of age when it is possible to shear or pluck them, although four months is considered better by some authorities because the fur at that time is of higher grade. Then a crop can be taken regularly four times a year. The wool is either plucked or sheared. Shearing is much faster and some prefer it, but the plucked wool brings a higher price, partly because it avoids the blunt ends which fray or shed. The plucking operation, when carefully done, seems to be satisfactory to the rabbit, and in some instances it is clear that this accommodating little animal prefers it to shearing.

Angora rabbit growers and also spinners and weavers claim that other factors being equal, Angora is considerably warmer than sheep's wool. When mixed with sheep's wool, even when as little as 15 per cent Angora is used, it makes such an excellent texture that some think there will be more demand for mixtures than for straight Angora.

SPINNING IN VERMONT

At a handicraft exhibition in Montpelier, Vermont, one of the most interesting features was the demonstration by Mrs. Eva F. Talbert of Middlesex, who had brought her spinning wheel and her favorite rabbit. The good-natured big white Angora sat on a chair beside the spinner, allowing her, as frequently as she desired, to pluck the wool from his generous coat. Mrs. Talbert would then spin it on her low wheel into yarn, which she would crochet or knit into small articles, thus giving a demonstration which in interest, completeness, and end product was a very satisfying rural experience. Little information at that time was available to spinners.

Mrs. Talbert said: "I learned to spin as soon as I was tall enough to turn the big Yankee wheel we used. I learned to knit before I went to school. Later I joined the Woman's Farm and Garden Association of New England, and it was through this Association that I learned of the Angora rabbit. During the depression I corresponded with the pioneer importer and breeder of Angoras in New England, Mrs. Dorothy Houle, who, when she learned that I could spin sheep's wool, made it possible for me to purchase nine rabbits. In 1932 I began to experiment with their wool. It is handled quite differently from sheep's wool, and I worked about two months before I produced salable yarn. I did some spinning for Mrs. Houle, who had been sending her wool to Ireland to get it spun. I demonstrated spinning for the president of the Farm and Garden Association, Mrs. Henry Ford, and won a diploma of merit on an exhibit I sent to the University of Vermont."

In expressing her preference for the spinning wheel over the electrically driven spindle, Mrs. Talbert says that she can pedal faster than she can spin anyway, and enjoys working both feet and hands more than her hands alone as on the electrically driven spindle. It may be a personal matter, she says, but she favors this coordination of hand and foot, in which the rhythm is often a relaxation.

Mrs. Talbert's brother invented a little contrivance for rabbits that would be practical for many people. It consisted of a kind of drum, about two feet across and four feet long, a rolling cage of chicken wire fastened onto wooden discs or wheels. Into this a single rabbit is placed; he can roll it about on the lawn getting his fill of green grass without running into the garden or getting away.

Mrs. Clarence R. Hall of Essex Junction began spinning about twenty years ago when she purchased a rabbit, called Peggy, that soon presented her with eight little rabbits. It was the possibility of using the wool from these rabbits that induced Mrs. Hall to learn to spin and to knit. The big wool wheel on which she learned had belonged

W. G. Pollak, A.R.P.S.

1. A MAKER OF LIGHTSHIP BASKETS

MITCHELL RAY IS A DESCENDANT OF A LONG LINE OF BASKETMAKERS. AT ONE TIME THE LIGHTSHIP BASKET WAS MADE ONLY ON LIGHTSHIPS; NOW IT IS MADE ON NANTUCKET ISLAND BUT NOWHERE ELSE IN THE COUNTRY.

Doris Day

2. EIGHTY-THREE-YEAR-OLD BLACKSMITH

BLACKSMITH GEORGE W. JONES IN HIS SHOP AT BAKERSVILLE, CONNECTICUT, WHERE
HE HAS WORKED SINCE A YOUNG MAN SHOEING HORSES AND OXEN AND MAKING
HICKORY AX HANDLES AND USEFUL TOOLS OF WOOD AND IRON.

Life Photographer, Fritz Goro, Copyright Time, Inc.

3. A POTTER OF NEW HAMPSHIRE

AMONG NEW ENGLAND POTTERS NO NAMES ARE BETTER KNOWN THAN EDWIN AND
MARY SCHEIER OF DURHAM. MOST OF THEIR PIECES ARE MADE ON THE WHEEL; HERE
MRS. SCHEIER IS THROWING A BOWL OF NATIVE CLAY.

4. A CHAMPION SHEEPSHEARER OF MASSACHUSETTS

Probably No Living Craftsman Has Sheared So Many Fleece from New England Sheep as William L. Dickinson of Whately. Shearing for More Than Fifty Years, He Has Won Many Awards for Speed, Skill, and Kind Treatment of the Sheared Animal.

Doris Day

5. KNITTING THE WOOL FROM HER OWN SHEEP

Mrs. Dorothy Howe of Pawlet, Vermont, Raises Thoroughbred Sheep, Has the
Wool Spun into Yarn, and with Her Neighbors, the West Roaders, Knits It
into Garments for the Market.

Doris Day, School Arts Magazine

6. A VERMONT AUTHORITY ON DOLLS

MRS. DORA WALKER OF RUTLAND IS OFTEN QUOTED AS AN AUTHORITY ON AMERICAN DOLLS. SHE HAS A COLLECTION IN HER HOME, WHERE SHE REPAIRS AND RESTORES DOLLS AND MAKES THEIR COSTUMES.

George French

7. A WEAVING LOOM IN A GREENHOUSE

Philip and Annie MacLean, Brother and Sister of Northeast Harbor, Maine, Weave on the Porch in Summer but in November Move into the Greenhouse, Which Makes a Comfortable Loom Room.

Doris Day

8. A MAKER OF WOODEN CLOCKS

CHARLES A. SMITH OF BRATTLEBORO, VERMONT, HAD TWO OUTSTANDING RECORDS.
HE WAS THE LAST MAKER OF WOODEN CLOCKS IN NEW ENGLAND AND KILLED MORE
WOODCHUCKS FOR THE FARMERS OF VERMONT THAN ANY OTHER MAN.

George French

9. AN OX-YOKE MAKER IN MAINE

John Fulton Collomy of Kezar Falls Is One of the Last Craftsmen to Make
Oxen Yokes. The Shaping of Them for Comfort, as Well as Appearance, Is an
Old Rural Art.

L. M. A. Roy

10. A PUPPETEER'S WORKSHOP IN VERMONT

RUSSIAN-BORN BASIL MILOVSOROFF AND HIS DAUGHTER, ANN, ARE CARVING PUPPETS IN THE HOME WORKSHOP NEAR THETFORD CENTER. WITH TWO DEGREES IN POLITICAL SCIENCE, MR. MILOVSOROFF TURNED TO PUPPETRY AS A SATISFYING LIFE WORK.

Doris Day

11. SPINNING ON THE HIGH WHEEL IN NEW HAMPSHIRE

Mrs. Eric Ingles of Center Sandwich Is Spinning Wool on the High Wheel, Sometimes Called the "Walking Wheel" Because the Spinner Walks Back and Forth in Propelling It.

Doris Day

12. HANDICRAFTS HELP PAY FOR CONNECTICUT FARM

John Royko, Born in Czechoslovakia, Revived in Connecticut the Traditions of His Homeland. Here the Family Made Farm and Home Utensils of Wood, Which They Sold About the Countryside to Earn Money to Help Meet Payments on Their Farm.

George French

13. A HOOKED RUG OF ORIGINAL DESIGN

Mrs. Mabel S. Bragdon of Kezar Falls, Maine, Makes Up the Designs for Her Hooked Rugs as She Goes Along. Rug-hooking Is One of the Most Widely Practiced Rural Arts in New England.

Doris Day

14. A MINIATURE FURNITURE MAKER

In His Small Shop in an Old Chicken House on His Farm Near Winsted, Connecticut, Charles Ormsby Made Tiny Furniture and Miniature Farm Implements by Hand.

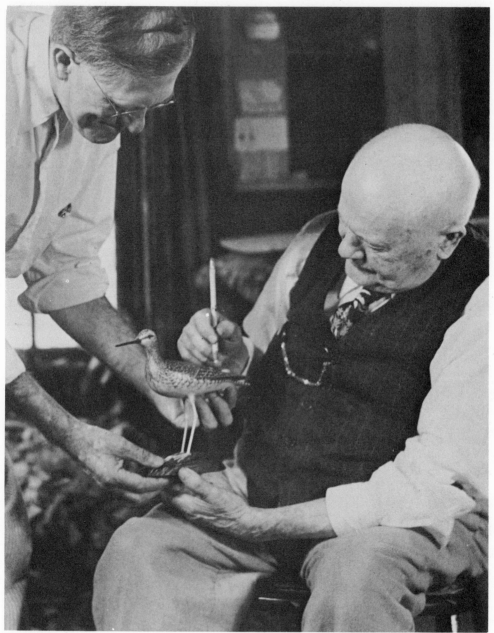

Doris Day

15. BIRDCARVERS ON CAPE COD

A. E. CROWELL OF EAST HARWICH, MASSACHUSETTS, WAS ONE OF THE BEST-KNOWN
BIRDCARVERS OF NEW ENGLAND. HE IS SHOWN WORKING WITH HIS SON, CLEON S.
CROWELL, WHO CONTINUES TO CARVE IN THE OLD SHOP.

The Providence Sunday Journal

16. A COLLEGE PROFESSOR TAKES UP BOOKBINDING

After He Had Retired as Professor of English at Brown University, Albert
K. Potter Took Up Bookbinding for the Practical Purpose of Putting into
More Permanent Condition His Own Books.

to Mr. Hall's great-great-grandmother and had not been used for generations. As Mrs. Hall learned to spin, the rabbits increased in number to twenty-three white, gray, and golden fawn, the last named having red-tipped hair. The fur on these rabbits, which were of English stock, grew to the length of four or five inches. She plucks the wool when it is long and ready, which in her judgment is about four months. For her best yarn she uses only the long lengths because she believes they make the garment "shed-proof," whereas the shorter wool may shed.

The wool is washed and dyed, moth-proofed with Larvex, and rolled on a small machine which is operated by hand. It is then ready for use or for sale. Mrs. Hall also spins sheep's wool. By combining hair of a German police dog or a chow with sheep's wool or that of an Angora cat with Angora rabbit fur, she produces a blend of yarn which is satisfactory for knitting various garments. She receives orders from distant states for her Angora wool, and she also spins and dyes wool sent to her and returns it to the owner. Mrs. Hall's young son has had full charge of the rabbits.

On a rugged farm near Worcester, where she and her sister-in-law used to care for twenty-two heads of stock, lives Mrs. Gertrude L. Wheelock, who learned to spin when she was seven years old. Mrs. Wheelock's maiden name was also Wheelock, and it was one of her family, Eleazar, who founded Dartmouth College. Her ancestors came to Vermont bringing their possessions on a handcart. Mrs. Wheelock once showed her pioneering spirit by tying her spinning wheel to a sled and hauling it a mile and a half through a Vermont blizzard to the grade school, so that teachers and children and thirteen assembled mothers might see a demonstration of carding and spinning wool. Mrs. Wheelock spins flax on the low wheel, also casein, a fiber made from milk, and almost any other fiber brought to her. When the writer visited her she was busily engaged in converting a poodle dog's fleece into yarn for Miss Anne Morgan. Mrs. Wheelock often demonstrates at fairs, for example, the Tunbridge World's Fair, and her work was shown at the Contemporary New England Handicraft Exhibition.

SPINNING IN MASSACHUSETTS

Mrs. Dorothy Houle, who cooperated with Mrs. Talbert and other Vermont spinners, is from Newbury. She is one of the earliest spinners and experimenters with Angora wool and has encouraged other New Englanders interested in raising Angora rabbits and developing the rural industries based upon them.

Mrs. Natalie S. Tarr of Essex was another early experimenter with

Angora fur. She and Mrs. Talbert agreed in saying that rabbit fur has been spun on both the low and high wheels. Mrs. Tarr said that the process of hand spinning Angora wool is moderately slow work. She found that it takes one hour to spin an ounce of wool into heavy yarn; finer yarns would require more time as there would be more yardage to the ounce. She had formerly sent yarn to Ireland in exchange for other yarns and for woven goods, the barter proving satisfactory.

SPINNING IN MAINE

Mrs. Alta M. Hale of Upper Gloucester makes a specialty of spinning rabbit fur during the winter, raising berries and vegetables in summer. She spins on an old flax wheel brought from England one hundred and twenty-five years ago, which belonged to her great-great-grandmother. Working five or six hours daily for about six months, she mastered the craft. "There is a knack," Mrs. Hale says, "to spinning Angora wool so that it will not shed. It is also easy to overspin it, that is, it can be made into a hard twist instead of being soft as Angora yarn should be."

Clayton O. Holloway of Winthrop spins a large part of the wool which he produces. Mrs. Holloway knits mittens and other articles for sale. Mr. Holloway is both scientific and ingenious. He has built himself a practical little shearing table, and uses an electric wool spinner, which he thinks is about twice as speedy as the spinning wheel. He has spun dog and cat hair, and has written of his weaving experiences generally for the *Small Stock Magazine*, published at Lamoni, Iowa.

Stewart Lord of Burlington has spun for thirty years or more, since a boy of ten or twelve. He writes: "All I spin is wool, whenever I have time. Some of my yarn is used for knitting stockings, mittens, sweaters, and some for weaving. It is so cold here and the winters are so long that many wool stockings and mittens are worn out. Men working outdoors wear usually two pairs of wool stockings and some wear three pairs, also wool mittens. Children all wear woolen stockings and mittens. Women do not wear the stockings as much as they did years ago. I have tried to interest people around here in spinning their own yarn, but have no luck. Many of them know how to spin but most send their wool to the mills to be spun, or buy their yarn. I weave some but I am not an expert. Last year I wove twenty yards of blanket cloth, using a cotton warp and homespun wool for filling. They were thin blankets to use like sheets in a cold room.

"I have my own sheep, twenty; I shear them, wash the wool, then

I have it carded at the mill. I can card by hand but it is slow work and I do not like the hand-carded batch to spin as well as I do the roll. The gray yarn is not colored but is made by mixing wool from black sheep with white wool. The brown wool is just as it comes from the sheep, no white with it. Hard to get this black wool now. My spinning wheels, loom, reels, and other things are very old—just like all that were used in New England one hundred or two hundred years ago."

A NEW HAMPSHIRE SPINNER

Miss Ruth Gaines, spinner and dyer, whom we mentioned earlier, lives in an attractive old red farmhouse near Meriden, New Hampshire. She not only spins the fibers of all kinds of plants and animals, chiefly the wool from her select group of Angora rabbits, but she raises flax and spins that as well. She is a specialist in natural dyeing, using both vegetable and mineral dyes as described in the chapter on this subject. Her extensive experiments with various kinds of fiber and her wide knowledge of the processes of coloring with natural dyes have contributed to her ability in judging the quality of handspun materials. She has demonstrated hand spinning at the fairs held by the League of New Hampshire Arts and Crafts. Her collection of early types of spinning wheels is unusual and she has written informingly about them.

Today there is probably more hand spinning done in New England than at any time since the Civil War. Much of this is due to the development of the Angora rabbit industry. If we wish to utilize new fibers, whether from plants or animals, spinning, at least in the early stages of the industry, will have to be done by hand because in present-day mills there are no appropriate facilities for converting unusual fibers into yarns, threads, or even string. It is hoped that the economic gain in spinning will continue to lead more craftsmen to practice this skill, also that the aesthetic experience will continue to interest more people, for spinning is one of the most graceful and fascinating operations of the human hand.

PART II. WEAVING

Hand weaving in New England today comprises many different types from the simplest and plainest web—a four-inch square made on a wooden frame called a Weave-It—to textiles woven on two-, four-, six-, eight-, ten-, twelve-, and sixteen-harness looms, including those complex patterns worked out on a drawloom or on a Jacquard.

Tapestry weaving in simple finger or laid-in patterns may be done on an ordinary harness loom; however, the Scandinavian and Gobelin tapestry techniques require especially constructed looms. Tapestry weaving of both these types is described more fully in the final section of this chapter.

TYPES OF LOOMS

Basically all looms are frames or other contrivances upon which threads of yarn can be intertwined to form a cloth or textile. Those threads that are fixed on the loom are the warp threads; those that are interlaced or woven into the warp are called the woof threads or the fillers. The warp and woof together make the web, the cloth, the textile as the completed weaving is variously called.

The simplest loom consists of a frame into which pegs or nails are driven at top and bottom. The warp threads are fastened on this frame like strings on a harp; the woof threads are then worked in and out with the fingers or with a needle or a shuttle. The Weave-It is of this type. The hand loom of the Navajo Indian is a Weave-It, but on a large scale, and the method of fastening the warp threads to the frame is different. The tapestry loom is also based on the same principle. In both the Navajo weaving loom and in some tapestry looms the weaver uses a thread or string, which acts to "shed" or divide the warp threads at points when the pattern requires it.

In a more advanced type of loom there is a mechanism which produces a shed or crossing of the warp threads, usually by means of a foot pedal though sometimes by hand, in which with each pedal stroke the shed is opened and a woof thread, carried by the shuttle, is shot or pushed through and fastened when the shed shifts back again. The action forms a V-shaped trough into the bottom of which the woof thread or weft is introduced, after which the threads of the trough cross each other to make a new trough or shed. Each time the warp crosses, it locks and holds tight the weft thread just placed in the trough. On some hand looms and on all mechanized looms the shuttle carrying the weft thread is attached to a spring or propelled by one so that it is shot through, or seems to fly through, the shed instead of being pushed through. This is called a fly-shuttle loom, on which it is possible to weave much faster.

There are two other types of looms used by a few craftsmen in New England. The drawloom, which was perhaps first used in China, has a number of drawstrings through which the pattern can be formed and repeated. The Jacquard loom, named after its French inventor, has a complicated harness arrangement of many cards having holes punched in them through which certain warp threads pass. The patterns are determined by stringing these cards above the weaving apparatus in such a way that the designs are reproduced with accuracy as the web is formed. All the elaborately decorated picture coverlets of early days in America were done on Jacquard looms, which were part of the equipment of some itinerant weavers.

Among the present-day New England weavers are some who make their own looms, others who have had looms built for them by good mechanics, and still more who have purchased them from the increasing number of loom-makers or manufacturers throughout the country. A majority of weavers use modern looms, but a few New Englanders have chosen the old box loom of their ancestors, an occasional one dating back to Revolutionary times. All told, the number of looms in New England runs into many hundreds.

EARLY TEXTILE OPERATIONS

There is no weaving without spinning and no spinning without fibers. We know that at first fibers were not abundant, and since twenty years after the Pilgrims came there still were intermittent shipments of cloth from England in exchange for lumber, fish, and furs, we may be certain that weaving was not among the arts to be extensively practiced in the earliest days of the settlements. However, it was not long until the need for cloth pressed upon the colonists, and under local encouragement and stimulation given to production of flax and wool, they were able before many years to make more cloth than that needed for their own clothes. In time the farm became a kind of manufacturing plant producing cloth not only for family use but as one of the items for barter.

In Massachusetts early laws passed by the colonists made it compulsory for each family to spin a given quantity of yarn every year under penalty of heavy fines. Flax-raising, which England did not oppose, was encouraged; and sheep-raising, which she had opposed from the first, was through dire economic necessity taken up by a few farmers; cotton was being raised in the West Indies, some of it finding its way into the colonies. The making of cloth at home was essential and inevitable.

Of the status and trend of early colonial cloth manufacture, the unknown author of the booklet entitled *New England's First Fruits* (published in London in 1643 and quoted by Rolla M. Tryon in *Household Manufactures in the United States, 1640–1860*) wrote, "With cotton-wooll which we may have at very reasonable rates from the islands [the West Indies] and our linnen yarne, we can make dimittees and fustians for our summer clothing. And having a matter of 1,000 sheep, which prosper well, to begin withall, in a competent time we hope to have woollen cloath there made. . . . So that God is leading us by the hand into a way of clothing." The "way of clothing" was made easier and more practical, economically speaking, by the development of linsey-woolsey; the actual wearing of this tough and often scratchy cloth, however, must have been a kind of penitential act—a symbol of American resistance.

One of the fascinating chapters in weaving, still to be fully explored, relates to the itinerant weavers who, beginning their country travels even before the War for Independence, continued in New England until after the Civil War. One, of whom we have a slight record, was Robert Northrup of Rhode Island, whose grandson "Weaver Rose," although probably never himself a roving weaver, had a shop in Narragansett where he made rag carpets, bed coverlets, and hap-harlots—earning his living entirely by his craft. In a book published in 1898, *In Old Narragansett*, Alice Morse Earle quotes from a letter written about that date by Weaver Rose: "My grandfather and grandmother, Robert and Mary Northrup, lived at what is now called Stuart Vale . . . in a little hamlet of four houses, only one of which, my grandfather's, is now standing. He owned a shore and fished in the spring and wove some at home and went out amongst the larger farms working at his trade of weaving, whilst his wife carried on weaving at home and had a number of apprentices. . . . He learned his trade of Martin Read, the deacon of St. Paul's Church. . . . He died in 1822, his wife lived until 1848."

Weaving is now done in many places in New England, but before it had been revived the old traditions were kept alive by occasional demonstrations in connection with historical places and events, such as the Pioneer Village at Salem, Massachusetts, where every year primitive ways of life and work are shown, and in the old historical house, Pilgrim Hall, at Plymouth, where during the summer months weaving and other old-time crafts are carried on. There have been comparable reminders of the merging of old and new ways, but in the main the weaving of today is of comparatively recent origin.

WEAVING IN MAINE

Maine has been outstanding in New England and even in the United States for the weaving by hand of yard goods for suitings and other purposes. Among the earliest to develop this type of weaving was Mrs. Florence Ives Gookin of Ogunquit, who has achieved a high place in the nation as a designer and weaver of textiles and who has also taught other weavers of Maine and neighboring states.

Mrs. Gookin, who was engaged in merchandising in New York, had a strong desire to do some creative work with her hands, and once when studying carefully a collection of hand-loomed textiles in a show window, she decided that she wanted to make some. After purchasing a small loom, she began to learn all the elementary processes involved in weaving, concentrating at night after her regular day's work until she had mastered these techniques and was able to open a workshop at Ogunquit. Mrs. Gookin's enthusiasm for good craftsmanship, her knowledge of materials and extraordinary enjoyment of color, as well as her rare talent for combining colors, are reflected in a wide range of work in wool, cotton, silk, and other fibers. Fine examples of the weaver's art are always to be seen in her workshop; once each year she holds an exhibition in New York. She has produced special webs for Lord and Taylor and other department stores.

Mrs. Florence Pratt of Kennebunkport brought together a few women of her neighborhood who were interested in hand weaving, and arranged with Mrs. Gookin to teach them. They work in herring-bone, plaids, stripes, and plain patterns. This group, known as the Kennebunk Weavers, have been meeting together since 1939. Among them are Miss Gladys Dalton, Miss Hulda Seavey, Mrs. Mary Parsons, Miss Lena Clark, and Mrs. Herbert Clough.

The weaving of yard goods by Ralph W. Haskell of South Portland, is noteworthy because of Mr. Haskell's cooperation in helping to develop the hand industries of Maine. His appointment in 1939 as supervisor of Maine Crafts marks the appearance of the state of Maine as a factor in the encouragement of handicrafts.

Mr. Haskell had been early trained in the textile industry, with which his father's family had been identified and knew the practical and technical aspects of fine clothmaking, the sources of supply for yarns, and the mills available for processing the raw wool. As executive of the state handicraft program he at once demonstrated his confidence in hand weaving by making the cloth for his own suits and overcoats. He has taught a number of men to follow his example. Probably more men in Maine have woven the cloth for their own suits than in any other state in New England. One of them, the late Dr. Bertram E. Packard, for many years State Commissioner of Education, said, "I never did anything which gave me more satisfaction. It was the best suit I ever had because I wove it myself."

In addition to individual weavers whom Mr. Haskell was able to encourage, he was concerned with certain groups of craftsmen and had a responsible part in the development, among others, of the Weavers Guild, a part of the Winter Industries Cooperative of Northeast Harbor on Mt. Desert Island, and the Cedar Grove group, known as the Kennebec Weavers, a few miles out from Damariscotta.

In Northeast Harbor Mr. Haskell had noted the interest of summer residents in British tweeds displayed at one of the smart shops of the town. This suggested to him the possibility that local people could make similar textiles which would sell profitably. The main responsibility for the experiment was assumed from the first by the Northeast Harbor people themselves, under the direction of Mrs. Henry Rawle. The state was prepared to offer encouragement, such as instruction in making looms and in weaving. In 1940 a group of the residents came together and decided that they would be willing to avail themselves of state assistance. It was not long before a number of looms had been made and an efficient setup worked out for the weaving and finishing of cloth. Practically all the original Winter Industries group became weavers. William Holmes, the postmaster, had his loom in a room above the post office; Charles N. Small, the local druggist, installed one at the back of his store near the prescription desk. If a customer came in while Mr. Small was weaving, he would call out above the clatter of the loom without missing a beat and ask what was wanted. Sometimes he would tell the customer to take his bottle of cough mixture from the shelf himself. The object of this concentration was to get cloth woven, but it also served to apprise the community of what was going on.

Most of the work was done in the homes or workshops of the weavers except for the winding of the warp. The local minister, the Reverend Richard B. Smith, took over this part of the work in the basement of his house. After a sufficient quantity of yard goods had been woven, a small exhibition for the summer residents was held in Northeast Harbor. Within a few days the textiles were all sold and orders taken for more. This first sale established a marketing pattern. The weavers' principle is to produce as worthy a textile as possible and sell it at a consistently low price in the community, and not be troubled with the problems or the added costs of shipment, consignment, correspondence, collections, and so forth.

A brief visit to the farm home of a brother and sister gives some understanding of what Winter Industries Cooperative means to its members. Philip and Annie MacLean, natives of Nova Scotia, are skilled craftsmen. Philip has made looms, many other objects in wood, including ship models, a wheelbarrow, and a violin for himself. Annie, like many Nova Scotians, can do any of the work on the farm and learned all the processes of clothmaking from her mother. The Mac-Leans weave on the same loom. In the summer the loom is in their cottage, usually on the porch, but in late fall or early winter they move it into the middle of their greenhouse, where there is abundance of light on the darkest days and sufficient steady heat. The writer visited this little farm with Mrs. Henry Rawle. Annie was not at home but Mrs. Rawle asked Philip if she might borrow a rug that his sister had recently finished, one of exceptionally fine quality, for the Exhibition of Contemporary New England Handicrafts to be held at Worcester. He replied, "I reckon you can, Annie would let you have the house if you wanted it."

The group of weavers living in and around the hamlet of Cedar Grove, a few miles from Damariscotta, number about nine. They weave in their own homes and make textiles similar in quality to those made at Northeast Harbor, marketing their products under the name of Kennebec Weavers. These craftsmen have made their own looms, with the exception of a few which were found in the neighborhood and reconditioned for modern textile weaving. The principal product of the group is suitings for both men and women. Mr. and Mrs. George Vaughan, both inventive craftsmen, were very active in the early weaving program of this group. Mrs. H. A. Everson, one of the pioneers, has possibly produced more cloth than any other member of the group. She and Mr. Everson are farmers specializing in strawberry culture. Work at her loom out of strawberry season is always recreation to Mrs. Everson. She manages to average perhaps fifty yards of suiting each winter, particularly herringbone patterns. Mr. Everson, who is a good mechanic, made the loom.

Mrs. Sadie Swett, who directs a group of weavers at Round Pond, is a designer and weaver of unusual ability. She was director and owner of an earlier enterprise known as Tenafly Weavers in New Jersey, and her group in Maine still retains that name. She markets suitings under the designation Pemaquid Tweeds. A variety of articles, including scarfs, bags, table covers, curtain hangings, upholstery fabrics, and many other items for personal and home use, is woven by this group. Hooked rugs and a few woven rugs in modern design are also made. Mr. Swett is an accomplished craftsman, his embroidery being a favorite form of creative expression.

Mrs. Lawrence J. Doore of South Paris, Oxford County, is a spinner, weaver, and needleworker, specializing in weaving suitings by the yard. She finds a market for many of her products in the neighborhood of her own home. Mrs. Doore has added to her textile arts linoleum blockprinting, which she does with the same skill that characterizes her other work.

Miss Barbara L. Page of Orono, although one of the younger weavers, ranks high among the designer-craftsmen in the state. She has extraordinary feeling for color and texture, two basic considerations in textile weaving, and has produced articles in considerable variety. As a graduate of the Boston School of Occupational Therapy, she became interested in handicrafts, especially weaving. She was a teacher at Northeast Harbor when the Winter Industries Cooperative was getting under way. Her tweeds are of high quality, and an extraordinary type of lap robe of heavy woolen yarn is one of her most satisfying achievements.

Miss Katherine D. Stewart of Bangor weaves for her own pleasure, making many articles of utility and decoration for her home. In addition to making designs in traditional New England weaves, she has mastered techniques and colors employed by weavers of South and Central America.

Mrs. Norma E. Korn of Kennebunk is known for her special interest in color. She weaves scarfs and other small articles and has developed a product consisting of a three-yard length woven textile to be used as a skirt, accompanied by twelve ounces of matching yarn for a sweater. These are called "matchies." The weavings are in many colors, solid, plaids, or stripes. Mrs. Korn has her yarn made to order at the Sheehy Mill.

Miss Mildred Lovejoy of Strong, Franklin County, is outstanding among the younger weavers of the state. Miss Lovejoy, who is blind, learned weaving in Perkins Institution, where she made many kinds of textiles. She has woven a considerable number of tweeds, the weaving of which has been made possible by a loom with a fly-shuttle, constructed for her by her father after the design supplied by Maine Crafts.

Up in Aroostook County, and especially along the Canadian border, perhaps more spinning, weaving, and knitting are done for home use than in any other part of New England. Mrs. Glouriess Ouelette of Frenchville is representative of a considerable number of French-speaking Americans who came originally from across the border, bringing to Maine the skills they had learned in their homes in rural Quebec and the Maritime Provinces. The blankets which they weave are usually of homespun yarn on linen warp, although the weavers would always prefer woolen warp if they could get it. However, the filler is pure wool yarn, for the most part from local sheep. The yarn is handspun usually on low-type spinning wheels.

In the town and neighborhood of Presque Isle there has been for some time a small community loom in the public library, or some other central location. The weavers could rent the loom for a nominal charge and weave such fabrics as they chose. At the time of the writer's visit Mrs. A. W. Higgins had just purchased an additional loom, which she was to make available to the people of the neighborhood. The plan was to charge a small amount per yard for weaving done on the loom. This would help pay for the new loom and also give people further opportunity to weave. Mrs. Higgins is a weaver herself and can instruct others.

WEAVING IN NEW HAMPSHIRE

From its beginning the League of New Hampshire Arts and Crafts has included spinning and weaving in its program. Among its early teachers were Mr. and Mrs. Eric Ingles, both of whom still practice these handicrafts in their home in Center Sandwich. Mr. Ingles had years of experience in the textile industries in Europe and is a graduate of a Swedish weaving school.

After coming to America he taught at the Worcester Art Museum School. Later he and his wife came to Sandwich to help develop a weaving project. He has raised flax, spun it into thread, and experimented considerably with native wool. In the old farmhouse which Mr. and Mrs. Ingles have reconstructed and on the land around it they will be able to carry out experiments with both plant and animal fibers. They hope to include the weaving of damask of which little, if any, has been done recently in New Hampshire.

Mrs. May Belle W. Seavey of Keene was a pupil of Eric Ingles and learned to weave in her home on an old loom that came from Deerfield, Massachusetts. It had been used for nearly a hundred years as a carpet loom, but Mr. Seavey made it into a four-harness loom for weaving luncheon sets, bureau scarfs, table runners, and an occasional rug. Mrs. Seavey is planning to weave a coverlet on the old loom from a colonial pattern such as was probably worked out on the same loom many years ago.

In 1940 Miss Elizabeth E. Marsland of Laconia set up her own studio and shop in an old barn where she produces textiles for the market. Many of the weavings are from her own designs.

Among early influences in the present handicraft movement and one of the most important, particularly in New Hampshire, is the Manchester Institute of Arts and Sciences, which was formed about half a century ago by the merging of the Manchester Electric Club and the Manchester Art Association. Its activities at first were chiefly in science and nature study, which then had great vogue, but instruction was also given in several handicrafts, including weaving. By the time the League of New Hampshire Arts and Crafts was organized teachers were already available from the staff of the older group. Manchester and the section around it have continued to make significant contributions to the work of the League. The general art program of the Institute in its earlier days was directed by Mrs. Maud B. Knowlton; weaving was under the supervision of Mrs. James Dodge. Mrs. Knowlton later became director of the Currier Art Gallery at Manchester.

For the past twelve years Mrs. Louise C. Martin of Manchester has had charge of weaving in Manchester Institute. She began to teach there when Mrs. Dodge resigned from her long service. Mrs. Martin is experienced in several types of colonial weaving, finger weaving, Spanish shadow weaving, but her chief interest is in plain weaving; she believes that some of the best examples of the weaver's art are in plain fine-textured linen. She is a strong advocate of the four-harness loom, on which so many simple but satisfactory patterns can be woven.

Miss Kate M. Gooden, one of Mrs. Martin's pupils, has developed a method for pattern weaving through the simple but little-used device of painting her design on the strung-up warp threads of the loom and then with carefully chosen yarn or thread of a neutral color weaving the web in the usual way. The painted design slightly diluted in color is thus retained and a pleasant pattern results. This method is capable of unlimited development. Miss Gooden has also done a number of unusual subjects in the form of pictures from twelve to eighteen inches square, in finger weaving. Another pupil of Mrs. Martin's is Mrs. Mildred P. See of Manchester. She weaves attractive textiles for suits. Mrs. See has built up a successful little home industry.

Mrs. Alma Hamilton, also of Manchester, specializes in the weaving of plain linen. She carefully selects a standardized mill thread and the product is of such smooth and uniform texture that one would have to examine it closely to discover that it was woven by hand rather than by machine. She also works in handspun materials but prefers a mill thread, especially when preparing a textile for petit point and other embroidery.

John W. Blake and Mrs. Blake were well-known and experienced weavers who worked together in the Blake Studio in Plymouth, New Hampshire. Mrs. Blake was one of the League's early teachers. Her work as a weaver was original and showed much imagination. The

Blake Studio contained twenty-four looms of the two-, four-, six-, and eight-harness types. Products of their eight-harness looms were shown by the American Federation of Arts at the International Exposition held in Paris in 1937.

Another instructor for the League is Robert F. Heartz, who lives in Exeter. He got his training in a textile mill, especially in carding and weaving and in the repairing of Jacquard and other looms. Both his grandmothers were spinners and weavers. He uses both a Jacquard and a drawloom, weaving damask and velvet; and has also done some oriental weaving. For nine years following World War I, Mr. Heartz was an occupational therapist in New York State, working with veterans. Recently he was associated with the School for American Craftsmen, and is now teaching special pupils under the Veterans Administration. He has also done some writing in the field of weaving.

Mrs. Mary J. Smith of Laconia began work on a table loom but soon found it inadequate. Finally she acquired a six-harness loom upon which she weaves many kinds of articles, including coverlets. Mrs. Smith feels that the weaver can put as much creative energy into the weaving of textiles as a painter can put into his canvases. She is not enthusiastic about weaving by the yard but feels that every woven article should be treated as a unit, and, for her, new designs are essential.

Mrs. Mildred Wentworth of Williamstown, Massachusetts, who at one time had charge of weaving at the Daniel Webster birthplace at Franklin, New Hampshire, is a painstaking craftsman who has the ability to combine colors in her web with extraordinary results. She makes suitings, upholstery material, and other practical fabrics.

Miss Berta Marken of Center Sandwich is a native of Sweden who, with her sister, was among the original teachers in the Sandwich Home Industries. Her work reflects the skill and taste of the weaving in her homeland.

WEAVING IN VERMONT

Among pioneers in the revival of hand weaving and the development of textiles in the United States, the Elizabeth Fisk Weavers of Isle La Motte and St. Albans hold a high place. Mrs. Fisk first developed in her home community a type of plain linen weaving with figures in color put in by hand, there called tapestry or finger weaving. She dyed all her linen thread herself and developed a color palette of rare beauty which, with the finger technique of weaving, set her work apart from anything done elsewhere, and has made it sought after by collectors.

In addition to teaching a number of young women on Isle La Motte, Mrs. Fisk worked with another group on the mainland at St. Albans, which was organized under the leadership of Mrs. Elizabeth Smith, wife of former Governor Edward C. Smith of Vermont. Thus the weavers of the two communities came to be informally known as the Fisk Weavers, although the St. Albans center is often called the Elizabeth Smith Looms. Some of the original pupils still carry on in these communities.

When Mrs. Fisk died she left a little stone cottage on Isle La Motte to the young women with whom she had been so intimately associated. Much of the work, including the dyeing of linen thread, has since been carried on there by Miss Cynthia Ritchie, who had assisted Mrs. Fisk in the experiments with dyes. The same formulas are still used. Among the weavers were two sisters, Miss Mabel C. and Miss Eleanor Holcomb, who continue the same type of weaving with similar emphasis on color, but who also do other kinds to meet present-day trends. The work of both was represented at the Worcester Exhibition in 1943.

The village of Isle La Motte is an example of what home industries can do for a community. Miss Mabel Holcomb has traced back the thread of handicrafts more than half a century through the records of the little church, which had burned and been rebuilt in 1856. In 1891 "The Ladies Aid paid Mrs. Rockwell $4.13 for weaving a carpet for the vestry"; it also recorded that cutting and sewing carpet-rags and weaving rugs brought in enough capital to enable women in 1895 to "hire a tent, borrow 75 cream pitchers" and give the first of the famous Fish and Game League dinners. Later they initiated "a period of face lifting for the old church." Proceeds from the sale of rugs were used for a new chimney, a stove, and redecorating; a kitchen was added, a belfry, and "all in all," writes Miss Holcomb, "these changes made it what it is today, as lovely a church as can be found in any town." The public library building was purchased by local women, and its restoration and development was largely due to the weavers of the island.

Among the weavers at St. Albans, Mrs. M. T. Dee, a native of Wales, has probably contributed most to advance the traditions of the Fisk weaving. Like Miss Ritchie she has experimented with dyes in accordance with Mrs. Fisk's palette. She also made the Vermont seal in finger weaving, with linen thread and colors, which is in the State House at Montpelier. Mrs. Margaret Armstrong and her associate,

Miss Elizabeth Ward, have developed worthy designs in yard goods and have woven special articles for home use.

Dr. and Mrs. Hubert Fowle have developed the Thetford Handicrafts at Weavers' Cottage in Thetford, where weaving in practically all fibers is done in a great variety of patterns. A selection of their weaving was sent to the Rural Arts Exhibition in Washington, D. C., in 1937. In recent years linen weaving has been their specialty, and they have also used high-grade Angora rabbit yarn from their own rabbits. Dr. Fowle was president in 1942 of Vermont Craftsmen, an informal group centering in Thetford, and both he and Mrs. Fowle have helped greatly in the advancement of weaving in the state.

Mrs. Fowle, who has woven for over twenty-five years, was at one time director of hand weaving for the New York Guild for the Blind. Since making her home in Thetford she has worked as teacher and designer as well as producer, and has styled neighbors' products for the market. Through her encouragement guilds have been developed in various branches of handwork.

The success of West Fairlee of the Homemakers Weaving Guild, part of a state-sponsored program for rehabilitating a farm neighborhood, is due in great measure to Mrs. Fowle. The West Fairlee weaving project is described in Chapter 19.

Mrs. Mary Maxham keeps a little store in the village of Worcester. At the back of the store is a loom where she works whenever there is time between customers. She has woven several old types of coverlets, including Orange Peel and Chariot Wheel, both traditional New England designs which are also found in the Southern Highlands, and has made luncheon sets, towels, and napkins which she sells in her store. Some day she intends to learn to spin on her grandmother's spinning wheel.

Mrs. Eugene C. Rhodes of Woodstock, director of the Crippled Children's Division of the Department of Public Health, is a serious student of handicrafts in therapy and a lover of beauty who realizes the need of each individual for some creative outlet. A large number of her pupil-patients have been persuaded to take up the kind of work that seems best suited to their disposition, talent, and general needs. Among them is Wilson Shippee of West Dover, about twenty years of age, who was a victim of infantile paralysis, which deprived him of the use of his right arm. With his left arm and hand he threads up his loom and with hand and teeth ties the knots in the warp thread. He has become a skillful weaver, and his enthusiasm for his work under so great a handicap impresses anyone who meets him.

Miss Bertha E. Hewitt of North Pomfret intended to weave only as a part-time hobby, but after spending a year in study she began to supervise the weaving in the North Bennett Street School of Boston, guiding Italian women weavers there in the making of tweeds. She has had charge of various weaving projects and has demonstrated at the Pioneer Village at Salem. Some old linen thread, found by a Burlington family, that was handspun during the Civil War is one of her prized possessions. This she has been using in her weaving.

Mrs. Jessie J. K. Westbrook of Benson, Rutland County, has produced beautiful runners in silk which are notable for originality of design. She takes time to produce an extraordinarily fine web and works in several mediums. Her sister, Miss Julia R. Kellogg, does needlework of equal quality.

WEAVING IN MASSACHUSETTS

The Weavers Guild of Boston, founded in 1920, is today one of the oldest and one of the largest and most active weaving organizations in our country, with over 100 members. Mrs. Lillian A. Sargent is the present dean.

A charter member and former dean of the Guild, Miss Myra L. Davis of Boston, is known as weaver, teacher, and supporter of handicrafts. Miss Davis spun and wove for the Worcester Exhibition a textile composed of the down or floss of native milkweed in combination with enough cotton to keep the feathery seed-bearing fibers from flying away.

Miss Kate Van Cleve of the Garden Studio, Brookline, author of *Hand Loom Weaving for Amateurs*, is a teacher of weaving of wide experience and a long-standing member of the Weavers Guild. She has taught hundreds of pupils from many countries and often demonstrates weaving on different types of looms, showing the various processes from original threads and yarns to the finished product.

Mrs. Marion P. Drew, custodian of Indian House, Deerfield, spins, dyes, and weaves. She taught weaving in public schools in Hawaii before taking up the work at Deerfield in 1936. Mrs. Luanna L. Thorn, also of Deerfield, has been weaving since about 1901; her specialty is called loom embroidery or shadow weaving. An example of this technique, The Sphinx Moth, done by Mrs. Thorn, was purchased by the Art Museum in Newark, New Jersey. In addition she does vegetable dyeing.

Dr. Mary P. Dole of Shelbourne Falls, a graduate in 1886 of Mount Holyoke College and a doctor of medicine, was known as well throughout New England as a "doctor in homespun." This is the title of her autobiography, in which she set forth in a vigorous and natural style the extraordinary experiences of her life, including her weaving and the part it played in her devotion to her Alma Mater. She learned to weave through prescribing this handicraft for a friend who was losing her eyesight. Upon retiring from the practice of medicine, Dr. Dole became so proficient as a weaver of marketable coverlets, knee blankets, dress and upholstery materials, and other items, that she began to provide medical fellowships for Mount Holyoke graduates. In 1943 she reported that the returns from her weaving since 1931 and from the sale of her book, which had been used for scholarships, amounted to $11,275. Among Dr. Dole's special pieces is an orange and brown coverlet of an old-time pattern called Sunrise and Dogtracks, copied from a coverlet woven by Mary Lyon, the founder of Mount Holyoke, for Dr. Dole's grandmother.

John Rehorka, a native of Czechoslovakia, now a farmer near Shutesbury, also finds time to weave. His fabrics are usually of open patterns in soft wool materials, especially shawls and scarfs. Examples of his webs are always to be seen at the Northampton Handicraft Fair, sponsored by the Hampshire Hills Handicraft Association, under the leadership of Miss Lena W. Barrus. They were also shown at the Worcester Handicraft Exhibition. Mrs. Rehorka and their son and daughter help with the weaving.

An unusually successful teacher of weaving is Mrs. William H. Hubbard of West Boylston. She provides the beginner with a loom which is strung up and ready for work. By this means a pupil soon feels a sense of achievement, after which an interest in stringing up a loom and other preliminary operations can easily be developed. These preliminary operations take time and patience, and can best be done when the need for them is understood.

Among other skilled weavers of Massachusetts, to name only a few, are Mrs. Phoebe K. Collins of Williamsburg, who specializes in old-type coverlets; Mrs. W. A. Sheldon of Northampton, who makes table covers; Mrs. S. T. Zappey of Greenfield, who exhibits at the Northampton Fair; Miss Irene V. Walsh, proprietor of Nantucket Weavers, who weaves chiefly articles for sale in her shop; Miss Amy P. Morse of Lexington, who makes attractive luncheon sets; Mrs. Gwen Maki of Ashby, born in Finland, who preserves in her weaving the traditions of her homeland; Miss Margaret Buchanan of Marblehead, who weaves Scottish tarlatans; and Mrs. Elizabeth G. Thorsen of Great Barrington, who weaves articles for household purposes.

WEAVING IN CONNECTICUT

Mrs. Nellie B. Burow of Stamford is a craftsman in several mediums and an excellent weaver, who makes many of her own designs. She likes to weave in the Swedish Dukadene technique, in which the decorative figures in the weaving are developed on practically a level with the rest of the web. Few do this Swedish type of weaving. Her contributions to the Crafts Project of the Connecticut Work Projects Administration in Stamford are referred to in Chapter 8.

Harry Miles Cook of Georgetown, who died before this book was completed, was an outstanding teacher and weaver. "To work with one's hands," said Mr. Cook, "and to create original things is my ideal of life." As a boy he did some fine work in knitting and needlework and was interested in learning all he could of carpet- and rug-weaving as it was done by his mother's friends in the home community. When illness interrupted his business career he determined to take up weaving seriously. He traveled, and studying textiles widely here and abroad, finally settled down as a weaver in a large log cabin in Ridgefield, Connecticut. Here at one time he had fifty looms, which he used for both teaching and production. Mr. Cook also taught weaving to the blind.

Warren C. Rockwell of Bridgeport weaves chiefly Scottish plaids in designs suitable for neckties and scarfs. Mr. Rockwell weaves them according to tradition, but he sometimes makes a free adaptation of the patterns.

Mrs. Agnes Barrington of the Puritan Weavers at Guilford weaves rugs, rag carpets, bags, scarfs, linen runners, and towels and has a variety of looms—as many as twenty-two—including two-, four-, eight-, and ten-harness looms. She reports that she "weaves everything from bookmarks to bedspreads," and has made shipments to England.

Mrs. George Weed Barhydt of Hartford began her training in the arts as a painter, but on considering the handicrafts decided that she would find in them an equally good opportunity for expressing herself and applying her standards. Mrs. Barhydt says of her progress, "It has been slow, not over-lucrative, but soul-satisfying. Now, as I grow older, here on my own farm alone I can have the same creative joy and satisfaction that an artist has with a fresh canvas before him."

Miss Martha Pasco of West Hartford teaches weaving, needlework, stenciling, metalwork, and clay modeling. She has two summer gift shops for which she and her sister make many articles. Miss Pasco is particularly active in research in the field of design and in the technology of the several crafts in which she is engaged. She is now directing handicraft work for cripples and the handicapped under the auspices of the Connecticut Society for Crippled Children and Adults.

Ranking among the most original and versatile New England weavers is Miss Alice Turnbull of Haddam, who has achieved special effects in tapestry, finger weaving, and other techniques. One of her textiles, Country Wedding, among other webs from her loom, was exhibited at the Worcester Exhibition. She wove in 1947 a theater curtain thirty feet wide by twenty-two feet high for the Bar Harbor Playhouse, which is one of the most interesting examples of modern hand weaving in our country. The curtain was designed by Alexander Crane. Carrying out so detailed a design was a real problem in technique. The curtain is shown here. Among Miss Turnbull's smaller weavings is a picture story of the Connecticut Valley, which she both designed and wove. She also weaves the rya type of rug originated by the Scandinavians. She is an all-round craftsman in both weaving and needlework and often combines embroidery with her weaving, giving it unusual interest, and sometimes a touch of humor.

Other Connecticut weavers deserving mention are Mrs. Allen Clark of Middlebury, a collector of textiles from near and far places and an experienced craftsman, who showed a plaid blanket at the Worcester Exhibition; Mrs. Louis H. Walden of Norwichtown, who weaves coverlets and textiles known as Walden Woven on looms made by Mr. Walden, these being among the fifty or more looms which he has built; Miss Ruth Potter of New London, who for the past twenty years has used the four-harness loom and woven with cards in carrying out her own designs; Miss Georgia A. Burroughs of Danielson, a pupil of O. B. Thayer; Mrs. Charles C. Piercey of Waterbury, who exhibits and sells through the Society of Connecticut Craftsmen. Mrs. Thomas L. Barrup of Roxbury taught herself to weave and has pursued this craft along with a professional interest in occupational therapy; she has taught weaving to patients suffering from nervous diseases. The Society of Connecticut Craftsmen awarded her the master craftsman insignia.

The Bridgeport Project

In the midst of the depression of the 1930's the Bridgeport Housing Company, owning and operating about 800 model tenement houses in the city, found itself with 350 vacancies and with an additional 200 tenants who could not pay their rent in full. It seemed clear to William H. Ham, the manager, that something ought to be done to enable his tenants to earn a livelihood in their own homes. There were two requirements for such undertakings: one, an inexpensive raw material; two, inexpensive home equipment for working the material into profitable form. Spinning yarn and weaving it on a hand loom seemed to be one of the answers. Mr. Ham was disposed toward weaving because he had long worn homespun suitings and recalled the traditions of spinning and weaving among his New England forebears.

His first concern was to teach his tenants how to spin and weave, and in this a young graduate from Yale Art School, Miss Marie Keller, was of the greatest help. Mrs. Catherine Maietto had said, "I can spin if you can get me a *fuso*." The primitive hand spindle, already described, which Mrs. Maietto and Mr. Ham together rigged up and which is now one of Mr. Ham's proudest possessions, earned for Mrs. Maietto more than $1,000 in the several years of the experiment. Other spinners on both high and low wheels were discovered, as well as other teachers, and a home spinning machine was built with an electric motor attachment by which the speed of the spinner was doubled. On visiting a family Mr. Ham saw one of these machines being used by a young man who was comfortably seated in the kitchen by the stove spinning his thread by sense of touch while his machine was in an unheated adjoining room. The yarn strand passed from his fingers to the machine through a narrow crack in the door. The distance from the spinner's hand to the machine was about eight feet. He could not see the machine, but like the blind spinners whom this young man taught, he was spinning entirely by touch, which is the correct way.

The story of the Bridgeport spinning and weaving project is a fascinating one which should be told more fully. But we must content ourselves with a brief account of the weaving as told by Mr. Ham: "I will never forget the day in 1937 when young John Henri came into my office and after waiting in line for his turn said to me, 'Mr. Ham, I am at the end of my resources. I haven't any income and I can't pay my rent; I guess I will just have to find a cheaper place to live.' I called for Mr. Henri's rent book. For several years he had paid his rent and his installments promptly; no payment had ever been more than a week late and he had never missed one. I said to him, 'Mr. Henri, you have never failed to meet your obligation to this company, you have established credit here, we don't want you to move, and it may be you would be interested in doing some weaving while you are not otherwise employed.' Then I explained the plan to have some of our tenants weave cloth and asked him if he would like to try it. He was eager to try and we lent him a loom at once, which he installed in the basement. He was quick to learn, and it was not long until he was making good wages weaving cloth for men's suits and overcoats."

A warping apparatus ingeniously made by Mr. Ham and an assistant in one day of actual work was, in his opinion, the principal key to the success of the enterprise. This made it possible for a weaver to continue his work for long periods without rewarping the loom. By this time- and labor-saving device he could greatly increase production. The homemade warping machine was in service ten years.

Mr. Ham undertook the marketing of the cloth, selling the yardage for over six hundred men's and women's suits and enabling sixteen spinners and fifteen weavers in the housing project to become self-supporting again. Their earnings under this project were more than enough to pay their rent or installments and they had time left over from clothmaking for other occupations. Other things were done by the tenants to earn money in this emergency, but it was the clothmaking at home which engaged most of them. They produced an outstanding product and in many instances discovered that they had hand skills of which they had not dreamed. The operation by this group of dyeing the yarn, largely with vegetable dyes, is referred to in Chapter 8.

Speaking of one of his own handspun, hand-woven suits, Mr. Ham remarked that, having just been fullerized and dry cleaned it looked much as it did when new six years earlier. "The colors are a little lighter, but better with age. I don't mean that this suit is just one of my old suits that I like because it fits and is a nice old-shoe kind of thing. I mean that this cloth has a sparkle about it that is real; it cannot be made with machine-made thread."

WEAVING IN RHODE ISLAND

The workshop of Mr. and Mrs. William E. Brigham and Mr. and Mrs. Hugo Linnell of Providence is known as Villa Handicrafts. These craftsmen are creators of a variety of handicrafts described in these pages. Their weaving is particularly good, and the loom room is beautifully designed to suit their needs. Their equipment, all of which they have made themselves, is probably not excelled in small studios anywhere. The looms range in size from the small portable kind to one eighty inches wide, which requires a weaver sitting on each side to throw the shuttle back and forth. One loom is called The Littler and Finer, and another The Bigger and Better; and webs produced on these looms are given the same names. The Linnells have recently made some large bedspreads on the eighty-inch loom, also large rugs. Both Mr. Brigham and Mr. Linnell are also skilled craftsmen in wood and metal.

Philip R. Sisson of Columbia University has a summer home at Hopkinton. Here he weaves during his vacations and is surrounded by his large collection of New England textiles, looms, wheels, and other devices for making cloth by hand. One of Professor Sisson's specialties is pattern weaving. On his favorite patterns he can sometimes weave as many as five yards a day. He uses a hand shuttle entirely and says that he and his wife can weave about one-quarter as fast as the work can be done on a highly mechanized loom. Professor Sisson likes to weave linen, although he does not limit himself to this fiber.

Miss Edith E. Tucker of Narragansett Pier has been a weaver for more than ten years and has taught weaving in the neighborhood; she has given much encouragement to local handicrafts. On the four looms in her home she produces both linen cloth and woolen suitings. Her mother does beautiful needlework, chiefly for their home.

Miss Jessie Luther of Providence is a distinguished weaver and has done praiseworthy work in therapy. Miss Luther started weaving and hooking for Sir Wilfred Thomason Grenfell, British physician and missionary in Labrador and Newfoundland. She is also an accomplished enameler.

Roger Potter of Wakefield is interested in weaving chiefly as a hobby; he has woven many rugs, table runners, luncheon sets, small pieces, and more recently tweed for jackets, vests, and topcoats for himself. In his workshop he has two old oak looms and a modern rug loom. Mr. Potter is a collector of textiles and owns a blue coverlet, said to have been woven by Weaver Rose.

TAPESTRY AND FINGER WEAVING

In tapestry and finger weaving, in the sense used here, the weaver puts the pattern in by hand rather than with a shuttle. The effect of tapestry weaving is more like a freehand drawing or a painting; that is, the design can be carried out in any form. Although the terms "tapestry weaving" and "finger weaving" are sometimes used interchangeably, tapestry weaving is to be differentiated from finger weaving by the type of loom and by the relative area given to the design. A tapestry loom has no shed mechanism by which the warp threads can be separated and the woof thrown in between the sheds with a shuttle; in tapestry every step is done with the hand or fingers, without the use of a shuttle. Finger weaving is usually done on a hand-shuttle loom, with only a small area, that containing the special figure or design, as a rule being laid in with the fingers; the remainder of the web above and below the laid-in design is woven with the shuttle.

Generally speaking, the methods for making tapestry which are used in New England can be grouped under two headings. One is the Gobelin tapestry (so-called from the name of a leader of Flemish wool dyers, Jehan Gobelin in the reign of Francis I) as woven and knotted in the famous tapestries of France, Belgium, and other European countries, where practically every thread laid in is tied around the warp in a tapestry knot. In the other kind of tapestry weaving, referred to usually as the Scandinavian or sometimes as the Norse or Swedish technique, comparatively few knots are made; the design is thus woven in by hand, and is comparable in technique to some of the Navajo rug figure weaving. There are variations for joining parts of a design, but the woof threads are turned back, folded, or worked into the web rather than tied. There are, of course, instances in this method in which some yarns are tied, but this is exceptional, while in the Gobelin type of weaving every piece of yarn used in the filling is tied.

Some Tapestry Weavers

Mrs. Clara G. Leavitt of Vineyard Haven on Martha's Vineyard is a tapestry maker who uses mainly the Gobelin technique, although she has also done some webs in the Scandinavian method—one an openwork Norwegian weaving of a tulip tree design. A large tapestry about five by seven feet, in the Gobelin style, is a reproduction of a medieval design, Pope Urban preaching the First Crusade, and was shown at the Worcester Exhibition. Other tapestries made by Mrs. Leavitt for her home include wall, as well as window hangings, and screens.

Mrs. Neil van Aken of Cheshire, Massachusetts, is a weaver and teacher of tapestry making, usually employing the Gobelin technique and originating her own cartoons, which are generally adapted to small pieces for chairs and similar purposes. In some of her work she uses the Scandinavian technique.

Mrs. Else Böckmann of Newtonville, Massachusetts, who is also a hand spinner, preparing and dyeing all her own yarns, is a skilled and experienced tapestry maker, working in designs of Scandinavian origin. She has executed several tapestries from drawings by John Bauer and has taught others to make tapestry.

Mrs. Brigham and Mrs. Linnell, of Villa Handicrafts already mentioned, are accomplished tapestry weavers. Both studied in Sweden.

Mrs. Brigham's tapestry, designed by John Bauer, was shown at the Worcester Exhibition and is illustrated here.

Among other tapestry weavers several deserve more space than can be given here: Mrs. Margareta Ohberg of Colchester, Connecticut, whose patterns in figures and flowers are finished in the Scandinavian tapestry technique; Mrs. Harry Hoffman, of Old Lyme, Connecticut, a leader in the arts of her community, whose beautiful tapestries of fish and undersea subjects are widely known; Alonzo J. Bloodgood of Middlebury, Connecticut; and Mrs. Rita M. Pettingill of Georgetown, Massachusetts, who has made a noteworthy St. George and Dragon tapestry, which took a year to complete. Mrs. Pettingill is one of New England's most versatile craftsmen; her home is filled with fine and original examples of her skill in many crafts.

As this chapter on weaving is being closed, word comes that the Reverend Theodore Sedgwick, at one time pastor of Calvary Church in New York, but now living in New England, has just completed in his eighty-fourth year a web of cloth to be made up as a suit for his son. Mr. Sedgwick took up weaving at eighty-one, and on a recent vacation in North Carolina could not be happy until he had found a loom on which to continue his weaving.

CHAPTER 6

KNITTING, NETTING, LACEMAKING, AND CROCHETING

T HE handicrafts treated in this chapter, although somewhat dissimilar in end product, have an affinity of method which makes it seem appropriate to group them together. Each of them uses a thread that is manipulated into a pattern by means of simple tools—the needle, hook, or bobbin. Knitting and netting are much the oldest of the four. Knitting goes back at least as far as the lake dwellings of Switzerland where, Dr. Ferdinand Keller assures us, in his book, *The Lake Dwellers of Switzerland and Other Parts of Western Europe*, linen thread was used for both knitting and netting; while netting, it seems reasonable to suppose, because of its simpler and more primitive form, must have been in even earlier use. Indeed it might be assumed that of all the handicrafts which this study includes, netting, in its broad sense—that is, the looping or meshing of fibers together to catch fish, to trap animals, to contain objects of every kind too large to escape through the meshes—is the oldest. Netting, for which special tools are now used, was probably accomplished at first with fingers as the only implement. "Flax was the material," Dr. Keller records, "for making lines and nets for fishing and catching wild animals." Now, of course, a great variety of threads is used in each of these ancient handicrafts.

Crocheting, certainly on the continent of Europe, is not nearly so old as knitting. The term "crochet" comes from the French word *croc*, meaning hook, one of the tools used in lacemaking. It is said that someone began using this hook to make patterns entirely independent of lace; from this experiment has developed one of the most extensive lines of patterns ever wrought from a single thread. It would seem then that crocheting in its European tradition—for there are other possible theories concerning the development of crochet in South and Central America—is the youngest of these four string handicrafts. As an offshoot of lacemaking, crocheting is said to have been first practiced in Europe by the nuns; perhaps its first popular development was in Ireland during the Great Famine of 1846. During its attendant poverty, large numbers of girls and women were able to earn a little by selling their crochet work. The art came to New England with the settlers from many homelands, England, of course, being the first; but possibly the largest number of crocheters came from Ireland for during the famine years, and afterward, half of the population of the Emerald Isle immigrated to America.

With the exception of personal and family sewing, it is probable that knitting is today the most widely practiced of the needlework arts in our country. The two world wars brought an unparalleled need for knitting. Besides this, scores of persons who previously did not know how to knit, having now learned to do so, are providing knitted articles for themselves and for their families which they could not otherwise have from gloves, mittens, and novelties, to dresses and suits.

This intricate and accurate machine of fingers, thumbs, and knitting needles, with its one-stock requirement, yarn, is portable anywhere; it generates its own power, is practically silent, and never intrudes upon the activities of others. It becomes so automatic that most persons say it does not interfere with thought, while some say that it even stimulates the mind. It may be done without using the eyes, and the operation is so pleasant that many like to do it and to be seen doing it in all sorts of places.

In New England knitting must have begun with the landing of the Pilgrims in 1620. Our main concern, however, is with knitting today, a period in which New England knitters have achieved a position of leadership. Not only do we find many individual knitters of exceptional skill and artistry, but we shall find several groups who have made outstanding textiles with their knitting needles. It is obviously impossible to mention more than a small number of the thousands who knit.

KNITTING IN MAINE

The people of Aroostook County, Maine, have made valiant efforts to organize their handicrafts, especially their knitting and crocheting, and to market their products beyond the state boundary. Prominent in this effort was the St. John Valley Handicraft Cooperative organized in 1937 by the Reverend D. W. Soucy of St. Joseph's Church of Sinclair, who undertook to find a wide market for products of his parish, extending throughout St. John Valley. The endeavor failed because it fell under the ban of the federal Fair Labor Standards Act, which applies to all products that cross state lines and thus come within the jurisdiction of the federal government. A number of labor unions invoked the law against the St. John Valley Cooperative, one of them stating that the handwork produced gave "serious competition to machine-made garments." The result was that the Cooperative was stopped, workers in more than a hundred families were cut off from their markets and so deprived of the privilege of earning; and some two thousand rural workers of the area, who were reported as having applied to the Cooperative for employment, were not able to realize their hopes. Here is an instance in which a large group of workers were prevented from earning any wage at all, because they could not earn the minimum wage prescribed by the national minimum wage law. The requirements of this law, unfortunately, pose recurrent problems for rural workers and industries throughout New England and elsewhere and are of importance in any consideration of handicraft activities.

Before the formation of the St. John Valley Cooperative, a number of manufacturers or jobbers had marketed some of the products of the knitters and crocheters of this area, and had facilitated their work in various ways; wages paid by these jobbers, usually on a piecework basis, however, were so low that unionized labor invoked the federal law and forced the jobbers to retire. In the hope of correcting the situation, Father Soucy and his sister, Mrs. Glouriess Ouelette, who had helped the women to bring their work to market standard, consulted with the people and organized the Cooperative.

Father Soucy spoke over the radio of his plans, a very colorful article appeared in a magazine of national circulation, and other publicity was given the undertaking. Upon reading the article a well-established New York jobber thought it might be possible for the members of this group to develop recognized types of knitting similar to those made in Europe, especially in the Scandinavian countries. The samples worked out for him were so excellent that he made a substantial investment in yarn, helped these knitters further in matters of styling and so forth, and procured orders for them. At this point the Cooperative learned that it could sell only to retailers unless it could meet the requirements of the minimum wage law. This automatically canceled the large order which was the basis for the expanding program, and the firm which had procured it could no longer function as an agent. Appeals to Washington by Father Soucy on behalf of the Cooperative were unsuccessful.

During the period of these developments the state of Maine, which through its Maine Crafts service had supplied yarn, recovered part of the funds advanced by selling some of the finished goods. The state decided, however, to withdraw its support. The Farm Security Administration also became interested in the plight of these rural knitters and seemed inclined at one time to make a loan to the Cooperative, but this plan also did not work out. The retail outlets were few and inadequate for the production which had been developed, and so the people whose hopes had been raised to a high point of expectation suffered both economic depression and spiritual disillusion, which at that time no person or group seemed able to alleviate.

One who has not visited this bleak and generally colorless section of northern Maine, which lacks many social and cultural advantages, and which subsists on its largely one-crop economy, potatoes, cannot easily imagine the hope which sprang from the very wide announcement of Father Soucy's Cooperative; indeed no one but the people themselves can know the tragedy of its failure.

The writer believes that when the Fair Labor Standards Act was passed few realized that it would affect handicraft production in rural areas as it has come to do; it is unquestionably true that the rural workers themselves had no thought of what was coming. Most of those with whom the writer has discussed the matter feel that the minimum wage provision, which after years of hard effort has been won by organized labor and accepted as a cardinal principle by the public, should not be made inoperative in rural districts, but that a way should be found by which the unquestioned inequalities of its operation there can be avoided. Where living costs are much lower than the average for industrial areas, as in most rural communities, it would seem reasonable to permit some adjustment of the standard which was undoubtedly fixed with urban areas and large factory production primarily in mind.

In Maine no way was provided by which rural people and those cooperating with them were enabled to work out the problem. Had there been a "reasonable time" clause allowing production to continue while efforts could be made to reach the minimum wage, the end result might have been different.

Since the time of the St. John Valley experience the Wage and Hour Division of the Department of Labor has formed a national committee whose members are familiar with and interested in handicraft production, especially that in rural communities. One of the intentions of the Division and the committee is to find ways in which rural workers may be guided to meet the requirements of the minimum wage law. Ways should be found by which rural people will not be prevented by generally desirable national legislation from using the opportunities that are most readily available to them to supplement their meager incomes.

There are women in Maine who are glad of the opportunity to knit even though the income from the work is very small. Ralph W. Haskell, when supervisor of Maine Crafts, told of a woman knitter who, when her returns were analyzed, found that she received about one and three-quarter cents an hour for her labor, whereupon her husband reminded her that he had said all along she was not getting enough for her work. To this his wife replied that other women among her neighbors were ready to do the work for nothing "if only they'll send us the yarn." The pleasure of having fine materials to work with, the social satisfaction of being able to show to neighbors their skilled, completed work are among the influences that make Maine women want to knit, especially in the winter when there is little work outside the house. How important it may be in the lives of a good many country women to do some creative work with a gleam of beauty in it, only they themselves know.

Mrs. Anna B. Cloutier of Biddeford, a native of French Canada, is an all-round craftsman. Not only does she herself make many useful and beautiful things, but as she expressed it in French, all her ten children likewise are *adroit*. Some knit and crochet, one makes ship models, and Medric, who is expert in woodworking, made the first-rate spinning wheel on which his mother spins her own yarn. The writer purchased a pair of warm white socks made from wool which Mrs. Cloutier had carded and spun and knit in beautiful simple stitches. Besides spinning and knitting she sews, crochets, and makes many kinds of rugs. Her own designs in these home arts have a very pleasant folk quality.

At Cornish, York County, is a group of women knitters, of whom Mrs. Marjorie Libby is one of the leaders. They call themselves the Cornish Knitters, and have knitted together ever since World War I, when they began working for the American Red Cross. When war work was not too exacting, they made stockings, sweaters, and scarfs, some of which they sold in the salesroom of Maine Industries at Saco. They are all self-taught and are excellent knitters. Mrs. Libby has knit for herself a sweater of yarn spun from the fur of her Russian sheep hound in its natural color.

At Mrs. Libby's home we met Mrs. Vivian Seakins, one of the original group, who is now a professional knitter. In addition to knowing many stitches she can reproduce in her knitting practically any pictured design. She was wearing a dress which she had knit over twice, and a favorite sweater of mothproofed yarn made seven years earlier. She had first made the dress in a certain style but later wanted to change it, so she unraveled it and knit it over again. This she repeated a few years later. After its third knitting it looked as fresh as if knit from yarn never used before. Mrs. Seakins makes many garments for her children, almost always knitting them over and over again and sometimes re-dyeing the yarn. Unraveling and re-knitting is a practice so common among thrifty country women that no one thinks of it as singular. The only wastage in unraveling and utilizing the yarn in an old garment is caused by holes or thin spots. This loss a knitter overcomes by careful joining of the broken yarn. The extraordinary longevity of yarn as used in knitting and crocheting has won for it deep respect as a handicraft medium.

Mrs. Rebecca L. Brophy of Fairfield, on the Kennebec, is also a knitter of experience, having made mittens, gloves, parkas, socks, and so forth for more than ten years. She writes that she is able to knit with two or three different colored yarns at a time, making special patterns; she uses mostly Norwegian and Swedish designs. Mrs. Brophy used to sell to stores and at one time had thirty women knitting for her, but now knits only for her own use.

In the neighborhood of Monson, in about the center of the state, are people from many parts of Europe, including Finns, Swedes, Norwegians, Scots, English, Russians, and Welsh, and almost all of the women knit and crochet, especially for their own use and for the American Red Cross.

Farther south and west, at Auburn, Mrs. M. C. Hansen is one of the principal teachers of knitting in the New England area. She has classes of from ten to twenty students and at the time of our visit was teaching about seventy-five knitters. They received a fixed amount for each sweater, and their agents sold the articles for whatever they would bring. This seems to be a very acceptable arrangement for women who would not be satisfied to put their work in stores on a consignment basis. Mrs. Hansen said she had taught perhaps a thousand persons in and around Auburn and Lewiston without making any charge before Mr. Haskell discovered her and worked out regular arrangements for classes. Now her pupils produce beautiful sweaters, which are sold in New York City, in Sun Valley, Idaho, and through other outlets. Mrs. Hansen learned to knit when she was seven years old in the folk schools of her native Denmark. She said knitting came first in the training course, then sewing, and next fine embroidery.

A project which has given Mrs. Hansen great satisfaction was one at Mechanic Falls, where paper mills owned by a Norwegian firm had closed down, leaving the people in very serious circumstances. At a friend's suggestion she talked with the women of the community and offered to teach them to knit, although she could not promise them a market. One of the neighborhood women accompanied her on all interviews so that everything was clearly understood by the group. The women responded with a will and into a good many homes where income had been cut off this work brought substantial amounts to help carry the family expenses.

Mrs. I. E. Ralph of Northeast Harbor is an expert knitter, specializing in children's socks of varicolored diamond patterns, baby-carriage robes, scarfs, and so forth. She works in sheep's wool and also Angora rabbit fur and in a combination of these. She is enthusiastic about color and confines most of her knitting to children's things.

Also of Northeast Harbor Mrs. Rebecca G. Stanley, known in her community as "Grandma Stanley," knits an excellent yarn glove with a slight intake around the wrist, which gives it a good fit and a pleasant feeling. She is in her ninety-seventh year but is still sending gloves knitted in fancy stitches to the Winter Industries Cooperative. These are eagerly bought. Mrs. Stanley is used to being busy; her father died when she was a little girl, leaving most of the work on the farm for the womenfolk. The family made many useful and beautiful objects from the fleece of their own sheep. When Grandma Stanley lost her sight in one eye the doctor told her that she should not use the other one, but she said with her accustomed gentle courtesy, "I thought I might as well use it while I could." Her blind eye is not noticeable and she certainly is getting much done with the help of the good one.

The annals of contemporary knitters in Maine must include the name of Edgar Quinn of Eagle Island, even though he died in 1942. "Uncle Ed" raised his own sheep, sheared them, carded and spun the wool, and knit mittens, socks, sweaters, and other garments for himself and sometimes for his friends. Neal Bousfield of the Maine Seacoast Missionary Society always looked in on Uncle Ed when the *Sunbeam* stopped at the lonely island on its mission trips. Mr. Bousfield has a pair of mittens which Uncle Ed made for him and sent with a note saying, "Thanks for looking after an old man."

Mrs. Albert Kennedy of South Brooksville, Hancock County, raises Angora rabbits and knits the yarn into beautiful articles. Someone else does the carding and spinning of the rabbit wool, but Mrs. Kennedy sees that the wool is carefully plucked or sheared, and that the yarn is just as carefully knitted. On the Kennedy farm besides the Angora rabbits are minks, foxes, and goats. It requires four hours twice daily to feed all of these animals, and this keeps Mr. and Mrs. Kennedy quite busy.

A rural enterprise encouraged by Mr. Haskell will be noted here because of its unique character, although it is not, strictly speaking, a handicraft. This is the power machine knitting project of Shirley Mills, known as Shirley Industries. When the collapse of the lumber business left the inhabitants of this sawmill town without work, the former superintendent of the mill procured three or four knitting machines that were turned over to the people or paid for by them at a nominal price. The machines were installed in the homes where electric power was available. The industry, now in the hands of local men and women, produces sportswear, especially socks and sweaters in Argyle and Fairlee plaids. The point of special interest to us is that, although the machines were modern and intricate, there was enough mechanical ingenuity among the people to master their use and prevent serious loss from breakdowns. The principal problems centered around styling and marketing. The industry has proved to be a great gain to the community, for its members continue to live and earn in a rural neighborhood where productive gardens help out income, and where there are opportunities to fish and hunt near at hand.

KNITTING IN NEW HAMPSHIRE

Among the early achievements in craftsmanship which brought the New Hampshire League to the favorable attention of the public was the excellent knitting of Miss Mary and Miss Sarah Potter, of Acworth, Sullivan County. The sisters received from the League their first instruction in blockprinting and designing, and although the group at Acworth whom they interested decided to work in material with which they were familiar—yarn for knitting—the Potter sisters applied the knowledge gained from their classes to making mittens. They are interested in producing beautiful things but not in making large quantities. Many of their designs are original; some are taken from the best Scandinavian or other sources.

Mrs. Maria Yorke of Kensington is reported in the *New Hampshire Troubadour* for February, 1944, as follows: "Even though she is in her ninetieth year Mrs. Maria Yorke is doing her part to aid the war effort. Mrs. Yorke has knitted more than 1,000 pairs of mittens for service men and has just completed a quilt of 1,872 pieces. This makes the third war in which Mrs. Yorke has done work for the service."

Whitefield Wintersportswear is one of the most important groups of knitters in New England. It was organized in 1936 with six members by Mrs. Mary Dodge, who based her first designs and experiments on mittens brought from Norway. With an associate Mrs. Dodge designs,

Edmund de Beaumont

17. HANDICRAFTS FOR FARM AND HOME

Brooms from Vermont and Massachusetts; Yoke, Gambrel, Flail from Massachusetts; Rake from Maine; Copper Measures, Root Basket, Butter Stamp, Rag Carpet from Vermont; Milk Stool and Handspun Yarn from New Hampshire; Wooden Implements from Connecticut; Wool from New Hampshire and Vermont.

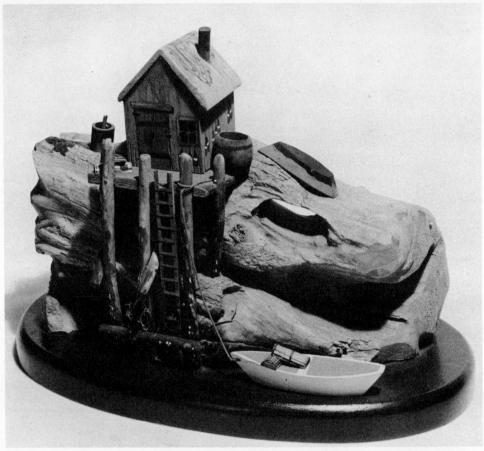

John D. Schiff

18. LOBSTER HOUSE, MAINE COAST

THIS SOUVENIR OF MAINE WAS WHITTLED AND PAINTED BY MAURICE DAY AND FAMILY OF DAMARISCOTTA. THE LAND AND ROCKS ARE CARVED FROM DRIFTWOOD. ALL THE DAY FAMILY CREATIONS ARE SOLD FROM THE HOME SHOP.

Edmund de Beaumont

19. HANDICRAFTS FOR SPORT

ARCHERY EQUIPMENT, SNOWSHOES, LAPROBE, FLYING DUCK, AND FISH FROM MAINE;
GUNSTOCK, BASKET, SWEATER, AND FISHNET FROM VERMONT; DECOY AND EEL SPEAR
FROM MASSACHUSETTS; MITTENS FROM NEW HAMPSHIRE AND VERMONT.

Courtesy of The Society for the Preservation of New England Antiquities

20. NEW ENGLAND TIN PEDDLER'S OUTFIT OF YESTERDAY

THIS COMPLETE TIN PEDDLER'S CART IN MINIATURE WAS CARVED BY DR. WALTER G. BRIDGE OF CAMBRIDGE, MASSACHUSETTS, WHO MADE MINIATURE MODELS AS A HOBBY. HE FOUND HIS DENTAL INSTRUMENTS EXCELLENT FOR THIS WORK, SUPPLEMENTING THEM WITH TOOLS OF HIS OWN MAKING.

Camercraft Studio

21. A HOMEMADE BIRD CAGE

E. Laurence White of Beverly Farms, Massachusetts, Had Always Wanted to Work with Tools but Never Did Until He Was Convalescing from a Serious Illness. Now He Has His Own Woodwork Shop.

Edmund de Beaumont, Worcester Art Museum

22. A MASSACHUSETTS SILVER SERVICE

THIS SILVER TEA SET AND CANDLESTICK WERE MADE BY MR. AND MRS. JOSEPH L.
SHARROCK OF PRIDES CROSSING, AND WERE SHOWN AT THE WORCESTER EXHIBITION OF
CONTEMPORARY HANDICRAFTS.

Edmund de Beaumont, Worcester Art Museum

23. A NEW ENGLAND TAPESTRY

Two Types of Tapestries Are Made in New England: the Gobelin and the Scandinavian. The Tapestry Shown Here, in the Latter Technique, Was Made by Mrs. William E. Brigham of Providence. John Bauer, the Swedish Illustrator of Folk Tales, Designed It.

Edmund de Beaumont, Worcester Art Museum

24. HANDICRAFTS FOR THE CHURCH

THE HANGING IN THE BACKGROUND, DESIGNED BY ALEXANDER CRANE OF BARNSTABLE, MASSACHUSETTS, WAS WOVEN AND THE FIGURES HOOKED IN BY MISS ALICE TURNBULL OF HADDAM, CONNECTICUT. THE SILVER ALTAR SET WAS MADE BY GEORGE C. GEBELEIN AND GEORGE E. GERMER, AND THE LACEWORK BY MRS. TERESA A. PELLEGRINI, ALL OF BOSTON.

Horydczak

25. A CRÈCHE OF NEW HAMPSHIRE PINE

Mrs. Susan N. Collins of Littleton Enjoys Most the Whittling of Traditional Religious Subjects. Among Her Well-known Carvings Are Nativity Scenes and Saint Francis with His Birds and Animals.

Clarence H. White

26. A PATCHWORK QUILT OF MAINE

THIS QUILT WAS DESIGNED AND WORKED BY MRS. WILL FIELD OF FIVE ISLANDS, MAINE.
IT PICTURES THE HOMES AND OTHER BUILDINGS OF THE LITTLE VILLAGE WHERE SHE
HAD SPENT MOST OF HER LIFE.

Henry Jewett Greene

27. POTTERY FROM MASSACHUSETTS

MR. AND MRS. HENRY JEWETT GREENE OF PETERSHAM, POTTERS OF WIDE EXPERIENCE, USE MATERIALS NATIVE TO THEIR NEIGHBORHOOD WITH FINE RESULTS. SKILLFULLY FORMED AND GLAZED, THEIR PIECES ARE THEN MOUNTED FOR EXHIBITION ON APPROPRIATE WOODEN PEDESTALS.

John D. Schiff

28. CLOTH ANIMALS FROM NEW HAMPSHIRE

MRS. R. GILMAN LUNT OF MEREDITH, A DISTINGUISHED NEEDLEWORKER OF THE LEAGUE OF NEW HAMPSHIRE ARTS AND CRAFTS, MAKES CLOTH ANIMALS THAT ARE UNUSUAL BOTH IN DESIGN AND EXECUTION. THOSE ILLUSTRATED ARE IN VERY ATTRACTIVE COTTON COLOR PRINTS.

Peter Nyholm, School Arts Magazine

29. STENCILED AND DECORATIVE TINWARE FROM NEW HAMPSHIRE

EXCELLENT STENCILING AND DECORATIVE PAINTING ARE TO BE FOUND THROUGHOUT NEW ENGLAND, OWING IN LARGE MEASURE TO THE PIONEER WORK OF MRS. ESTHER STEVENS BRAZER, CRAFTSMAN AND AUTHOR. THE THREE PIECES, COMBINING STENCILING AND FREE-HAND PAINTING, WERE DONE BY WILLIAM P. DUDLEY OF EXETER.

Life Photographer, Fritz Goro, Copyright Time, Inc.

30. WOODCARVING AND WOODTURNING

THIS LIFE-SIZED MALLARD DUCK WAS CARVED BY A. E. CROWELL OF EAST HARWICH
ON THE CAPE; SMALLER DUCK BY CHARLES CHASE OF WISCASSET, MAINE. . . . THE
SALAD BOWL WAS TURNED AND THE MAPLEWOOD FORK AND SPOON WERE CARVED BY
ALFRED ROSSITER OF REDDING RIDGE, CONNECTICUT.

Edmund de Beaumont, Worcester Art Museum

31. FARM VEHICLES OF MAINE

AFTER A LONG ILLNESS WILLIAM COLBY, A FARMER NEAR WISCASSET, LOOKED FOR A
SUITABLE WAY TO EMPLOY HIS TIME. HE CARVED IN MINIATURE ALL THE VEHICLES
THAT HAD BEEN IN USE ON THE FARMS IN MAINE DURING HIS LIFETIME.

Doris Day

32. FOLK ART CREATIONS IN WOOD

Archie Gilbert of Landaff, New Hampshire, Constructs in Wood Many Objects of Folk Art. These Deer Are More Than Life-sized Landscape Decorations, and Are Often Seen Along the Fencerow of His Place.

inspects, packs, and markets the output of mittens, caps, and socks of the double strand Norwegian type, the peasant type with embroidered designs, and a utility type. The purchase of the yarn (many hundreds of pounds a year), the weekly payments to the knitters, and the marketing of the finished work, chiefly to large retail stores in Boston and New York, are financed by a fund set up by the management. Any surplus is divided annually among the knitters. It is thus a profit-sharing enterprise.

Mrs. Dodge writes: "Our little industry has grown in eleven years to include 40 knitters. Last year we did $10,000 of business and made 5,200 items. . . . I set the retail price, taking off 40 per cent for the store's discount, less the price of the yarn; then the knitter is paid the rest. The women are fine hard-working farmers' wives, women with children, or shut-ins—all unemployed and all loving the few dollars a week they earn in their evenings and spare time."

For several years the women have met in the directors' room of the Whitefield Savings Bank and Trust Company, offered by the bank to further the success of this hometown industry. "Not only is it a meeting place of faithful workers," reports Mrs. Dodge, "but it has become a friendly social center welcomed by many women who come into town from their farms only once a week."

KNITTING IN VERMONT

Mr. and Mrs. Arthur Shores and their six children live on a farm at Granby, Essex County, in remote and mountainous country. Mrs. Shores is an excellent knitter and uses yarn which comes from her own flock of sheep, among which are usually one or more that are black. The Shores send the clip from their sheep to a small woolen mill for carding and spinning, where the charge is moderate. Mrs. Shores says she can better afford to knit her wool prepared in this way than she could to card and spin it herself—supposing she had time to do so.

The Shores family and their neighbors suffer from the depredations of bears, and recently one of their black sheep was killed. Mrs. Shores felt the loss keenly because, like other craftsmen, she especially enjoys combining natural black and white wool in her patterns. These are very thoughtfully worked out, and the contrasting white and black, which is really a deep rich brown, gives distinction to much of her knitting. The skill and artistry of this modest and inventive rural knitter were impressive. On the day of our visit the children proudly exhibited several examples of their mother's craftsmanship which she had forgotten. Mrs. Shores has designed a "hunter's mitten," with a special trigger finger. A pair of these was exhibited at Worcester.

Miss Clara M. Hemenway of Manchester Center, Bennington County, raises rabbits and knits their yarn into mittens, gloves, scarfs, and even some yard goods. She has about 150 rabbits all in fine condition, and said she could take care of 500 herself if she had no other work to do. The trade name of this rural industry is Wailiilii Angoras. Miss Hemenway does not spin by hand because it is too slow for her purposes, but she has an arrangement by which a Canadian firm does the spinning for her. The dyeing is also done in Canada, where rapid advances have been made in the rabbit fur industry. Miss Hemenway maintains that an overcoat of rabbit's fur is warmer and more comfortable than an overcoat of sheep's wool weighing several times as much.

Among the knitters of Vermont who have brought much credit to rural industries is Mrs. Ed Burrows of Northfield. On her hilly farm she raises Shropshires, the sheep with black faces, and on "three long days" in the spring she and her two sons do the shearing. She carefully cuts the fleece about the head and neck while the boys do the rest of the shearing with a machine. She is a great lover of animals, and when visited was planning to blanket all her sheep the following winter—an unusual procedure in Vermont. She believes the sheep would have cleaner wool, be free from burrs, and be more comfortable, and she says she would be also.

Mrs. Burrows washes the wool, cards it by hand, and spins it into yarn on a small wheel brought twenty years ago from her home in Canada. She also dyes the yarn as required and knits caps, cablestitch sweaters, cardigans and slip-ons, many in patterns of her own design. These well-styled accessories are in demand not only by the winter skiers at Mount Mansfield but by visitors to Vermont shops and at the summer Craft Fair. Some of Mrs. Burrows' socks are natural color with alternating bands of red and blue; others are of brilliant red yarn; sometimes black sheep's wool is used. An added feature which makes these articles sought after by the skiers is the fact that some of the lanolin, or natural oil, is left in the wool, making it water repellent. Mrs. Burrows is also an expert quiltmaker and at the time of our visit had just completed a quilt for her son called the Glistening Star, the predominant color of which was yellow. Mrs. Burrows knits very rapidly as she sits rocking back and forth with a parrot perched on her shoulder and a collie at her feet, but one wonders how she and other busy farm women find time for their handicraft accomplishments in addition to the demands of farm and household.

Mrs. Dorothy Howe of Pawlet raises sheep and knits. She is not only an expert knitter herself, but she has encouraged the West Roaders, a group of knitters who take deep pride in their skill and who help her in working up the yarn from her sheep's wool into a variety of sweaters, suits for women, socks, mittens, and a few examples of bed coverings, for which she finds a market. Among the many kinds of birds which she raises are ducks, geese, pheasants, peacocks; she also raises several domestic animals. Her fascinating kitchen has a fireplace and a grand piano, and in the spring she uses this room for the lambing center.

KNITTING AND NETTING IN MASSACHUSETTS AND RHODE ISLAND

At Vineyard Haven, Martha's Vineyard, Mrs. A. L. Webster is the proprietor of the Come-and-See Shop. She especially enjoys working with Iceland wool, which she imports and keeps in her shop for local knitters. This she uses for her own sweaters, shawls, and yarn flowers, of which she sells a great many. Mrs. Webster combines teaching and her own work in handicrafts with the salesroom. She has a rug-hooking frame, teaches rugmaking as well as knitting to the people in the community, and encourages handicrafts generally in her neighborhood.

Mrs. Patrick Dillon, wife of a fisherman well known around Point Judith, Rhode Island, lives in the hamlet of Jerusalem across the breakwater from Galilee. Ever since she was ten years of age, when she made a pair of hunter's mittens for her father, she has been an expert knitter. The Dillons' typical fisherman's cottage, near the shore, is surrounded with old-fashioned flowers and on the morning of the writer's visit was lovely in the summer sunshine. It was built on the foundation of their old house, which had been completely demolished by the tidal wave and hurricane of September, 1938, that overtook every cottage in the settlement except the four on higher ground; these served as a refuge to the people of the village on that terrible night. Days afterward Mrs. Dillon found hanks of yarn—remnants of a new stock she had just laid in—festooned on the trees several miles distant from her home. These and a portrait of Pat Dillon painted by a summer visitor were all that ever was found of what had been home. The income from her knitting, said Mrs. Dillon, had been a real help in getting started again.

NETTING

An early home art practiced long ago in America was the making of testers or canopies of net for the four-poster beds of colonial days and also nets for dressmaking purposes. In *American Needlework* Georgiana Brown Harbeson tells us that a guest at Mount Vernon, writing to a friend in Virginia, said of the First Lady, "Her netting is a source of great amusement to her and is so neatly done that all the younger members of the family are proud of having their dresses trimmed with it."

Deerfield, Massachusetts, seems to have been a center for netting in recent times. Mrs. Gertrude C. Smith is an able netter of today who has revived old patterns and has repaired and replaced many wornout historic canopies and edgings for curtains, valances, and so forth. Miss Rachel Hawks is noted for her netted testers for high-post beds, which she makes only to order. The material which Miss Hawks uses is as near like the handspun thread as is possible to obtain.

Mrs. J. C. Sawyer of Durham, New Hampshire, mother of Charles H. Sawyer, former director of the Worcester Art Museum and now dean of the Division of the Arts, Yale University, learned the craft of netting from one of Deerfield's experts. Mrs. Sawyer made many canopies for four-poster beds and taught her neighbors and friends how to make them. She had long been interested in handicrafts, and during his lifetime her husband, who shared her interest, was a sponsor of the beautiful Ship Room in the Addison Gallery of American Art at Andover, Massachusetts.

Mrs. Marie E. Masales of Woodstock, Vermont, writes that netting is now her principal work although she embroiders, does needlepoint, hooks rugs, and knits. She has made handicrafts almost since her babyhood in Canada over seventy years ago and is still filling orders. Mrs. Arthur Teeri of Durham, New Hampshire, is another maker of fine canopies.

Netters, whose skill is in making nets for fishermen or is an outgrowth of fishnetmaking, are noted in Chapter 15.

LACEMAKING

One of the best-known lacemakers in New England, a teacher, and a restorer of fine laces, is Mrs. Teresa A. Pellegrini of Boston. In Santa Margherita, Italy, where she was born, Teresa learned from her mother to thread bobbins for the fascinating art of pillow lacemaking. At the age of five she attended, as did all other little girls of the neighborhood, a school for lacemaking in the morning and a public school in the afternoon. She continued at school and practiced at home until she could make Genoese, Milanese, Venetian, Flemish, French, Irish, and English designs. Later, when she came to America, she was able to restore fine pieces of old lace for the Metropolitan Museum of Art and the Boston Museum of Fine Arts; and now as a master craftsman of the Society of Arts and Crafts, she makes special lace on order. In her pillow lacemaking she has sometimes used more than 650 bobbins in the working out of a single pattern.

A number of Massachusetts lacemakers are connected with a group known as the Worcester Folk Stitchery, described in Chapter 11. Three members of this group showed their lace at the Worcester Exhibition. Miss Berzelia Bagdasarian was represented by a doily with lace edges; Miss Lucia Parsekian showed two examples of Armenian lacework; Miss Ankine Shamgochian exhibited a runner with insertions of Armenian lace.

Mrs. Louise Walker of Mount Hermon, Massachusetts, made a very attractive altar piece of crocheted lace about two and one-half feet wide by six feet long, which was also shown at the Worcester Exhibition. It was made in a Catholic school, where lacemaking and other handicrafts are carried on, and was for use in a local church. Mrs. John P. Bainbridge of Hingham is another well-known lacemaker of Massachusetts.

CROCHETING

No one need worry that crocheting will die out; the number who practice it is legion and the purposes for which it is carried on are amazing. Its range is from a simple chain of thread to a cover for a dining-room table or a bedspread, and the technique is such that feet could be extended to miles if there were need for it, for crocheting is limited in size only by the length of the yarn or thread. Crocheting in simple stitches is the most elementary of the string arts in which tools are used. In the field of personal adornment crochet stitches are often combined beautifully from dainty edgings for a handkerchief to a complete dress.

With all its fascination, its versatility, and the countless practical uses to which it is put, crocheting is not generally accorded the high rating it deserves as a hand art to be included oftener in American handicraft exhibitions. There are, it seems to the writer, several reasons why this has been true. One reason that has tended to exclude crochet is that the concept of handicrafts, popular among those who promote handicraft programs, put on exhibitions, and write on the subject, is none too broad. Perhaps another is that, when crochet is included at all in exhibits or in books on handicrafts, good placing and lighting of real or pictured articles are too often absent. Among guides that might be mentioned as helpful on these points is the excellent treatment by Elizabeth L. Mathiesen in *The Complete Book of Crochet*. The illustrations here are a model not only for a book but also for purposes of exhibitions, the principles being similar in both. A third factor which would bring crocheting into greater favor would be more originality in design.

From the standpoint of the number who participate, crocheting is one of the most democratic of handicrafts. It is also one of the most exact—yarns, threads, and hooks having been thoroughly standardized. Furthermore, it is economical, measured in terms of what a little material and a small investment will yield in articles of use and beauty. For these and other reasons—including the ease with which crocheting can be learned, the availability of materials and the fact that, like knitting, it can be practiced almost anywhere, at any time—it merits increasing consideration. There are few crafts which are so elastic, and it is to be hoped that the crocheters of the United States who have received so many stitches and patterns from Europe and have adapted them to such varied uses will enrich this popular craft with more designs that are new and beautiful.

CHAPTER 7

HANDMADE RUGS AND CARPETS

THE word "rug" as used here means a partial floor covering; carpet means an entire floor covering. Our interest is in rugs and carpets made by hand. Rugs may be divided roughly into seven classes: hooked, braided or plaited, hand-loomed, knitted and crocheted, needlework, rugs or mats made of cornhusks, and those made of tanned animal pelts. The most widely made and used are the first three kinds: the hooked, the braided, and the hand-loomed or hand-woven rug. This chapter is limited largely to these three.

Many rugs produced in New England derive their names from the method of making, the materials used, or sometimes the design, but most of these can be classified under one of the main heads listed above. For instance, there are the patchwork, appliquéd, scalloped, cross-stitched, embroidered, and needlepoint types, which are all needlework rugs because they are made mainly with the sewing needle. The Oriental type of rug, of which there are a few specimens in New England, belongs to the hand-woven group. Although it is not woven with a shuttle, the filler is tied to the warp. However, this type is not to be confused with the Oriental rug designs that are worked in the hooked technique. The tapestry rug also belongs to the hand-woven or hand-loomed group.

The hooked, pulled, or drawn-in rug is made in every state of the Union and in every province of Canada. Measured in terms of the numbers who participate in the making, in the variety and beauty of design, in the extent to which it is used in the homes of its makers, or even of those who buy it, the hooked rug is the most outstanding form of present-day American folk art. To this folk art New England artists and craftsmen have made great contributions. Probably the first rugs to be hooked in America were done in New England; certainly many of the finest have been produced there.

Literature on the hooked rug is perhaps as voluminous as that on any phase of handicrafts. The subject has been approached in many

113

ways: from the standpoint of research into origins and the evaluation of designs and craftsmanship; from the standpoint of the development of the art in New England, as seen through the eyes of a teacher and craftsman; or as part of a general survey of handmade rugs and carpets by a specialist in the field.

Several factors contribute to the popularity of rug-hooking, the principal one being that this is a form of folk art that almost anyone can carry out. There are excellent hookers even among the blind. Tools and equipment required are simple and materials are inexpensive. They consist of canvas, burlap, or some other fabric stretched upon a frame as a foundation, and a hook to push the yarns or cloth strips through the fabric. Even the frame is omitted by a few rugmakers who prefer to hook on their laps. With some types of rugs this is a pleasant thing to do, but the best hooking requires the steady control that a sturdy frame will give.

Almost every individual, and certainly every family, has cloth of some kind that can be worked into a hooked rug. Mill ends, yarns, and other bought materials often make good rugs, but the commonest and frequently the most cherished are those made from clothing that has long since worn out, or perhaps from only fragments of cloth, as, for instance, small pieces of old Paisley shawls. All members of the family can work on the same rug, from grandmother to granddaughter.

The New England states should be given credit for pioneering and for maintaining high standards in the art of hooking, but recognition should be made of the influence of eastern Quebec and the Maritime Provinces. Each country is indebted to the other; the Canadian hooked rug has been important in the development of rug-hooking on this side of the border, and many craftsmen from Canada are now taking a noteworthy part in this popular home industry in their adopted communities.

ORIGIN OF THE HOOKED RUG

As to the origin of the hooked rug, opinions vary from naive announcements such as "the first hooked rug was made by my grandmother in New England," to the authentic statement that the Copts employed the hooked-rug technique as far back as the sixth and possibly the third century. From observation of ancient textiles still in existence William Winthrop Kent has discovered that Coptic craftsmen employed basically the same technique as that used by New Englanders today. In his book, *The Hooked Rug*, he gives a photograph of a hooked or drawn-in textile of the sixth century from the collection of the Metropolitan Museum of Art in New York. He has found examples of this technique elsewhere, including Spain, but that part of his research which is of most immediate interest is the investigating he has encouraged in the British Isles. It has resulted in conclusive evidence that hooked rugs, bearing other names such as "thrummed" and "brodded," have been made in the British Isles for a long time, possibly four hundred years or more. This is also the considered judgment of Mr. Kent's valued collaborator, Miss Ann Macbeth, chief instructor at the School of Art in Glasgow. After due study she concluded that rugs called "hookie rugs" had been made in northern England, southern Scotland, the North of Ireland, Wales, and in Norway. The fact has thus been established that the hooked rug did not originate in America. It probably came to us from the British Isles.

EARLY DEVELOPMENTS IN RUGMAKING

More important than the origin of the hooked rug are the facts as to the perfection in design, color, and technique to which it has been brought in Canada, New England, and other parts of the United States. The period between the two great wars, including the years of depression, probably witnessed more widespread activity in this handicraft than New England had ever known. There are some who feel that the peak of hooked-rugmaking was reached in this section during the 1860's. That the craft received a great impetus soon after the Civil War there is no doubt, but with a few exceptions the rugs made then did not equal those made toward the end of the nineteenth century, the beginning of the twentieth, and those being made today.

How long hooked rugs have been made in New England has not been satisfactorily established. We know that the technique of hooking was employed for bed covers in the Revolutionary War. Mr. Kent shows a photograph of one of these covers initialed "EH" dated 1779, and another, "made by Mary West for self and husband, Nathan," of unclipped wool on a wool base dated 1763. Very few hooked rugs are dated, but the approximate time of the making of several early New England rugs has been set in the first half of the 1800's. We are sure that the art had developed well in both New England and Canada before the 1860's.

Frost the Rug Man

Something happened in New England soon after the Civil War that had more to do with the encouragement of rug-hooking in our country than any other single occurrence. It was the return to his home in

Biddeford, Maine, in 1863 of a twenty-year-old soldier, Edward Sands Frost, whose health had become so impaired that he could not continue in the service or resume his former occupation in a machine shop. An outdoor life without too strenuous labor was imperative, and young Frost became a tin peddler. His own account of this experience follows:

> By close economy, I saved my first thousand dollars, and it was the proudest day of my life, when in January, '69, after taking account of stock, I found I had invested in household goods $200, in team outfit $175, in staple goods and cash in bank $700. As the profits did not average over two dollars per day, it had required the strictest economy to support my family, and save that amount. It was a hard struggle, but that is the only way a poor man can get capital to go into business. It is easy enough to make money, if a man has money to work with.

The story was originally told to a reporter of a newspaper of Mr. Frost's native town, the *Biddeford Times*, in 1888. It has been reprinted both by Mr. Kent, and by Mrs. Pearl K. McGown in her book, *The Dreams Beneath Designs*, and is given here in briefer form.

Frost's great contribution to rug-hooking was his practical inventions for making patterns, many of good quality, which were available to countless workers throughout New England and the country. He thus popularized a rural art for which New England women had long shown marked aptitude.

In the course of business Frost collected a quantity of colored rags which his wife decided to make into a rug. A pattern was marked out on burlap with red chalk and Mrs. Frost went to work with the kind of hook then used, which was often made of a nail or an old gimlet. Frost's first contribution was to make a crooked hook of the type now in use. He soon spent his evenings in hooking; he had "caught the fever." The pattern pleased the neighborhood women so much that they wanted others like it. Twenty orders came in within three days.

> So you see I got myself into business right away. I put in my time evenings and stormy days sketching designs, giving only the outlines in black. There was not money enough in it to devote my whole time to the business, and as the orders came in faster than I could fill them I began, Yankee-like, to study some way to do them quicker. Then the first idea of stencilling presented itself to me.
>
> Did I go to Boston to get my stencils made? Oh, no, I went out into my stable where I had some old iron and some old wash boilers I had bought for their copper bottoms, took the old tin off of them and made my first stencil out of it. Where did I get the tools? Why

I found them in the same place, in my stable among the old iron. I got there some old files, half flat and half round, took them to the tin shop of Cummings and West and forged my tools to cut the stencil with. I made a cutting block out of old lead and zinc.

After fitting myself out with tools I began making small stencils of single flowers, scrolls, leaves, buds, etc., each one on a small plate; then I could with a stencil brush print in ink in plain figures much faster than I could sketch. Thus I had reduced ten hours' labor to two and a half hours. I then had the art down fine enough to allow me to fill all my orders, so I began to print patterns and put them in my peddler's cart and offer them for sale. The news of my invention of stamped rugs spread like magic, and many a time as I drove through the streets of Biddeford and Saco, a lady would appear at the door or window, swinging an apron or sun bonnet, and shouting at the top of her voice, say, "Are you the rug man? Do you carry rugs all marked out?" I at once became known as Frost, the rug man, and many Biddeford citizens still speak of me in that same way.

My rug business increased and I soon found that I could not print fast enough; I also found it difficult to duplicate my patterns, or make two exactly alike, as many of my customers would call for a pattern just like Mrs. So and So's. Then I began to make a whole design on one plate. At first it seemed impossible, but I was willing to try, so I obtained a sheet of zinc and printed on it and cut out a design. This process I continued to follow till I had some fourteen different designs on hand, ranging from a yard long and half a yard wide to two yards long and a yard wide. . . . It required a great deal of patience, for I was just thirty days cutting the first one and when I laid it on the table the center of the plate would not touch the table by two and a half inches. As the plate of zinc lay smooth before being cut, I knew it must be the cutting that caused the trouble; I studied into the problem and learned that in cutting the metal expanded, so I expanded the uncut portion in proportion to that which was cut and the plate then lay smooth. This I did with a hammer, and it took about two days' time.

When the plate was finished I could print with it a pattern in four minutes that had previously required ten hours to sketch by hand. I then thought I had my patterns about perfect, for I began to prepare them for the market. I remember well the first trip I made through Maine and a part of New Hampshire, trying to sell my goods to the dry goods trade. I failed to find a man who dared to invest a dollar in them; in fact, people did not know what they were for, and I had to give up trying for a while and go from house to house. There I found plenty of purchasers, for I found the ladies knew what the patterns were for.

Next I began coloring the patterns by hand, as I had some call for colored goods. The question of how to print them in colors so as to sell them at a profit seemed to be the point on which the success of the whole business hung, and it took me over three months to settle it. I shall never forget the time and place it came to me. . . . It was March, 1870, one morning about two o'clock. I had been thinking how I could print the bright colors in with the dark ones so as to make good clear prints. My mind was so fixed on the problem that I could not sleep, so I turned and twisted and all at once I seemed to hear a voice in my room say: "Print your bright colors first and then the dark ones." That settled it, and I was so excited that I could not close my eyes in sleep the rest of the night and I tell you I was glad when morning came so I could get to town to buy stock for the plates with which to carry out my idea. At the end of a week I had one design made and printed in colors.[1]

The colored patterns were such a success that Frost sold his peddling business and opened a salesroom in Boston. Before long he had four men working for him in Biddeford. He continued making patterns until 1876 when he sold his Biddeford interests and went to California to regain his health. Many of the Frost stencils and his equipment were kept together and a few years ago were purchased by Mrs. Charlotte K. Stratton of Montpelier, Vermont. Mrs. Stratton and her husband built a special studio in a barn on their home property and have made a remarkable workshop and museum with every possible convenience for showing and using this priceless collection.

While the advent of stamped patterns facilitated the process of rug-hooking and was a permanent advance of importance, the quality of design and craftsmanship showed no general improvement in the period following the Civil War. In fact, there was general deterioration in commercial designs until toward the end of the nineteenth century and the beginning of the twentieth. Since then much has been done to improve designs and craftsmanship by individuals, some of whose work is to be mentioned here.

Abnákee, Sabatos, and Subbekashe Rugs

At about the turn of the century there were a few evidences of a new and vigorous interest in both designing and making rugs of various kinds. An account of this development is given by Max West in *The Revival of Handicrafts in America*, published in 1904 as a bulletin of the United States Department of Commerce and Labor.

The development was particularly marked in the Abnákee neighborhood rug industry in Pequaket (Silver Lake), New Hampshire; the

[1] McGown, Pearl K., *The Dreams Beneath Design*. Boston, Bruce Humphries Co., 1939, pp. 61, 62-64.

Sabatos rugs in Center Lovell, Maine; the Cranberry Isles rug industry at Cranberry Isles, opposite Northeast Harbor, Maine; the Subbekashe rug industry at Belchertown, Massachusetts.

There were some other small fires burning. The Deerfield Rug Makers, who were weavers of rag rugs, were a part of the handicraft movement revived at Deerfield, Massachusetts. At the summer School of Art held at Ipswich, directed by Arthur W. Dow, blue and white "willow tree" rugs were worked. The Ladies Aid Society of Isle La Motte, Vermont, made a number of rugs designed by Mrs. Elizabeth Fisk, whose work in weaving has been noted elsewhere. "Pilgrim" rugs were woven at Pittsfield, Massachusetts, from cotton strips prepared by women of Pilgrim Memorial Church.

The time about which we are now writing coincided with the beginning of the arts and crafts movement, but it is difficult to say what if any effect the movement had upon the rugmaking development; it is a matter of record, however, that the Abnákee rug experiment in New Hampshire did influence the development of some of the community groups.

Mrs. Helen R. Albee established her home in Pequaket, New Hampshire, in 1899. As a designer she had noted the rugs made in the neighborhood and thought that better designs might create a market for them. Accordingly she worked out some simple, conventional designs with restrained colors. Several rugs were made and exhibited in the village hall, where all were sold and orders taken for more.

This was the beginning of a project which developed in the community and encouraged rugmakers elsewhere. In addition to designing the rugs, largely with Indian motifs, Mrs. Albee made stencils for marking the burlap base, bought materials, dyed flannel, trained about thirty workers in the course of five or six years, arranged for exhibitions and sales, and finally wrote a small book, long since out of print, *Abnákee Rugs: A Manual Describing the Abnákee Industry, the Methods Used, with Instructions for Dyeing.*

The rugs were made of flannel strips a quarter of an inch wide, the hooked loops forming a close pile about three-eighths of an inch high, of which only the higher loops were cut. The uncut loops made a firm texture, while the slightly frayed ends of the cut loops lent a velvety quality. Each finished rug was labeled "An Abnákee Rug."

In 1900 Mr. and Mrs. Douglas Volk, at Center Lovell, Maine, began to encourage neighborhood handicrafts. Mr. Volk was an eminent painter. Mrs. Volk developed an all-wool hooked rug known as Sabatos, and invented a knot resembling that used in Oriental rugs. Native homespun wool was used for both base and filler. All processes were carried out by hand except the carding of the wool, which was done at an old water-power mill near Center Lovell. Vegetable dyes were used, indigo produced by the age-old vat method being one of the most important. The Volks arranged exhibitions at the village hall in which the Sabatos rugs were shown at every stage in the process.

When the women of Cranberry Isles heard of the Abnákee rug experiment, they undertook a similar enterprise as a winter industry to raise money for church purposes and for a wharf. In these rugs a somewhat firmer texture was obtained by using two yards of flannel to the square foot instead of one and one-quarter to one and one-half as at Pequaket. The dyestuffs used were procured from Mrs. Albee. All the Cranberry Isles rugs were marked with "CR".

The Subbekashe rug industry, with a product quite similar to the Abnákee rugs, was started at Belchertown, Massachusetts, in 1902 by Miss Lucy D. Thomson. Her designs were drawn largely from American Indian motifs. None of these projects is now in existence, but they all strove to improve design, color, and craftsmanship, unquestionably influencing the handicraft movement.

The interest of certain fine furniture and department stores was enlisted in the furnishing of homes with hooked rugs. B. Altman and Company of New York was a particularly vigorous and discriminating pioneer in the field of handmade rugs, under the direction of James A. Keillor. All these factors, often emphasized by books and magazine articles, had their due part in stimulating the hooking of rugs.

RUG-HOOKING IN MAINE

For forty years or more the Maine Seacoast Missionary Society has ministered to the needs of 10,000 people living on the lonely headlands and islands off the coast from Kittery to Calais. It has more than a hundred ports of call along a coastline 300 miles long as the crow flies but 2,500 as the boat plies along the shore. During the 1920's the Mission encouraged the making of Seacoast Mission rugs, which developed into an interesting revival of the rug-hooking art. Its hookers could hardly be called a "group" because they were scattered along the coastline, seldom more than two or three in a single neighborhood, and numbering only about a score in all, but there was among them a strong solidarity of interest and effort. The teacher and leader, Mrs. Alice M. Peasley, now dean of the Mission, is a well-known character to every old inhabitant of the islands.

"Ma Peasley," as the island folk call her, is a painstaking worker, and the women whom she taught to hook were just as particular in their choice of motifs and colors. Of the score of rugs made in the period of their activity, several, still constantly in use, can be identified. There is also a collection, largely reminiscent of the sea, in the small memorial museum at the ferry landing on Islesford, Maine. Good material, careful work, and freedom to follow the imagination made most of these rugs true expressions of folk art. One, designed by Mrs. Peasley and still in her possession, was made by Miss Mary Bunker in nature's colors. It is called The Haith Old Meadow and the Partridges—a realistic scene of partridges on the heath or "haith," as it is still known along the seacoast.

Mrs. Peasley likes to talk of the interest the women show in their work, the appeal that beauty makes to them, and how they welcome the opportunity to express their creative urge, sometimes with reverence, as did the one who said, "This is nature's design, and I bow to it." More than one of the hookers, after finishing a rug, would say, "I don't know how I can let this one go." One of the rugs was called Methuselah because so much time was required to make it. The worker felt that she just had to hook in a big yellow rose that had nothing to do with the design. When it went to the exhibit, Ma Peasley made sure that it was well hidden in a pile of more respectable rugs, hoping that no one would see it, and to be doubly sure that it would never get away to disgrace the Mission, she marked on it the exorbitant price of $50; but an inquisitive lady from the city spied the yellow of the rose, pulled it out of the pile, and to the amazement of all gladly paid the $50.

In another instance a rough sketch of a Maine pasture had been given to one of the women to fill in, and it was suggested that since she had a little bull calf she might work him into the design. When the rug came back there was a big buffalo instead. None thought that a buffalo in a Maine pasture would do, but the rugmaker explained that she had always been more interested in buffaloes than in calves, and when she began to hook, said she, "That's the way I saw it." She thought maybe other people might see it that way too. The buffalo rug turned out to be one of the best sellers. Another favorite was a heap of autumn vegetables and fruit, outlined in black with some of the fruit raised above the surface. This was an original idea carried out by Mrs. John McGinnis of Southwest Harbor. Among the most beautiful of the rugs produced were those depicting scenes along the coast of Maine.

Ma Peasley and her rug-hooking neighbors sometimes have business in New York. On one occasion, after viewing some of the extremes of fashion in a shop window, one of her friends turned to her and remarked, "I guess rich people really wear things like that. It's kind of nice to be poor, ain't it?" Ma Peasley's own comments are pointed:

"Up here in Maine we have twenty-four hours—but you don't have a split second to spare in New York." However, she respects the differences she observes and would have them respected. "You can have your chilled grapefruit for breakfast, but give me my pie."

It will be remembered that some of the pioneers in the organization of the Winter Industries Cooperative of Northeast Harbor were hooking rugs before hand-loom weaving was begun. Among the hookers were Mrs. Charles N. Small and the MacLeans. The work of these and other hookers now makes the output of rugs by the Winter Industries Cooperative one of its main products.

Miss Henrietta H. Ames of Matinicus Island hooks rugs for the floor and pictures for the wall, of which she has made about sixty since 1934. Her interpretation of local scenes or happenings is recorded in pleasant color harmonies. Her own house on the edge of the woods with the local ice pond in the foreground, partly bordered with evergreen timber, makes a pleasing composition. Another study is of the sailing vessel *Julia Fairbanks*, seining for mackerel. This rug is an authentic record of the old days when, as Miss Ames remembers, perhaps a hundred of these seine-boats and dories, not omitting the larger boat carrying the seine, were to be seen from the island. Miss Ames's rag pictures have both artistic and documentary value. She contributed a chapter on local church history to the book on Matinicus by Charles A. E. Long, referred to in Chapter 3. In a letter written in 1947 she reports, "for emolument I make bait bags which the lobstermen use, and for entertainment I paint pictures."

Mrs. Hazel W. Bullard of Alfred is a collector of rugs, a teacher, and a rugmaker of note. She has in her collection a rug with a design of strawberries and blue-green leaves, which was bought from Edward Frost and worked by Mrs. Bullard's mother in Columbia, New Hampshire, about 1870. In her home Mrs. Bullard has other fine examples of both old and modern rugs. As an instructor she has given encouragement to classes formed under the Maine Crafts service and is teaching privately as well as in schools. She knew personally Miss Minnie Light of Burkettville, Maine, who drew several original floral designs for Edward Frost. These are now in Mrs. Bullard's collection and are known as the Minnie's Garden Series. Miss Light's flower garden was the inspiration for her work; her method was to select the flowers, lay them on paper, cut them out, and then place the paper designs on the burlap for tracing. Some of the results of this simple but ingenious method were among the most beautiful of the floral rugs of Maine. Mrs. Bullard also owns the original patterns of another early hooker, Miss Lilla Bumps of Thomaston. These original designs in folk art were derived usually from scenes near at hand. Mrs. Bullard's own rugs and designs, some of them introducing bees and butterflies, have been illustrated in various magazines—particularly a beautiful reproduction of the Harriet Emery rug in the *Christian Science Monitor* of March 25, 1936.

Mrs. John P. Winchell of Freeport is an acomplished rugmaker and teacher, having had charge of classes for the state in Freeport, Bath, Camden, and other nearby towns. She has taught more than sixty women how to hook. One of the finest hooked rugs made in recent years in Maine was designed and hooked by Mrs. Winchell for Robert P. Tristram Coffin. Both Mr. Winchell, a safety engineer in the shipyards at Bath, and Mrs. Winchell are discriminating craftsmen.

Mrs. Sherman Abbott of Eliot is an expert hooker of rugs. It is not always, however, that she feels like it. "Some days I just can't do it," she explained, "when the mood is not just right; but when it is, then nothing else takes its place." She remembers vividly a rug which her grandmother made, a kind of crazy-quilt pattern which they called The Broken Dish, and has hooked a large one of the same pattern for her own home. The design is made up of forms like broken dishes. The rug has unusual beauty because of the careful selection of colors and their harmonious arrangement. Much of the dyeing for Mrs. Abbott and other women who make rugs in the community is tastefully done by Mrs. Clara Jane Brown, who sells the dyed materials to neighbors at a uniform price.

When the writer called, Mrs. Abbott had a large quantity of her materials arranged in compartments on the wall of her "rag room," and with the sun coming through the windows this display itself was a beautiful pattern in color. She was working on a floral design with blues in the background, for which she had prepared the dyes herself. The rug was about three by six feet. It was, in the writer's opinion, good enough for a museum piece. A pleasure which she shares with friends and neighbors is her scrapbook about rugs, including many clippings and quotations. One of her favorite "scraps," cut from a Maine paper, thus describes an old rug: "This was a garden of warm colors lying on the oak floor before my mother's fireplace. Deep carmine roses and blue bowknots and a spray of heart's desire."

RUG-HOOKING IN NEW HAMPSHIRE

With the growth of the League of New Hampshire Arts and Crafts, skilled rugmakers came into being and their products were shown at annual Craftsman's Fairs and in the League's shops throughout the

state. Miss Harriet M. Cilley of Plymouth, often an exhibitor at the
Fair, is one of the best hooked-rugmakers in New England. She has
made two rugs of special interest to New Hampshire: one showing a
map of the state, another of Main Street in the village of Plymouth.
Miss Cilley is self-taught and delightfully original. A member of the
League said, "I think she is one of our finest artists—collectors are
always waiting for her next piece of work."

Mrs. R. A. Eggleston of Newport both designs and hooks rugs. She
learned the craft from her mother, a native of Nova Scotia, who, like
many other Canadian-born Americans, did much to improve standards
of craftsmanship in New England. Mrs. Eggleston made a fireplace
rug shown in the New Hampshire building at the World's Fair in
New York in 1939.

Mrs. Ada M. Ericson of Claremont has probably hooked as many
doll house rugs as anyone in New England. She writes: "I began
hooking some seventeen years after one false start and thirty years of
anticipation. My relatives had been rug-hookers of the old school—for
economical and salvage reasons." Since she started to count she had
made 167 chair seats, innumerable doll house rugs and "well within
shooting distance of 200 regular rugs," selling mainly through the
League of New Hampshire Arts and Crafts, and the Women's Educational and Industrial Union of Boston. "I use choice wool rags, old if
possible, and new if necessary. Rug-hooking . . . has all the earmarks
of being a disease from which I seem unable to recover."

Mrs. Lillian B. Prescott of Exeter specializes in hooking rugs. At the
1943 Craftsman's Fair at Manchester she exhibited one of the best
large hooked rugs shown there. In fifteen years she has made more
than a hundred rugs, some of them very large. Her most prized work
is a series of wall hangings depicting scenes from the Bayeux Tapestry
done in hooking technique. Often these are mistaken for needlework,
which disappoints Mrs. Prescott, who says, "I am always pleased to be
known as a hooker."

At the Boston Garden Show in 1943 a rug considered by many to be
the finest shown there was designed by Mrs. Bruce Zeiser of Providence
and worked out by Miss Claire F. Ingalls, then of Nashua, now of
Fitchburg, Massachusetts. This beautiful piece, folklike in character,
was called the Rockweed design because the border was derived from
a kind of rock seaweed. The background was a sandy tone against
which was a blending of garden flowers informally arranged. Much of
the dyeing of the rags had been done by Miss Ingalls. Her father, a
native of Germany and a craftsman in wood, makes records in color
photography of his daughter's most important rugs.

Mrs. Elizabeth Morse of the Scrap Bag in Warner directs the work of a group of hookers in her neighborhood who have made many rugs to order, ranging from the least expensive to some selling for as much as $300 each. Mrs. Morse usually selects the colors and patterns for them.

RUGMAKING IN VERMONT

The work of Mrs. Charlotte K. Stratton of Montpelier has already been mentioned in connection with the stencils of Edward Frost. She and Mr. Stratton have been of great help in combining old methods and new in the preparation of designs, the transfer of patterns, and the final hooking of a rug.

A group of Vermont women in and around Johnson have worked together for more than ten years making hooked, braided, knitted, and crocheted rugs, as well as quilts of many patterns, crocheted bedspreads, tablecloths, and various types of needlework. Their organization is the Helen Collins Handicraft Club, named after its founder, who although an invalid always worked with her hands. She felt that by meeting and working together the neighborhood women could accomplish more than by working separately, and that much would be added to their good times. Since Miss Collins died the women have continued to meet regularly every month. Mrs. Belle Kneeland, one of the group, conducts a gift shop in her home, where she sells the work of the members. She does both hooking and knitting, and sent knitted lace to the Worcester Exhibition of Contemporary Handicrafts.

Mrs. Will Davis, known locally as "Aunt Essie," has been a member of the Club from the beginning. A portrait of Mrs. Davis with some of her rugs is shown. Her favorite she calls Maple Leaves in Autumn. It is in natural colors in a design made by laying the leaves down on the burlap and remembering how they looked. Mrs. Davis said she always loved to walk through the leaves when she was a little girl. "Things that you have seen all your life," she remarked, "you don't really see until you are interested in them." She showed the writer other rugs, and described how she had made a special scalloped design with a teacup, "Oh, it was a lovely design!" On the wall behind her was a rug featuring a big Maltese cat, a favorite with her and her husband. They often lamented that they did not have photographs made of him while he was alive. Finally Mrs. Davis felt she had to make the best likeness of him she could in a rug, although she had never drawn a cat before. Glancing in the direction of the kitchen where her husband was reading she said, "I guess he must like it; he's never said anything against it."

An inquiry about a set of wooden knitting needles revealed that Mrs. Davis had made them herself for a niece who wanted to learn to knit. She had just made a rug portraying Uncle Sam, a standing figure with his hands in his pockets, where Mrs. Davis put them because she "did not know how to draw them." Suddenly Aunt Essie asked if we knew whether the seeds in an apple pointed toward the stem or toward the blow. Of course, we did not know. She had other rural conundrums.

Another member of the Helen Collins Club is Mrs. Seth Washer of Morrisville. We got to her house early one fall morning and found her hard at work on a flowered rug stretched on a frame twelve feet long. The frame reached from the kitchen stove to the single window, the sill of which was lined with ripening tomatoes. Pushed as far into the corner as it would go was a big loom on which Mrs. Washer weaves both rag rugs and home textiles. The days were getting short, and light from only a kerosene lamp made work difficult, so Mrs. Washer was making the most of the precious morning light coming through the kitchen window. We begged her to go on with her hooking while we talked. It did not seem to her the right thing to do, for visitors came seldom, but she consented to work till she got a big flower hooked in.

Mrs. Washer is not only one of the best hookers, she has the great human quality of gratitude for the blessings of life—strength to work, a clear conscience, and, as an extra resource, a hand clever in craftsmanship. Her rug won for the Club the first prize of $100 in a national competition in which 3,300 clubs had entries. It has a beautiful yellowish background with cornucopia and flowers, an adaptation of a folk design made in Vermont a long time ago. A corner of it appears in the frontispiece. Mr. Washer says he will never forget the day of the award. His wife was "glummer than a beetle" that morning, but when word came that she had won the national prize all was right with the world. Without interfering with the hooking Mr. Washer played his favorite tunes on his fiddle—"Zipp Coon," and "The Irish Washer Woman," and finally at Mrs. Washer's suggestion, "The White Cockade," of which she said, "I like it best, you get the most out of the fiddle for it."

One of the rugs which its maker had most enjoyed hooking was a study of the famous trotting horse Jay Eye See, that held the 2:10 record in 1882. "The only thing I have always wanted that I never have had is a genuine Morgan horse." This seemed an unusual preference, but it was expressed with such conviction that no one could doubt it.

Among many others who are doing hooked rugs in Vermont are Mrs. Von Dette of Bennington, whose designs are original; Mrs. Charles

Wishart of Barre, who designed the Bride's Rug shown at the Worcester Exhibition; and Mrs. Herta Moselsio of Bennington College, whose designs and fine sense of color give her creations distinction.

RUG-HOOKING IN MASSACHUSETTS

In 1923 the South End House in Boston began making hooked rugs under the auspices of the South End House Industry. To this settlement, located in a lodging house section of Boston, came men and women from Maine, New Hampshire, Vermont, and the Canadian provinces, among whom were always some who had learned rug-hooking in their former homes and who were eager to put their skills and experiences to use. The attractive and spacious workrooms were well equipped; skillful teachers, designers, and supervisors were employed; and it was not long before this workshop was busy making salable rugs.

The floor rugs made at South End House were usually oblong in shape, of standard sizes, and in interesting designs. New and carefully chosen materials were used and the dyeing was done on the premises, which was one of the special features of the project. During the depression of the 1930's rug-hooking was discontinued and has not yet been resumed.

Mrs. Caroline C. Saunders of Clinton is an honored pioneer teacher of rugmaking. Probably no one has had a wider influence, both direct and indirect, upon the development of this branch of handicraft in New England. Aside from her appreciation of the best qualities of hooking, she has a real understanding of the need of people, especially of women, to find some outlet for their urge to create, where the effort culminates in a useful and beautiful thing for the home.

Realizing the necessity to do something to relieve the tension which her neighbors and their friends were subjected to during the depression years as factories closed down and general morale ebbed, Mrs. Saunders, at the time president of the Woman's Club, thought that rug-hooking would bring to many the satisfactions which come from creative work, and to others an opportunity to earn something with their hands.

The story of her learning all she could about hooking, and teaching and having others teach the rudiments of the craft, making her home the center for work and exhibitions and hospitality, is too long to outline here. It is not too much, however, to say that from her interest and efforts much of the revival of rug-hooking in New England and elsewhere can be traced.

Mrs. Pearl K. McGown of West Boylston has helped to preserve the best traditions of rugmaking. In addition to being a designer and craftsman she is a teacher, lecturer, collector, and writer. Each year special exhibitions are held of the work of Mrs. McGown and of her pupils, usually at Horticultural Hall in Worcester. These exhibitions are attended by persons from all parts of New England and from many other states. The various processes of dyeing and hooking are demonstrated. Prepared materials, with instructions as to how they may be used with some of the patterns, are available at reasonable cost. There is a general interchange of ideas and experiences among hookers and teachers. This is probably the most important annual gathering of rugmakers in our country. With its exhibitions, demonstrations, and general information, it is the starting place for many workers in this popular folk art.

At least one dealer in Massachusetts must be briefly mentioned in this record, Ralph W. Burnham. His widow and successor, Nellie M. Burnham of Ipswich, continues to sell early patterns collected by Mr. Burnham and to repair and restore rugs. Mr. Burnham was not only a distributor of patterns and materials for rugmakers and a buyer and seller of old and fine rugs, but a close student and observer who wrote considerably. Mr. Kent included Mr. Burnham in a list of eleven "who were the first to renew the early appreciation and encourage the revival in America of rug-hooking," and reproduced a number of choice rugs from the Burnham collection. The business at Ipswich is still a center of interest and information for rug-hookers. Mr. Burnham's valuable article on "The New England Hooked Rug" is published in the latest edition of the catalogue issued by Mrs. Burnham. His standing offer is there renewed of a reward for exact information as to "when and where the first hooked rugs were made in America."

Mrs. C. E. Anderson of Holyoke, whose work is mentioned again in the next chapter, has demonstrated the process of rug-hooking at the Handicraft Fairs held at Northampton. She once showed a beautiful rug which she was finishing for herself, a large floral design with a tan background and a border in which she had worked parts of a worn-out Paisley shawl.

People get into rug-hooking in an infinite number of ways. Mrs. Royal F. Manson of Hudson writes: "The business of designing hooked rugs and teaching rugmaking was established by my son. After four years at the School of Practical Art and the Museum School at Boston, he was unable to find work. That was during years when so many people were desperate to find something to do. Hooked rugs caught his interest and he wondered why they were always copies of old rugs, some good, some bad. He had the idea a hooked rug could be good with an original design. Immediately I became interested and started to make designs under his supervision to prove that his idea was sound. Since then I have continued to make rugs and I have never worked at a craft which has given me so much pleasure. . . . Being a housewife, I do not make many rugs in a year, three last year, two of which I sold. . . . I make patterns and dye rags to sell."

One of the most extraordinary hooked carpets discovered in making this study was the floor covering for the altar in the Church of Our Lady of Lourdes at Wellfleet on Cape Cod. The carpet had been made by the local sewing circle about 1913. The Reverend Joseph Eikerling had designed it and instructed the women in hooking. The designs were of folk-type hooked in woolen yarn. Irish, French, Portuguese, and other Americans of European lineage participated in the work.

RUG-HOOKING IN CONNECTICUT

Because of an eye injury when she was younger, Mrs. Josephine M. Davis of Somers was not able to satisfy her love of color until she took up hooking. This gave her an outlet that was not a great strain on her eyes and enabled her to earn at the same time. During the decade and a half that she has been hooking she has produced about seventy-five rugs, her only tools being a pair of shears and a crochet hook. She works without a frame. She likes to use animals in her designs, getting help from the best available pictures in color.

Mrs. Richard Wampler of New Britain has made hooked rugs for her own pleasure for more than twelve years. She has copied some of the Oriental rugs in the Ballard Collection at the Metropolitan Museum of Art in New York. Her rugs have been exhibited by the Society of Connecticut Craftsmen.

Mrs. Vida Jopson of West Hartford is one of the most skillful New England rugmakers. She was represented at the Worcester Exhibition by a beautiful runner with autumn leaves, notable for its design, color combination, and perfection in hooking.

RUG-HOOKING IN RHODE ISLAND

Mrs. Molly Nye Tobey of Barrington, near Providence, is known as one of the most original designers and makers of hooked rugs in our country. All her rugs are individual and are modern in spirit and execution. The design of the Victory Garden rug, which was shown at the Worcester Exhibition, was inspired by the Tobey family garden. It received first prize in the *Woman's Day* national hooked-rug competition in 1942. This rug is shown in the frontispiece. Mrs. Tobey's coloring is strong yet very harmonious and the technique impressionistic. At Worcester she was represented also by The Farm, a rug in which a few excellent colors are combined in barnyard motifs. The texture of these rugs is fairly coarse, yet firm, and in keeping with the rural subjects, which she prefers.

Mrs. Bruce Zeiser of Providence, already referred to, has designed many rugs for others, as well as for her own hooking. Among those hooked by her perhaps the best known was reproduced in color in *Woman's Day* for August, 1943. It was called a Flower Medley, a room-sized rug in tawny and muted colors on a warm ecru background. The scroll-type border picks up the flowers from the design in the center. The hooking of this large rug was an unusual achievement in craftsmanship.

BRAIDED RUGS

The braided rug has also experienced a wide revival in New England with the development of some excellent designs. In a braided rug the mechanics of the process are: first, the cutting of the cloth into strips; second, the braiding of the strips; and third, the sewing of the braided strips together in flat coils to form the rug. An illustration shows the process of braiding by Edwin Pease of Warren, New Hampshire, with one of his finished rugs on the work table in the background.

Miss Belle D. Robinson of Williamstown, Vermont, as anyone who sees the picture of her shown in this book will know, is an expert rugmaker, although it is but one of her achievements. Her flower garden, which she tends entirely herself, and her brother's picturesque tin shop at the rear of their quaint little house against a hill make a beautiful unit in this old Vermont village.

Mrs. Arthur Fitzgerald of Waldoboro, Maine, is the director of a group of braided-rugmakers of Lincoln County that have been very successful as a cooperative. Several braiders who represent the third generation to have plied this craft are members of the cooperative, many of whom are fishermen's and farmers' wives. Good rugs are made both for general sale and on order. About seventy braiders make up the group and of these fifty work steadily. Most of their rugs go to the Colonial Rug Company of Maine.

HAND-LOOMED RAG RUGS AND CARPETS

There are several weavers in New England who still make the old-fashioned hand-woven rugs and carpets for their own use and also to sell. In tracing the craft of hand-woven rugs and carpets we might be able to follow clues back to colonial days when the making of rag carpet was one of the most popular handicrafts. It is probable that rural weavers in New England have made rag rugs and carpets during all the years since the Republic was established.

In the early part of the present century we find that the Woman's Club of Plainfield, New Hampshire, organized a Mothers and Daughters Industry, which wove rugs according to color designs made by Mrs. Frances Houston of Boston and Mrs. H. O. Walker of New York. Mrs. G. S. Ruggles was manager. A trademark with distaff and with the letters "MDI" was sewed in the corner of each rug. When the community ran out of cloth, white cotton flannel was bought and dyed as desired. Exhibits were sent out and hundreds of rugs were made and sold. Six looms were brought into the community, twenty-five workers were kept busy, and the Mothers and Daughters Industry branched out into other forms of weaving.

Albert Oughtibridge of Sanford, Maine, born in England and now an American citizen, is a weaver of rugs on a specially designed loom of his own construction. He was wounded during World War I, and on his return to this country was unable to work again in the Sanford Woolen Mills, where he had learned textile processes. When it became necessary to choose a light occupation in which he could make a living, he naturally turned to hand weaving. His special loom has a foot equipment adapted to his needs, which helps him to weave rapidly, although he does not use a fly-shuttle. Most of his rugs are in small standard sizes, very firm in texture, and can be made in almost any color combination. He finds a market for them at his own door.

Weaving of this character is usually done to order and frequently with materials furnished by the purchaser. Mrs. Alice O. Fleet of Essex is among the best known Connecticut weavers who make floor coverings. Mrs. Caroline E. Banning of Westerly, Rhode Island, specializes in colonial patterns and hit-or-miss rag carpets and scatter rugs. Occasionally figures are woven into the textile as in the nursery rug designed and woven by Miss Mabel C. Holcomb of Isle La Motte, Vermont, for the children's corner of the Worcester Handicraft Exhibition. The work of Miss Holcomb and her sister, Eleanor, both experienced craftsmen, has been mentioned in Chapter 5.

CHAPTER 8

THE DYEING OF MATERIALS AND THE DECORATING OF SURFACES

THIS chapter deals with some of the various processes employed in changing the surface appearance of a product. Sometimes the entire surface, or even the product throughout, is changed, as in dyeing by immersion—a process which may be applied to fibers, yarns, and cloth. Sometimes only part of the surface is changed, as in block-printing or stenciling on cloth, paper, wood, glass, or metal; or in decorative painting, illuminating, lettering, or calligraphy.

DYEING BY IMMERSION WITH NATURAL COLORS

There is renewed and growing interest in the ancient method of dyeing with vegetable and other natural dyes, and in New England unique work has been done with this method.

Paralleling the interest in extracting color from the plants of garden, field, and woodland is the interest with which they are studied as sources of food, drink, cosmetics, and medicine. Plants for medicine, as in pioneer days, are still common in some places, and a number of New England men and women give much time to growing, gathering, blending, and vending herbs. Often at craftsmen's fairs there will be exhibits of dried herbs and extracts in attractive containers. In the Country Store next to Wiggins Old Tavern in Northampton, Massachusetts, there is an old apothecary's cabinet filled with blown-glass containers holding herbs. Native nut trees, such as walnut, butternut, and hickory, supply food and medicine as well as excellent color for dyeing materials. Occasionally someone will be found who knows equally both the dye and medicinal properties of plants, reminding us of the fact that for centuries medicine and chemistry were a single and united science.

The term "natural dyes" comprises the coloring matter obtained from plants, animals, insects, or minerals. The majority of these dyes are of plant origin except, for example, the red and pink coloring extracted from the insect cochineal, the orange and yellow made from copperas, and a few other colors derived from minerals and shells. Most of the dyes with which this chapter deals are vegetables dyes from plants familiar to people of New England.

Interest in the subject, however, is much more than regional. No section, for instance, in recent years has done more in the home manufacture of vegetable dyes than the Southern Highlands. Canadian craftsmen, too, have carried out a considerable number of experiments with good results, while in Mexico the use of colors from plants is an unbroken tradition older than history. The thorough student of the subject should not be limited in his observation to what has been accomplished in our own country, but should include our neighbors to the north and south.

Commercial and Natural Dyes Compared

Something should perhaps be said on the relative merits of home or vegetable dyes as compared with store or commercial dyes, and suggestions made in justification of a wider use of the former, particularly in rural districts where there is an abundance of dye material.

The claim that vegetable dyes are always permanent while commercial dyes are not is a common error. No such general assertion can be helpful, for comparison must be made between a specific vegetable dye and a specific commercial dye, and must take into consideration the operations that attend the process of dyeing. Absolute quality is not alone in the dye itself, but partly in the way in which it is prepared and applied. Moreover, fastness is a relative matter; that is, a dye may be comparatively fast when exposed to light but may fade when washed. Or the reverse of this may happen. Also fastness may vary with the material used, whether wool, cotton, silk, or some other fiber. Thus some natural dyes may be applied successfully to one kind of material but with less assurance to another. The best commercial dyes are prepared to be used on a specific fiber. The only conclusion, therefore, at which one can arrive as to the relative permanence of vegetable and commercial dyes is that a number of the former are more lasting on certain fibers than some of the latter; again the reverse is true. On the whole, the record for fastness is with vegetable dyes. They have been in use for centuries; synthetic dyes are a fairly recent invention.

There is one fact about the fading of the two kinds which gives real advantage to natural dyes. Generally speaking, when natural dyes fade they still bear a definite relation to their original color, often becoming softer and more beautiful without losing their character; a faded synthetic dye, on the contrary, may bear little resemblance to its original tone. Since few colors in any fabric are absolutely fast, the fact that those obtained from natural sources do not usually deteriorate in quality but sometimes improve is a definite advantage.

A question often asked by craftsmen wishing to experiment with native dyes is, "Can I get a sufficient color range to ensure good results?" A satisfactory answer depends upon two basic things: first, the color range desired; and second, the whereabouts of the craftsman. It is true that in choice of colors synthetic dyes generally far out-number natural dyes even when one has access to a large variety of dye-producing plants, but wide variety is not always the need of the artist. A few carefully chosen colors will usually bring better results than experiments with many, just as in the graphic arts much of the best printing is achieved with a few well-selected type faces rather than with the endless variety made available by type foundries. However, a greater range of colors than is generally known has been developed from plants of the New England states, and experiments to increase the number are still in progress. A complete list of colors derived from plants growing in New England would be of interest but we can mention only the following: black, blue, brown, tan, gray, green, orange, purple, red, yellow, and many shades of these. It would seem that the New England craftsman need not feel greatly handicapped by color limitations.

To many the relative costs of the two kinds of dyeing is important. For city dwellers synthetic dyes are preferable because, besides being cheap, they are more easily obtained; native dye plants are inaccessible. The country dweller, too, can now purchase synthetic dyes at a low price, but often he has little cash, and to make his own dye from plants that he can gather is for him often an economy.

Synthetic dyes are certainly easier to use but a craftsman will not always measure his task in terms of work involved; he often experiences great satisfaction when he can engage in the complete process and thus thoroughly control his medium. To know all the reasons for the choice of a natural dye is obviously not possible. Those who spin and weave by the old processes and who wish to complete the cycle will understand the enthusiasm of the old mountain weaver in her gaily striped skirt who said, "I like to see my petticoat all the way from the sheep's back." Others will find in vegetable dyes an opportunity to create a color palette of individuality and perhaps of rare beauty; this is a unique experience. There is always a new plant to discover, a new dye to make, and a worker can frequently trace his methods back to the homelands of Europe and to recipes used there for centuries.

Some Principles of Dyeing

Directions for using natural dyes may be found in many publications but a few basic processes in the preparation of nearly all vegetable dyes will be briefly given here. These basic steps include: first, gathering the dyemaking materials; second, preparation of the dye; third, preparation of the fibers to receive the dyes; finally, the actual immersion of the fiber followed by the rinsing and drying of the colored product.

The material of which the dye is made may be native wild plants, such as sumac berries and hickory bark, or from cultivated plants or trees such as apple bark or coreopsis flowers, or from a plant or tree that is both wild and cultivated, like the black walnut. The dye source may be any portion of the plant—roots, stems, barks, leaves, nuts, flowers, fruit, seeds, or sometimes the complete plant. In many cases the time of year when the parts are gathered is important. This would be obviously true with flowers and fruits, but it is also true with certain roots and barks. From the sumac blossom and fruit, a different shade varying from a light to a deep tan is obtained according to the state of fruit or flower.

Some materials when gathered must be made into dye at once, others can be dried and used months and sometimes years later. There are dyes which can be kept in liquid form for a considerable time without losing their potency, and still others in which a part of the dye solution, for instance indigo, can be used over a long period. A few years ago an indigo "blue pot" was discovered in the Southern Highlands. Members of the family who owned it said it had been in continuous use for more than ninety years.

Wool is generally the fiber which in New England is colored with vegetable dyes; rabbit fur and dog hair are sometimes dyed, and probably a little linen is also colored in this way. Some dyes will color both wool and cotton without any preliminary preparation; this is true of indigo. But in most cases the application of a mordant is required to prepare the fiber to absorb the dye and hold it. Different solutions, in addition to acting as a mordant, sometimes serve to modify the shade. For instance, when alum is used as a mordant, wool dyed with madder becomes rose color; but if the mordant is muriate of tin, the result is brick color.

The actual process of dyeing follows the treatment with a mordant, if one is needed, and calls for great care with respect to timing, right temperature of the dye bath, and careful handling of the material, including constant stirring (with intermittent lifting and draining) so that it will not be crowded in the vessel and thus dye unevenly. The kind of vessel—tin, brass, copper, or iron—often has a bearing on the color that is obtained. The manner of removing the material from the vessel, of rinsing, and of drying it is also of great importance in obtaining an even color. It is generally held that best results from vegetable dyes come from drying in the open air. Certainly anyone who has ever smelled an indigo blue pot will agree that outdoors is the proper place to work with this dye. The dyeing process may be used equally with woven cloth, thread or yarn, or with wool before it is spun—when it is "dyed in the wool."

Experiments in Vegetable Dyeing

In early days all dyes were derived, of course, from natural sources, for synthetic dyes did not come into general use until the second half of the nineteenth century; but in recent years further experiments with vegetable dyes have been made by craftsmen who have felt much satisfaction in controlling the entire process of dyeing, or who wished to use colors that could not be had through commercial products. Only a few such experiments can be referred to here.

Miss Ruth Gaines of Meriden, New Hampshire, an expert spinner, has developed dyes for wool, Angora rabbit yarn, and linen thread. In addition to a number of special vegetable dyes, she has a particularly beautiful mineral vermilion and also a chrome ochre dye, a cinnabar, and other mineral colors.

Writing in the *Chronicle of the Early American Industries Association*, of May, 1941, Miss Gaines describes a "little exhibit from my farm in New Hampshire which seemed to me typical of my state," prepared by her for one of the informal meetings of the Association held at Wiggins Old Tavern: "It consisted of a wicker basketful of yarns, hand spun and hand dyed, together with a tray of dyes hastily gathered in the autumn fields: brown plush butternuts; sun flower seeds, in their round, dried, containers; magenta sumac spikes; grey tips of the same, like antlers in the velvet; crimson-thorned blackberry stems; coral madder roots; goldenrods, canary yellow; and, added to these, mineral dyes our ancestors used . . . chrome ochre, and hematite—that primitive red which decorated with war paint the bronze skin of the Indians before we used it to color our barns and farm houses and flannels with an illusion of warmth. Almost unnoticed, I laid in a tiny skein of Upland, home-grown flax."

In her search for information about home dyeing, Miss Gaines corresponds with a number of craftsmen throughout the United States who use vegetable dyes. One of these is Miss Pearl Becker of Scappoose, Oregon, who has cultivated her own madder bed and experiments widely with dyes from native plants of Oregon.

Another scholarly experimenter was Miss Lucy Cabot of Boston, a statement of whose formulas and experiences is now in the hands of John Ralph Geddis and Francois Martin, dyers, spinners, and weavers of originality, and puppeteers, whose skill in the last-named craft is described elsewhere. Besides her outstanding experiments with New England dye materials, Miss Cabot also worked with Indians, especially those of the Southwest, in efforts to recover some of their old formulas and to help them develop new colors for their textiles.

Extensive vegetable dyeing was done in Deerfield, Massachusetts, at the beginning of the century by members of the Society of Blue and White Needlework who, being unable to buy the colors they wished for their thread and yarn, developed their own palette. Further reference to their work is made in Chapter 11.

Cushings dyes, made at Dover-Foxcraft, Maine, are generally used in Mrs. Pearl McGown's classes because she considers them the most permanent commercial dyes to be had. Ingenious formulas have been worked out, and dyed strips for separate flowers, figures, and even for extensive rug patterns in different color combinations are produced. But the use of vegetable dyes in preparing material for rugs was shown in 1945 at Worcester by some of Mrs. McGown's pupils.

One of these experimenters, Miss Anna M. Boynton, from Maine, wrote:

I was pleased to learn that you noticed the vegetable dyeing, for I was very much intrigued with it. It was purely a matter of its capturing my interest, for it is infinitely easier to open a package of dye and get it over in half an hour or so, whereas with the vegetable dyes you have to make your decoctions and then still go through the process.

I once shared a camp in a rather isolated place, with a friend, so I tried some experiments with what was around me. I used first Alder bark, and got some lovely golds with that, reddish golds. Then the Poplar bark gave paler tones.

I had never heard anyone mention them as a source of dye, but I found that sarsaparilla berries, which grew in profusion in the neighboring fields, stained my hands deeply whenever I touched them, so I made a lot of that decoction. I got some lovely dull plum shades, and had one very interesting accident. I wanted some paler shades, so I was adding rags at intervals after part of the dye was taken up. I forgot to rinse the soap out of one piece after I washed it, and it turned the whole batch a lovely shade of pale green. I suppose it was some chemical action of the lye in the soap. There were literally acres of goldenrod about me, so I tried that. It gave some very rich shades of clear yellow, rather on the canary, and the flowers do make very powerful dye. One of my loveliest shades came from rhubarb roots, a beautiful bronze or old gold shade, very powerful dye. I also got some bronzy green from cedar tips.

My interest in the work was further stimulated by an article in the *New York Sun,* issue of August 3, 1942, describing the work of Mrs. Chester G. Marsh with the Girl Scouts. She was teaching them to dye clothing and yarns with natural dyes, but I have never been interested to use them for anything but rug material.

In Connecticut the group of workers in the Bridgeport Housing Company, led by William H. Ham, experimented extensively with vegetable dyes in connection with their weaving project described earlier. Old recipes yielded vegetable colors with which a large amount of yarn was dyed. "Some of our best results," reports Mr. Ham, "were with the local Iceland moss, walnut shells, maple and oak bark, birch bark, alder bark, and local lichens. We used many other materials and prepared samples for 190 colors, some of these very permanent as shown by tests by the Bureau of Standards in Washington."

DECORATING SURFACES

Methods of applying color other than by immersion include wood and linoleum blockprinting on cloth or on paper; stenciling; freehand painting or decorating on wood, metal, and glass; the silk-screen process known as serigraphy; illuminating and other arts of the book; and possibly other processes. In referring to blockprinting, that is, the transfer of a design from the face of a block to a textile or other material, the term "linoleum block" should usually be substituted for "wood block" because materials so decorated in New England today are being printed largely from linoleum blocks.

Blockprinting on Fabric

Linoleum blockprinting in New England owes a great deal to experience gained in the Connecticut Work Projects Administration, an undertaking which through its several craft units exerted wide influence on taste and standards of workmanship. Organized mainly to provide employment, the blockprinting unit was so well managed from its headquarters at Stamford that, soon after classes were formed,

Doris Day

33. A FOLK WHITTLER OF NEW HAMPSHIRE

When Archie Gilbert of Landaff Lost a Leg Through an Accident, He Turned to Making Toy Oxen and Carts for the New Hampshire League. Mrs. Gilbert Helps to Paint Them.

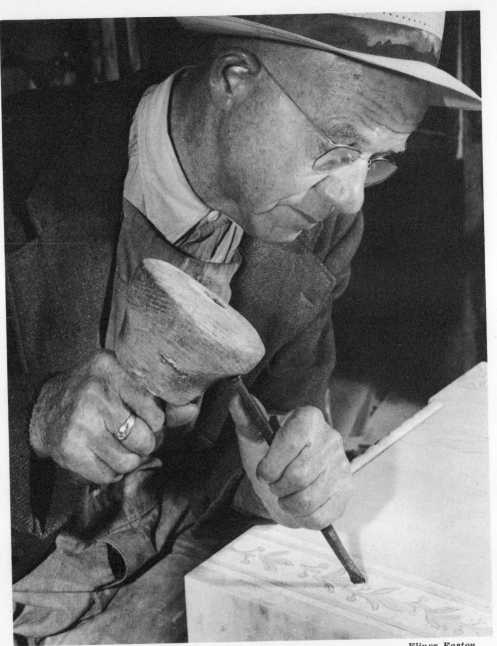

Elinor Easton

34. CUTTING TOMBSTONES IS AN OLD NEW ENGLAND CRAFT

VIRGIL FLOOD OF NORWAY, MAINE, IS CUTTING AN ORIGINAL DESIGN IN VERMONT
MARBLE. HE HAS CUT LOCAL TOMBSTONES FOR YEARS, SOMETIMES BARTERING THEM
FOR OTHER FORMS OF CRAFTSMANSHIP.

R. D. Snively

35. NETTING A TESTER FOR A HIGH-POST BED

Miss Rachel Hawks of Deerfield, Massachusetts, Has Helped to Preserve the
Old Art of Netting Canopies for Four-post Beds, Which She Learned Many
Years Ago from an Old Resident of the Town. A Finished Canopy Is Shown
in Place.

Doris Day

36. EARLY KNITTERS OF NEW HAMPSHIRE

MARY AND SARAH POTTER OF ACWORTH WERE AMONG THE FIRST KNITTERS FOR THE NEW HAMPSHIRE LEAGUE. MANY OF THEIR DESIGNS ARE ORIGINAL AND THEIR CRAFTS-MANSHIP HAS RARELY BEEN SURPASSED.

37. A SAILOR MAKES FINE SHIP MODELS

CHARLES SAYLE OF NANTUCKET FOLLOWED THE SEA AS FISHERMAN AND SAILOR FROM HIS EARLY TEENS. HE HAS BUILT AND REPAIRED BOATS, CARVED MINIATURE WHALES FROM IVORY AND TEAKWOOD, AND HAS MADE SOME OF THE MOST ACCURATE AND BEAUTIFUL SHIP MODELS IN NEW ENGLAND.

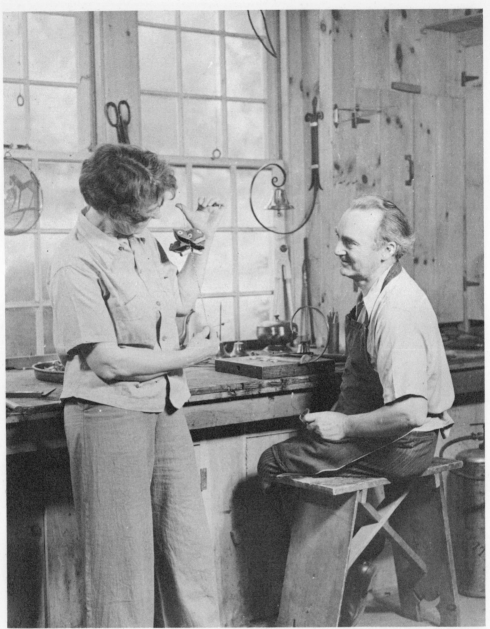

Doris Day

38. PIONEERS IN CONNECTICUT HANDICRAFTS

Leonard and Myra Rankin in Their Workshop Near Bakersville. Mr. Rankin, a Metalworker, Was the First Director and Field Secretary of the Society of Connecticut Craftsmen; Mrs. Rankin Is a Designer and Craftsman in Many Mediums.

W. G. Pollak, A.R.P.S.

39. A CONTEMPORARY TINSHOP IN NANTUCKET

There Are a Few Old-time Tinshops Left in New England, Among Them William
H. Barrett's on Nantucket Island, Where Tin and Sheet Iron Articles Are Made
by Hand.

George French

40. KNITTING IS ONE OF THE OLDEST HOME ARTS IN MAINE

MRS. FRANCENA FRENCH OF KEZAR FALLS HAS KNITTED ALL HER LIFE. HER SON, ONE OF AMERICA'S LEADING PHOTOGRAPHERS, CHOSE HER AS A SYMBOL OF THIS AGE-OLD DOMESTIC ART.

George French, School Arts Magazine

41. A FISHNETMAKER OF MAINE

ALPHEUS A. PENDLETON OF ISLESBORO WAS NOTED FOR HIS EXCELLENT FISHNETS. HERE
HE IS MAKING ONE FOR HIS NEIGHBOR, MAURICE L. DECKER, WHOSE WOODEN DECOYS
ARE SHOWN. MR. PENDLETON ALSO MADE SHIP MODELS, GARDEN RAKES, AND OTHER
ARTICLES FROM LOCAL WOODS.

Eames Studio

42. A BIG LOG IN GOFFE'S MILL, NEW HAMPSHIRE

GEORGE WOODBURY OF BEDFORD OPERATES A SAWMILL AND A GRISTMILL, AND MAKES FURNITURE. HE IS OF THE SEVENTH GENERATION FROM THE JOHN GOFFE WHO ESTABLISHED THE MILL ON BOWMAN'S BROOK IN 1744.

George French

43. A ONE-MAN BALL-BAT INDUSTRY IN MAINE

ERNEST HUSSEY OF KEZAR FALLS, A LOCAL BASEBALL PLAYER AND A SKILLED CRAFTS-
MAN, SHAPES ON HIS LATHE EXCELLENT BALL BATS AND OTHER WOODEN ARTICLES
FROM NATIVE HICKORY, MAPLE, AND ASH.

George French

44. A PHARMACIST OF MAINE TAKES UP WEAVING

Charles N. Small of Northeast Harbor Was One of the Earliest Weavers of the Winter Industries Cooperative. He Set Up His Loom Near the Prescription Desk of His Drugstore and Invited Customers to Look on the Shelves for Whatever They Needed.

Doris Day

45. FAMOUS FOR HER BRAIDED RUGS AND ROCK GARDEN

Miss Belle D. Robinson, Living on the Old Homeplace in Williamstown, Vermont, Is One of the Best-known Makers of Braided Rugs in New England, but Is Even Better Known for Her Beautiful Rock Garden on the Small Hill Behind Her House.

R. D. Snively, School Arts Magazine

46. A METAL CRAFTSMAN OF MASSACHUSETTS

LEWIS WHITNEY AT WORK IN HIS METAL SHOP IN ROCKPORT. MRS. WHITNEY IS A DESIGNER, AND TOGETHER THEY HAVE PRODUCED NOTABLE ARTICLES IN COPPER, PEWTER, ALUMINUM, AND SILVER.

Doris Day, School Arts Magazine

47. A CRAFTSMAN FROM CHIPPING-CAMDEN

EDGAR KEEN OF WARNER, NEW HAMPSHIRE, IS A TRAINED SCULPTOR IN WOOD FROM THE CHIPPING-CAMDEN SCHOOL IN ENGLAND. HE HAS CAST HIS LOT WITH THE CRAFTS-MEN OF HIS ADOPTED STATE, HELPING THE NEW HAMPSHIRE LEAGUE UPHOLD HIGH STANDARDS.

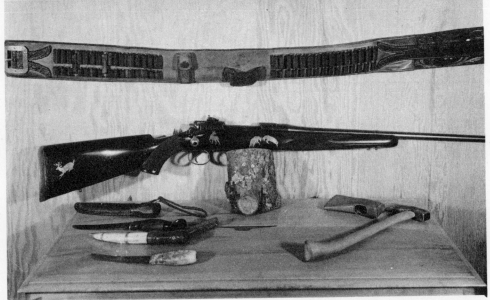

George French

48. A CRAFTSMAN MAKES HIS HUNTING OUTFIT

ROBERT L. SMALLIDGE OF NORTHEAST HARBOR, MAINE, MAKES FINE SHIP MODELS,
SNOWSHOES, AND ARCHERY EQUIPMENT, AS WELL AS THE ARTICLES SHOWN: THE GUN-
STOCK, METAL FIGURES IN THE STOCK, LEATHER CARTRIDGE BELT, HUNTING KNIVES
AND SHEATHS, AX HANDLE, AND LEATHER COVER FOR THE BIT.

a demand for curtains, table covers, upholstery material, and wall decorations came from many public institutions. So many persons learned how to do such work that the project became an important factor in utilizing the unemployed during the prewar depression.

The administrator of the WPA for Connecticut was Howard Staub, and Miss Eleanor B. Finch was state supervisor of crafts. The Stamford Crafts Project was under the direct supervision of Mrs. Nellie B. Burow, already referred to as a weaver. The major part of the designing was done by Mrs. Myra W. Rankin and Mrs. Marion R. Voorhees. Mrs. Rankin, a graduate of the Art Institute of Chicago, and a designer of wide practice and versatility, brought to her work a sense of humor not often found in the general field of design. Some of her subjects have a whimsical quality in addition to charming color combinations. The gay and colorful designs by Mrs. Voorhees of Hamburg also have an original, playful quality. The work of both these designers extended to the making of patterns for hooked rugs, in which the Connecticut project achieved a high record in both design and craftsmanship. One of these large hooked rugs and a few wall hangings are illustrated.

Among the best-known blockprinters of our country are the Folly Cove Designers of Annisquam, near Gloucester, Massachusetts. This group of young craftsmen developed under the leadership of Mrs. Virginia Demetrios from a class in design which she conducted. Mrs. Demetrios, who is a skillful designer, and an illustrator of children's books, continues to teach the members of the group, and is sometimes assisted by Mrs. Aino Clarke, her first pupil. The group consists of about twenty-five designers, all residents of Cape Ann. A yearly exhibition and sale is held in Rockport in which all members cooperate to make the occasion beautiful and pleasurable, as well as conducive to sales.

According to a letter received from the secretary in 1947: "Each designer is required to make and print his or her designs. They must be original work. In order to maintain the quality, each design bearing the name, Folly Cove Designers, must be approved by a jury of five of the more experienced members of the group."

Names of some of the designs are A Country Fair, Noah's Ark, Calendar Wall Hanging, The Farm, Merry-Go-Round, Horse and Buggy, The Circus, together with other home and village scenes, or animal and bird subjects. Some are reminiscent of earlier days— American designs with native roots in our own past. At the Worcester Handicraft Exhibition a special cottage alcove was decorated with hand-blocked wall fabric designed and printed by Mrs. Louise Kenyon of the Folly Cove Designers, and the window drapery was a textile, The Gossips, a design created by Mrs. Demetrios. The products of the group, now sold in several large stores throughout the country, include wall hangings, curtain fabrics, luncheon sets, tablecloths and napkins, scarfs, skirts, aprons, dresses, and blouses.

Mrs. Gladys Wilkins Murphy of Fall River, Massachusetts, has done textile printing from linoleum blocks and, in addition to making blocks for hand production, has prepared designs for manufacturing in quantity. Hers were among the blockprint textiles shown at the Worcester Exhibition. During the summer Mrs. Murphy and her husband, Herbert A. Murphy, conduct a shop and gallery in Rockport, in which they display their blockprints and paintings.

Blockprinting on Paper

Carl Tait, formerly of Manchester, New Hampshire, now living in Beverly, Massachusetts, has achieved a wide reputation with Christmas and other cards printed by hand from linoleum blocks in from two to four colors. Trained as an artist in the Manchester Institute of Arts and Sciences, the question of making a living was the practical one which he faced when he completed his art courses. He drew several designs of uniform size, used as few blocks as possible to get pleasing results, and developed a technique of rapid printing by hand which enabled him to sell the cards at an unusually low price. His pictures are more like those of the French artist, Henri Revière, than anything yet developed in this country, although he had never seen any of Revière's prints. Most of his work is done in three colors. His subjects are flowers, seashore scenes taken at Rockport and Gloucester, Christmas scenes and motifs, and a number of others. Mr. Tait does all the processes himself—designing, cutting the block, mixing and applying the colors—and has become expert in the technique of printing. His work was interrupted by army service, but he has since resumed his card-printing, now using the silk-screen technique, and has brought out several new designs, some in brilliant colors.

Miss Ruby G. Allen of Antrim, New Hampshire, uses linoleum blocks for the printing of nature subjects. She records flowers and animals native to the state on small cards appropriate for Christmas and other occasions. She often demonstrates the processes at the annual Craftsman's Fair of the League of New Hampshire Arts and Crafts.

We shall mention only two other linoleum blockprinters in New England, both identified with the printed word. Fritz L. Amberger has a well-planned but almost miniature rural printshop a few miles from Washington Depot, Connecticut. The press is in a room barely large enough to hold it and its ample owner. Mr. Amberger makes linoleum block Christmas cards of his own design cut by hand and printed in his shop, but he also combines blockprints for display cards and posters, which he runs off on his small press. For these he is able to draw and cut designs and select colors which he runs separately from the printed matter, giving the whole an original and interesting effect. Sometimes if he wishes to print a large poster he will feed it into his small press four times, once for each corner. When finished it looks as unified as a single printing could have made it. Running four or more impressions in order to complete a design is more economical for him, Mr. Amberger says, than supporting a shop with large presses. Mrs. Amberger does much of the typesetting. Although Mr. Amberger's printshop is located far in the country, he works also for some large industrial enterprises. For the local trade he makes letterheads, billheads, statements, and so forth. Thus the tradesmen and storekeepers of Washington Depot are supplied with printed forms that they are proud to use. Good taste costs no more in the village than in the city, and here, with overhead cut down to a minimum, it is really to be had for less.

This rural American craftsman comes of a long line of Swiss printers famous since the 1700's and perhaps earlier. His forebear, Joseph Magg, founded about 1715 in Zürich what is now the second oldest printing business in the little Alpine republic. Among several Swiss keepsakes Mr. Amberger displays in his shop an almanac done in the printing house of his grandfather in Zürich. He prizes above all the original type stick which his father gave him when he left Switzerland for America, with strict instructions as to how to use it.

One of the most interesting examples of linoleum blockprinting ever done in our country is the first copy of *Found Horizon's Herald,* conceived, written, edited, illustrated, cut from one block, and printed by Frederick Robbins, an early member of the League of New Hampshire Arts and Crafts. Mr. Robbins, or "Robby," as his friends call him, lived at the time in Alexandria, about six miles from the town of Bristol, New Hampshire, and carried on his work in the small house which he built for himself, much of his living coming from his garden.

A reproduction of *Found Horizon's Herald* is shown. The linoleum block from which it was printed is 22 by 27½ inches, a very impressive spread. "Of course," said Mr. Robbins, "a linoleum block could be yards in length if there was a reason for it." When Mr. Robbins had prepared the text, which gave the neighborhood news, and had laid out the illustrations, which recorded local scenes, he cut the entire text and illustrations on one block and printed them with one impression on his large etching press; he then carried the finished papers from his cabin to Bristol on his bicycle. From here he shipped them to the Craftsman's Fair at Dartmouth College.

The printing of the newspaper still goes on. Mr. Robbins writes the text, prints it by hand, and draws in the illustrations; but to save time he now has the original material reproduced in a zinc linecut through arrangement with a country newspaper office. Thus, while mechanically the later numbers are not wholly a one-man product, they retain much of the individuality, freshness, and charm of the first issue.

There are in New England several excellent wood engravers who cut their design on the end grain of the wood and print the image usually on paper. One of these, a craftsman of unusual originality and skill, is Herbert Waters of Campton, New Hampshire, who is mentioned here because he often demonstrates at the annual Craftsman's Fair of the League of New Hampshire Arts and Crafts.

Although we regret that we cannot include in this book references to the work of New Englanders in the graphic arts, especially those eminent in the field of typography, it is pleasant to be able to include as craftsmen, in quite diverse fields, at least three men who stand very high in the printing arts. Bruce Rogers of New Fairfield, Connecticut, whose work in typography is known and admired throughout the world, is referred to in Chapter 16, where his singing cuckoo weathervane is described; William A. Dwiggins of Hingham, Massachusetts, famous for his type designs, decorations, and illustrations, and book designing, appears in this record because of the superior quality of his marionettes and his fine calligraphy; and Carl Purington Rollins, Printer Emeritus to Yale University, who has long been interested in handicrafts, is mentioned here as both the designer and maker of a small working model of the famous Gutenberg printing press, the first to use movable type.

Stenciling as a Process

Stenciling is an old art practiced in America in colonial days and by skilled craftsmen in one form or another up to about the middle of the nineteenth century. Now it is being revived as a popular art, and it would probably be accurate to say that, with the exception of rug-hooking and needlework, more New Englanders practice some form of stenciling combined with painting for decoration than any other craft. The revival of stenciling and what we shall call decorative painting is but a part of the new and wide interest in many forms of home decoration. Although credit for the revival must go to a number of pioneer teachers in New England, it is hardly possible to overestimate the influence of the research, writing, and teaching of Mrs. Esther Stevens Brazer, whose definitive and delightful book, *Early American Decoration,* is clearly instructive as to each process in stenciling. It includes remarkably adequate photographs, drawings, and color plates. A Memorial Exhibition of Mrs. Brazer's work and of some of the best examples done by her pupils was shown in Springfield, Massachusetts, at the Eastern States Exposition in the fall of 1947, and later as a part of the Exhibition of Maine Crafts and Decorative Arts in Portland, Maine. This is a continuing memorial exhibition with educational and aesthetic potentialities.

According to Webster, a stencil is "a piece of thin sheet metal, parchment, paper, or the like, so perforated that when it is laid on a surface and color or ink is applied, a desired figure is produced." The process may be as simple as cutting a hole through a piece of paper, or it may be as elaborate as having a dozen or more stencils to be used in completing a single composition. Stencilers apply their craft to more purposes than could be enumerated here, including the decoration of chairs, benches, tables, beds, boxes, metal trays, and any number of household conveniences, and even walls, ceilings, and floors. The list of amateurs and professionals is very long. Of those known to the writer comparatively few can be named here owing to lack of space.

A Few New England Stencilers

Among those who combine taste and skill in excellent proportion, Donn Sheets of New Milford, Connecticut, ranks high. As a decorator and designer, Mr. Sheets has added interest and charm to many a room in New England by his artistry in applying stencils to furniture and to parts of plastered walls. His work in metal and wood is also distinguished.

In New Hampshire regular courses in stenciling given for several years by the League of New Hampshire Arts and Crafts have trained many persons to apply this craft successfully. Among the members of the League William P. Dudley of Exeter is perhaps best known for the extent to which he has developed the art of stencil and freehand painting. He is a master of technique and possesses a fine sense of color and form. Mr. Dudley is always represented at the annual Craftsman's Fair, and the pieces which he lent for the Handicraft Exhibition at Worcester showed a wide variety of technique.

In the state of Maine Mrs. Adele E. Ells has carried out many important commissions in stenciling and has also served as a regular instructor in the League of New Hampshire Arts and Crafts. Mrs. Ells applies her stencils to various kinds of surfaces from living- and dining-room walls to the smallest piece of furniture. Many of her designs are original and among them are scenes of local interest. One which she did for her own house in Eliot includes likenesses of the lobster fisherman's wife, the tax collector, and other local characters. She has also made a series of stenciled scenes of the town of York, which she worked out on valance boards in one of the rooms in her home. She used a similar design on the furniture of a neighbor. The local landmark of Eliot, Newell's Bridge, is represented in one of Mrs. Ells' designs.

Much of the stenciling in New England is done on tin, some of it on large or small trays, boxes, and other objects. During the war the difficulty of getting tin for decorating was almost unsurmountable, but there were certain New Englanders who were able to overcome the handicap, at least in part. Among these were L. B. Worthly, a tinsmith and plumber of Johnson, Vermont, who made his own trays and boxes and decorated them; Mrs. Lenda W. Gove of Burlington, who became interested in stenciling through an adult education class, exhibited in Worcester in 1943 a tray made of maple syrup cans; and Mrs. Arthur Chivers of Hanover, New Hampshire, exhibited also at the Worcester show several trays made from ordinary tin cans.

A number of craftsmen in Rhode Island decorate tin trays and other objects. Mrs. Arthur B. Holmes of Kingston specializes in stenciled trays. At Worcester, Mrs. Exene Meyersham of Barrington exhibited a tray with floral design; Mrs. Delos A. Howland of Cranston showed two trays; Harry B. Sherman of Edgewood was represented by chairbacks and trays; and Miss Miriam Spicer of Providence showed painted chairs, trays, and toleware.

Free-Brush Painting

Even more extensive than stenciling in New England is the free-brush painting of articles of household use, furniture, and the interior decorations of the home. Often free-brush painting and stenciling are combined, but there are a large number of craftsmen who do only decorative painting; the few selected from among these will illustrate the wide practice of the art in this region.

Peter Hunt, of Provincetown on the Cape, is probably the best-known decorative painter in the New England states. For several years he and his associates have turned out a great number of objects of all forms with gay peasant decorations, including many pieces of furniture that have found their way to all parts of the country.

Up in Calais, Vermont, Rome Van Ornam and his brother run a

little farm, where they raise much of their food and specialize in Toggenburg goats. Rome was once a sign-painter and carriage striper. Sign-painting he learned through an apprenticeship of two years, during which time he was paid fifty cents a day and boarded himself. He has done most of the post office signs in the Calais region of Vermont. He and his brother used to play the fiddle and organ for country dances and other social events. Now Rome spends considerable time in decorating furniture.

Mrs. Ruth G. Mould of Williamstown, Vermont, a member of a talented family, is a decorator whose designs are usually original; she also teaches. Her abilities are reflected throughout her home; the treads on her stairway are covered with attractive pieces of hit-and-miss hooked carpet, the risers painted to harmonize with the carpet. Mrs. Mould is also an accomplished portrait painter, and among her interesting local subjects are Mrs. Will Davis, "Aunt Essie," the hooked-rugmaker of Johnson, Vermont, referred to earlier.

Mrs. Deering Edson of Lebanon, New Hampshire, has decorated many pieces of furniture. One notable example was a large chest shown at the Craftsman's Fair in Portsmouth, which was copied from an original in New York's Metropolitan Museum of Art.

Among other free-brush decorative painters are Mrs. Bertha S. Dobrien, Brockton, Massachusetts, and Mrs. Marion Y. Greene, Boston, both of whom do work for the Society of Arts and Crafts. Mrs. Emily Gordon, also of Boston, decorates furniture for the Women's Educational and Industrial Union, and was represented at the Worcester show. Mrs. Katherine F. Arms and Mrs. Wesley B. Foss, Deerfield, members of the Society of Deerfield Industries, do decorative painting.

Mrs. Lois Warren of Amesbury, Massachusetts, exhibited four trays, each quite different, in Worcester. Miss Pauline Hopkins of Guilford, Connecticut, is a professional painter but has adapted her skill both to wood and metal decoration. Mrs. Katherine Lusk of Unionville, Connecticut, has decorated many Hitchcock chairs and is well known for her tolework, of which examples were shown at Worcester. Edward Paine of Mason Island, Mystic, Connecticut, makes a specialty of screens. Mr. and Mrs. William E. Brigham of Providence have also painted a number of fine screens for their home, as has Carroll T. Berry of Wiscasset, who was well represented in the exhibition of Maine Crafts and Decorative Arts at Portland in 1947.

Decorating on Glass

Throughout New England are craftsmen who specialize in painting clock faces and decorating glass doors and other parts of clock cases. Much of this work is done by stencils and in part by freehand painting.

Mrs. Mary E. Stephenson of Plainville, Connecticut, does fine reproductions and restorations of clock glasses, mirrors, also hand-painted trays, and so forth. It is, however, her decoration on glass in clocks for which she is best known. This is a technique requiring special judgment and skill, for the scenes are painted on the back of the glass, to be viewed through the opposite side in just the reverse from ordinary painting. As someone put it, "Everything has to be done backward." Mrs. Stephenson's father, William B. Fenn of Plymouth, Connecticut, who had charge of all the decorating in the Seth Thomas Clock Company at Thomaston, was among the outstanding decorators of glass of his time. Mrs. Stephenson has the large and rare collection of stencils used by him. She has devoted herself since 1917 largely to the accurate reproduction and restoration of old painted clock and mirror glasses and trays, and has done some exceptionally fine designs for mirrors. Her subjects are flowers, scenes, and conventional designs, some of which are embellished with a gold-leaf border.

Also connected with the traditional decorating of clocks is Mrs. Kathleen W. Laumann. She is the daughter and successor of Edward E. White of the Old Curiosity Shop in Belmont, Vermont. She continues to make up stencil sets as he did, and also teaches stenciling. She writes, "I have added many nice old patterns, copying and preserving any possible original that I find on old chairs and trays."

High on the hills above the village of South Royalton, Vermont, Miss Josephine E. Miller lives on an old farm settled in 1785. The farm commands a beautiful view which Miss Miller often interprets, sometimes through the difficult medium of reverse painting on glass, combining paint and tinfoil—a craft which she has mastered through the encouragement of Mrs. Eugene C. Rhodes. Miss Miller as a child suffered from infantile paralysis, but through work with her hands she has created many objects of interest and beauty, some of which she sells.

H. N. Bunker of Brewer, Maine, a clock repairer and collector, painted and stenciled a number of attractive faces for old clocks and also made cabinets to house them. Miss Beulah True of Hancock Point, just before she died at the age of ninety, did a painting of the *Mayflower* at sea, which Mr. Bunker set in a clock he had repaired.

E. W. Bartlett of Cornish (Old Dingleton), New Hampshire, taught himself as a young man to paint and to work in wood. While he was making a mirror frame for Mrs. Augustus Saint-Gaudens of Cornish, she suggested that he might enjoy painting on glass in the traditional technique. He experimented and found this a very congenial medium in which to work. Some of his original paintings on glass are small, almost miniature, and for these he whittles special frames, finishing the work carefully in tones that harmonize with the paintings.

John Copps, a retired salesman who lives near Bedford, Massachusetts, is now over eighty-five years of age. He thinks he should not make too many plans for the future but always has something to be done on his workbench. His interest in crafts began a few years ago when a friend brought him an old mirror to repair. He soon started making reproductions of mirror frames, using old woods from his former New Hampshire home. His wife and daughter help him with the glass-painting and laying on gold leaf. Mr. Copps, who does all the work of his apple orchard, even spraying the trees, was picking apples on the day of our visit.

Stenciling and painting on glass is carried on by Mrs. Dorothy Weir Ely of Old Lyme, Connecticut, who learned her craft in a Czechoslovak factory. She began by decorating tumblers and other forms of glass with sport motifs, which were very popular, but the decorations at first were not permanent. She finally developed a method by which she could apply her design to the glass with a stencil, and by using a heat-resisting mineral pigment she was able to fire the glass and so make the decoration permanent. This method has increased both the value and the demand for her product.

A variant of the usual decorating on glass is seen in the work of Mrs. C. E. Anderson of Holyoke, Massachusetts, who uses tinfoil almost entirely for her beautiful floral compositions. This decoration, like much of the glass-painting for clock doors is put on in reverse. Mrs. Anderson is as careful in selecting her frames as in her pictures, often using the handsome old walnut frames in oval form.

Decorating Boxes

There is a special method of decorating pasteboard boxes which should probably come under this section of decorating surfaces, although instead of stenciling, wood blockprinting, or free-brush painting, the effect is achieved by decorative papers carefully pasted on the object.

An interesting revival of a very old handicraft of this kind is carried on by Fred B. Tuck of Kennebunk, Maine. Mr. Tuck as an antique dealer has acquired a fine collection of old wallpapers. He has developed the skill of decorating bandboxes with these papers very much after the style employed by the famous pioneer in this field, Miss Hannah Davis of Jaffrey, New Hampshire, on her wooden boxes two generations ago. The boxes Mr. Tuck covers are usually old forms, although there are some that are modern, and the decorations with fragments of the old papers from walls of the fine homes of New England are often handsome. At Windsor, Vermont, H. L. Rockwood uses wallpaper to decorate boxes which he markets through outlets in New York.

Mr. and Mrs. R. D. Snively of Colerain, Massachusetts, both good country craftsmen and excellent photographers, make special photographs and apply them as attractive decorations on wastepaper baskets and other receptacles. Some craftsmen apply maps to the outside of boxes, wastepaper baskets, and so forth, often giving them an antique finish.

Serigraphy

One of the newest developments in the art of transferring designs to surfaces is the silk-screen process known as serigraphy. This method is a multicolor stencil process and one of the most elastic yet to be invented in the entire history of the graphic arts. In using it a silk cloth is stretched tightly over a wooden frame and stencils are drawn of that part of the design which is to be transferred. Other parts of the composition are stopped out, that is, filled up. The pigments are then spread on the screen and forced through the open areas with a squeegee. One advantage of the process is that it can be used to print on almost any base—paper, plastic, textiles, metal, and so forth, and the design can be repeated many times through the same screen.

The widest and one of the most attractive uses of the medium by New England artists known to the writer is an extensive line of special wrapping papers in sheet form and some wallpapers developed under the direction of Miss Eleanor B. Finch of Clinton, Connecticut, already mentioned in connection with the Crafts Project of the WPA of that state.

Illuminating, Lettering, Calligraphy, and Some Arts of the Book

Among the fine traditional craftsmen of the United States, Miss Elisabeth H. Webb of Mystic, Connecticut, achieved a high place in the field of hand lettering and illumination. Fortunately a comprehensive collection of her work has been preserved in the Newark Art Museum, where students of calligraphy, illumination, and fine bookbinding can study it at leisure and with profit.

Miss Webb developed an early interest in the arts of the book, and her father, appreciating her feeling, sent her to England, where she studied lettering and writing under the great English master, Edward Johnston. Miss Webb soon found her interest centering in the techniques practiced by the scribes and illuminators of the fourteenth and fifteenth centuries; she used gold, vermilion, and other materials much as they were used in that day. In her studio at Mystic, Miss Webb wrote, printed, illuminated, and bound her work, doing every part of it with the conscience and accuracy of the free craftsman. She referred to herself in one copyright note as "Printer and Scribe by the Grace of God." Examples of her work are to be found in different parts of the United States, one of the best known and one of her last being the baptismal service book made for the Cathedral of St. John the Divine in New York.

Calligraphy in New England is admirably represented by John Howard Benson of Newport and Providence, Rhode Island. This everyman's craft has descended to a low level in our time of mechanical devices for writing letters, but happily is now experiencing a revival of interest. Mr. Benson not only follows the best traditions in the practice of calligraphy in his studio and workshop in Newport, where he is also a notable stonecutter, but he teaches it and the art of lettering and design at the Rhode Island School of Design, Providence. Through his course in handwriting many students have learned to write legibly and beautifully as well.

William A. Dwiggins has executed some of the finest pages and broadsides in the field of contemporary handwriting, and those who know American calligraphy place the work of Dwiggins among that of the topmost artists. Mr. Dwiggins, whose Caledonia type is used for the pages of this book, is especially noted for his happy and effective use of calligraphy, hand printing, and printing types. As a designer, craftsman, and writer, "Dwig," as his friends call him, is equally versatile and delightful.

Even the shortest list of calligraphers in New England should include the name of George F. Trenholm, whose study at 80 Boylston Street looks out over Boston Common. Here this distinguished worker in graphic arts creates many of his best designs in hand lettering and handwriting. Long a leading member of the American Institute of Graphic Arts, and the Society of Printers, his contribution to the arts of the book are outstanding. He has brought fine handwriting into many of his designs and uses it continuously in his personal communications.

The appearance in 1947 of the book, *An Old New England Village*, extended the acquaintance of Charles D. Hubbard of Guilford, Connecticut, to thousands of people who had not known of his remarkable talent as hand printer and hand writer. Author of the book, he also printed every page of it by hand and drew all the illustrations. Reproduced by offset, it has extraordinary interest and charm. Mr. Hubbard, now past seventy, has the steady hand and the imaginative fire of youth, and his letters, always written by hand, are pages of beauty. He writes: "For several years I have admired the work of the old scriveners of long ago. It is possible, of course, to space letters more evenly than in printing from a type face. Then each letter is born for that particular place and has an individuality not possible in printing. I went to the trouble of learning some of the older alphabets such as uncial and Gothic and made my pens from reeds." Mr. Hubbard is preparing, in the same way, a book to be called *Camping in the New England Mountains,* which he believes will be completed within two or three years.

Associated in a less finished way with handwriting is the experimenting of Frederick F. Black of Searsport, Maine, who takes pleasure in making his own ink and penholders. The ink is made from blackberries, blueberries, and elder bark; the penholders from cattails after a suggestion made by John Burroughs in a book Mr. Black was reading, entitled *John Burroughs Talks: His Reminiscences and Comments* as reported by Clifton Johnson.

"I use," says John Burroughs, "ordinary steel stub pens for writing, and my favorite penholders are those I make myself of cat-tails. I gather the cat-tails in the swamp, and when the stems are dry, I cut them up into the proper lengths. These penholders are very light and I can easily push the pens into the pith. Once I got a fountain pen and used it two or three days. Then I went back to my beloved cat-tail. That suited me best. . . ."

Related to the arts of the book and belonging in this chapter because of the change wrought in the surface appearance of the paper are marbled and paste papers. The old craft of marbling, that is, of floating pigments in liquid and transferring them to paper, is practiced by several New England bookbinders. A wide variety of decorative marbled papers was shown by Arno Werner of Pittsfield, Massachusetts, at a recent exhibition of bookbindings and figured papers in New York. Mr. Werner makes the papers in large sheets, uses them in his own work; his fellow bookbinders have access to them. A less familiar method of paper decorating—paste papers—is accomplished by covering a sheet of paper with paste upon which a pattern is worked with some tool or by the fingers.

Mrs. Rosamond B. Loring of Boston a few years ago sought suitable end papers to harmonize with her bookbinding and also to use as book covers. Being unable to find what she wanted, she undertook to make the decorative papers herself; soon she became one of the foremost practitioners of the art. Her mastery of the subject is the result of much practice and of intensive study. She has long been an enthusiastic collector of decorated papers, showing the collector's instinct for obtaining the finest examples from worldwide sources. She has possibly the most nearly complete library on the subject in existence, in which every obtainable book is represented. Examples of Mrs. Loring's own work form an important part of the collection. Many handbinders and makers of fine books use Mrs. Loring's papers. She has written a comprehensive and scholarly book, *Decorated End Papers*, which is replete with historical data and clear explanations of a technique that she herself practices so successfully. Generous in sharing her experiences and enthusiasms with others, she has helped many students along the happy road of this fascinating handicraft.

CHAPTER 9

NEW ENGLAND POTTERY

THE words "pottery" and "ceramics" might be used interchangeably in this report, but pottery is given preference because it is a good descriptive word familiar to most people and, like the handicraft itself, ancient in origin.

Pottery in its broadest sense includes all earthy objects, from building bricks to fine dishes, which have been changed by fire from a pliable state of clay to a hard, permanent form. Mud pies baked in the sun are not pottery although they may be on the way. Unless their form and substance are permanently changed through the process of firing, they will, when soaked in water or exposed to the elements, go back to mud again.

Not only is pottery a very inclusive term, it carries a specific meaning within itself, so to speak, one which will serve us well here by separating the usual run of pottery from porcelain. This is a clear distinction which John Spargo of Bennington, Vermont, has made in his *Early American Pottery and China*. For practical purposes Spargo classifies all ceramic products under two main divisions, one to be called "pottery," the other "porcelain." Under pottery he includes all those earthy products which when held up to the light appear opaque, and under porcelain all ceramic products which appear translucent. Anyone can recognize these two main divisions. Some writers on ceramics make a third division by putting stoneware into a separate classification, placing it between pottery and porcelain since it requires firing at a temperature between the two. That, however, is a rather technical classification which the layman cannot recognize by the appearance of the piece. Therefore, since stoneware is opaque, it seems logical to classify it as Spargo does with pottery.

Although the variety of forms, surfaces, and even uses of pottery seems infinite, processes employed in its making are comparatively few and easily understood. The materials are all taken from the surface or below the surface of the earth, clay forming the body of the myriad

152

objects that man has made for his use and contemplation. The finishing coats or glazes, which give special color or smoothness or density and which render the piece waterproof, require other and usually harder mineral substances.

All pottery is constructed or built by one of four processes: (1) It may be entirely hand built of coils, or ropes of clay, one coil laid upon the other and all pressed together before firing; (2) it may be "thrown" or turned on a revolving disc or wheel set parallel to the ground, such throwing of pottery on a wheel being one of the most magic of all handicraft processes; (3) it may be modeled with the hand and a few tools, a process by which a figure is built up as a sculptor would model his clay; (4) the potter may use a mold into which the moist clay is pressed or into which a mixture of clay and water is poured and shortly poured off again, leaving a layer of the right thickness for the vessel or object desired. Certain cups and saucers, bowls, and much other tableware are poured in this way. Molding and pouring processes are used generally when objects exactly alike are to be made; yet in some potteries, as we shall see, uniformity of shape and size is accomplished through skillful throwing on the wheel.

The body of an object of pottery is often finished simply by firing it as soon as it has dried to the required hardness, as a garden flowerpot or a plain brick, but these forms are porous and will not hold water. Therefore, if it is desired to make the pottery waterproof or to give it a smooth or hard surface, a glaze is prepared and applied either with a brush or sponge or by dipping or spraying the object. Then the piece is fired again and the glaze either fuses with the body or otherwise hardens into permanent, one might almost say everlasting, form. Of all the arts of man, pottery in its broad sense is one of the most enduring.

The coloring of pottery may come through the firing of the clay at certain temperatures, through special glazes (or glasses) applied to the body, and in a few instances by means of some element used in the fire itself. In the last-named method certain hardwood ashes burned with the clay produce special colors. It is said that in attaining the intense black of the Ildefonso pottery of New Mexico, the Indians fire the pottery with sheep manure.

The simplest form of ceramics or pottery in New England, as elsewhere, is the ordinary red building brick. The processes employed are elementary and direct: the clay is mixed and pounded to the right consistency; it is then pressed into a mold; and when dried out enough to handle, it is piled up in such a way that the stack of brick itself forms the kiln with openings or channels at the bottom, where fuel is placed and "the kiln fired." This makes a brick a ceramic product, but it is not an example of handicraft in the sense of this report; that is, its character has not been determined by the touch of the hand.

However, Mr. and Mrs. John Turnbull of Haddam, Connecticut, have through very elementary methods produced some bricks that are clearly within our definition of handicrafts. They had no wheel, no special kiln, no glazes, nothing for tools but simple sticks and a pocket-knife. But, much in the spirit of children making mud pies, they incised and modeled common bricks into forms of interest and beauty.

As a member of the office staff of a large brick manufacturer, Mr. Turnbull was able to study common brick from the clay bank through the kiln. He watched the varied results of the firing on the outer, middle, and inner walls of the kiln, and conceived the idea of incising some simple patterns in the bricks while they were soft and before stacking; the experiment would cost nothing except a little time and a few bricks. In this he had the cooperation of Mrs. Turnbull, an experienced designer.

A wide variety of experiments in pottery making is going on in New England where kilns range from the simplest backyard oven, home-made and fired with wood, to the latest and most scientifically constructed studio kiln.

Professor Randolph W. Johnston of South Deerfield, Massachusetts, and the Department of Art of Smith College, has invented a method for firing pottery and terra cotta by imbedding electric resistance wires in the clay body of the object to be fired, burying the object in a loose heat insulator such as asbestos, and connecting to a house circuit. The temperature is raised from within until the clay is brought to a bright red heat. He also developed a method for firing the molds for casting bronze sculpture, using the resistance wires in the same way. A photograph of Professor Johnston embedding a wire in a vase which he is molding is reproduced here. He has not confined himself to a single art; his versatility embraces work in wood, stone, terra cotta, pottery, metals, stage design, and fresco painting.

POTTERY IN MAINE

It so happens that the Rowantrees Pottery, the farthest "Down East" of any in Maine, is of particular interest to us because it is a community undertaking concerned with both people and products. It was established in Blue Hill between Ellsworth and Bucksport in 1934 by Miss Adelaide Pearson, who built the first kiln there. She had worked in Boston settlement houses and had organized folk handicraft classes

A CHRISTMAS GIFT IN NEEDLEWORK

THIS CHRISTMAS GIFT WAS DESIGNED AND MADE BY MRS. MARGARETA OHBERG OF
COLCHESTER, CONNECTICUT, FOR HER GRANDDAUGHTER. A DELIGHTFUL EXAMPLE OF
FOLK ART, IT REFLECTS THE TRADITIONS OF SWEDEN.

and exhibitions among non-English-speaking immigrants. Largely because of her interest in both social welfare and the arts she determined to provide for Hancock County cultural opportunities similar to those accessible in cities. Miss Laura S. Paddock, who had been graduated from Western Reserve University and also from the Department of Ceramics of the Pennsylvania Museum and School of Industrial Arts, was enlisted at once as a volunteer. Since that time Miss Paddock has had charge of the Pottery. When opportunity permits, she and Miss Pearson travel extensively, gathering materials for their arts and crafts museum, which is a mine of information. After a trip to India in 1939, which included a fortnight's visit with Mahatma Gandhi, the ancient craft of pottery took on new dignity and meaning, and the real achievements of Rowantrees Pottery began.

In 1941, according to Rowantrees records, $5,000 worth of pottery was sold, and the next year the business was doubled. Since that time the output has increased annually. Over an acre of floor space was added in 1942 and two new kilns were built. Thus the Pottery, established primarily as a summer school for the community, has developed into a village industry of permanence and stability. Eighteen craftsmen are working in the plant (as of 1947), all natives of the township, which has a population of something over a thousand.

An extraordinary feature that distinguishes Rowantrees from any other pottery in our country is that not only the clay used in the body of the product is local, but the twenty or more glazes, beautiful in luster and depth, are practically all evolved from ores and rocks found in the vicinity. The clay used in the body of the pottery fires to a red. It is given greater durability than is usual by firing at 2,000 degrees Fahrenheit. According to the potters themselves, in a leaflet they issued, "the foundation of all the glazes is Blue Hill white granite colored by copper ore (greens, blues, and one red), manganese (black and lavender), and iron (rich red). Other ingredients are feldspar, quartz, lermondite, pegmatite, galena, diatoms, calcopyrite, and the calcined clamshells, which give the Rowantrees turquoise its peculiar lustre." The minerals used in the glazes are collected "from the seashore, mountain top, abandoned mines, bottom of bogs, and edges of ponds," and are ground to fine powder with all the impurities left in.

Each piece of pottery is wheel thrown or modeled by hand into excellent shapes, most of which require no other decoration than the beautiful glazes, although painted designs are occasionally applied. Rowantrees craftsmen often turn to sea or woodland for their decorative motifs; the deer is a favorite subject. On some of the covers for jam pots and other dishes the forms of wild flowers and berries are modeled and glazed in nature's colors. Wild strawberries, blueberries, cranberries, and other native berries with their foliage make delightful decorations.

But one does not see the Pottery in full through its products alone, admirable as they are, or even as they express the joy in work of the potter. To get the complete picture one would have to go behind the immediate scene and view sympathetically the human elements which are so important. Not only has the Pottery brought a steady income to many in the community; it has brought educational, social, and aesthetic values, which often attach to a handicraft when thoughtfully conducted. Mrs. Blanche Butler, for instance, a farm woman, who does not often go to the plant, models at home many of the attractive decorations on the tops of jam jars referred to above. She modeled and glazed a miniature farmhouse and garden as a top for one of her own dishes. This was fired at the Pottery. Mrs. Butler is typical of thousands of rural women throughout our country who welcome opportunities for creative expression, and when she said, "I do not know what I would do without our Pottery" it was plainly not alone the economic return that she had in mind.

All those who work steadily at Rowantrees are from families who have lived in that neighborhood for a long time. A surprising fact in this connection is that some of the workmen have become expert craftsmen after two or three years' practice, but nearly all of them have used their hands in some kind of rural work from childhood, and children who have played around the Pottery take to it like ducks to water.

There is probably no experience which exceeds in satisfaction that which one feels in creating some object of use or beauty, but ranking close to it is the satisfaction of having an indispensable part in the production of a needful and worthy thing. It is not generally realized how important such an experience is to many individuals; it comes out at Rowantrees in the keen feeling which the different workers have for their part in the entire product. They all know that a defect anywhere along the line spoils the work of all the others; so from the men who grind the clay, to those who shape the pieces, and spray or brush on the glazes, all feel their responsibility and have a pride in the finished piece. Hardly a family in the village but is building up a dinner set of pottery, some part of which members of the family have made.

Mr. and Mrs. Charles E. Abbott live in a beautiful old rambling farmhouse on the slope of a low hill above the valley in South Berwick, York County. Here they carry on the Quamphegan Crafts of pottery and weaving. Mr. Abbott has developed an excellent product including stoneware, all done with a rather high fire, giving the body great strength. Form is always a prime consideration, most of the pieces being thrown on the wheel. The glazes are low in color, beautiful in tone, and harmonious when shown together. In addition to single pieces of pottery which Mr. Abbott sells, he has made for home use a number of handsome and efficient baking dishes of clay native to Maine. Some of his pottery was shown with Mrs. Abbott's weaving at the Exhibition of Contemporary New England Handicrafts in Worcester, and at a more comprehensive exhibition in the L.D.M. Sweat Memorial Art Museum at Portland, Maine, in 1947. The combining of weaving and pottery as carried out by the Abbotts is one of the pleasantest achievements known to the writer in these two arts. While it is not often that weaver and potter are found in one family, it would frequently be possible for weavers and potters from different groups to work together.

Mrs. Noah R. Bryan of Orono is contributing new and very attractive products in ceramics. She conceived the idea of interpreting native wild flowers and other plant motifs in the form of ceramic jewelry. The response to this was so marked that she determined to specialize in this field. The clay used is native and the firing is done in a small homemade kiln. Mrs. Bryan's figures are often full of humor. One, a white horse ambling along with a flower pot filled with gay blossoms curled in his tail, she calls the Drunken Horse. It is an excellent piece of modeling and beautiful in color. Mrs. Bryan has named her home industry the Merry-Go-Round Pottery and uses as her trademark a horse from an old merry-go-round.

Linnwood Pottery is the creation of Linn K. Phelan, whose studio was for several years at Saco, Maine, adjoining the house of the Maine Industries. Here he produced pottery of many shapes and sizes, including some large bowls and jars all wheel thrown. He prepared the clay, did the throwing and modeling, also the glazing, decorating, and firing. There is an individuality about the pottery not often attained by those who produce such a considerable volume of work, some of it in plates, bowls, cups and saucers, and other tableware. Two characteristics are outstanding: one, Mr. Phelan's glazes; and the other, his painted decorations. He developed a range of harmonious glazes, including grays, blues, a few greens, and some especially attractive yellows and blacks. His decorations, usually inspired by local subjects, are achieved through applying the slip with a brush. This has been done with such evident skill that the craftsman's pride in his work is shared by those who own an example of it.

Richard Coolidge and Luigi Balestro conduct a tearoom and gift shop, The Dan Sing Fan, in Ogunquit during the summer months; in the winter they find time to make a small but choice selection of pottery. The objects are mainly for household decoration, and the potters use a few selected glazes, including blues and greens, which suggest old Persian pottery. Both craftsmen learned to make pottery at Greenwich House in New York as a hobby, and found at Ogunquit the opportunity to combine their hobby with business.

Miss Margaret L. Vincent of Norway, Maine, has done some notable things in ceramics, her pieces having gone to many parts of the country. She is also well known for her woodcarvings. Examples of her ceramics are on display, with other selected American pottery, at the Art Museum in Syracuse, New York.

POTTERY IN NEW HAMPSHIRE

Edwin and Mary Scheier of Durham came to the League of New Hampshire Arts and Crafts from the Southern Highlands. No two contemporary potters have made more progress in the development of ceramics in New England than these talented and enthusiastic artists. Most of their pieces are made on the wheel. They reflect not only qualities of skill and a high sense of beauty, but they are lively symbols of that "joy in work" which William Morris identified with art itself. Their pottery ranges from small simple cups in burnt red or gray earthenware to stoneware with the ring of metal. If decorations are employed beyond the simple and effective striping which follows the motion of the wheel, a characteristic of Scheier pottery, they often take a sculptural rather than painted form and may be incised, or modeled, or both. Whatever else these decorations may express, they invariably say to one who has a feeling for materials, "I am made of clay." The Scheiers' pottery is often the medium for delightful expressions of humor; Adam and Eve on a cider jug or Juggled Babies modeled on a stoneware vase are typical examples.

Mr. and Mrs. Scheier have received high recognition in national shows and competitions, but the best opportunity to enjoy their work is afforded by their demonstrations and exhibits in their adopted state of New Hampshire. One or both of them are almost always at the annual Craftsman's Fair, where they demonstrate their work and often give others an opportunity to take part. At the Hanover Fair in 1941 they not only had an extensive and beautiful display of their own pottery, but they let school children work at all the processes. The Scheiers are experimenters; they use materials of many kinds, their principal pieces being made of New Hampshire clay. For some years they have taught ceramics at the University of New Hampshire.

Two former art students, Mr. and Mrs. Robert Bailey of Hopkinton, came into the League of New Hampshire Arts and Crafts through their blockprinting. After a few lessons in pottery, however, they decided that this was the medium for them. Their kiln and equipment have been ingeniously and inexpensively built by Mr. Bailey, who is known as a very practical Yankee. From the beginning he and Mrs. Bailey have operated a small workshop in their home, where they make their living by combining subsistence farming with pottery making. The pottery products, which have a utilitarian value, are in the form of attractive tableware, although a few very interesting larger pieces are made. The Baileys have developed markets through the League and other outlets.

POTTERY IN VERMONT

Mrs. Herta Moselsio of Bennington models and fires ceramic figures of high quality in both design and the technical and artistic use of glazes. Her best-known pieces are sculptural, although sometimes she makes objects of household utility. The work of Simon Moselsio, who is director of the Art Department of Bennington College, in advancing the arts generally and encouraging their appreciation, is an outstanding instance of relating them to the life and work of college students. Mr. Moselsio is a sculptor of national reputation. He and Mrs. Moselsio are interested in both the fine and the minor arts; they draw no arbitrary line between them and are particularly concerned with their educational and social values.

Having learned the technique of motion-picture making, Mr. and Mrs. Moselsio have contributed some of the most valuable films on the arts and crafts yet produced in this country. One such film illustrating the processes of sculpture, or more specifically the process of making a portrait in sculpture, is an outstanding achievement. A typical Vermonter was chosen for the portrait. The motion picture opens with a long shot of this native resident making his way uphill in an old-time buggy, getting out at the sculptor's studio, and arranging to sit for his portrait. All the processes of making the portrait, from Mr. Moselsio's quick penciled strokes on the surface of the stone, the roughing out of the head and shoulders, and the stages of chiseling, to the completion of the sculptured study, are shown so that the observer, in the short space of half an hour, follows sequences which would require months if observed in the workshop, if indeed he could have the opportunity to see them. The culminating scene is thrilling when the Vermonter and the sculptured portrait of him in stone, a remarkable likeness, are shown on the screen together.

Mrs. Lydia K. Winston, whose home is in Michigan, spends her summers in West Dover and has done some notable experimenting with the local clay of Vermont in making pottery of high fire, approaching stoneware, examples of which were shown at the Worcester Exhibition. She has produced a vase of local red clay glazed with wood ashes from her own fireplace.

POTTERY IN MASSACHUSETTS

Massachusetts has produced more potters than any other New England state. At least four potteries more or less identified with the arts and crafts movement of the early years of this century made a lasting impression on New England ceramics. They were the Marblehead Pottery of Marblehead, the Dedham Pottery of Dedham, the Grueby Pottery of South Boston, and the Paul Revere Pottery of Brighton. They were all among the early "studio potteries" in our country.

Marblehead Pottery was first started in connection with the sanitarium of Dr. Herbert J. Hall of Marblehead, and developed under the direction of Arthur E. Baggs, then a young potter of great promise. He made important contributions to the art of pottery in this country and was director of ceramics at Ohio State University at the time of his death. At Marblehead Mr. Baggs developed a very superior pottery which compared favorably with anything done then or since. The glazes are in low tones of gray, blue, green, yellow, red, and black, each a fine color in itself and all harmonizing when used together. It took the form of plates, bowls, cups and saucers, mugs, sugar bowls, creamers, and other articles for table use and household decoration, including ornamental tiles, which found their way into many American homes.

Dedham Pottery, oldest of this group of four, was originally established at Chelsea prior to 1866 but moved later to Dedham. It was noteworthy for the experiments carried on there by its Scottish founder, especially for its popular blue and white crackleware. James Robertson, the fourth in line of a family of potters, came to the United States from Scotland in 1853 with three sons, one of whom, Hugh C., was the true founder of the Pottery.

The Pottery at Chelsea was started not far from Powder Horn Hill, where flowerpots, ferneries, and beanpots were made for a time but not until 1867 did it produce any painted or glazed decorations. In 1878, however, the Pottery was awarded first prize by the Massachusetts Charitable Mechanics Association. After 1884, when Hugh carried on the pottery works alone, he produced a fine apple-green glaze. He had seen at the Centennial Exhibition in Philadelphia in 1876 the Korean exhibit, which included examples of Chinese crackle and also of Dragon's Blood vases of the Ming Dynasty, known in England as oxblood. He at once attempted to recapture the lost art of producing this rich color. The experiments were so costly that they left Hugh penniless, and in 1889 the Pottery was closed. He had succeeded, however, in getting the fine red color of the original oxblood (sometimes referred to as "Robertson's Blood") and as a by-product of his experiments he learned how to make crackleware, which was to become famous.

The pottery works were reorganized in 1891 with the financial backing of Boston men and women, and the development of blue crackleware with glaze decorations was undertaken. The dampness of Chelsea proving unsuitable to such work, the Pottery was moved to Dedham, with Hugh Robertson and his son, William A., in charge. Production of crackleware began again in 1895 and together with Dragon's Blood received high awards at Paris, San Francisco, and St. Louis. Hugh Robertson died in 1908. He held the rank of master craftsman conferred by the Society of Arts and Crafts, of which he was a charter member. The Pottery continued to produce under the leadership of the Robertson family, and specialized in crackleware with various charming designs by Denman W. Ross and Charles E. Mills. The rabbit pattern, devised by Joseph Linden Smith, became the firm's trademark. The pottery works closed for the duration of World War II.

Grueby Pottery of South Boston produced some of the finest examples of ceramics ever made in our country. Many of the forms were designed by Addison B. LeBoutillier, now of Rockport, and these fine shapes gave them immediate distinction; most pieces were without decoration, although occasionally a stem and a bud of a plant would be modeled in low relief to give both the composition desired and the effect of one glaze color over another. The glazes, developed by William H. Grueby, were few but excellent, especially the blues, greens, and yellows, and the melonlike textures of both pottery and tiles have never been surpassed in American ceramics.

Paul Revere Pottery was established and conducted for many years in the neighborhood of the Paul Revere house in Brighton. The objects made were chiefly tableware, especially pieces for children, the treatment of which introduced a new and interesting note in the development of small potteries in this country. The decorations were underglazed in many attractive colors; the designs were usually incised; the painting done freehand with an outline filled in with black.

The pottery just referred to was always known as Paul Revere Pottery. A somewhat more recent establishment has been called Revere Pottery because it is made in Revere, Massachusetts. There is no connection between these two potteries and no similarity except in the word "Revere." The confusion between them is lessening since Paul Revere pottery is now no longer produced.

Revere Pottery is also sometimes called Roman Pottery, an appropriate name when one comes to know the potter and his background. Frank Cacciagrani, the proprietor, specializes in earthenware much like that made by his family in their old pottery in Rome. There were sixteen Cacciagrani boys, all of whom learned pottery when they were young. Frank's father had fourteen kick wheels, all about the same size, and driven by primitive foot power, lined up along the wall of the old Roman shop; here the sixteen sons learned the art of throwing pottery. Frank, who began to learn when he was seven years old, was the only one to come to America. Five of his brothers were killed in World War I, and some of them were in service during World War II.

After working for Arthur Baggs in the Marblehead Pottery, Mr. Cacciagrani went into business for himself, making practical baking dishes and other utilitarian forms usually turned out without glazes, except such as would be necessary for the inside of dishes used in cooking. He throws all the pieces on a wheel, never using molds. Occasionally for his own pleasure he makes a special piece and applies a favorite glaze. He finds that it pays him best to stick closely to objects of utility. His wife and sometimes the children lend a hand in the workshop, but he does most of the throwing and the firing. Among his treasures is a piece of pottery which someone had picked up in Italy and brought to this country. When Frank recognized the Cacciagrani family mark on it, the traveler gave it to him; it is now one of his proudest possessions.

In the oldest settlement of New England, Plymouth, Massachusetts, are situated the Plymouth Pottery and the Plymouth School of Pottery, both presided over by Miss Katharine Alden. She is a direct descendant of John and Priscilla Alden, who practiced handicrafts when life depended upon individual effort, dexterity, and skill. Katharine Alden had been an experienced craftsman for some years at the time the Richard Sparrow House in Plymouth, built in 1640, was restored in the 1930's. When the architect, Sidney P. Strickland, suggested to Miss Alden that it would make an ideal setting for a handicraft shop and school, she eagerly took advantage of this opportunity.

In 1936 the Vocational Division of the Massachusetts Department of Education arranged through the local schools for this new undertaking in ceramics under Miss Alden's direction. Resources were very limited, but trained and experienced as she was, she brought together a mass of stone, a heap of brick from a local gas works, and slate from a disused old mill not far away, and, with the help of neighbors and those interested in the establishment of the school, built a kiln and a little house around it. A kick wheel, still in use in the Pottery, was constructed from an old wagon wheel filled between the spokes with cement; the turning platform Miss Alden made of plaster of Paris.

All methods of making pottery are employed at Sparrow House. The products of the Pottery depend upon the pupils, but the line which is made available to the public through the attractive salesroom usually includes articles of utility, cups, saucers, and other tableware. The well-known succotash dish is made in several sizes and when sold is always accompanied by the recipe for succotash used by the Plymouth settlers. The clay comes principally from the Kingston clay pit which was used by local potters a hundred years ago. White clay is also dug along the beach at Plymouth and mixed by boys associated with the Pottery. Miss Alden is concerned not only with the product, but with the cooperative way in which every problem is worked out.

Mr. and Mrs. Henry Jewett Greene of Petersham, probably the most widely traveled potters in New England, have worked with some of the best potters of the world, including Bernard Leach of England and Tomimoto of Japan. They have made a careful study in various countries of this almost universal handicraft. In their own pottery making Mr. Greene does most of the forming and Mrs. Greene does all the glazing. They took up pottery as a hobby, and while they are able to get materials from many sources, their greatest satisfaction comes from working with those closest to home. They use local clays entirely in their products. Some of the pieces resemble choice examples of the pottery of Japan. The Greenes are not, however, limited to any single influence but are always searching for new and better expressions in this basic earth material. Whenever they exhibit, their pottery is displayed on specially made wooden pedestals in harmonious forms and against a background appropriate in color and texture.

A book could be written on the ingenuity of New Englanders in making things which they could not have any other way. For example, Robert E. Thayer of Amherst, a very inventive youth, watched Henry Greene throwing pottery on his wheel. It was young Thayer's first sight of this magic process, and he was eager to try it himself. He had neither tools nor materials, but to make a kick wheel he brought together what he could get his hands on, including wheels and spare parts from baby carriages, toy wagons, and an old automobile. With borrowed tools he put these various parts together and made a contraption that worked. It was not much for looks, but any boy seeing it in operation would be encouraged to make one for himself. The platform upon which the clay was thrown was an old flywheel from a discarded Nash engine. Filled with plaster it worked perfectly. He used tricycle bearings for weights, and where he did not have metal for ball bearings he made them of oak and maple so carefully turned and shaped that when oiled they ran smoothly.

This kick wheel and its maker were features of the Northampton Handicraft Fair in 1943. The young potter got his clay from an abandoned brickyard near Amherst, and since he did not have access to a kiln he dried out his pieces gradually, first in the air, then near a stove until they were hard enough to transport to a commercial pottery where they were fired.

Mrs. Rowena W. Hallowell and Mrs. Carol M. Nickerson of the Clay Craft Studios, Winchester, have been making pottery cooperatively for about fifteen years, and along with their accumulated experiences have acquired complete equipment. Mrs. Hallowell uses an electric power wheel for throwing, but Mrs. Nickerson prefers the coil hand-building method for her product. Each has a Norton kiln in her home. These kilns are fairly large and permit high firing, even stoneware. The bisque is fired in Mrs. Hallowell's kiln and the glazed pieces at Mrs. Nickerson's. These craftsmen manufacture their own glazes from carefully tested formulas and from minerals ground in their own home-constructed ball mill.

Russell G. Crook of South Lincoln, who one time worked with Augustus Saint-Gaudens, has achieved considerable success in developing decorative stoneware in salt glazes—the ambition of many potters. Mr. Crook came to Massachusetts from California fifty years ago, constructing both a large and a small kiln and a brick building behind his home. Now past seventy-five years old, he is still an adventurous craftsman. He was represented at the 1943 Worcester Exhibition by a large gray stoneware vase with a decoration in blue showing an elk in the forest.

George F. Frederick is director of Dreamacre Pottery, Vineyard Haven, Martha's Vineyard. Mr. Frederick was a student and became a teacher in the School of Industrial Arts in Trenton, New Jersey, where he had his first experience in ceramics. Later he was graduated from the Department of Architecture at the University of Pennsylvania, becoming a member of the American Institute of Architects.

The clay used in Dreamacre is obtained from various deposits on the island of Martha's Vineyard. Most of the pieces are thrown on the wheel; bowls and similar objects are sometimes cast in molds or built up with coils. After the "green" ware is dry it is fired at a temperature of about 2,000 degrees Fahrenheit, then glazed and again fired at the same heat. The glazes used are pulverized ingredients of glass, some opaque, some transparent, others dull. The Persian blue glaze, a favorite, is an alkaline mixture containing soda and sand. Copper oxide is used for the warm blues and cobalt for the sapphire. Other glazes are composed principally of lead colored with mineral oxide as follows: copper for green, cobalt for blue, manganese for brown, iron for yellow. Unusual effects are obtained by repeated firing of one glaze over another. Mr. Frederick specializes in tableware, tiles, flower and salad bowls, garden and terrace jars, and lighting fixtures and pierced lanterns. An all-round craftsman, he has served as president of the local arts and crafts organization.

Dreamacre presents another example of the combination of pottery making and weaving. Mr. Frederick's mother is a weaver; her textiles are as notable as the pottery for their color and are often planned to harmonize with it. She is particularly accomplished in weavings of Swedish type. Dreamacre Pottery with its tastefully designed studio and beautiful formal grounds is one of the most attractive handicraft plants in New England.

Mrs. June York, who has a showroom in the little yard back of the metalwork shop of the Lewis Whitneys on Bearskin Neck, Rockport, uses local clay, does her modeling by hand with the coil method, and has a kiln where she fires small receptacles for household and personal use. She makes attractive buttons of clay in a wide range of sizes and colors.

Norman E. Arsenault of the Pottery Work Shop of Boston is both a teacher and a potter. He has developed some exceptional examples of stoneware, and was represented in the 1943 Worcester Exhibition by two large cylindrical pieces notable for their form, their texture, and coloring.

Miss Edith H. Tracy, who received her preliminary experience in pottery working with Miss Maude Robinson in Greenwich House, New York, has for about ten years had her own pottery and shop in Stockbridge. She has taught a number of people in the village and also a few selected patients at the Riggs Foundation. Her kiln is in her backyard, and she has good facilities for teaching in her studio.

Bill Shakespeare of Massachusetts Institute of Technology has been doing special research in glazes for himself and for other interested potters in the New England region. Several amateur potters have been greatly helped through his experiments and his cooperation.

It is with regret that some description of the work of many more Massachusetts potters cannot be given here. Among them mention should be made of Edward Norman of Deerfield, who entered the Navy in the early days of World War II, and whose processes of making pottery were photographed by Mr. and Mrs. R. D. Snively for their book on *Pottery*; Paul Wieghardt of Pittsfield; Miss Mary White of Northampton; Miss Jennie Newhill of Greenfield; Miss Louise Baldwin and Miss Gail N. Kernan of Brookline, and Mrs. Ursula Decius of Cambridge.

POTTERY IN CONNECTICUT

Mrs. Dorothea Warren-O'Hara of Darien is one of the pioneer potters of New England. Her studio home, transformed from a barn with a separate pottery adjacent, is a happy combination of beauty, order, comfort, and efficiency. Here for many years Mrs. O'Hara spent her summers making fine pottery, examples of which are to be found in the museums of the country, including the Metropolitan Museum of Art in New York. She has also won recognition in Sweden, Finland, France, England, and Germany.

Writing for the *Christian Science Monitor* of June 10, 1941, Amy Bonner quotes Mrs. O'Hara thus:

> I work no set number of hours each day . . . but get up when dawn breaks and the light comes into my eastern window. . . . I usually keep early hours at night, too. But if a piece interests me I work far into the night. , . . Unlike most women potters, I do everything myself. I even get down and clean out the carbon from under the kiln, and lift the heavy glaze mill. I feel I must understand everything about my work, beginning with the chemistry of it. Each summer I try to get out a new glaze which I perfect by test after test. . . . The colors all look alike before they are fired—a gray color. After firing, however, the coppers are bright blue or green under the heat, and sometimes it takes much experimenting to work out a satisfactory glaze.

Mrs. O'Hara uses clay from many parts of the country. She decorates most of her pieces, sometimes carving or incising the clay but often turns out a piece in single color to show beauty of form alone.

Mrs. Marian M. Rowand of New Canaan has written several articles about pottery and given lectures and demonstrations. Recently she said:

"I have worked in pottery since 1932, making objects for home use and for sale. Though I have used the wheel I much prefer the hand-built type of work. The pieces of mine which have been exhibited at

Syracuse and other places all have been of that type. I use various kinds of decorations but I am against over-ornamentation, believing that purity of line is of first importance. I try to show that pottery can be a satisfying and not too expensive a craft for even a beginner."

Luman P. Kelsey of North Canton is a potter of a wide range of experience, having done work in all types of ceramics, including stoneware and porcelain sculpture. Mr. Kelsey and his wife, Dorothy, are both accomplished designers and craftsmen. Mrs. Kelsey's specialty is hooked rugs and linoleum blockprints. Both were instructors in the outstanding Connecticut Work Projects Administration; they have been active members of the Society of Connecticut Craftsmen and have exhibited under its auspices. Mr. Kelsey was represented by some of his ceramics at the Worcester Exhibition.

A craftsman who gives more attention to demonstrating than to the making of pottery is Harry W. Austin of the Potter's Wheel, Old Lyme. He takes much satisfaction in the educational side of his work, and while he made art pottery for about thirty years he now devotes almost all his time to exhibiting the wheel and talking to groups in Connecticut, Massachusetts, and New York.

CHAPTER 10

CARVING AND WHITTLING

MEASURED in terms of quantity, quality, and the reflection of environment upon the craftsman, woodcarving and whittling take high rank among the handicrafts of New England. Over ninety carvers and whittlers, who have become known to the writer, will be brought into the present chapter. These do not include all the shapers of wood mentioned in this book, for some who carve and whittle have been grouped in other chapters.

The simplest statement of the difference between whittling and carving is that the whittler uses only a pocketknife while the carver, although he may use a pocketknife, employs primarily carving tools, that is, chisels with cutting edges on their ends. There are many small carvings on which only the craftsman himself could tell whether he had used chisel or knife, or both; therefore the terms "carving" and "whittling" may be used here interchangeably in describing both the process and the final product.

Woodcarving is a very old handicraft, coming to our country mainly by way of Europe; many woodcarvers in New England demonstrate skills and traditions familiar to the lands in which they were born. Three outstanding examples, each from a separate country, are I. Kirchmayer, a native of Austria; Karl von Rydingsvärd born in Sweden; and Edgar Keen from England. Mr. Kirchmayer and Mr. von Rydingsvärd are not living now, but both have left their imprint upon New England culture and both were influential contributors to the arts and crafts movement. Mr. Keen has been in a sense a double contributor, first as a carver in England trained under the influence of the arts and crafts movement there, bringing those standards and ideas to the United States, and later as a carver here definitely related to the new handicraft movement.

Mr. Kirchmayer was known to architects as one of the best ecclesiastical carvers in our country and as the creator of the "American Gothic" style in wood sculpture. Although most of his work was done

168

in America, his woodcarving traditions were rooted in the medieval village of Oberammergau, where part of his boyhood was spent. Later, after a few years of study in London and Paris, he came to America early in the present century and developed elements of thought and technique that set his work apart as among the best examples of design and craftsmanship ever done in our country. Examples of his carving are in the Church of Saint Mary the Virgin in New York and in the Detroit Institute of Arts, including Christmas in Heaven; several small pieces are in George G. Booth's collection of the Work of American Craftsmen at Cranbrook, Michigan.

Karl von Rydingsvärd was recognized as a craftsman and teacher of woodcarving on both the Atlantic and Pacific coasts, but he became greatly attached to New England, and passed the last years of his life in East Lovell, Maine. Mr. von Rydingsvärd enriched the handicrafts of his adopted country by adding traditional motifs of Sweden to American motifs. As an early teacher at Manchester Institute of Arts and Sciences, New Hampshire, he influenced several pupils who have found their places in the present handicraft movement. He also worked out important experiments in the therapeutic value of woodcarving.

Edgar Keen, now of Warner, New Hampshire, received his early training in the Chipping-Camden School of England, which carried on the fine traditions of design and craftsmanship for which William Morris and his associates stood. In America Mr. Keen has done outstanding ecclesiastical carving, first while a resident of New York and later after he made New Hampshire his permanent home; examples of his work can be seen in Boston, New York, and other American cities. Mr. Keen has influenced the handicrafts of New England in two ways: first, through his encouragement of amateur country craftsmen; and second, in his relations with the League of New Hampshire Arts and Crafts as member, teacher, and, at one time, director. Some native whittlers, admiring his skill and achievement, were inclined to follow his patterns in their work, but Mr. Keen urged them to pursue their own aptitudes with honesty and sincerity in the ways most natural to them.

A boy in New Hampshire, Tommy Strong, son of the late Dean Strong of Dartmouth College, will, for reasons of his own, always remember Mr. Keen. When the writer met this lad at the Craftsman's Fair in Portsmouth in 1944, he was conspicuously wearing a round, medal-like decoration of wood on his coat lapel. Closer inspection revealed a mouse skillfully carved in low relief. Mr. Keen, while working on a portrait study of Tommy's sister, had learned of her small brother's prowess in catching mice. The sculptor not only voted him a medal as a mouser, but carved it.

Apart from a few professionals, the majority of carvers and whittlers in New England are self-taught. The range of subjects which interest these craftsmen, roughly classified, includes likenesses of men and women; animals both domestic and wild; birds of land, inland waters, and the sea; decoys; fish; flowers and fruits; figureheads, ship models, driftwood figures; wooden chains; and miscellaneous objects, large, small, or miniature.

Among carvers and whittlers referred to in this chapter nearly one-half are birdcarvers, some carving birds only; but obviously this list is incomplete because there are any number of hunters who make their own wooden decoys and who are usually not known for their craftsmanship outside their own neighborhoods.

Something should be said of the little hand tool that has made much of this work possible—the pocketknife. It is usually omitted from the books on carpenter's tools, probably because it is never in the carpenter's tool chest but always in his pocket. A pocketknife is a part of the equipment of practically every man, and wood of some kind is within the reach of almost everyone, especially in the country; therefore "whittling" has long been a common practice with countless boys and men. But whittling to a purpose, so to speak, is a comparatively new development, and is one of the most promising in the whole range of American handicrafts.

Maine. Beginning well "down East" the first whittler to be recorded is "Uncle Harry" Wass of Addison, who has made hundreds of decoys. He also whittles out of native pine miniature ducks, which he gives to his friends, and which are sometimes sold for the benefit of the Maine Seacoast Missionary Society. Uncle Harry, besides being a fisherman and a gardener, with a fine strawberry patch, is handy with tools and can do the things essential to good living on this part of the Maine coast. When the day's work is over, he is always ready to take his fiddle to a neighbor's house to play for an evening's entertainment or to help with a church service.

The carvings of Dany Carter, a youth of Augusta, include imaginary subjects sometimes suggested by books or motion pictures; several compositions were inspired by Walt Disney's productions. Dany's masterpiece, and one of his largest carvings, is a trotting race in which three horses are almost abreast as they near the judges' stand in a spectacular finish. Every detail including horses, drivers, sulkies, harness, and drivers' costumes is done with vitality, and the spirit of this favorite Maine sport is perfectly recorded.

Life Photographer, Fritz Goro, Copyright Time, Inc.

49. WHITTLED BIRDS OF NEW ENGLAND

WATERFOWLS AND WOODLAND BIRDS CARVED BY JESS BLACKSTONE OF CONCORD, NEW HAMPSHIRE; GULLS AND TERNS BY ARTHUR M. BLACKSTONE, MELROSE, MASSACHUSETTS; RED-HEAD DUCK AND KING EIDER DUCK BY GODFREY B. SIMÔNDS OF PROVIDENCE, RHODE ISLAND.

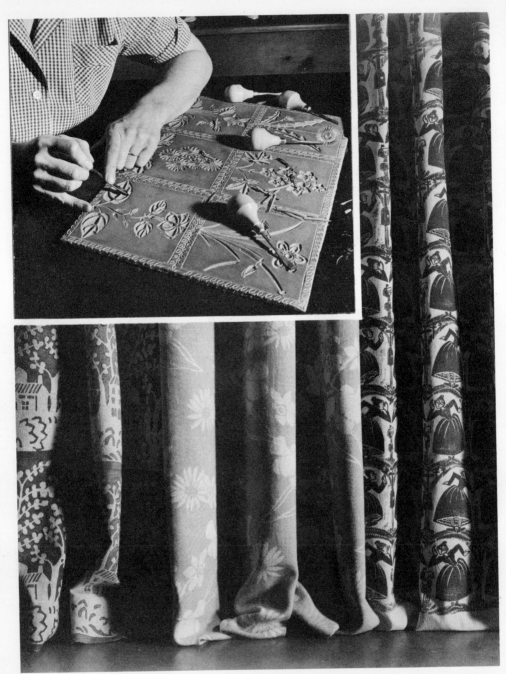

(Inset) Life Photographer, Fritz Goro, Copyright Time, Inc.

Edmund de Beaumont, Worcester Art Museum

50. LINOLEUM BLOCKPRINTING

THE DESIGN IS BEING CUT IN THIS LINOLEUM BLOCK BY MRS. LOUISE KENYON OF FOLLY COVE DESIGNERS, ANNISQUAM, MASSACHUSETTS. . . . THE HAND-PRINTED FABRICS, FROM LEFT TO RIGHT, WERE DESIGNED BY MRS. MYRA W. RANKIN OF CONNECTICUT, MISS MARGARET STEDMAN, RHODE ISLAND, AND MRS. VIRGINIA DEMETRIOS, MASSACHUSETTS.

Lifshey Studios

51. A BUTTER STAMP FROM VERMONT

THIS BUTTER STAMP OF A TRADITIONAL PATTERN WAS CARVED IN 1947 BY GEORGE
MILLIGAN OF BARNET, WHO IS PROBABLY THE ONLY CRAFTSMAN NOW MAKING BUTTER
STAMPS. HIS BLOCKS ARE OF VERMONT BIRCH OR MAPLE; THE ENGRAVING IS ON THE
END GRAIN.

Let others tell of storm and showers
I only count the sunny hours

Marchese Studio

Edmund de Beaumont, School Arts Magazine

52. SUNDIAL OF CONNECTICUT CLAY AND A VERMONT CARVING

MR. AND MRS. JOHN TURNBULL OF HADDAM HAVE MADE MANY DECORATIVE OBJECTS FROM COMMON CLAY, FIRING THEM IN AN ORDINARY BRICK KILN WITH THOUSANDS OF OTHER BRICKS. . . . VERMONT COUNTRY STORE AND POST OFFICE CARVED FROM NATIVE PINE BY N. F. DEGUISE OF WATERBURY.

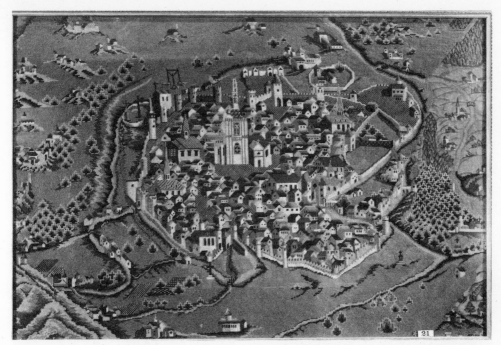

Juley and Son, School Arts Magazine

53. NEEDLEPOINT WALL DECORATION

MRS. NATALIE HAYS HAMMOND AND HER ASSOCIATES OF SAINT BRIAVEL GUILD OF
GLOUCESTER, MASSACHUSETTS, MADE THIS NEEDLEPOINT WALL DECORATION. THE
DESIGN WAS DERIVED FROM AN OLD WOODBLOCK PRINT OF THE CITY OF COLMAR.

Life Photographer, Fritz Goro, Copyright Time, Inc.

54. CONNECTICUT FURNITURE AND HOOKED RUG

THE WINE CABINET WAS DESIGNED AND MADE BY MISS LOUISE TAYLOR OF HARTFORD; THE LARGE RUG ON THE FLOOR WAS MADE BY THE CRAFTS PROJECT OF THE WORK PROJECTS ADMINISTRATION AT STAMFORD FROM A DESIGN BY MRS. MARION VOORHEES OF HAMBURG.

55. CREWEL EMBROIDERY IN MASSACHUSETTS

CREWEL STITCHERY HAS BEEN PRACTICED CONTINUOUSLY IN NEW ENGLAND FROM PIL-
GRIM DAYS. THE CHAIR COVER WAS DESIGNED BY MRS. LOUISE CHRIMES OF BOSTON;
THE EMBROIDERY IS BY MRS. HELEN S. DYER OF HINGHAM.

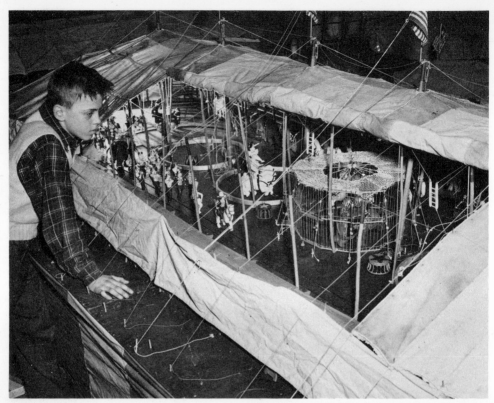

Al. Aumuller for New York World Telegram

56. UNDER THE BIG TOP

PART OF A MINIATURE CIRCUS BY WILLIAM BRINLEY OF WALLINGFORD, CONNECTICUT. THE FIGURES MARCH AND THE ANIMALS PERFORM AS A VISITOR WATCHES THROUGH THE TENT OPENING.

Myrton S. Reed

57. MODEL FOR A PARADE WAGON

THE ALICE IN WONDERLAND FLOAT IS ONE OF SEVERAL PARADE WAGONS IN THE
MINIATURE CIRCUS BUILT AND CARVED BY ERIC F. OLSON, JR., OF WORCESTER, MASSA-
CHUSETTS. THE COMPLETE MODEL COVERS A SPACE OF TWENTY-TWO BY FORTY-TWO
FEET AND WEIGHS NEARLY A TON.

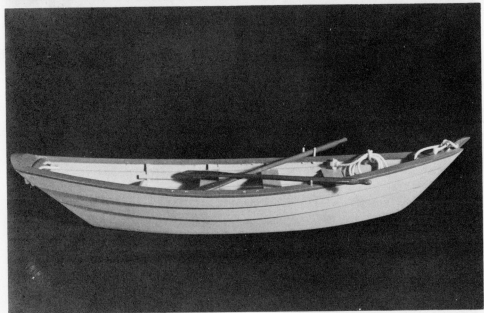

Lifshey Studios

58. BLACK CHERRY BOWL AND MINIATURE DORY

THIS BOWL WAS DESIGNED AND TURNED BY ARTHUR W. LAUGHTON OF WEST BRATTLE-
BORO, VERMONT, ON AN OLD-TIME FOOT-POWER LATHE. . . . MINIATURE DORY, TWENTY-
SIX INCHES LONG, WAS BUILT BY RAYMOND T. COLE, TOYMAKER OF NEWCASTLE, MAINE.

59. KNITTING AND CROCHETING DOG-WOOL YARN

This Samoyed Puppy Represents One of the Best Wool-producing Dogs. Miss Martha E. Humphriss of Westerly, Rhode Island, Raises Thoroughbred Samoyeds, Combs Their Wool, and Has It Spun into Suitable Threads for Her Handwork.

Edmund de Beaumont, Worcester Art Museum

60. COMMUNITY SERVICE IN CRYSTAL AND SILVER

THE SERVICE ILLUSTRATED HERE WAS DESIGNED AND WROUGHT BY WILLIAM E. BRIGHAM OF PROVIDENCE, RHODE ISLAND. IT WAS SHOWN AT THE WORCESTER EXHIBITION OF CONTEMPORARY HANDICRAFTS.

George French

61. A TROTTING RACE IN MAINE

The Miniature Woodcarving of a Trotting Race Is but Part of a Larger County-fair Racetrack Scene Made by Dany Carter of Augusta. A Young Craftsman of Unusual Skill and Taste, He Has Caught the Spirit of One of Maine's Favorite Sporting Events.

Goodman, Waterbury Republican American

62. A PAINTING IN YARN

PROBABLY NO ONE HAS DEVELOPED FINER TECHNIQUE IN PICTURE EMBROIDERY THAN
MRS. MARIAN STOLL OF WATERBURY, CONNECTICUT. THE BASE CLOTH ON WHICH THE
STITCHERY IS WORKED IS COMPLETELY COVERED; OFTEN FIFTY THREADS OF VARYING
COLORS HANG FROM HER NEEDLES.

John D. Schiff

63. SCRIMSHAW IN NEW BEDFORD MUSEUM

THERE ARE STILL A FEW WORKERS IN SCRIMSHAW IN AND AROUND NEW BEDFORD, MASSACHUSETTS, ENCOURAGED IN PART BY THE FAMOUS WHALING MUSEUM ON JOHNNY CAKE HILL. THESE BOOK-ENDS WERE DESIGNED AND MADE BY MANUEL P. S. MACEDO AND THE WHALE'S TEETH WERE ETCHED BY WILLIAM PERRY, BOTH OF NEW BEDFORD.

Bruce Burroughs

64. SINGING CUCKOO WEATHERVANE

THIS WEATHERVANE WITH ITS SINGING CUCKOO AND WHIRRING WINDMILL WAS DESIGNED AND BUILT BY BRUCE ROGERS OF NEW FAIRFIELD, CONNECTICUT. AS THE WINDMILL TURNS, THE CUCKOO OPENS ITS BEAK, SPREADS ITS WINGS, AND SINGS UP-AND-DOWN NOTES AFTER EACH EIGHTEENTH REVOLUTION.

Delmont Potter of Bar Harbor is a carpenter and general handyman who has always liked to whittle and now is carving in miniature all the wild animals of the state of Maine. A group of these is illustrated. Association with his son set Mr. Potter to thinking seriously about whittling as a hobby.

Kenneth Potter, encouraged by his parents, learned to whittle ship models while he was an invalid—activities which not only filled the day with pleasure but were largely responsible, his family thinks, for his recovery. His mother used to spread a sheet on the bed to catch the chips from his carving. Kenneth whittled out dogs, ducks, and birds, and finally, working from newspaper photographs, he made a model with movable parts of the U.S.S. *Kearney.* The more he studied this efficient little vessel, the more he fell in love with it. A year after he had completed his model he was so well recovered that he enlisted in the Navy. His first asignment was, as he had hoped it would be, to a ship built like the *Kearney.* Kenneth said that he could have gone over the whole vessel with his eyes shut.

Several carvers and whittlers of Maine produce work so strongly influenced by the sea that they might well have been put into Chapter 15. One is Lloyd Thomas of Camden, a young carver of fine feeling and great versatility. He has made many chests carved in low relief with motifs of the sea and seacoast, and has carved ships, also in relief, on pine planks. One of his best-known large carvings, about four feet square, is a full-rigged sailing vessel in color, which hangs in the public library at Camden. Mr. Thomas is a skillful carver of birds and fish which, as hunter and fisherman, he understands well. Small examples of his work are the flying green teal duck and the pickerel shown here in a composition of objects connected with sports.

Maurice Day, proprietor of The Whittle Shop in Damariscotta, although an artist of all-round ability, takes great pleasure in his whittling. Besides being a water colorist Mr. Day is an expert photographer. He has made photographs and sketches for Walt Disney, particularly in connection with the motion picture *Bambi.* It is, however, his whittling of Maine scenes and subjects for which Mr. Day is best known to his neighbors and to travelers who stop at his shop. He gives special charm to the birds he whittles by mounting them on native driftwood. Mr. Day and his family have together worked out characteristic scenes of fishermen's huts, especially those of lobster fishermen, to be seen along the rugged cliffs of the Maine coast. These miniature huts, as the Days contrive them, with wooden piers, a ladder or two, nets, boats, buoys, and other fishing equipment, touched up in their natural colors against the driftwood backgrounds, perhaps outrank any souvenirs in our country in their artistic interpretation of a fascinating region.

Down at Darkharbor, a village on an island off the Maine coast, Maurice L. Decker carved and painted favorite birds for years. When the writer visited Mr. Decker he was coming in with a small catch of mackerel, just enough for the day's lunch. He pointed out the beauty of the fish and was soon enthusiastically talking of bird life on the island. He showed to his caller a small eagle which he had carved as a boy of sixteen; it reflected a fine feeling for his favorite bird.

Mr. Decker's knowledge of birds was greatly increased through practice in taxidermy, which he had taken up earlier for friends who wished to preserve proof of their marksmanship. It was when a huge eagle was brought to him to mount that the idea of perpetuating this bird in the form of woodcarving took definite shape in his mind. He carved usually from native cedar, sometimes using island oak for the eagle's feet and other parts which needed strengthening; a jackknife, a chisel, and a new kind of gouge which he made himself were his tools. He never made designs beforehand but carved the birds "out of his head" as he worked. The price he charged for carving a bird depended a great deal on the feathers because they take a lot of time to shape.

The Malmstrom brothers, Arthur, Carl, and Just, sons of Scandinavian parents, are natural carvers. Carl, the oldest, lives at Longcove and worked in a shipyard during World War II. He specializes in sea birds, beautiful in form with natural markings in color. His wife, who is a good craftsman, often carries out the painted details. Mr. Malmstrom's favorite subjects are native ducks, especially on the wing, which he carves in low relief and in the round. These sensitive carvings are the work of a man trained originally as a cutter of paving stones. Arthur, who lives in Rockland, has done a wide variety of subjects, one of his favorites being the American eagle. He exhibited a six-foot spread-eagle at the Worcester show in 1943 and has made many reproductions of it in both flat and round. Just, the youngest, lives in Worcester, Massachusetts. He has made studies of bird life, and carves comical figures in low relief, one of the latter being of a famous Rockland character, John Killuberger, working at a marine handicraft. It is locally considered an excellent likeness.

Wayne Buxton of Searsport, writer, artist, and craftsman, cooperated with his father, Henry Buxton, in preparing the book, *Assignment Down East*, for which he took hundreds of photographs of old-time Maine people. Mr. Buxton's carvings, usually from three to six inches high, show excellent construction and good motion, as well as fidelity to character. One such figure representing an old man going down the road exercising his "constitutional right" to walk in the middle, as described in *Assignment Down East,* is a first-rate character study seen either from back or front. At the Worcester Exhibition Mr. Buxton was represented by a small sitting figure of Moses Chandler, grandfather of Mr. Buxton's neighbor, Charles Worth. This character study was worked up by Mr. Buxton from an old family group photograph.

Mr. Buxton cuts out his blanks from native pine with a handsaw, then whittles them into shape with a pocketknife. The figures are painted with dry pigments mixed with oil, a filler having been used to prevent the paint from going too far into the wood. They are finished with a non-glossy drier. His color palette is low and harmonious. Although self-taught, his carvings would rate high in any exhibition of small wood sculpture.

Probably the pioneer birdcarver of New England was Sylvanus McFarland of South Bristol, who began to whittle when thirteen or fourteen years old. A traveler from Germany brought him a small carving of a swallow and asked him to copy it. He soon found himself making sea gulls, herons, and sandpipers for other visitors seeking souvenirs of the region. Sylvanus developed into a true naturalist, and it is unfortunate that his diaries and much of his correspondence were destroyed at his request. John Burroughs was one of hundreds of friends that the birdcarvings made for Sylvanus; their encouragement and criticism helped in many instances to perfect the character of his work. A letter from Burroughs is quoted: "Thank you for the pretty little pine Oriole. It is very cleverly done. There is but one feature about it that I do not like—the open beak. This prevents your giving it characteristic shape. I feel that no bird should be painted or carved with an open beak unless the beak has food in it. . . . The open beak soon becomes tiresome, we wish the bird would close it. All the bird artists do it and they all make a mistake in doing so."

Sylvanus became more and more interested in the wild life around him, and began to carve songbirds about three-fifths their natural size; of these he completed about forty to fifty varieties. For eleven years he whittled only songbirds of the region, making in all over 22,000, which he shipped to all parts of the world, a collection of over fifty going to an Indian maharajah.

Sylvanus' brother, George, wondered whether he too might be able to whittle. Sylvanus assured him that he could, and it turned out that he was right, for George whittled butterflies out of basswood, sandpapered to delicate thinness and beautifully colored. He also made gulls and ducks. These, like the birds of his older brother and teacher, were in great demand.

Gillman, the son of Sylvanus, has inherited his father's talent. One of his earliest orders was from Rachel Field, the author, who was so well pleased that soon he was receiving requests from her friends. His favorite subjects now are water birds, and from his workshop on the shore he can see living models in almost any direction. He sometimes carves his birds in unusual poses which others may not have had an opportunity to observe. The wings of his birds he carves from basswood, the bodies from "punkin" or white pine, and mounts them on carefully selected pieces of driftwood; he says that getting the appropriate mountings is the most time-consuming part of his bird production. He has carved about one hundred varieties, practically all the birds of Maine and some from elsewhere, including flamingos and pelicans.

Wendell Gilley, a young tinsmith and plumber of Southwest Harbor, holds a high place among bird whittlers of New England. First he made decoys, and then, through closer study of native birds, began whittling them singly and in groups. Some are life-sized, others miniature. Among his notable pieces are a pair of ducks, an owl, a loon, and a sea gull. Each piece is carved with great pains and then as carefully painted. He is a taxidermist and the painting is often done directly from the mounted specimen, which he thinks better than working from pictures.

The delightful whittling of William Colby, a farmer who lived near Wiscasset, is both a symbolical record of his countryside and a tribute to the therapeutic value of whittling as a handicraft. Following an attack of pneumonia which made him unfit for hard out-of-door work, Mr. Colby felt deeply discouraged, and to while away the time he began to whittle. His miniature oxen and other subjects were so well done that, much to his surprise, they proved to be constantly in demand. The Portland *Sunday Telegram* and *Sunday Press Herald* of September 15, 1935, described Mr. Colby's carving of a tiny log cabin "being hauled on a sled by six yokes of oxen"—the representation of a scene in the children's story, *Away Goes Sally*, by Elizabeth Coatsworth Beston of Nobleboro.

During the last years of his life, Mr. Colby whittled practically every form of vehicle that he had ever seen on the farms of his neighborhood. Mr. and Mrs. William Seaver Warland, for whom Mr. Colby had worked for many years and who were much interested in his whittlings, have a complete set of these really important recordings presented to them by the maker. A few of these are shown in illustration.

Charles Chase, also of Wiscasset, began to carve during the depression. He bought his tools from a mail-order house and adopted a unique plan of making a flat charge of a dollar an hour for his labor, selling all his pieces on that basis. Thus a number of persons were able to form collections of his birdcarvings who could not have afforded them at prices usually charged by professional sculptors. Mr. Chase's work is usually in mahogany or walnut and always finished in the natural wood without color, so the effect of his interpretation lies in the sculptured form. A mixture of half oil and half shellac is well rubbed in when the piece is completed. The carving is done with great restraint, the purpose being to catch essential characteristics of the bird. Mr. Chase is often able to record extraordinary poses, and his feeling for birds and for the qualities of the wood in which he works results in something satisfying to both naturalist and sculptor.

In the beautiful old house that shelters the Wiscasset Public Library a room was for several years set aside for showing the work of local craftsmen. Mrs. Henry Webb, who was the librarian, felt a special interest in handicrafts and was one of the pioneers in bringing handwork to the attention of the public. She helped the workers of the neighborhood by holding frequent displays, buying for the Library books of special interest to them.

New Hampshire. Swedish by birth, Leo Malm of Concord came to this country when he was four years old. Twenty-odd years of his life in America were devoted to designing and modeling in silver, but like other New England craftsmen, he finds much satisfaction in working in both metal and wood. Mr. Malm served his apprenticeship under Louis Lang, Augustrofus Van Stry, and I. Kirchmayer, and has become well known as a woodcarver. He makes small, beautifully proportioned statuettes, and for the League of New Hampshire Arts and Crafts he carved some excellent miniature animals.

Another craftsman now of Concord is Jess Blackstone, who was with the Army overseas during most of World War II. His interest in bird life was then a source of much help to him under exceedingly trying experiences. In his letters home he wrote of hearing bird sounds at night from foxholes, and on one strenuous march he found a piece of wood from which he managed to whittle a German land bird. Jess was encouraged to take up whittling by his father, Arthur Blackstone of Melrose, Massachusetts, also a carver and a linoleum blockprinter. For some time father and son worked together, but when Jess moved to New Hampshire he undertook independently the whittling of the land birds of that state. Since returning from service his advance as a whittler has been steady.

Omar Marcoux came to Concord from French Canada. He has been greatly encouraged in his whittling by the League of New Hampshire

Arts and Crafts, which has given him opportunities to demonstrate at the annual Craftsman's Fair and an outlet for his products. One of his best whittlings is a span of oxen hauling lumber on a sled. President Franklin D. Roosevelt purchased one of these ox teams. Mr. Marcoux enjoys experimenting with the qualities of different woods, such as mahogany, basswood, black walnut, gumwood, and maple. He makes a specialty of carving dogs and has whittled out eighty-five different breeds in miniature size. At the Rural Arts Exhibition held in Washington, D.C., in 1937, Mr. Marcoux had twenty-five varieties of dogs for which he built a number of stalls, giving his miniature creation the appearance of a professional dog show. He usually paints his figures in their natural coloring. Photographs of some of his miniature dogs are shown.

Like his friend, Marcoux, Octave Dufresne also of Concord, is a native of Canada. On coming to Concord as a young man, he worked for many years in a silversmith factory and later did fine cabinetwork, but he always whittled at home for amusement. He carves in ivory as well as wood and particularly enjoys working in miniature forms. One of the subjects he likes best is a farmer feeding his pigs, and another a pig with his nose in a pail of food, the latter whittled out of one piece of wood. Mr. Dufresne also makes table landscapes. He fills in a woodland composition with miniature creatures—herons, ducks, rabbits, bears, squirrels, and perhaps adds a group of hunters or fishermen preparing meals or engaged in some appropriate way. His finely carved Conestoga wagon is now a permanent possession of the Concord Arts and Crafts Shop.

Charles Clough of Bristol, eighty-seven years of age at the time these notes were made, may be truly called a folk whittler. He never makes a pattern but cuts his subjects directly out of the wood. Mr. Clough has always worked with his hands, doing blacksmithing, cabinetmaking, and general repairs. A friend writes, "Perhaps his most amusing carving is a figure of a hunter sitting on a log with a bottle in his pocket and his gun ready for a squirrel, and all the time a saucy squirrel is perched on the log just behind him." One of his own favorite pieces is a fat girl sitting on a fat boy's lap. Another is an old-time politician.

One of the best-known folk whittlers in New Hampshire is Archie Gilbert of Landaff, who is always represented at craftsmen's fairs by ox teams and gaily painted carts. Mr. Gilbert used to farm, and worked in a local sawmill where through an accident he lost a leg. Forced to sell most of his farm property, he took up whittling and woodworking. He uses no power tools, and his material is often rough wood salvaged from slab piles. His large figures of people and farm animals are striking examples of folk art. They are made for his own amusement and give him much satisfaction. His own rural mailbox is on the lap of a full-sized sitting figure of a man waiting for the mail to be delivered. His dependable span of red and white oxen with the blue cart, of which he has made several hundred, is a real source of revenue. Mr. Gilbert is a hard worker despite his physical handicap, averaging twelve to fourteen hours a day. His wife assists him, particularly in the finishing of his oxen and carts, which when finally painted are lined up behind the kitchen stove to dry. There is a continuous demand for these through the League.

Mrs. Susan N. Collins (Suen Collins) of Littleton, whose son, Laurence, is a notable craftsman in iron, says of her own hobby, whittling, that it has at least three justifications: it costs little for materials and equipment; it is not overdone; and there is no limit to the useful and ornamental things to be made. Of her first carving, undertaken as a result of seeing a small wooden figure at an arts and crafts exhibit, she says: "I was as much surprised as anyone to see a little woman emerge from the wood, crude and funny, of course, but it made me want to try again; and little figures have been crawling out of sticks of wood ever since, each a little better than the one before. And so an interest became a joy and a pastime, a source of income commensurate with the time I have to give to it. I don't suggest that anyone may expect income from a hobby. If it works out that way by being unusual or unusually well done and you need the money, well and good, but ride without saddle and spur as long as may be."

Mrs. Collins uses mostly native pine, and has created figures and scenes of true folk quality, of which the crèche shown is a good example. Saint Theresa the Little Flower and Saint Francis with His Birds are other carvings in similar mood.

Hans Brustle of Raymond, near Manchester, a native of the Black Forest, Germany, is a professional carver of exceptional skill and experience who has recently cast his lot with the New Hampshire League. His small carvings of fish and birds he often makes into pins and other decorations. Mr. Brustle is happy in having procured a farm where he has built his own house and combines agriculture with handicrafts.

George Boyd, who lived at Seabrook, was the pioneer whittler of New Hampshire birds, known for years to every summer visitor to the seaside resort. He recorded the bird life of his vicinity in hundreds of miniature forms and in decoys. A few weeks before Mr. Boyd died, David Campbell, director of the League of New Hampshire Arts and Crafts, wrote of him: "To my mind he is one of the outstanding craftsmen of New Hampshire. We have never been able to have any of his articles in our shops because he has such a ready market; thus he is able to meet his daily needs through the sale of his finished work. Mr. Boyd is very generous and has helped every craftsman that I have brought to him, withholding no so-called secrets but encouraging others to venture forth as he did."

A complete collection of Mr. Boyd's birds, which number about two hundred pairs, is owned by Sam Allen of Rye Beach. The Boyd family also has many birds whittled and ready for painting. These, Mr. Boyd's son, Clarence, who sometimes helped his father, may complete. Clarence, who likes to whittle fish, has done an excellent study of a tuna fish.

Vermont. In the most northwestern corner of rural Vermont near Alburg Springs, Gerald Tremblay has built his Duck Decoy Shop and there makes bluebills, whistlers, buffleheads, blacks, coots, canvasbacks, mallards, mergansers, wood ducks, and other varieties of decoys, twenty-seven in all, for hunters of the region. Handicapped by infantile paralysis but courageously overcoming obstacles to complete his schoolwork, in which he learned the rudiments of woodworking, Gerald has carried along his decoy business happily and efficiently. He has supplemented it with work on his turning lathe and the repairing of furniture. Although he has developed a sturdy body by using his hands and arms in walking, more than his crippled knees, building a shop was no easy task. But this he did after earning money enough to buy materials. For his first five hundred decoys he chopped the blocks out himself with an ax but now he finds that he can save time by having this done at the sawmill. He generally uses cedar or pine, strengthening the neck or other weak parts of the bird with a harder wood, and in his best decoys he joins the head to the body with a dowel. He saws the blank roughly into the desired shape; with his drawing knife he gives it body form; and with his jackknife he whittles out the head and more detailed parts. The painting he does rather sketchily, but coloring and markings are true to the species and the wooden birds serve well not only as decoys but as attractive ornaments. Gerald makes an average of about three hundred regular decoys each year and often whittles out smaller birds for which he finds a market through the Arts and Crafts Service of Vermont. He works quickly and systematically; having almost no overhead, he is able to sell the birds at very reasonable prices.

Among his best bird groups are mother ducks with their young. Out of a single block Gerald whittled two young ducks as though they had bumped into each other while swimming. This feathery collision forms a heart-shaped base, on the underside of which he prints "To my valentine." Gerald knows much of the lore that comes only to those who have lived with waterfowl the year round. He says that whistler ducks do not get their feathers until they are nearly a year old.

He invented a wooden duck bank with a sliding back, a duplicate of which he used to send every year to President Roosevelt on his birthday, filled with dimes collected in Alburg Springs. He painted by hand the wooden sign for his Duck Decoy Shop and mounted a decoy above it on the top of the pole. This small shop is a model of neatness and efficiency. With bird skins and wooden decoys, it is almost a miniature museum of the American duck family.

Charles G. MacDonald of Red Echo Farm, Topsham, is a whittler of unusual versatility who shapes his blanks roughly on the jigsaw and finishes the figure with a carver's chisel and a pocketknife. For some of his round figures he uses a turning lathe. The carvings, usually of human figures of an attenuated type, are ultramodern in style. Apple farming is the main activity of this rural carver, whose orchard is on one of the highest hills of Vermont. Mr. MacDonald was formerly a Wall Street man with five telephones on his desk, but he got tired of business and decided to raise apples. The combination of apple-raising and woodcarving brings him much satisfaction.

V. Despot of Johnson, proprietor of the meat market and general store, is a kind of natural carver who is more concerned about the fun he is having than how the product strikes his neighbors. He has carved some fantastic scenes and portraits on wooden planks, and has arranged them on the walls of his store. One is a picnic group with an enormous winking pig in the foreground waiting for the party to go away so he can clean up. Another is the King of England done on the end of a Swift and Company packing box, which Mr. Despot is not sure "is proper and fitting for the King, but it was all I had."

Henry Waldo lives in the country near Middlesex. His Shop Without a Wheel is so called because everything in it is done by hand; there are no wheels to make the machine go 'round. Mr. Waldo is an excellent example of a person following a craft in spite of great handicaps and maintaining a cheerful and helpful attitude. He makes dominoes and other games, and seeks naturally colored woods for paper knives and so forth.

Mr. Waldo's one machine is a typewriter, which he uses chiefly for his "verse writing." On this he expresses his enthusiasm for the things of everyday. He recently put together a collection of these "verse writings" neatly typed, the sheets bound in native birch bark. In the words of one of his own verses he is of the kind who "will never say die 'till we're dead." Writing of childhood in a family of "one small girl and six big boys," he tells of a vacation in an old Chevrolet car when:

> Mother got somehow excited
> When a hornet flew into the car,
> She thought it a little too crowded
> If he wanted to ride very far.

Of an old bobsled of his childhood days he writes:

> . . . no architect drew the plan
> But the artisans that designed it
> Were father and the hired man.
>
> . . . .
>
> The runners were solid and heavy,
> And were some over six feet long,
> They hewed the bunks from an old red elm
> For they wanted it good and strong.

Dwight J. Dwinell of Montpelier, though making no pretense to being a woodcarver, when the need came supplied for the Vermont State House a monumental likeness of Ceres to take the place of an earlier carving. Arnold Nicholson, in the *Saturday Evening Post* of January 1, 1944, tells the story:

Ceres is a white painted, fourteen-foot wood statue perched on the gilt dome of the statehouse in Montpelier. She is the second in her line. Five and a half years ago Ceres No. 1, known familiarly in Montpelier as the "old lady" or "Agriculture" but rarely by her mythological name, began to disintegrate with age. She was eighty years old and entitled to retirement. . . . But she couldn't come down without a replica to take her place.

No one thought of sending to New York or Boston for a high-priced, long-haired sculptor to create a new Ceres. The authorities turned instead to the state's sergeant at arms, the late Dwight J. Dwinell. He had tried his hand at art not long before, whittling out a handsome cow to ornament the state coat of arms that hangs on the wall of the House of Representatives. The cow was a minor piece of carving compared to the Brobdingnagian proportions of Ceres, but it was argued that if the sergeant at arms could jump from occasional cabinet work at home to a satisfactory job of bas-relief, why couldn't he progress to statuary on the heroic scale?

Mr. Dwinell, at eighty-seven, allowed as how he could. Six weeks from the day the original Ceres came down, the elderly sergeant at arms and two assistants—one a former tree surgeon and the other a carpenter—completed the new goddess, sawed and chiseled and whittled from pine blocks in a workshop in the rear of the State House.

Mr. Dwinell "personally chiseled out the head and facial features," a Montpelier newspaper recorded in 1938, and that's about all the public notice the eighty-seven-year-old carver ever received. Vermonters, although proud of the homespun origin of their statehouse Ceres, are inclined to take the job for granted. They are used to seeing skilled, patient hands turn to craftsmanship, to whittling and spinning and the creation of useful and artistic things.

Mrs. Frank Lawrence of Lawrence's Dairy Farm, St. Johnsbury, has eight well-cared-for children and with the dairy there is plenty of work to be done. But whenever she can Mrs. Lawrence turns to carving. She gets her inspiration from every source; her carved salt and pepper shakers, for instance, have designs inspired by Campbell's soup advertisements from the Atlantic and Pacific store. "I see a scrap of design here and another scrap there and manage to put them together somehow. Everything I see reminds me of something I want to carve." She has made a fine piece of redwood into a beautiful tray with simple scalloped edges. "I like useful things best of all," she said, and explained that it was the county farm agent who encouraged her to take up carving. She had just finished whittling roughly a sketch of the South Church steeple of St. Johnsbury. It is a beautiful steeple with a clock in the base, and she was planning to set a watch into the base of her own carving to make what she termed "a nice and authentic ornament." At the time of the writer's visit, she was carving a Madonna in native pine, which promised to be one of her most successful compositions. "Farm work is wonderful," said Mrs. Lawrence, "but after all there is nothing like creating something with your own hands."

N. F. DeGuise, locally known as "Napoleon," is the proprietor of a barber shop in Waterbury, but he is much more than a barber, important as that is for the village. "Napoleon" writes poetry, paints in oil, is a carver and an inventor. He began to carve in talc "just for fun" when he got some "pencil stock," used in marking hot metal, from the local talc mine. He carves figures of people seen from the large window of his barber shop. He will catch the droop of shoulders, the way an umbrella or handbag is carried, the tilt of the hat, and in some cases the actual facial expression. Sometimes he removes the head of the barber's electric clippers and converts it into a temporary drilling and carving machine.

Among his subjects is a country store with a man in a heavy coat and muffler warming his hands before a pot-bellied stove, another reaching into the cracker barrel, another reading the *Waterbury Rec-*

ord by the light of a kerosene lamp, two old men playing checkers, and a lady "all dressed up," who has come to town with her children to shop. Another favorite scene is a complete blacksmith shop, and a recent production is a full orchestra. At Christmas time he makes for the shop window a kind of crèche which he calls Gloria in Excelsis.

The skilled craft of carving butter molds or butter stamps as they are often called in New England, once widely practiced throughout the country, has almost disappeared. The only man of whom the writer knows who still makes them, on order, is George Milligan of Barnet, Vermont. He is a carver of unusual skill who taught himself long ago to make butter stamps when he thought them too expensive for his father to buy. Among several molds that he has recently carved, his bundle of grain done in delightful outline is his best. He carves on the end grain of birch or maple, which he cuts from the tree himself, being responsible for all the processes. John Varnum of Peacham carved butter stamps extensively and well until a few years ago when he discontinued taking orders and gave his tools away. He knew many butter-mold carvers throughout his part of New England when butter stamping by hand was a general practice.

Massachusetts. A writer, carver, and naturalist, David Aylward of the National Federation of Wild Life, with headquarters at Boston, has long been interested in the out-of-doors as a sportsman and wildlife photographer. He carves ducks, geese, shore birds, and to a lesser extent song and insectivorous birds, in relief and in the round. After carving he paints them in their natural colors. Most of Mr. Aylward's tools are those used by his grandfather, a fine cabinetmaker and woodcarver, from whom he thinks he may have inherited his bent. He feels that woodcarving gives an outlet for the enthusiasm that nature stirs in him. "The birds seem so beautiful to me that I just have to give some expression beyond the spoken word."

A. E. Crowell of East Harwich was among the pioneers in birdcarving. His subjects were native birds, both water and land, but particularly game birds, which as hunter and student he knew well. Mr. Crowell worked out his own blanks from large chunks of wood with ax and hatchet. Many of his carvings were life sized and the painting was done with great skill. The workshop on the morning of the writer's visit was fragrant from the chips of native red cedar, a favorite carving wood. His son, C. S. Crowell, continues carving in the well-established tradition. A characteristic study of father and son working together is shown.

At Martha's Vineyard, Fred Chase, a carpenter and practical craftsman, reproduces in wood subjects in nature which interest him most—

local birds and landscapes. These are painted, or burned with a pyrographic needle in low relief. He has made a number of wood sea chests, book ends, and wall decorations. He has also decorated swords of swordfish in low carving, rubbing coloring matter into the design to bring it out.

Frank Adams of Tisbury, Martha's Vineyard, was an old carpenter who in later years made weathervanes and ship models and whittled ducks, geese, and other water birds of the island. He had been a hunter a good deal of his life but explained that he got much more satisfaction in carving the images of ducks than in shooting them. His weathervanes are of wood. One design is a fishing boat, another a two-masted schooner, and a third a brig, all subjects from Martha's Vineyard and the surrounding sea.

John H. Trivola of Norwood carves spoons, forks, table utensils with beautiful flowing lines reminiscent of his native Finland.

Travelers through West Gloucester will recall the display of birds, especially penguins, carved by Charles H. Hart, an old hunter who thinks he may hold the local record for the number of game birds shot in his area. He has whittled many of these birds including ducks and geese in giant sizes; he has carved over 1,500 penguins and finds them among the most popular of his subjects. His experience tells him that the public demand is for inexpensive carvings, and this he undertakes to satisfy. He has an unusually fine collection of decoys, many of his own make.

At the Sea Shore Dining Room in Marblehead, its proprietor, S. C. Duffield, carves and teaches woodcarving, especially to children. His own carvings are often monumental—totem poles, figureheads, large eagles, naturalistic in style but sometimes planned for their architectural effect. He has made some large nautical decorations in cast cement. He is also interested in finding natural, or almost natural, forms in branches or roots of trees—such as a group of squirrels, a goat's head —and these "imprisoned" images it is a pleasure for him to bring out, with a minimum of carving. His associate in the studio, Miss E. L. Post, has done notable needlework some of which, along with Mr. Duffield's carvings, decorates the dining room.

Miss Carrie L. Blake of Reading, formerly a teacher of languages, found that she could interest her students in reading favorite French fairy tales and legends by whittling the figures and arranging them in scenes. Before Miss Blake had finished her work as a teacher she had thus learned much of the technique of woodcarving. At eighty-three she was still carving, finding in it, as she said, a satisfaction which those who do not work with their hands cannot understand. She became so well known for her carvings of bears that her orders for them outran all others. She was one of the most spirited demonstrators at the Boston Garden Show of 1943. An example of her work is illustrated.

Addison B. LeBoutillier is an artist and designer in several mediums. Perhaps his most famous designing was for the Grueby Pottery. The small house which he designed and built himself in Rockport contains much of his delightful woodcarving, especially in connection with its structural features. Mr. LeBoutillier has made a model of a dream village of old France, the homeland of his forebears, including carved figures of the inhabitants. The artist together with the model village fashioned by his mind and hand is shown.

Francisco Peviri of South Framingham is a blind chair caner and woodcarver. It is in the carving of ancient and medieval scenes, and particularly the recording of biblical legends that Mr. Peviri delights most. A carving of a crucifix in the little Church of the Holy Spirit at South Orleans on the Cape led the writer to make further inquiry concerning his work. A visit to South Framingham revealed a workshop filled with his creations in wood, among which those most vividly recalled are St. John the Baptist, Romulus and Remus, the Last Supper, and Flight into Egypt. All are true examples of folk art, and it is with regret that the illustration must be limited to one, Romulus and Remus.

A decoy maker at fourteen and later a bird painter, John Templeman Coolidge of Milton began carving water birds a few years ago in about forty different types of grouping. Among these is an extraordinary arrangement of Asiatic white crane. The birds are in a composition of driftwood branches and hand-carved flowers which lend an oriental quality particularly appropriate to the subject. A pair of Canadian geese, mounted on driftwood slabs, is beautiful in both execution and composition. Mr. Coolidge is generous with his method of work, carrying his experiences to other craftsmen and often writing, as in a recent number of *Craft Horizons,* a description of his methods and materials.

Another whittler of Milton is Dr. Janice Rofuse. Her objects cover a wide range: Madonnas, elephants of teakwood, ship models, birds, dogs, and deer, but her favorite subject is horses. She has whittled from pine a fine pair, a Percheron waxed in natural color, and a colt. An exceptional whittling is an Arctic tern alighting.

Russ P. Burr of Hingham whittles birds on the wing, for which he thinks the demand is greater. He first made a small grouse just for want of something to do; a friend liked it and others requested replicas. From this accidental beginning in 1937 he has now come to devote all his time to carving birds. "Whittling, however," writes Mr. Burr, "was not new to me. I had always made my own shore birds and duck decoys since I was a kid with an air rifle." Like some other New England carvers, Mr. Burr is very particular about how he mounts his carvings, and derives about as much fun from hunting appropriate pieces of wood as from hunting grouse. Nor is this as easy as it seems. One good mount to a mile of tramping is a fair average. "You can go on a man's land with fishpole or gun and no one pays much attention but try it with bag and saw and everybody's head is up wanting to know what is going on. If you explain that you want little pieces of wood to mount little birds on, they look at you as though you're crazy. So it's a case of keeping out of sight, which gives the added excitement of feeling you are being hunted as well as hunting yourself."

Miss Cornelia van Geuns born in Delft, The Netherlands, spent much of her childhood in Java, and later lived in European countries. She finally became an American citizen and is now carrying out a desire to promote folk arts in her adopted city of Boston. "The urge and ability to make use of what is available at the stretch of the arm to meet our need for comfort and beauty underlies all folk arts, and should be, I believe, at the foundation of all art." She is teaching several handicrafts for the Cambridge Community Center. Her woodwork and carving, which brings her into this chapter, is well represented by a four-foot Flop-to-the-Wall table, carved, painted and decorated with the symbolical designs of a Frisian legend, a type of table made only in Friesland.

Eric F. Olson, Jr., of Worcester has been working for years on a circus patterned mainly after Ringling Brothers and Barnum & Bailey's, which he has visited and studied many times. Olson's is probably the largest miniature circus in New England; the big tent is approximately twenty-two by forty-two feet, and the total weight of the entire circus is about one ton. Included are all the facilities for moving the circus and setting it up. There are ninety-five horses besides all the other animals in the menagerie. The small shaping machines, which he used to rough out his work, are mounted on one movable stage, but the elaborate carvings of animals and of decorations on cages and parade wagons he does entirely by hand. Mr. Olson never carved wood until the needs of his circus called for it, but he has acquired great skill and unusual artistry.

Connecticut. Another circus builder is William Brinley of Wallingford. As a boy he spent nine years in making a miniature five-ring circus, which has been often displayed in New England, and he is still adding to it. Complete in every detail, it has given many people much pleasure. While in service during the recent war he looked forward to enlarging and improving his circus, which since his return he has been able to do. He has made not only the tents, performers, and animals, but all the equipment for putting on a full circus parade and a show under the big top. Many of the figures have been mechanized so that they parade and perform. In addition he has built cook-wagons, transportation facilities, tools and machines for moving the show and setting it up again.

Rhode Island. Gino Conti of the St. Luke's Art Guild, Providence, is a carver who sees in the tree trunk of the oak or maple limb the final image which he wishes to record. A characteristic example of Mr. Conti's work shown at the Worcester Exhibition was a section of the trunk of a small tree, split, or rather sawed, in the middle and carved on the inside of both halves. The two sections were again joined with concealed hinges so that when opened the carvings are revealed, but when closed only the outside or the natural trunk of the tree is to be seen, a remarkable blending of the work of nature and the art of man.

Gustav Hellstrom of Providence is fond of carving Viking subjects. He does them in solid pieces of wood whenever possible, applying his carefully worked-out design in lightly restrained carved surfaces. He enjoys working in very hard woods, and the nearer he can complete his idea in block or solid form with a minimum of decoration, the better it suits his feeling.

At North Scituate Allen J. King and his son, James A., work together in the carving of birds and small animals. Their miniature subjects, particularly those of pairs and small families of birds, are technically and artistically among the finest things in small wood sculpture ever done of American birds. The father, a naturalist, has long been a careful observer of bird life in his home and neighboring communities. His groups of mallard ducks with their young, quail families, woodcocks, and other favorite game birds beautifully arranged, carved, and painted, would attract attention in any exhibition of fine wood sculpture; the son's carvings of dogs and other animals take equally high rank.

When the present fish and game warden of Rhode Island, Harold N. Gibbs of Barrington, was growing up he whittled, as most boys do, just to be whittling. A favorite aunt insisted that he make something of his efforts, so he began by carving decoys for himself and some of his neighbors. Later, when he made some miniature ducks as playthings for his little girl, he discovered that the children did not play with them but were carefully keeping them. When adults began to show interest in them Mr. Gibbs undertook in his spare time to whittle the birds of Rhode Island, and now each piece is eagerly awaited.

There is a salt marsh nearby, which was a cedar grove three or four hundred years ago, and cuttings from these old trees make ideal mounts for Mr. Gibbs' birds. Their legs are strengthened with thoroughly seasoned birch saplings and the feet are molded from plastic wood. His realistic painting of the feathers adds to the charm of his birds.

CARVERS FROM SEVERAL STATES

In addition to those already described there are a number of carvers throughout New England who deserve fuller treatment than can be given. In Maine John J. Hern of Camden, a pupil of Kirchmayer, does ornamental carving and lettering; Lawrence W. Carver of Lincolnville has a lobster pond and has decorated his dining room and the outside of the building with carvings of fish and birds; Charles Garcelon, Jr., of North Lovell makes furniture and carves it beautifully for home and to order; Wendell E. Hall, a farmer near Newcastle, whittles replicas of his farm animals. John L. Hawks of Falmouth Foreside excels in fish carving; sometimes a salmon carved in wood is covered with a carefully removed salmon skin. Miss Margaret L. Vincent of Norway, well known for her pottery, has carved in relief a three by four-foot decoration for the local post office; examples of her woodcarving are also on display in the War Department building in Washington. Dr. Freeman Brown of Rockland carves fish, boats, and other native subjects as a hobby for his office and home; a prized piece is a miniature replica of a "Johnny Boat" once used to bring cordwood from Nova Scotia. Robert Morse of Southwest Harbor, a painter and whittler, is indebted to handicrafts as therapy; while suffering from a serious form of arthritis he did one of his best carvings, a set of chessmen from native wood. B. M. Thornburg, a whittler at Wiscasset, carved boxes which were shown in the public library.

In New Hampshire Edwin H. Richardson of Concord has carved, to the delight of children, carnival scenes with revolving ferris wheels and dolls for passengers; Don Lenox of Whitefield has whittled New England birds; Francis Farrer of Chester carves small animals and human figures; a former blacksmith, William Morrison of Lower Waterford, has carved horses and made a model of an old country blacksmith shop. Clinton Cheney of Manchester, a master craftsman and teacher at the Manchester Institute of Arts and Sciences, has produced several extraordinary carved chests. Miss Nell G. Lamson of Bristol has carved for the League of New Hampshire Arts and Crafts a seasonal panel entitled Sugar Time in New England, and others depicting the seasons, one winter scene with a covered bridge. Nathaniel Garland of Windham took up woodcarving in his seventy-eighth year after losing his poultry business by fire. At grange fairs and other gatherings in his area he exhibits his whittlings of great variety, including a long linked chain cut from one piece of wood.

In Massachusetts Ernest Hermann of Boston became an expert whittler of birds and animals after his retirement from the Sargent School of Physical Education. Carl F. Turner of Lowell, a newspaper man, carves animals in his spare time. Lovell P. Pearson of South Deerfield makes hollowed-out birds with a joint construction which causes their bodies to swing like some of the carvings of Russian peasants. Roy W. Stanley, a banker of Boston, took up painting of birds and modeling in his spare time, and later turned to woodcarving. He thinks his first carving, a woodcock, is his best. He uses cedar, willow, and basswood. Samuel G. Colt of Pittsfield carves birds and fish, from one to three inches long, from wood and ivory, colors them with oil paint, usually making breastpins of them. The fish are chiefly salmon, trout, or bass.

In Vermont Lempi Miettinen of Bethel inherited her Finnish-born father's talent for whittling, including beautiful spoons, forks, and other home utensils and small original figures. W. S. Dodd of the Old Mill and Chair Shop, South Newbury, carved many fine pieces of furniture which Mrs. Dodd often designed. They and their talented son David of Springfield, a puppeteer, worked together at their home and studio, The Twinflower, named for the lovely little plant, said to have been the favorite flower of Linnaeus, which with rhodora grows in that locality. Frank Hackett of Tunbridge neighborhood lost his right hand at fifteen but learned to whittle with his left. His necklaces with pendant of acorn are charming, but most Vermonters know better his whittling of a complete up-and-down sawmill model shown annually at the Tunbridge World's Fair.

In Connecticut we record briefly two additional carvers: Clark Voorhees of Hamburg, who is also a potter of unusual ability; and the Reverend H. W. Perkins of North Woodbury, whose carving shows good craftsmanship.

In Rhode Island should be noted the carvings of Otto Carlburg of Providence, a native of Sweden now over eighty years old, who delights in whittling and painting small New England birds.

CHAPTER 11

DECORATIVE NEEDLEWORK:
EMBROIDERY, QUILTMAKING

NEEDLEWORK," said Walter Crane, "is the most domestic, the most delicate, and the most beautiful of all the handicrafts." It was in an effort to give needlework its rightful and dignified place in the realm of the arts that Walter Crane, William Morris, and their associates stressed its importance in the arts and crafts movement of England.

The field of needlework in New England, as elsewhere in the United States, is so vast and so varied that only a small segment of it can be included in a single chapter. Therefore only two of the great branches of decorative needlework have been somewhat arbitrarily chosen: embroidery and quiltmaking.

Embroidery is the decorating of a material by working patterns in thread or yarn onto a carefully selected base. As to quiltmaking, this term has been intentionally used in the present chapter because it is both more exact and more inclusive than the word "quilting," which technically is the process of fastening layers of cloth together by stitching—originally for purposes of warmth and economy. Quiltmaking is one of the greatest folk arts in America, a handicraft practiced for the longest continuous period of any of our highly decorative domestic arts. In some parts of our country it is still the most widely practiced of the home arts, its main rival in recent years being the hooking of rugs.

We have spoken of the emphasis on needlework in the English arts and crafts movement, which extended its influence to America near the opening of the present century, with special effect upon the New England states. A much earlier influence, however, stamped the English stitchery tradition upon New England—the influence which came with the pioneer women, who brought with them needle and thread, and also a few fine materials to meet the wear and tear of life in the New World, and to work into objects of beauty that would brighten their homely surroundings; among the latter, for instance, are the samplers of early days.

It will help us to realize the great part which the sewing needle played in the economy of those first years if we recall two facts: first, that such a thing as a sewing machine had not yet been conceived, much less invented; and second, that little or no spinning and weaving of cloth for wearing apparel or bedcovering was yet being done in the colony. Therefore it was a period when making every garment last its longest depended upon the skill of the Pilgrims with that tiny but powerful tool for thumb and fingers, the sewing needle. The need for this is plainly set forth in some of the New England poetry of that time. One verse of the *Forefathers' Song,* written probably about 1630, ten years after the landing at Plymouth, reads:

> And now our garments begin to grow thin,
> And wool is much wanted to card and to spin,
> If we can get a garment to cover without,
> Our other in-garments are clout upon clout.
> Our clothes we brought with us are apt to be torn,
> They need to be clouted soon after they're worn,
> But clouting our garments they hinder us nothing;
> Clouts double are warmer than single whole clothing.[1]

It must indeed have been an era of much patching and darning, for all the conditions were present for rents, tears, and break-throughs. It is doubtful if any examples of mending, especially that branch, darning, which often produced beautiful results, have remained from the earliest days, but skill and artistry in this type of needlework are still manifested by many a New England woman. The most interesting example of modern darning anywhere that the writer can recall is a child's dress from Mexico containing eighty-four darns. Darning, it would seem, is an art reserved for the poor and the particular.

SAMPLERS—TRADITIONAL AND CONTEMPORARY

The earliest examples of decorative needlework in New England were probably samplers. We are fortunate to have in Pilgrim Hall, Plymouth, a sturdy yet beautiful sampler, dated about 1640, made by Loara, daughter of Miles Standish. Although more than three centuries old, it is in a fair state of preservation. The legend reads as follows:

> Loara Standish is my name
> Lord guide my hart that
> I may do thy will
> Also fill my hands with such

[1] Stearns, Martha G., *Homespun and Blue.* New York, Charles Scribner's Sons, 1940, p. 8.

convenient skill
As may conduce to virtue
devoid of shame
And I will give glory to
thy name.

Loara's sampler is more than a bit of needlework; it is a symbol of those domestic arts of our earliest forebears—arts to which we owe so much and of which we know so little. Samplers are one of the oldest and perhaps to many of us the most precious form of hand stitchery ever done in our country, furnishing as they often do abundant and vital details of contemporary life, skills, and aspirations, and reflecting above all the character and spirit of the worker. Some day an inquiring New England mind will put together from the samplers, in which New England is so rich, much of the story of the people of this region, for these unique examples of stitchery provide both text and illustration. Certainly in no other part of America, and perhaps in no part of the English-speaking world, have so much human history and personal sentiment been recorded in samplers as in the New England states. Georgiana Brown Harbeson, in her beautiful and comprehensive book, *American Needlework*, states that "In America alone there are more than twenty-five hundred recorded examples of this type of needlework." She does not say so, but it is probably true that a large percentage of these samplers is in New England.

A great many of the New England samplers were dated. The Miles and Abigail Fletwood sampler—a beautiful piece of needlework viewed from either side—is dated 1654 and contains the cryptic observation based, we may suppose, upon the sad experience of Miles Fletwood: "In prosperity friends will be plenty; but in adversity not one in twenty."

We know that the art of sampler stitchery was well advanced in the seventeenth century in New England, influenced mainly by English tradition. Each one of the New England states has preserved examples worked in the 1700's and also in the 1800's; a few have been made from 1900 to the present. But the age of the sampler, especially as a pastime and duty for the child, is passing, and those who still follow closely the traditional forms are but few.

Among needleworkers who still follow the unmistakable sampler tradition, using the characteristic sampler cross-stitch and confining themselves to approximately the sampler dimensions, is Mrs. Kendall Dunbar of Damariscotta, Maine, who has made many samplers, some traditional, some original in design, and has also done a great variety of other needlework. Mrs. Marian Hubbard of Bangor has designed and worked some fine contemporary samplers. She also does excellent pieces in cross-stitch and other forms of embroidery applied to handbags.

In Massachusetts Mrs. Elizabeth Graves of Northampton made a sampler, Mexican in subject, which was an attractive exhibit in the Northampton Handicraft Fair in 1943. Her principal interest is in crocheting, but she is a versatile worker who has made dolls and pottery. She is a member of the Hampshire Hills Handicraft Association, through which her work is sold.

Mrs. Edna S. Perk of Hillsboro, New Hampshire, a native of Holland but now an American citizen, has created through her remarkable artistry and industry the largest number of contemporary samplers which the writer knows of in New England. Her work excels in design, which is always attractive and lively, and often original, in color harmony and in fine stitchery. She is especially sensitive to the "feel" of textures. Mrs. Perk has exhibited widely and filled commissions throughout the country. Her samplers are often shown at exhibits of the Hampshire Hills Association and in Boston.

In Connecticut Mrs. Isabelle Wright of Willimantic has made several samplers in cross-stitch, entitled Old-Fashioned Mottoes, which have a charming flavor of the past in sentiment and appearance. She has also made a sampler of her own home in apple-blossom time, beneath which is a quotation from *Homesick in Heaven* by Oliver Wendell Holmes:

> Where we love is home
> Home that our feet
> May leave but not
>   our hearts. . . .
> The chain may lengthen
> But it never parts

Some of Mrs. Wright's samplers were reproduced in the *Woman's Home Companion* for November, 1930, and November, 1931.

PICTURE EMBROIDERIES

One of the most artistic and skillfully executed needlework pictures done in recent years in New England was designed and carried out by Mrs. George Peirce of Boscawen, New Hampshire. The subject is a pictorial map of Old Boscawen, her home village, on King's Highway. The map is worked on linen in fine colors representing the Highway and the town, with its homes, its church, academy, parsonage, blacksmith shop, and other buildings, all shown in charming miniature and beautifully stitched. The country roads are lined with trees, the Merrimac River and the mountain are shown in pleasant color and faultless technique. Mrs. Peirce is a member of the Saffron and Indigo Society, to be described presently.

Mrs. Grace W. Hill of Concord, New Hampshire, is another maker of needlework pictures, among which two representations of her own town are outstanding. One shows the state capitol and grounds at Concord; the other, which required a great amount of research, is a pictorial history of the industrial life and development of that city with symbols of industries for which Concord has been noted since pioneer days— among them an anvil, a boot, a beaver hat, a Concord stagecoach, a bible to represent the printing industry. Mrs. Hill is one of the earliest members of the League of New Hampshire Arts and Crafts and also of the Saffron and Indigo Society.

Another maker of picture embroideries in New Hampshire is Mrs. R. Gilman Lunt of Meredith, one of the most artistic needleworkers of New England. An embroidered picture map made by her recently records events and associations connected with the boyhood of her son. It is an original design, worked in beautiful colors on linen and portrays the familiar places of the home town and countryside. At the Worcester Exhibition Mrs. Lunt displayed an adaptation of sampler strips which she had worked up from examples of old Chinese embroidery in five shades of blue. These showed some of the characteristic border designs which deeply influenced our New England needleworkers in colonial times. Illustrated in this book are Mrs. Lunt's fascinating cloth animals made from selected prints, which were shown at a Craftsman's Fair of the New Hampshire League. She was president of the Saffron and Indigo Society at the time of this writing.

In Massachusetts Mrs. Benjamin G. Higgins of Chesterfield has exhibited at the Northampton Handicraft Fair several examples of picture embroidery done in simple outline, not unlike drawing, very interesting in design and color. It seemed hardly possible to achieve in needlework the hundreds of curves so smoothly executed as were employed in a bible scene, in which the heads and faces of the populace were outlined.

Mrs. Rita H. Pettengill of Georgetown, Essex County, Massachusetts, who sometimes lectures and calls her talk The Needle and the Eye, has made several beautiful pieces of needlework as part of the decorative plan for her home. This work also includes rugs and hooked wall hangings, tapestries, wall coverings in needlepoint, and even stained glass window panels. One of the needlepoint decorations illustrates Chaucer's Prologue to the *Canterbury Tales*. Mrs. Pettengill has served at different times as president of the Arts and Crafts Societies of Reading, Melrose, and Haverhill.

Mrs. Marian Stoll of Waterbury, Connecticut, has developed a type of embroidery properly described as painting in wool. Her needlework creations are usually on linen, of which not a thread of the base shows in the finished work. The designs are all original and their maker developed her own technique of getting brush stroke effects with needle and woolen yarn. Sometimes as many as fifty needles strung with different wools are in use at once. Mrs. Stoll was born in New England but lived and studied abroad, where her invention of picture embroideries was made. "My work," she says, "was conceived in Vienna, born in Oxford, and educated in Paris." Her paintings in wool have been exhibited in Edinburgh, London, Antwerp, and Paris.

The needlework by Mrs. Margareta Ohberg of Colchester, Connecticut, done in the Swedish tradition, is outstanding. She is one of those finished craftsmen who control their medium from beginning to end; she dyes her colors "in the wool" with vegetable dyes, which she herself makes, and also spins the yarn. She is both a needleworker and a tapestry weaver, and often lectures on these subjects to interested groups.

MEN WHO EMBROIDER

Frederick S. Youngs of Bangor is the treasurer of the University of Maine in nearby Orono; he does cross-stitch and intricate embroideries of high quality and in great volume, some of which decorate his home. Mr. Youngs has made original designs but prefers to execute good designs by others. Although he works very rapidly, needlework, he says, is a genuine relaxation to him.

Alexander Crane, formerly of Cheshire, Connecticut, but now of Barnstable, Massachusetts, and referred to also in other chapters, is mentioned here because of his achievements in embroidery. Black sheep from his own flock on No Mans Land sometimes provide the natural black yarn for his embroidery; combining it with white he produces some of his color effects. Mr. Crane, who has executed many of his own designs in embroidery, has also created designs for woodwork, metalwork, and pottery.

INFLUENCES IN MASSACHUSETTS AND NEW HAMPSHIRE

In Massachusetts and in New Hampshire needlework has been practiced under forms of leadership which has established worthy traditions and exerted strong influence. In New Hampshire the development of handicrafts generally in recent years has been, first, under private and cooperative leadership, then, merged into state participation in the League of New Hampshire Arts and Crafts, to which Chapter 18 of this book is devoted. Later in the present chapter an example of organized group work in New Hampshire will be described.

The Deerfield Society of Blue and White Needlework deserves recording here as the earliest and by far the most important needlecraft development related to the present handicraft movement. It took the definite form of a revival, flourished for nearly thirty years, until 1925, and exerted its influence upon needleworkers throughout the United States.

Deerfield Society of Blue and White Needlework

This important undertaking grew out of the association in Deerfield in 1896 of two gifted women, Miss Margaret C. Whiting and Miss Ellen Miller, both painters, who had studied with Robert C. Minor in his camp in Keene Valley and had known there other artists of the Adirondack School; they were drawn to the beautiful old village of Deerfield and settled there in a congenial community.

The trained and sympathetic eyes of these young women soon recognized the beauty and historic interest of old examples of needlecraft treasured among Connecticut Valley families, specimens of which were in Deerfield Memorial Hall. A portfolio of designs gathered from old embroideries on bedspreads, bed curtains, and petticoat borders was the starting point for this revival of a lovely art, one which drew the women of the community together under scholarly and vigorous leadership. Their special gift was perhaps their excellent taste, which led them to discard the ornate and sophisticated in favor of purity and boldness of line and balance in proportions and arrangement. They set themselves to develop new and simplified patterns based upon the best of the old designs, and patiently taught the village women to bring their needlework to perfection in executing the curtains, bedspreads, dresses, table linen, and so forth, which the Deerfield Society of Blue and White Needlework began to make. Upon each piece the Society put its own insignia—a "D" in the center of a spinning wheel. This protective emblem is treasured by collectors to this day.

In carrying out the designs linen thread imported from Scotland was substituted for the earlier wool. Much of the old crewelwork had been destroyed by moths. The use of linen thread is fully as authentic as that of wool, but in the old days wool was more available, easier to use, and with it, as Miss Whiting herself explained, "bad workmanship could more easily be disguised." The foundation material used was linen, much of it hand woven in Russia, which Miss Whiting considered "the most distinguished fabric the loom has ever produced."

One of the most admirable features of the revival was the fidelity with which the lovely colors of the eighteenth century originals were reproduced. To acquire the blended and subtle shadings of Bengal indigo dye, the "blue tub," from deepest blue to palest azure, became an early task of Miss Whiting. Otherwise the study and use of dyes devolved upon Miss Miller. All the operations called not only for great patience and for aesthetic appreciation of color, but for technical knowledge of the chemistry involved, the effect of weather conditions upon dyes, and other factors that were almost unpredictable until checked by long and careful experiments. The colors used with characteristic restraint and discretion by the Deerfield needleworkers have survived laundering and hard use over many years.

During World War I, when materials were hard to get and when the women were called upon for other duties, the output of the Society diminished. The death of Miss Miller, its secretary, and Miss Whiting's own failing health and eyesight influenced the latter in 1925 to withdraw the sign of the Spinning Wheel. Miss Whiting had said of the Society that "it was one of the earliest associated groups of craft workers brought together in a single enterprise in our country. Though entirely under the control of the two heads, the number of needlewomen engaged in the work varied from a half dozen to thirty, according to circumstances" and always on a part-time basis.

Mrs. Martha G. Stearns of Hancock, New Hampshire, author of the delightful book on New England needlework called *Homespun and Blue*, from which we have already quoted, and founder of the Saffron and Indigo Society, lived as a child not far from Deerfield. She has given a vivid description of the early exhibitions and sales inaugurated by the Society of Blue and White Needlework when "throngs of tourists and customers" arrived every summer at the appointed time.

I remember seeing four women sitting in hollow-square formation under the trees on a lawn in the hot summer afternoon, each at work on a corner of a large linen bedcover in blue and white needlework. They must have reached a high degree of skill to be able to merge their work on one piece so that no variation from the different hands would be noticed in the finished production.

Each house had a sign to indicate the nature of the work carried on within. There was the pine-needle basket house, and another where beautifully patterned raffia baskets were made; the house where the netting worker could spread out her lacy "canopy-tops" for beds, with their thousands of knots and deep fringe; the rug maker, and the worker who drew knotted patterns into white linen, and the Miss Allens who took wonderful photographs. But our favorite, the magnet among them all, was the large square house before which the sign of the Spinning Wheel hung, denoting the headquarters of the Blue and White Society. Brought up by my mother to love the needle and all its works, I was spellbound by the graceful designs and the soft colors with their little variations in tint between green and blue, and the general air of artistic competence in a kind of work so utterly different from that practiced by the ordinary maker of "fancy-work" of those years. . . .

The prices were high, but it was explained by the directors that every piece was as perfect as possible, and although such work was a luxury, full value was given. An embroiderer of the Society in its early days remembers how every stitch on a large coverlet so carefully embroidered was laboriously taken out after the discovery had been made that the color of the thread was not absolutely fast. Better that weary job beforehand, she said, than to have the imperfection discovered after the first washing and the whole piece ruined. This was the spirit which animated the Deerfield Industries.

The influence of the Society is still to be traced in other groups, as for instance the Saffron and Indigo Society, the work of whose members is reminiscent of Deerfield achievements. Individual workers also, some from the original group, are carrying on the tradition. Mrs. Gertrude C. Smith of Deerfield, to whom reference has been made as a netter in Chapter 6, continues to keep alive the delicate arts of candlewicking and netting. It is hoped, because of her unusual knowledge of the work done under the leadership of Miss Whiting and Miss Miller, and her long association especially with the former, that she will prepare some written account of them and their group.

Worcester Folk Stitchery

An associated group of Massachusetts women, which is very active today, is the Worcester Folk Stitchery, numbering variously between twenty-five and forty-five members. It was organized in 1919 by Mrs. May Harrington Gray. Max W. Sullivan, director of the Exhibition of Contemporary New England Handicrafts held in Worcester, and now president of the Rhode Island School of Design, prepared a sketch of this stitchery group upon which the writer has drawn. The idea was born, he says, with a handsome lace-edged handkerchief shown at a fair in the Syrian section of Worcester.

This group admired the exquisite beauty of the piece, realizing that this ancient art of needlecraft was in acute danger of being engulfed and eventually lost by the rush and progress of the New World. Mrs. Gray decided to organize a group called the Worcester Folk Stitchery. Her purpose was twofold: one, to revive the art of needlecraft done mainly by the foreign-born women in Worcester; and two, to encourage these people who needed it most in their effort to help themselves and their families.

The organization, established first in the Syrian section, then in Neighborly House under the auspices of the Civic League, expanded to receive the Italian population; later the Syrian, Assyrian, Swedish, and Armenian groups were included and finally native-born American women as well. The Stitchery now has fourteen retail outlets in different parts of the country. "Our purpose," states the organization, "is the sale of Worcester Folk Stitchery. This beautiful work is done by the foreign-born women in Worcester. We help them to help themselves. Will you help us?"

When a new member needs training and wishes to learn new stitches, she receives such training free of charge. Only the most nearly perfect work is acceptable for sale. In 1942 the Society of Arts and Crafts of Boston conferred on the Worcester Folk Stitchery the master craftsman award, given only to those who have shown superior ability both in design and technique over a period of time. Planning and designing of the needlework is done by Miss Lucia Soule and Mrs. Gray without cost to the workers.

Several members of Worcester Folk Stitchery are among the lace-makers of New England and are recorded in Chapter 6.

Saffron and Indigo Society of New Hampshire

This Society, an offshoot of the League of New Hampshire Arts and Crafts, was organized by Mrs. Martha G. Stearns. Soon after the League was launched it was observed that there were many skillful needleworkers in the state who could not find a market for their work, and it was Mrs. Stearns' opinion that the difficulty lay chiefly in the character of the designs used. She set about helping the needleworkers to seek, appreciate, and adapt to their needs the good designs often to be found on early New England household articles of glass, pottery, china, linen, in old embroidery, or other handwork, and even on tombstones. The Saffron and Indigo Society's continuing purpose is "to encourage needlework and to stimulate native designs." Its name was suggested by the lining of an old-time quilt in Mrs. Stearns' collection. Anyone is eligible for membership; there are no dues. The only requirement is a desire to learn. The meetings are held now in one part of the state, now in another, and sometimes last two days. Problems of needle-workers are discussed and progress is made in design, workmanship, and marketing techniques.

EMBROIDERERS FROM SEVERAL STATES

Miss Emma E. Cole of Hampden Highlands, not far from Bangor, Maine, exhibited thirteen pieces of her needlework in the National Needlework Bureau Exhibition held in New York some time ago. She is a rapid worker, executing many pieces in petit point and a variety of embroidery stitches. She also crochets extensively. Her work is usually original in design. Her mother, also a craftswoman, carves with a jackknife.

Mrs. Rosalia Namaka, who lives near Amherst, Massachusetts, does beautiful embroidery after the traditions of her native Ukraine. At the Northampton Handicraft Fair she showed a shirt and blouse which she had done for a member of her family. The shirt, which was borrowed for the Worcester Exhibition, was strikingly embroidered in black and red thread on front panel, collar, and cuffs. The closely stitched pattern of fine workmanship covered all the surface in line with the old Ukrainian custom.

Mrs. G. Wolf of Cummington, Massachusetts, was also an exhibitor at the Northampton Fair and showed some excellent embroidered work, particularly on lamp shades in all-over designs. Mrs. Wolf was one of a group of refugees engaged in handicraft work in the Sangree Workshop in Cummington, part of the activities of the Cummington Refugee Hostel.

There are several excellent needleworkers in the Petersham Handicrafts group in Massachusetts. At the Worcester Exhibition three of these were represented: Mrs. C. Frederick Bryant showed an Assisi linen runner with a red and blue border; Mrs. Eleanor Lamb, a well-executed Assisi runner with a green border; and Mrs. Lester B. Stone, a square runner with Italian hemstitching.

Among producers of individual pieces of needlework Miss Julia R. Kellogg of Benson, Vermont, is known especially for her handbags decorated with Marash embroidery. The word "Marash" comes from a town so named in old Armenia noted for its rugs and embroideries. Most of the needlework is done on a dark foundation which brings out the decorative colors, usually restrained, but there are occasional brilliant combinations which produce charming effects. Miss Kellogg also makes purses in Barjello embroidery.

Miss Petronilla Asselin of St. Johnsbury, Vermont, is a sensitive craftsman in needlework and also a good whittler. As a designer she had charge in her community during the depression of the sewing classes and embroidery workers, under the Vermont Work Projects Administration. Miss Asselin is of French parentage and seems to have retained the artistry and skill of the French needlewomen.

Mrs. George D. Hersey of Morrisville, Lamoille County, Vermont, is a craftsman of versatility. She is a good designer with an unusual sense of color. Needlework seems to be her favorite medium, although she has done excellent hooked rugs. She designed and executed a large piece of crewelwork, perhaps five by eight or nine feet, which is an outstanding example of this type of contemporary needlework. Mrs. Hersey belongs to a talented family. Her sister, Mrs. Ruth Mould, is an artist mentioned in Chapter 8; and her uncle, Porter C. Greene, is a genius at designing machines, one of which cleverly turns out heads for violins. Mr. Greene also makes grandfather clock cases and does other fine cabinetwork.

Mrs. Anna J. Pettersen of Broad Brook, Connecticut, is a clever needleworker and an excellent designer. Mrs. Pettersen uses floral and plant designs almost entirely, and her appliquéd patterns on felt with pleasant color combinations are unusually attractive. She was responsible for designs for needlework and textiles in Connecticut WPA projects.

One of the contributions to modern needlework in New England deserving special note in this record is that made during the depression by WPA workers under the direction of Miss Alice Turnbull, who supervised weaving and needlecraft. This work, often taking the form of spirited wall decorations, emphasized stitchery done usually in gay colors and original designs, many of these being humorous in character. Delightful results were obtained by using the skill in stitchery of many foreign-born women, who brought to their craft Old World techniques and traditions, lending it vitality and charm.

QUILTMAKING

For many years the Eastern States Exposition at Springfield, Massachusetts, has held a national annual contest and exhibition of quilts, possibly the most extensive in the country. Between five and six hundred accepted entries come from nearly every state in the Union, many from New England, to whose women a reasonable number of awards have been given. Thousands of New Englanders have thus had an opportunity to see what is going on in quiltmaking in this country.

The basic process of quiltmaking is the putting together of two or more layers of cloth, usually with padding between, the layers being then stitched together by the process known as "quilting." All quilted bed covers are made in this way but within this classification there are three general types.

1. The "pieced quilt" in which the top cover or layer is made up of pieces of cloth sewed together in regular or haphazard design. These are known as patchwork quilts. The haphazard type or "crazy quilt" is always colorful and may be charming if its maker exercises ingenuity and taste. It is sometimes of rich materials put together with embroidery stitches.

2. The "appliquéd quilt" has a top layer made of a single piece of cloth upon which a laid-on pattern of cut-out cloth is sewed with simple stitchery or sometimes with elaborate embroidery as a further embellishment.

3. The "quilted counterpane" is usually of one color, although the top layer may be figured. The characteristic decoration, however, is achieved by the quilting process itself, in either a simple or a complicated pattern; it thus acquires decorative qualities of its own through the use of a conscious design in the stitchery. Padding may be used to give different levels to the quilted surface.

Fine quilting is one of the most beautiful and restrained forms of textile decoration. The technique dates back to ancient times when layers of stitched or quilted cloth were used for clothing, for protection under heavy armor, and for other purposes besides bed coverings. Although quilting is now used extensively in clothing, upholstering, and so forth, it is the decorated bed quilt to which craftsmen of the United States have made an outstanding contribution. Fine quilting applied to bed quilts was one of the skills brought to America by the Pilgrim women, at which time emphasis was placed upon the quality of the quilting itself, which often formed the only decoration on the bed cover. This very restrained form of embellishment has long characterized the quiltmaking of old England, and it also marked the work of the early American needlewomen in New England and in other states wherever English people settled.

Much early quilting and stitchery done in America was like that of the mother country, but American women were soon to make a definite departure from traditional techniques. The women of the New World made the quilt a medium for a variety of patterns and kinds of ornament heretofore undreamed of. In adapting appliqué and patchwork to quiltmaking they probably developed more patterns, that is, more designs that can be repeated, than have all other countries combined.

Many hundreds of designs have been worked out. With a minimum sense of limitations, our women have used every idea that seemed to them worthy and have developed on this continent one of the most picturesque folk arts to be found anywhere in the world.

A majority of modern quilts in New England, as throughout the country, are of the appliquéd variety, although many are pieced. Embroidery, as we have indicated, may be added to either type. Various techniques may be used to achieve a desired result: in an autographed quilt signatures are sometimes outlined in thread, or written with a fairly permanent ink; a story quilt may have photographic transfers on some of the pieces or patches; sometimes drawing or painting is applied; but it is when the decorations are achieved entirely with needlework that the quilt possesses its greatest charm and interest. In a recent exhibition of the Hampshire Hills Handicraft Association held in a school gymnasium, fifty or more needlework quilts were hung on a high line like great flags or banners, rich in color and pattern. They circled the large gymnasium completely and shut off the structural steel caverns and brought unity, warmth, and color to the entire exhibition.

At the Tunbridge World's Fair in 1946, Mrs. Leon Grant of Chelsea, Vermont, showed for the first time her Remembrance Quilt, containing 172 decorated patches, which she had been working on for eight years. On each alternate patch she had embroidered a rural scene, a favorite bouquet, a neighborhood character, a country house or barn, a span of horses, or something else of significance in the life of her family.

Shown among the illustrations is a quilt of local historical significance, done by Mrs. Will Field of Five Islands, Maine, in which she pictures all the principal buildings of the little village in which she reared her family. On Matinicus Island Miss Henrietta H. Ames has preserved a pieced Memory Quilt which she began over eighty years ago and completed when she was twelve. It contains a scrap of dress, apron, coat, or necktie of nearly every inhabitant of Matinicus at the time it was being made. Miss Ames also cherishes a china doll brought from the mainland by her father as a present on the night he carried the news of President Lincoln's assassination to the island.

Quilting bees are still carried on in Maine and Vermont, and probably in other New England states. A group of quilters of Marshfield, Vermont, have been meeting regularly once a week over the local undertaker's headquarters for many years and always have plenty of quilting to do. The members of the group are Mrs. Lon Carpenter, Mrs. Lillian Davis, Mrs. Ella Lilley, Mrs. Gertrude Mears, Mrs. Florence Morris, and Mrs. Flora Packer.

George French

65. GRANDFATHER AND GRANDSON WORK TOGETHER

BILLIE THOMPSON AND HIS GRANDFATHER, UNCLE HARRY WASS OF ADDISON, MAINE.
THE GRANDFATHER MAKES DUCK DECOYS; BILLIE IS MODELING A SEA GULL WITH THE
APPROVAL OF HIS PET MALLARD DUCK.

Doris Day, School Arts Magazine

66. A RUG-HOOKER OF VERMONT

"Aunt Essie" Davis of Johnson Makes Her Own Designs for Hooked Rugs. Her
Favorite Pattern Is Maple Leaves in Autumn.

Doris Day

67. AN EARLY NEW HAMPSHIRE WHITTLER

The First Whittler for the League of New Hampshire Arts and Crafts Was a Country Girl, Mary Whittier, Who Lives at Bow. Her First Creation for the League, a New England Farmer and His Wife, Is Still Popular.

Doris Day

68. BUILDING A SMALL BOAT MODEL

Captain Charlton Smith, Who Was Proprietor of the Home of the Brutal Beast at Marblehead, Massachusetts, Built Models and Full-sized Boats, Sailed the Main, and Wrote Sea Stories.

Doris Day

69. A FINNISH-BORN BASKETMAKER

Mrs. Anna Miettinen of Bethel, Vermont, Learned to Make Baskets, Shoes, and Other Useful Articles from Heavy Birch Bark in Finland. She Has Taught Her Children Many of the Home Arts.

Doris Day

70. AT WORK BETWEEN CUSTOMERS

IN HER SMALL CROSS-ROADS STORE AT WORCESTER, VERMONT, MRS. MARY MAXHAM,
AN ENTHUSIASTIC WEAVER, HAS A LOOM WHERE SHE WORKS WHENEVER TIME PERMITS.

W. G. Pollak, A.R.P.S.

71. A CRAFTSMAN IN WOOD AND TOYMAKER OF NANTUCKET

LINCOLN J. CEELY IS AN AMATEUR PAINTER AND A FINE CABINETMAKER, BUT TO THE
CHILDREN OF THE ISLAND HE IS "THE TOYMAKER." ON A SUMMER DAY SCORES OF MR.
CEELY'S WIND TOYS ARE TO BE SEEN IN ACTION ON THE FENCE SURROUNDING HIS
WORKSHOP.

William F. Winter, New York State Museum

72. SHAKER CRAFTSWOMAN

ELDRESS SADIE NEALE, A SKILLED SHAKER CRAFTSWOMAN WHO SPENT HER LAST DAYS
AT THE PITTSFIELD, MASSACHUSETTS, CENTER.

Ben Greenhaus

73. A PIONEER HAND WEAVER OF MAINE

MRS. FLORENCE IVES GOOKIN OF OGUNQUIT IS AN EXPERIENCED TEXTILE DESIGNER, HAVING STYLED MANY PATTERNS FOR MACHINE PRODUCTION, BUT HER GREATEST SATISFACTION COMES FROM THE WEBS WHICH SHE MAKES ON HER OWN HAND-SHUTTLE LOOMS.

Doris Day

Doris Day

Doris Day

George French

74. FOUR NEW ENGLAND CRAFTSMEN

A. H. Eaton of Collinsville, Connecticut, Repairing a Copper Weathervane. . . . Henry Anderson of New Sweden, Maine, Making Skis. . . . Mrs. Mary Curtis Cobb of Osterville, Massachusetts, Who Specializes in Miniature Ship Models. . . . Charles Clough of Bristol, New Hampshire, a Folk Whittler.

Doris Day

75. BIRDCARVERS OF RHODE ISLAND

Two of the Finest Birdcarvers and Plumage Painters in Our Country Are Allen J. King and His Son of North Scituate, Both Keen Observers of Bird and Animal Life. James King Specializes in Animals.

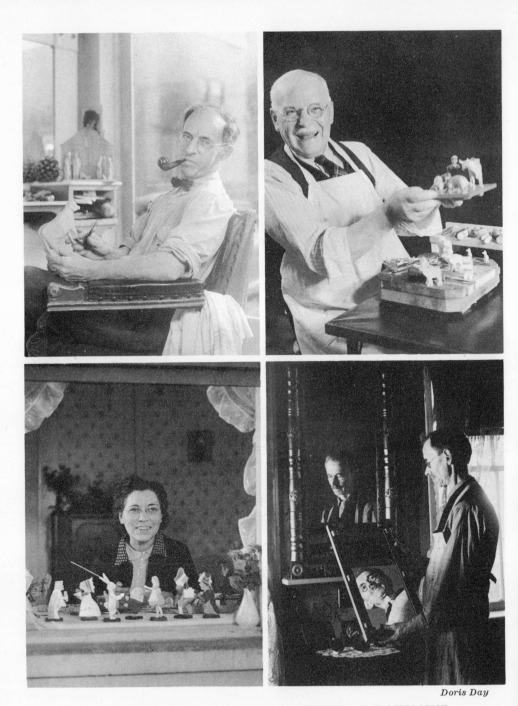

Doris Day

76. WOODWORKERS FROM NEW HAMPSHIRE AND VERMONT

N. F. DeGuise of Waterbury, Vermont, Whittles Between Haircuts. . . . Octave Dufresne of Concord, New Hampshire, Carves a Rural Scene. . . . Miss Ila E. Fifield of East Calais, Vermont, Creates Alice in Wonderland Characters. . . . Elmer W. Bartlett of Cornish, New Hampshire, Carves Mirror Frames and Makes Pictures in Tinfoil.

Doris Day

77. THE ARTS OF THE BOOK

Miss Elisabeth H. Webb of Mystic, Connecticut, Was a Talented Calligrapher,
Illuminator, and Bookbinder, Working in the Best Old World Traditions of Her
Chosen Crafts.

Dora Portraits

78. A WEE WEAVER ON THE CAPE

In New England Little Children Are Learning to Weave on Simple Looms. Here Alexandra Crane of Barnstable Is Weaving in Her Father's Shop, The Leading Wind, While He Operates a Large Loom in the Background.

Doris Day, School Arts Magazine

79. A NEW HAMPSHIRE CRAFTSMAN AT HOME

JOHN G. HERRICK OF HILLSBORO, ONE OF THE EARLIEST MEMBERS OF THE NEW HAMPSHIRE LEAGUE, WORKS WITH EQUAL PROFICIENCY IN METAL AND WOOD. THIS VIOLIN-CELLO IS ONE OF MANY INSTRUMENTS HE HAS MADE. AT EIGHTY HE BECAME A LAPIDARIST.

L. M. A. Roy

80. RUNNING CANDLES IN NEW HAMPSHIRE

L. M. A. Roy Has Photographed His Mother in Old-fashioned Dress Making Candles in the Old-time Way. They Live in the Famous Ocean-Born-Mary House, Not Far from the Village of Henniker.

One of the most charming quilts recalled from many seen in the New England states is a crib quilt made by Mrs. Dahlov Ipcar of Robinhood, Maine. For years she has been collecting attractive remnants of cloth, for animal figures especially, and these she uses in her homemade quilts and toys for her own children and those of other members of the family. On the crib quilt are appliquéd twelve animals, including a snake which any unprejudiced child would like. She has used native stitchery depicting plants, flowers, and fruits, which gives it added charm. Mrs. Ipcar is also a talented painter, but her fine feeling for color, form, and texture could hardly have a happier outlet than through the toys and quilts she makes.

CHAPTER 12

TOYS, DOLLS, AND MINIATURE OBJECTS

TOYS, dolls, and miniature objects are linked together in this chapter mainly because of their relation to children—children young and old. The invention and artistry involved in each of these separate subjects might fill a chapter or even a book; in one short chapter combining all of them the most that can be accomplished is to point out in introductory fashion something of the character of what is being done in New England in these crafts by referring to a few craftsmen and their work, selected almost at random from the contemporary scene. Accounts of some of the finest examples of miniature objects built to scale will be found in Chapter 15, especially ship models; therefore this particular branch of miniature craftsmanship is omitted here. For the serious student of these objects, approaches are possible through museums and collections, in which New England abounds.

TOYS MADE IN NEW ENGLAND

It seems appropriate to open the story of toys with an account of the Toy Division of the Work Projects Administration in Connecticut, the general headquarters of which were in Stamford. This project accomplished much more than its primary purpose of giving employment to a considerable number of persons in the designing, making, and circulating of toys throughout the state, particularly in libraries and other public institutions. The patterns set by the Toy Division in lending toys to children, just as the libraries had lent books for many years, worked out so successfully in Connecticut that the plan was copied in other parts of the country. Besides designing and making toys, this project included repairing and reconditioning old toys. It yielded a maximum of happy results for many of the children of Connecticut, and, of no less importance, probably no other single project in the region or in the whole United States brought more pleasure to the workers from day to day.

Although the center of the WPA toy project was in Stamford, other towns—New Haven, Norwich, Manchester, and Waterbury—came into the plan, each having a branch office, toy depot, workshop, or other connection with the central agency. Experiments following the pattern in Connecticut were later instituted in California, New Jersey, Louisiana, Illinois, and perhaps in other states.

We may note some of the types of persons who worked on these toy projects while the depression was at its height, and indicate some of the results of the work. A veteran of World War I who had been badly crippled found himself a victim of the unemployment crisis. He was first assigned to the sanitation department in Waterbury to work on sewer construction. Not being able to perform such heavy work satisfactorily he was about to be discharged when the workshop and toy project of WPA got under way. The story of this workman's plight reached Miss Eleanor B. Finch, state supervisor of crafts and director of the Toy Division, who was just then in need of assistants, and she offered to try him out at making toys. In this he proved to be an excellent worker, taking pride in his efforts and contributing to the quality of the toy output. He became a first-rate craftsman and a very loyal member of the project's staff. During World War II he was employed as a cabinetmaker in a defense plant.

A one-armed man found employment in the workshop where he could serve faithfully and effectively at a machine cutting blocks of wood for hand carving and for toy construction. He also devised special pieces of equipment for the workshop. An unusually heavy woman whose size would seem a handicap in a factory was skillful in cutting linoleum blocks. "It's nice on the nerves," she jovially remarked, "even though a little hard on the hands." A patient in an institution for mental cases found congenial employment with toys in the Stamford project, where he showed his special aptitude in joinery. Putting together the parts of small boxes brought him pleasure and a certain degree of adjustment.

Among the special toys identified with the Connecticut experiment was a Noah's Ark, worked out at the Manchester center, with all the paired animals made strictly in accordance with the story. Another was a remarkably long hobbyhorse which carried several children at one time made at the shop in Norwich. One of the favorite circulating toys was a small tool chest for woodworking and another for metal-work made especially for boys but lent occasionally to girls who like to work in these materials.

To emphasize good design, some well-established craftsmen of the community were engaged to prepare samples for the guidance of beginners working on toys. Mrs. Myra W. Rankin designed a dog with movable parts, a penguin, a duck, and a bear. These were characterized by the note of humor which marks, as we have said elsewhere, many of Mrs. Rankin's designs, and also those of Mrs. Marion R. Voorhees, whether of animals or of people. Mrs. Rankin's bear was almost completely round and still lifelike. Mrs. Voorhees designed a Billy Bull which the craftsmen liked to reproduce and which delighted children.

Whatever the personal needs that brought the toymakers to the project in Connecticut, they found their tasks interesting with glimpses of beauty and humor, and heartening experiences in human relations. The skills of many reached a good degree of proficiency, and at the close of the project such persons found employment in the normal channels of production. Both Miss Finch and Mrs. Nellie B. Burow, in directing the toy projects, were unfailingly conscious of the importance of the human element in all their endeavors, never omitting to inquire of a prospective worker if he or she liked people. In addition to furnishing employment to scores of persons, this experiment served to demonstrate how a workshop could take its place beside the local library as an instrument of community culture.

Among the toys of New England best known to the general public are those made by Raymond T. Cole in the attic workshop of his farm home near Newcastle, Maine. Mr. Cole calls them seaside toys since many of them are made for children to use at the seashore and are suggested by the ocean or by that magical spot where land and ocean meet. Mr. Cole has created over 140 different types of toys, ranging from a small model of a dory to miniature water birds an inch to two inches high; he also carves a fine sea gull in natural size and smaller gulls in flight.

At one time a civil engineer, Mr. Cole found work in the drafting room did not satisfy him; he yearned to get out of the office and make something entirely with his hands. He recalled that his grandfather used to make miniature windmills. His father-in-law, who ran a store on Monhegan Island, wondered if Mr. Cole could make something to sell as a souvenir. Together they developed a miniature dory which was laid out very accurately. Mr. Cole built it with extreme care and it was a beautiful piece of craftsmanship. Other pieces such as lobster traps, miniature lobsters, buoys, and a variety of objects characteristic of the Maine seacoast were worked out and sold on Monhegan Island, but the dory is still the toymaker's favorite. "People love that toy dory; I think the dory is the prettiest boat that ever was made."

Mr. Cole derives much satisfaction from studying his customers.

"A toymaker," he says, "should put into form some of the things that people carry around in their heads." He admits that he is strongly influenced by the work of other craftsmen and by their ways of doing things, although his greatest pleasure is in creating something which no one has done before, and "making it both nice and reasonable in price." "I get carried away by the work other people do, but in order to do anything creative myself I have to get back to my old shop, and by working alone I can get something original." He still consigns to some of his early cooperators, explaining, "They helped me when I began and I want to help them now." He likes the leisurely way of the natives on Monhegan Island, where time is never crowded and deliberation marks all occupations and activities; where two men meeting unexpectedly may sit down for a couple of hours to converse. Mr. Cole is an amateur horticulturist of unusual accomplishments, raising varieties of pears, grapes, and other fruits which the old-timers told him it was no use to try to grow in Maine. If people come to the shop and do not like his toys, he gives them fruit from his orchard.

Philip L. Martin of Auburndale, Massachusetts, author and designer of toys, has made many animals and birds of wood, partly shaped on the bandsaw and often completed by hand carving. At the Worcester Exhibition of Contemporary New England Handicrafts his painted animals were among the most attractive toys in the children's corner. Possibly the most ambitious of his toys and one of the best examples of his work is a Noah's Ark with about fifty animals, which he made for his son when the latter was five or six years old. Later he wrote and illustrated a book entitled *Animals for You to Make*.

Kenneth Audibert of Littleton, New Hampshire, a 4-H Club boy, made when he was sixteen years old a complete circus of eighteen wagons, nine elephants, six camels, four llamas, and twelve caged animals. The exhibit covers an area of about fifteen to twenty feet when all are in line for the parade. Kenneth did this work before he had seen a circus, being guided by pictures on a billboard in his part of the country.

Outstanding among the toymakers of Vermont is Miss Ila E. Fifield of East Calais. Her delightful *Alice in Wonderland* figures, wooden cutouts from two to four or five inches high, are based on the famous Tenniel illustrations, and attract much attention wherever they are shown. A victim of infantile paralysis, this cheerful, industrious, and artistic craftsman shapes all her work with one hand on a small machine consisting of jigsaw, drill, and disc sander. The machine is so constructed that Miss Fifield can tilt it back by hand and move the thin wood on a tiny platform where, as it comes in contact with saw,

drill, or sander, the required shape, holes, and finishing are all accomplished. With the use of other appliances which she has invented,
she can complete all the processes in creating these miniature figures.
A set of these figures was shown in the children's corner at the
Worcester Exhibition. Miss Fifield is a symbol of other happy and
productive craftsmen who, through contact with Vermont's Crippled
Children's Division of the Department of Public Health, have profited
from the teaching and guidance of Mrs. Eugene C. Rhodes, its director.

Although well past seventy years of age, Mrs. William Dorner, who
lives near Vergennes, Vermont, is one of the enthusiastic toymakers of
the state. Her specialty is cloth animals, which she markets through
the Three Green Doors at Stowe, Vermont. Among Mrs. Dorner's
popular creations is Ferdinand the Bull. Largely, states Mrs. Dorner,
through the income provided by Ferdinand she has been able after
several years of savings to install plumbing in her home. Many of
Mrs. Dorner's toys are original, and like Ferdinand, are usually humorous in appearance.

DOLLMAKING IN NEW ENGLAND

How many types of dolls were included in the Connecticut WPA
toy project has probably never been computed, but no doubt the
number was large. Without venturing to guess at the actual number of
doll types or dolls made in this important project one can recall some
of the scenes in the workrooms. One visit was to the costume room
where dresses, coats, hats, gloves, and a full array of accessories, all
in miniature, were displayed in vast numbers on small racks constructed by hand for the purpose. Likewise the cobbler shop was
crowded with many varieties of shoes, boots, slippers, sneakers,
rubbers, and galoshes. An unemployed shoemaker was in charge. He
had made scores of small wooden lasts and other equipment suitable
for carrying on his work. Especially numerous in this showroom were
doll shoes needing repair which were placed row by row—awaiting
buttons, new soles, and patches.

In the general repair shop one saw hundreds of dolls that had come
from all parts of the state needing hands, arms, legs, heads, or a new
wig. Selecting or making new parts for worn or injured dolls was one
of the important features of such work; it called for a true eye and
unusual skill in matching the remaining part of the body. One woman
in the workroom was extremely skillful in doll "face lifting"; she
worked arduously in reviving hands and faces of dolls sent in for repair.

In Orono, Maine, Miss Abbie Jo Wilson has for fifteen years designed dolls and animals. Her toys may be divided into two classes: cloth dolls and animals to be cuddled by children, and sophisticated character dolls designed especially for doll collectors. Miss Wilson models the character dolls' faces and hands from pulp and paints them in such manner as to give each face a distinct personality. Her dolls and animals are very lifelike, and she looks upon them as things alive. "I never knock a doll over without apologizing," she remarked while showing them. She has great faith in her dolls and is very sensitive about them. She makes her own contacts with retail places largely in order to find out for herself how the buyer will feel about them. All her dolls have names. Naming a doll, she said, is as important to her as "christening a child is to a mother."

Mrs. James Lowry of Lexington, Massachusetts, designed and originated the well-known colonial dolls, sometimes called Little Ladies. These dolls were a family product. Mr. Lowry carved the doll bodies from wood, then Mrs. Lowry assembled the parts, painted the faces, and completed the costumes. The series consists of the School Teacher, the Housekeeper, the Lady in Afternoon Dress, and several other types reminiscent of early New England. Mr. Lowry also made miniature ladder-back chairs frequently sold with the dolls. The Lowrys were early members of Minute-Man Crafts, through which they marketed their products.

Mrs. George Hauman of Lexington comes into this list through the character dolls and the crèches which she and her husband have made. They are primarily illustrators of children's books and so with them carving is only a hobby. As Mrs. Hauman says, "Most of the little people have been made for our own pleasure." She has made two complete Christmas cribs and many single features for nativity scenes. A favorite among character dolls made by the Haumans is the Old Lady Street Vendor.

Such ingenious character dolls, made chiefly for collectors or to illustrate the fashions of a particular period, bring to mind the first folk artist to come forth in New Hampshire after the arts and crafts program was initiated early in the 1930's. The League of New Hampshire Arts and Crafts had just engaged its first director, Frank Staples, and a statewide study of active and potential craftsmen was well under way. Among the workers this study revealed was Miss Mary Whittier of Bow, New Hampshire, who was recorded in the report as skilled in rug-hooking and handy with her father's tools on the farm. She was especially good at whittling, having made for her own pleasure a miniature farmhouse and barn with furnishings in complete detail.

In working out a list of products for its salesrooms to be established presently throughout New Hampshire, the League saw the need of a craftsman who could provide small figures in wood characteristic of New Englanders. Miss Whittier believed she could whittle out some. In the old farmhouse which Mr. and Mrs. J. Randolph Coolidge had acquired some years earlier near Center Sandwich, the former owners, the Hodges, had left old photographs of members of their family, veritable likenesses of them as they lived and worked in their time. Mrs. Coolidge chose the photographs of Grandma and Grandpa Hodge as typical New Hampshire folk, and turned them over to Mary who began to whittle out their rugged faces and erect bodies. She dressed them in precise fashion, even to Grandpa's vest with strap and tiny buckle across the back, and Grandma's plain waist with dainty buttons down the front and narrow white lace bordering the straight collar which was fastened with a "breastpin" of that period. They were exactly what the League members wanted, and they are as popular today as when they were whittled out of the native pine.

Recently someone asked Miss Whittier how she came to do whittling. She said, "When I was a little girl my grandfather had a jackknife which I always wanted; after he died I got it." She still uses her grandfather's jackknife to carve figures characteristic of his day. A portrait of her, out-of-doors among her beloved farm animals, is shown.

Mrs. J. J. Fallon of Concord, New Hampshire, began modestly several years ago restoring and costuming period dolls. She is scrupulous about the minutest detail, and is an exceptional needleworker whose doll costumes are creations of taste and beauty. Mrs. Fallon extended her endeavors later to historical characters, and this provided ample opportunity for continuing her search for authentic types and costumes. Among her historical dolls are a delightful Betsy Ross and, perhaps her best, a charming Sarah Hale. A unique group by Mrs. Fallon represents a traditional quilting party of New England. This is adapted from a similar creation made over one hundred years ago and now in the Historical Society building at Concord. The dolls of the quilting party have heads and faces made of hickory nuts; with their authentic rural attire they reflect the character of country people energetically practicing this old folk art.

Among the more recent dollmakers of New Hampshire is Mrs. Helen Hoffman of Manchester, who specializes in faces of dried apples, a handicraft practiced long ago in some of the Indian tribes. It was the League of New Hampshire Arts and Crafts that encouraged Mrs. Hoffman to show her dolls and to develop her little home industry. At first she did not feel that they were worth while, but visitors to the Craftsman's Fair assured her that they liked them and proved it by purchasing a considerable number. Interest in her dolls has now extended quite beyond the borderlines of New Hampshire. Mrs. Hoffman says she prefers Baldwin and Winesap apples for her doll faces because they last well.

In a little house on Strawberry Hill in Meredith lives Mrs. Ralph F. Flather, maker of the Strawberry Patch Doll, so-called because the hill on which Mrs. Flather lives with her family abounds every spring with wild strawberries. She also makes clothes and accessories for her dolls, and a good friend reproduces in miniature early American chairs which fit some of them. At the time these notes were made Mrs. Flather had made over a hundred of these character dolls, one of which is illustrated.

Mrs. Dora Walker of Rutland, Vermont, is a specialist in repairing and restoring dolls but her knowledge goes quite beyond that of the usual person interested in restoration. She is exceptionally well informed on the dolls of New England and probably no one else in the area has had so many native dolls, both homemade and factory-made, pass through her helping hands. A visit to Mrs. Walker's home is a rare experience, for one then has an opportunity to see her own fine collection, including some very old dolls, and also a large aggregation of dolls in transit, waiting to be restored, costumed, or otherwise embellished.

In the scholarly work of Janet Pagter Johl, *The Fascinating Story of Dolls,* the author refers often to Mrs. Walker's opinion on a controversial point, and frequently accepts her judgment in clearing up a moot question. Mrs. Walker occasionally buys a doll of good pedigree in order to restore it properly and attire it correctly after which she may sell it or attach it to her own collection. She and her daughter are both pioneers in the New England rabbit industry. Fur from her rabbits is often used for the costumes of her dolls. Beautiful fur capes of white or tan, coats lined with fur, small fur hats and caps, or dainty fur accessories adorn some of the doll wardrobes in very effective fashion.

Mrs. Grace Banzhaf of Southport, Connecticut, was over fifty when she began to create her lifelike and charming figures. They are called "characterettes," for they are authentic reproductions of famous characters. Mrs. Johl says of her: "Mrs. Banzhaf made her first characterette, Ann of Cleves, as a project for a course in costume designing. She found the modeling so fascinating that she continued until the group was finished including Henry the VIII and all of his six wives. All these figures, twelve inches high, were copied from the Holbein paintings and dressed authentically."

Mrs. Banzhaf builds her doll bodies on wire armatures, stuffed with cotton, and covered with satin. After making the first group of dolls she began the study of sculpture and has continued learning as she has advanced in her art. In correspondence with the writer she wrote: "I am enclosing a picture of one of my best sellers, Queen Victoria. The details of her dress are very accurate, being copied from Von Angelin's portrait in Windsor Castle. Each figure is made by hand; the head and hands are modeled in clay, then painted to look quite lifelike. . . . Among my later characterettes the most outstanding ones have been of Maurice Evans in his various roles such as Hamlet, Falstaff, Malvolio, Richard II, and Macbeth."

Among the notable collections of dolls and dollhouses in New England is the one owned by the Society for the Preservation of New England Antiquities in Boston. At Essex Institute in Salem is also a collection of dolls, among them one of the first dolls ever sent over to America.

THE MAKING OF MINIATURE OBJECTS

The practice of making miniature objects, aside from the delight which their achievement and appearance give, stems probably from two main purposes: first, to satisfy a child by making toys and small furniture for a dollhouse or playroom; second, and more utilitarian, to make small accurate work models or to reproduce old furniture or other objects on a diminutive scale. Neither of these explanations stresses sufficiently the attraction that is felt quite naturally by most of us for the diminutive, which so often leads a craftsman to find special pleasure in his work. Whatever the various reasons may be that account for the growth of this fascinating branch of handicrafts in New England, one finds craftsmen in every state who produce charming small objects, some of them original and others which follow minutely all the details of the full-sized model.

Edson W. Fletcher of Searsport, Maine, superintendent of the Armour Fertilizer Plant, began his work as a craftsman by making miniature furniture for a dollhouse. It was not long before he learned that he had exceptional skill in making miniature objects, and fine woodworking then became his chief spare-time interest. Almost all his tiny pieces are constructed entirely by hand and are made to exact scale. They are usually simple in line without much ornamentation; some are perfect reproductions, and others are original. Drawers of the chests and tables are equipped with small knobs and open easily; the chests and tables are moved about readily on casters.

Mr. Fletcher has undertaken to produce the furnishings of an entire house in miniature. He has already completed full dining-room and bedroom sets, a fireplace with andirons made of solid brass, a pair of pewter candlesticks, and brass candelabra, as well as a concert grand piano and console piano equipped with benches; even the tiny pedals move. Other finished pieces are a gate-leg table, a library table, and two end-tables. Picture frames of apple wood enclosing diminutive oil paintings on canvas were executed by Mr. Fletcher's father-in-law, Herbert J. Friselle, of Boston.

Ernest L. Washburn of Brewer, near Bangor, now in his late seventies, has also won much praise for his miniature work. When about sixty years old he turned from housebuilding to the less strenuous though still exacting work of building in miniature excellent reproductions of authentic pieces of furniture. His chairs of apple wood resemble ivory in texture. Among Mr. Washburn's notable commissions have been furniture and dollhouses for Mrs. Mary Dorgan of Great Neck, Long Island, New York, a well-known collector and authority on dolls. Some of his work is in the Franklin Institute in Philadelphia.

Charles Ormsby, who lived at Norfolk Road, three miles north of Winsted, Connecticut, made miniature tools, furniture, and other objects, including stage scenes and sets and some mechanical toys. In his miniature shop, formerly a chicken house, were to be found small-sized machines, which he made out of odd pieces of material; all run by foot or hand power. In order to get the right-sized spindles and rungs for his Windsor chairs, and teeth for his garden rakes, his technique was to pull tiny pieces of straight-grained wood, commonly hickory, through a metal plate similar to the usual treatment of steel for making wire. Mr. Ormsby liked to sell his own products, partly because he could charge a low price and partly because he enjoyed the social contacts made in negotiating sales.

Arthur D. Knight of Barre, Vermont, a superior craftsman in the miniature field, was a machinist by trade until he suffered partial paralysis of his legs when fifty years of age. He then took up handicrafts, specializing in early American miniature reproduction. His work is delicate and precise, all pieces made to scale, which is usually one inch to a foot. Among his subjects are highboys, desks, tables, and several types of early American chairs. His work has been exhibited at America House in New York. During World War II this skillful and energetic craftsman laid aside his miniature work to teach in a war production school in New England.

Perhaps as fine miniature furniture as has ever been made in our country was that done by Edward R. King of Fairhaven, Massachusetts. Mr. King was for a long period an instructor in a manual training school in New Haven and for thirty-two years was never absent for a day from his work. He encouraged hundreds of pupils to follow his own motto of "order, industry, accuracy, economy." He built many pieces of beautiful full-sized furniture, both original and period, and continued to his eightieth birthday to make these large pieces for his home and for friends; then he began working on miniature furniture— exact scale copies of pieces which he had done formerly in full size. He used similar materials, exercising the same expert skill, and marked each piece with a legend minutely printed by hand, sometimes on the back of the piece, sometimes on the bottom of a tiny drawer. In addition he made photographs of every piece, and recorded in a book in his own handwriting the complete story of his adventure in miniature furniture making.

Three other miniature furniture makers in Massachusetts should be recorded here: Wilfred T. Victoreen of Pittsfield, E. F. Bliss of Springfield, and W. B. Douglass of Dunstable. Mr. Victoreen, a native of Sweden, began his career in toy furniture in 1943, when he furnished playhouses he had built for two grandchildren. For years he taught manual training in Pittsfield, inculcating the work principle that "nothing is too good." He had made many pieces of full-sized furniture and copied them in miniature, a penknife being his principal tool. For grandfather clock faces he uses small wrist watches. His work has been described in *Popular Mechanics*. In addition to making miniature furniture, Mr. Bliss has made a tiny spinning wheel which runs by the touch of the finger. Mr. Douglass writes, "After having spent the first six months following my retirement leisurely in Florida, I decided one day that life was too aimless." Remembering pleasantly the collection of miniature rooms made by Mrs. James Ward Thorne, he got books and photographs to work from and was soon making furniture on a one-inch scale. One of his best pieces is a miniature copy of the dining room built by his great-great-grandfather in 1791 at Hebron, New Hampshire. At the Fiftieth Anniversary Exhibition of the Society of Arts and Crafts in Boston Mr. Douglass showed a high-post bed, a replica of the original in the Metropolitan Museum of Art. For this bed Miss Myra Davis wove a small coverlet and Mrs. Louise Chrimes did some tiny needlework.

CHAPTER 13

PUPPETS AND MARIONETTES

ACCORDING to Webster a puppet is "a small image in the human form . . . often with jointed limbs, moved by the hand or by strings or wires, as in a puppet show or a mock drama; a marionette." And he defines a marionette as "a puppet moved by strings or by hand, as in a puppet show," which would seem to indicate that there is little or no difference; and to the layman there probably is none.

But the puppeteer makes a distinction between puppets and marionettes, and that distinction we shall recognize in general here. It is that a puppet is manipulated directly by hand, as in a Punch-and-Judy show, or sometimes with a rod or a stick from below; a marionette is manipulated by strings or wires, or occasionally by a rod, from above. Both are figures under human control but marionettes are usually manipulated by strings. And, of course, neither puppets nor marionettes are now limited to images of the human form; both often include animals and insects, and sometimes objects, when the action calls for them. There are several forms of puppets—"string," "rod," "shadow," and others—but our concern is mainly as they come within the scope of handicrafts.

These little images are included not because they provide a favorite and to many a choice form of entertainment, but because they are handicrafts of importance. Actually few objects anywhere are as thoroughly handicraft. In the first place, the images are themselves handmade and are costumed by hand; in the second place, they are always hand shown or hand manipulated. In some instances they represent a handicraft continuity, as when the puppeteer conceives and writes his play, creates and constructs the images and their appurtenances in his workshop, and finally manipulates them with his own hands in the miniature theater which he has designed and constructed. Such a puppeteer is both artist and craftsman.

There was some question as to where in the plan of this book, which does not consider the arts of the theater, puppets and marionettes should go. They might have been put in the chapter on toys, dolls, and other miniature objects; but, although they delight children, they are not in their long tradition children's playthings. They are much more the playthings of adults who create them and make them act. They are not miniature because one of their most fascinating qualities is that they appear to be life sized to the beholder, who forgets for the time his own world and the scale on which it is built. Having a special and an honored place because they are so truly handicrafts, they are here given a chapter of their own.

In the New England area a considerable number of persons, both amateurs and professionals, make puppets in wide and often delightful variety—some for their own entertainment only, the majority for the amusement of others. In this study over a hundred such persons were discovered. Of these, many were found with the assistance of Paul McPharlin, who undoubtedly did more to bring puppeteers together than anyone else in our country. His last writing, *The Puppet Theatre in America*, has recently been published.

But no one can know all the puppetmakers of New England, for they reach back into remote and hidden places. Brief reference to a few, including some who stand high among the puppeteers of America, and also some who both make and manipulate their puppets or marionettes, together with a note on a few of the many uses to which puppetry has been put, will serve to bring out the importance of this very personal handicraft. It may be possible also to suggest some of the social values connected with the making and manipulating of these handmade images.

SOME PROFESSIONAL PUPPETEERS

The chapter may well begin with a reference to John Ralph Geddis and François Martin, "Actors with Puppets," as they appropriately call themselves—both actors and craftsmen, whom we shall see at work on all the varied handicrafts of their diminutive theater, making their own characters and equipment by hand and bringing to life again the best traditions of an art and a craft which flourished in ancient Greece and in Europe centuries ago. These two young men turned from careers on the so-called legitimate stage to produce plays with puppets, "which," they say, "are convincing symbols of actors capable of expressing the full scale of emotions with the power to move an audience to laughter or to tears."

Because Geddis and Martin are concerned with a rising popular appreciation of "this distinct art of the theater," they often give a lecture and demonstration entitled Design for Puppets. In this they distinguish between the "string operated figure which is a marionette" and the puppet, quite a different creature "worked from below stage on the arm of the producer" and which they have critically chosen as their medium of expression and communication. Mr. Geddis as spokesman says, "The marionette is a mechanical novelty; the movement is interesting but it can't act. On the other hand, the puppet with its limitations is an exciting theater medium" in which the performer "has to create by his own power, the expression of his hand and arm, all the qualities of the solid person."

In their combination puppet show and lecture, Geddis and Martin say they came to choose the puppet stage from the standpoint of producer, director, scenic artist, costumer, playwright, stage manager, actor, and financier, all of which responsibilities these two young puppeteers assumed when they "pooled their skills in the arts and crafts of the theater" and opened a puppet theater on Beacon Hill in Boston called Mr. Punch's Workshop. During the seasons of 1931 to 1936 they designed, produced, and acted in about twenty plays, among them *Alice in Wonderland, A Midsummer Night's Dream, Bourgeois Gentilhomme, Médecin Malgré Lui, Little Flowers of Saint Francis*, three plays based on Hans Andersen stories—*Little Mermaid, The Swans, The Nightingale.* Finally they produced *Uncle Tom's Cabin.* Their puppets for *Alice in Wonderland* were faithfully copied from a set of the famous Tenniel illustrations that had been hand colored by Lewis Carroll. Their figures are originally designed and are sometimes whittled directly out of wood without a preliminary sketch.

In 1935 they restored an abandoned meetinghouse in Dartmouth, Massachusetts, and established a summer theater there. Traveling from this base throughout the year, they gave puppet plays in various parts of New England, at museums, circuses, universities, amusement parks, churches, country fairs, and summer performances on Boston Common. Geddis and Martin have now returned to their native California.

Jumping in imagination from Massachusetts to rural Vermont, which is no trick at all when make-believe images are the subject, one climbs a high hill, some miles from the village of Thetford Center, and there on the edge of the timber from which he cut the logs and built his house and shop lives Basil Milovsoroff, with his wife, Georgia, and their two children, Ann and Peter. And here is the Folktale Marionette Theater (when it is not away visiting some school, art museum, children's theater, or other group) where the audience is waiting to see *The Two Blind Beggars, The Peasant and the Imp, The Little Humpbacked*

Horse, The Hut on Chicken's Legs, The Tale of Tsar Sultan, The Rabbit and the Fox, The Golden Fish, Grandma and Her Little Gray Goat, The Crow and the Fox, or some other Russian folk tale arranged and presented by Basil, sometimes with the assistance of Mrs. Milovsoroff, who helps with both acting and playwriting.

Basil Milovsoroff is not a product of the theater, nor is he conscious of its influence as he carves his figures and sets his miniature stage for the presentation of folk tales. His point of view is that the puppet is a subject for an artist's creative effort, and he finds that usually the marionette form is best suited to his folk plays; but he speaks of all of the images as puppets and uses both types. Mr. Milovsoroff asks, "What could be more honest for a puppet than to tell the story of his own world of fancy, a world of make believe of which he himself is a part." Mr. Milovsoroff was born in Siberia, where old tales are still recounted to children and adults, and thus he brings to this much younger nation of which he is now a citizen gifts of fantasy—the best heritage of his own childhood—to be woven into the myriad-colored tapestry of American folklore. The puppets which he creates, and which help to convey the spirit and the letter of the folk tales, are as Russian as though they had been carved by a talented ancestor of our puppeteer in his old homeland. He works directly from native wood, whittling the strongly individual figures "out of his head" without sketches or models. They delight equally the simplest and the most sophisticated.

Rufus and Margo Rose, who were first associated with Tony Sarg, have worked with their own marionettes since 1938. Over a period of six years they gave three thousand performances in five hundred cities and towns in the United States. These professional programs were sponsored by schools, colleges, theaters, and civic organizations. The Roses now have a permanent Marionette Theater in Avery Lane, Waterford, Connecticut, designed entirely and partly built by them, where they present a repertory of plays and variety acts each season. They work individually and as a family in shaping and restoring the hundreds of figures in their repertory. Soft pine and plastic wood are the materials most often used. In their workshop, neatly arranged in small closets and wardrobes, are the almost countless costumes needed for performances at home or on the road.

Some of the shows, for which they have made all the marionettes and equipment, are remarkable examples of construction in achieving realistic performance and balance. Possibly their circus scenes rank highest from the standpoint of clever and often amazing manipulation. Togo, their famous clown, is a show in himself and a fine reflection of the Rose genius for unexcelled craftsmanship. Rufus Rose is an expert in manipulation and has invented a marionette controller of great practical value. Their famous Rip Van Winkle production requires all the resources of the entire family, Margo, Rufus, their two young sons, James and Rufus, Jr.

The National Puppetry Festival

The Puppeteers of America during their National Puppetry Festival made their headquarters at the Rufus Rose Marionette Theater from June 27 to 30, 1946. It was the seventh national festival, but the first since 1941, when war cut off the meetings of this group of craftsmen. It would be hard to imagine—and puppeteers are very imaginative— a more appropriate place for the reunion of this group than the studio-theater-home of the Roses. No mere visitor could tell where home, workshop, or theater begins or ends. The small but conveniently planned auditorium in which many of the sessions of the Festival were held is at other times a spacious and comfortable family living room with a generous wood-burning fireplace. This room, which will seat from one hundred and fifty to two hundred persons, is on a slightly lower level than the rest of the house and has on one side a movable curtain-wall, which, when rolled up, reveals the proscenium opening of a regular stage used for special gatherings and performances. The stage is so large and so arranged that a truck can be driven onto it from an outside entrance.

Group discussions at the National Puppetry Festival brought out the fact that, in addition to the problems of budgets, publicity, play material, and other common problems growing out of efforts to start and maintain marionette productions in a community, there is considerable sensitivity on effective presentations because of their influence upon the taste, social thinking, and the general culture of audiences. Instances were given in which entire programs were changed when their ethical quality had been questioned.

It appeared also that people made and worked with puppets because of the satisfaction they derived. The element of make-believe is not to be underestimated if judged by those representatives of more than thirty states. Puppetry would seem to be an art practiced not because of its money return, for few can depend on it as an entire source of income. But many feel it even worth a sacrifice because of the opportunity it gives for creative thinking and doing; also because the plays bring pleasure to so many persons, including some to whom other forms of entertainment are not so easily available.

OTHER PUPPETEERS

It is not possible to characterize accurately all who follow in one way or another the craft of puppetry, and only a few can be referred to here. Of these some teach and some exhibit; some do both; some do neither; but all are craftsmen in the sense that they make puppets.

William A. Dwiggins, already referred to in Chapter 8, is both maker and manipulator of puppets. He has also made an outstanding contribution to the art and science of puppetry by developing controls for perfect balancing, which he applies to many marionettes, whether men, beasts, or fantastic figures. In his workshop at Hingham, Massachusetts, planned entirely and partly constructed by himself, is his marionette theater, the proscenium and curtains of which he designed and decorated in brilliant colors. Here he and his friends have given many performances.

A useful little book, *Marionette in Motion*, was written by Mr. Dwiggins and printed as Handbook 12, Puppetry Imprints, 1939, with diagrams, drawings, title heads, and lettered text all from his skilled hand—a very pleasant combination of calligraphy lettering and drawing. In this text Mr. Dwiggins sets forth "under the Püterschein Authority," which for many years has "conducted a private experimental theater in Hingham Center," his own discoveries in counterbalance, "adopted by some of the leading American puppeteers." In outlining his views on puppetry as an art Mr. Dwiggins says: "It is not possible to reproduce . . . all the motions of a human figure—nor is it desirable. . . . As in all the arts a simplified or abstracted presentation is often more vivid than an exact reproduction. The designer watches to see just how a wrist joint moves, for example, and then works out mechanized ways and means for *suggesting* that motion." The "Püterschein system," described in this book, "succeeds very nicely," remarks Mr. Dwiggins, "in suggesting a number of the natural motions of the human body."

Miss Lillian A. Phillips, who has studied puppetry in England, France, Czechoslovakia, Germany, and Italy, teaches the making of puppets, shadow puppets, and marionettes in the Massachusetts School of Art, Boston. Among graduates of the School, Mrs. Barbara Marshman, now of Lexington, a member of Minute-Man Crafts, directs The Jolly Capers Company; and Philip DeRosiers has given his outstanding shadow plays during the summer at the Springfield, Massachusetts, Art Museum. Miss Phillips said that at least once a year her pupils give a puppet play which emphasizes international relations. One of the latest of these was on the life of President Thomas G. Masaryk of Czechoslovakia.

Mrs. Mary Dean, of the Curry School of Speech, Boston, who also has a studio-theater at Manchester-by-the-Sea, has made many of her own puppets and marionettes. By organizing regional puppetry festivals she has done much to bring together cooperatively the puppeteers of New England.

Miss Harriet Peasley of Cheshire, Connecticut, has given public and private performances throughout New England, at first with string puppets, latterly with hand puppets. Her Merrie English Puppets did much to raise relief funds during World War II, and she personally made hundreds of toy hand puppets to send to English children who were evacuated or orphaned. Herbert H. Hosmer, Jr., makes puppets for his Toy Cupboard Theater, West Newton, Massachusetts, and has given a summer season of children's shows for the past several years, and occasional performances for civic, church, and school audiences. He is a teacher by profession.

The Midsummer Marionettes, made before World War II at the Schola Pictorum in Boston and sometimes called the Marionettes of the Schola Pictorum, differed from other puppets or marionettes in the use of special small masks for faces designed and made by Miss Meta K. Hannay, then director of the school. It was Miss Hannay's purpose to produce "faces," to use her own words, "that would be expressive and mobile under light. . . . The identical mask may be used to represent a variety of characters so that evil may become good in another interpretation." The words "Laughter is the only way of destroying evil without malice" are on the *Schola Pictorum Bulletin*. In 1941 Miss Hannay joined the Navy Department, taking her supply of masks with her, about five hundred at the time, and continued teaching and demonstrating to groups in the Army and Navy. Altogether she made and distributed about four thousand of these masks.

Mrs. W. Clarke Haywood of Laurel Gables, Salem, Massachusetts, makes puppets, miniature masks, and figurines mostly for her personal use. She gives occasional performances and also lectures on Puppets Through the Ages. Mrs. Haywood models the heads and then makes a plaster mold, usually in two sections in which the final head is cast in plastic, wood, or papier-mâché. The hands are carved from the kind of wood, smooth, grained, or gnarled, most suitable to the character. Mrs. Haywood makes all the costumes and stage settings and paints scenery for the little plays or sketches.

Among other puppeteers who as craftsmen should be noted are the following, all from Massachusetts: Mr. and Mrs. B. J. Jarvis of Sandwich, who make stage sets, marionettes, and puppets. They give two full plays, *Jeppe of the Hill* and *Ali Baba*. For specialty acts they use a mouse as master of ceremonies. Mrs. Ralph Morse of Wellesley centers her interest in actually making, costuming, and developing the personality of hand-controlled puppets as opposed to string-controlled. She and her neighbor, Mrs. Lester Holman, have given shows and hope their children will adopt puppetry as a hobby. Mr. and Mrs. Charles C. Rollins of West Springfield work with a group of thirty young people in Leominster and have given Christmas and Easter shows there and in Worcester. Holmes C. Hurll of New Bedford maintains a Jolly Puppet Show in which the characters are marionettes except for Mr. Punch, a hand puppet and master of ceremonies. Mr. Hurll's first shows were combined with his brother's performance as a magician.

Certain phases of the subject of puppetry and those who devote themselves to it indicate to the writer its importance socially and culturally in the American scene. Roughly stated these are: the element of family cooperation in puppetry; the appropriate use of puppetry for the handicapped; social and educational uses, of which a significant instance is teaching the rights of animals to children.

FAMILY COOPERATION IN PUPPETRY

The programs of the 1947 National Puppetry Festival must have led others besides the writer to feel that, although art is often spoken of as an individual matter, the art of puppetry appears to give unique opportunities to work in groups, especially family groups. It suggests in this respect families of musicians or of craftsmen who were to be found so often among Europeans of past generations. The Rose family and the Milovsoroffs are outstanding examples.

Mrs. Elizabeth H. Fuller of the Fuller Studio, North Quincy, Massachusetts, writes that their "company is a family affair"; the other members are the sons, John W., Buell R., and A. Edson Fuller. The family has made about a thousand puppets and produced more than thirty plays. Their puppets are hand carved; pine is used for marionettes and balsa wood for puppets. When balsa was unobtainable and pine difficult to get, they used fine sawdust and paper-hangers' paste in combination, modeling the images in the rough and then carving them. They liked the method of modeling the heads and painting them because even though cracks may form after the first modeling these can be filled in, and any kind of surface can be built up with paint. During World War II the sons went into the armed services or into an essential industry.

One, an air mechanic, used puppets on programs at Gunter Field, Alabama, and marionettes at Brooks Field, Texas, where they were well received.

Mrs. T. C. Clark, a teacher of art in the Junior High School, Burlington, Vermont, and director of puppet plays, writes of puppet making and playing as a family activity: "Once when faced with an Easter vacation with four healthy, active children at home, we began in self-defense doing rag-doll marionettes. We all worked together around the kitchen table—the oldest child learned to use an old electric sewing machine by sewing up the dolls, and the smallest one could mess around with a spoon stuffing the marionettes with sand and sawdust. Last spring we gave a fairly elaborate production of *The Three Wishes* to a group of adults. The marionettes had carved wooden heads and hands and rag bodies. I don't know anything that is more fun for a family than to get together on something like this."

Mrs. Lyda Flanders of Worcester, Massachusetts, writes, "Ten years ago my son, when about twelve, worked with marionettes at the Worcester Art Museum, and I dressed them for him and began to study them. Then I made a theater and puppets for the Worcester Gas Company for their commercial work." This is one of the many uses of puppets in advertising.

PUPPETEERING FOR THE HANDICAPPED

In Massachusetts three puppeteers who have extended their programs for the benefit of the handicapped have come to the writer's attention. No doubt there are others carrying out similar activities in other states.

Miss Louise B. Spier of Attleboro taught puppetry to deaf children at the Clarke School in Northampton from 1933 to 1945 and produced a marionette show every year. She reports as follows: "The older girls made the stocking type of marionettes with airplane controls. Many of these girls were unusually clever in designing and making puppets and costumes. The speech of the deaf is not always intelligible and does not carry well, so we developed pantomime plays and vaudeville acts. . . . The Puppet Show was an event looked forward to all year. All the action of the play had to be shown on the stage. The puppeteers were trained to put on the show themselves with their own stage managers, property and lighting 'men.' Girls who had some hearing were in charge of the victrola records. A parade of the puppeteers with their marionettes around the hall after the performance was not only a satisfaction to the puppeteers but an interesting feature for the audience. Perhaps the greatest value of this work, still carried on at the Clarke School, is the personal satisfaction to the students in doing something which is also being done by those without handicaps."

Miss Edwina Goodey of Lincoln School, Melrose, writes, "My class is composed of mentally deficient pupils, and I find puppets and marionettes of interest to them and a grand source for developing them mentally, morally, and physically." She explained that both hand puppets and string marionettes are made and operated by the pupils who have also made a stage with backdrops and have written plays. All this contributes to their sense of self-esteem, for "with marionettes or puppets there is a place for each—those who can draw, sing, talk, write, or just shift scenery."

Miss Mildred L. Houlihan of Rockland is a teacher of mentally retarded boys. She studied puppetry with Tony Sarg in New York. She writes, "I feel the producing of a marionette play is one of the best all-round activities for boys of this type. They learn to make their own marionettes, costumes, scenery, properties; it gives them a splendid opportunity to develop teamwork." The boys have presented marionette plays for both school and teacher groups. Miss Houlihan believes that boys will take part in marionette shows when they are too self-conscious to act in an ordinary play.

SOCIAL AND EDUCATIONAL USES

The writer has been much impressed by evidence of the wide use of puppets and marionettes in the broad field of social work. Many puppet makers in New England and elsewhere appear to use their creations for social and educational purposes. A number of replies to our inquiries made in New England about puppets indicate they have been employed in classrooms, hospitals, community houses, in church programs, and so forth.

Miss Stella B. Forrest, Fitchburg, Massachusetts, makes marionettes of religious and historical characters which are used in churches and schools. She thinks that old ladies' homes are pleasant and satisfactory places in which to perform. For adult entertainment she also makes characters from opera. "I make these for my own programs, carving the heads of wood and sometimes the hands if they are important. Lately I have discontinued the use of a stage." Miss Forrest now hangs the marionettes on stands and takes them off one by one, then demonstrates and explains the characters. She says the audience likes to see a puppeteer in action. In this way she can entertain in private homes. Her marionettes, which include animals, "for even adults like them," number about twenty-five or thirty.

Two members of the Schola Pictorum faculty, Miss Marcia J. Cline and Miss Minnie G. Gass, used marionettes in a program of safety education for children.

Miss Alice J. Kennedy, a teacher of Newton, Massachusetts, reports that she became interested in marionettes about fifteen years ago when a junior-high-school boy brought one to show at school: "I visualized the possibilities of a good theater on a small scale. . . . I had always been handicapped in producing actual stage productions with school children because school authorities rarely care to spend money enough for good settings, lighting, and so forth. On the tiny stage required by puppets settings can be magnificent at small cost."

Miss Helena A. Kelly of Holyoke, Massachusetts, uses puppets as aids in the teaching of modern foreign languages. She writes: "I have had a large puppet theater built by the manual training department of our school, designed and painted by the art department, with a curtain backdrop made by the domestic science classes. Boys in our local trade school wired the theater for footlights. We have given puppet shows using original plays by talented members of the classes, and we have also dramatized such favorites as *Le Voyage de M. Perrichon, La Petite Chaise, Don Quixote,* and others. Pupils make puppets, paint backdrops, and read various parts."

Miss Ernestine M. Baxter, children's librarian of the Pawtucket, Rhode Island, Library, has been making puppets and giving shows in libraries, schools, hospitals, institutions, and playgrounds for more than ten years. An opportunity to learn puppetmaking came through a government recreation project during the depression, after which she made puppets to supplement her storytelling.

Miss Dorothy Jennings of Saylesville, Rhode Island, has constructed three marionette stages, has made over fifty marionettes for her own use, both eighteen and twenty-four inches in height, and has written her own plays. She gives performances in Rhode Island and neighboring states.

Miss Helen A. Haselton of West Hartford, Connecticut, encouraged her pupils in high school to make and use puppets and marionettes in connection with classes in drawing, modeling, costume and stage design, "and for general Yankee handiness with tools and inventiveness with materials." Her students constructed a folding stage and four hand puppets for a Punch-and-Judy show to be used annually, with new lines, by the French Club. One of Miss Haselton's former pupils, Miss Virginia Boyd, now working for the State Health Department, developed marionettes who could wash their hands and faces and brush their teeth properly, and with them Miss Boyd visited rural schools throughout the state, where health lessons were received with enthusiasm and profit.

Alwin T. Nikolais and Michael Adrian of Hartford built at Southington two seven-foot marionettes and produced Dunsany's *Glittering Gate.* In the depression years Mr. Nikolais organized and supervised the Hartford Parks Marionette Theater, under the Work Projects Administration, which utilized at one time seven actors, four stagehands, a woodcarver, and a seamstress. Through arrangements with the Board of Education, the Marionette Theater played an average of nine shows weekly, covering each of the city schools twice during the year, and maintained in Bushnell Park a cottage workshop, where hundreds of puppets and props were made. In summer puppet shows were given in the parks through the "show wagon."

In 1936 this organization was sent by the state to all county fairs, to many schools, parks, and other institutions and clubs. Earlier, during the Connecticut River flood of 1935, the company was sent to the refuge centers. While this statewide service operated, covering about two and one-half years, more than six hundred performances were given of puppet plays appropriate to both children and adults. Mr. Nikolais gave a course in puppetry to school teachers who received point credit for their work, and *Index to Puppetry,* a book classifying material available in Hartford libraries, was compiled under his direction. This use of puppets was perhaps the most extensive and intensive program in education and recreation by puppetry ever carried out in New England.

Teaching Children the Rights of Animals

The chapter may appropriately close with a reference to uses of marionettes by the Animal Rescue League of Boston in the teaching of "kindly consideration for every living thing."

In 1945 the League reported that 327 marionette shows were presented to 67,820 children in Boston, and through the fine cooperation of teachers, many thousands of letters and pictures reached the League which were written and drawn by children. The "fan mail" gave evidence of the value of this form of combined education and entertainment. Mrs. B. Maude Phillips, director of education for the League, writes: "We make all our own puppets and marionettes, our scenery, and in fact everything that is required for the plays. We write our own scripts and adapt them to the educational work of stressing every possible phase in the development of character and find that the plays the children know and love are fine mediums for getting across the lessons."

Mrs. Phillips' first experience with marionettes was with Sir Wilfred Thomason Grenfell's mission one summer at St. Anthony in Labrador, an experience which she reported to the Animal Rescue League. In 1934 the League was granted permission to go into the schools of Boston where the work has continued since without interruption. Mrs. Phillips reports further: "No talks or lectures would ever impress the children as the little marionette characters do, and it is wonderful how much good is being accomplished with this type of program. . . . We feel that what we are doing is not only achieving desirable results in teaching kindly consideration for every living thing but in stressing many other fine points in character development."

One result of presenting *Peter Rabbit, Hänsel and Gretel,* and other plays especially devised by the Animal Rescue League to the thousands of Boston school children is the building of marionette theaters by the children themselves, to be used for purposes devised by them. In connection with such a project they learn to do all that is necessary to put on a puppet play, an experience that those who take part in it will always remember.

CHAPTER 14

METALWORKING, SILVERSMITHING AND JEWELRY MAKING, ENAMELING, GEM-CUTTING

M ETALWORK in New England covers a wide range from sturdy pieces in iron and steel made by blacksmiths, and objects of lead, copper, brass, and aluminum, to those made of silver. Most of the metals used come from other states. As to jewelry there are scores of both professionals and amateurs engaged in this craft. They can find many semiprecious and precious stones that are native to New England, with Maine having first place, and lapidarists to get them into usable form.

From the early years of settlement until now there have been black-smiths in every state of our Union, but it is doubtful if in any area other than New England so large a number of blacksmiths are at work today who have combined with their repair and patching services to the native countrymen the making of useful and beautiful things for the tourist and city dweller. These country blacksmiths of an older day, whose usefulness to their community has diminished with the mechanization of the farm and who have had the resourcefulness to apply their skills elsewhere, make an interesting group of craftsmen. It is the blacksmith who does some work for household decoration and utilities whom we shall consider.

BLACKSMITHS IN MAINE

At Blue Hill, where he has always lived, Charles Wescott stood at the forge in his commodious blacksmith shop, which he calls The Hammer and Tongs, with many products of his craftsmanship about him and a great number of his designs still to be worked out. "Peace and poverty," said Mr. Wescott, "is what we represent in this old shop." His "fancy ironwork," as the local people call it, gives him pleasure, for he likes to make nice things."

228

Mr. Wescott's work is usually heavy in character; he is known the country 'round for his ability to make iron gates, metal signs, and objects designed for use in fireplaces. He also makes light, thin, and graceful patterns in iron, many from his own designs. Candelabra are among the most attractive of the latter; for these the suggestion came from a motion picture Mr. Wescott saw in Blue Hill. Although the candelabra appeared only momentarily on the screen, he was able to hammer out from iron a replica, which made a very favorable impression at the Contemporary New England Handicraft Exhibition in Worcester. It is shown in the frontispiece.

Among the best-known ironworkers of New England is Ernest S. Rice, once the village blacksmith and now a designer and master craftsman in iron forging. Much of the work done in his shop on Highway No. 1 is light and has grace and delicacy, although some of his executions are massive. A pleasant feature of Camden, his home village, is his metal boxes filled with gay flowers on the lampposts, a mark of beauty in which Camden feels a just pride. Many of the mailboxes on the doorways were also made by Mr. Rice. He has made a variety of well-designed fixtures for fireplaces, also a number of weathervanes, and carries out special orders from customers along the eastern seaboard.

Henry W. Merrill of East Hiram, a blacksmith and botanist as well, writing in November, 1943, in his eighty-sixth year, said, "I enclose an article which tells what some writer had to say about me, so better put a little salt on that." The article, part of which is reproduced here, did not, in the opinion of this reporter, require much salting. Its title is "The Village Blacksmith Turned Botanist" and was written by Mary Carpenter Kelley, published in *American Forests,* July, 1934. It begins by describing Mr. Merrill's blacksmith shop on the Saco River.

Should you enter his shop . . . he would more than likely be twisting a slender support for a bridge lamp, bringing the end into a delicate scroll resembling the tendril of a climbing fern or fashioning the finial for the top of the standard in the likeness of a half-opened bud. Or he might be hammering a strip of iron into an andiron with a double scroll base like a reversed pair of the stout young croziers of the Osmunda [fern]. But whatever Henry Wilson Merrill . . . may be making . . . you may be certain that . . . it is . . . thoroughly original. . . . He never makes duplicates and folk who want something different have indeed worn a path to his door.

" 'The Botanist Blacksmith!' How did you come by that name?" I asked the first time I called to see the man whose treatise on Maine Ferns I had read in the *American Fern Journal.* . . .

"Well, sit down here on this box and I'll tell you." . . .

"I had to go to work young and was apprenticed to a blacksmith over in New Hampshire. After I had learned the trade I came back to Maine and opened this little shop in East Hiram fully determined to learn something outside my work so that I would not always be just the village blacksmith. Well, along about the time I was twenty-two I happened to get hold of a Maine Agricultural Report that had an article on 'Grasses and Sedges.' I read it over and over. The subject interested me and I made up my mind to learn all there was to be learned about it. I did. Then I branched out into trees, then flowers, and then ferns and after that into other realms of natural history. I had opened a door into a vast and beautiful world and I saw no reason why I should not combine botany with blacksmithing. For more than fifty years I have studied botany, collected specimens, and lost no opportunity to gather information concerning the great world about me. Just lately I have been doing some writing and folks have been asking me to talk to them about my ferns and flowers. I love to do it and I never let them pay me, for I get more fun out of it than they do.

"You say you would like to know particularly about the ferns? I haven't been outside of Maine to gather specimens but I have a fine collection just the same—more than 600 kinds. There are only forty . . . that grow here in the state and out of those I have found thirty-three in the Saco valley within a radius of ten miles of my shop.

"Yes, I've had the honor of having a variety named for me. I found a Christmas fern with an irregular, torn edge, that none of the botanists had ever seen, and so they call it '*Polysticum Acrosti choides Laciniatum* Merrill!' Naturally I am pleased about it and after I am gone that will be my monument." . . .

[Referring to his need for books this blacksmith-botanist told a delightful tale of how he acquired these precious tools]:

"One day, some years ago, in the summertime, a palatial affair, a sort of bungalow-on-wheels, rolled up to the door here. The owner came into the shop and asked if I could fix some gadget or other in the dining-room end of the concern; said he'd stopped at several blacksmith shops and hadn't found anybody who knew what the trouble was. Said he'd heard that I was clever with my hands and didn't do things like everybody else.

"Well, I looked the thing over, found the trouble—just a simple affair that didn't take any time to fix, repaired it and told the man I guessed fifty cents would be all right for pay. He was pleased and seemed in no hurry to get away so we began to talk. Pretty soon I started off on my favorite subject—botany—and as he seemed interested, although it was plain enough that he didn't know much about such things, I mentioned that if I could only study certain books I could make sure of some matters that were puzzling me. We chatted a spell, and when he got up to go he said rather casually that when he got back home in Pennsylvania perhaps he'd hunt up some books that his uncle had left when he died and send them down to me.

"To tell the truth, I didn't think much about it and in fact had almost forgotten the whole incident when one day I got a notice from the freight office down at the depot that they were holding some packing-cases addressed to me and that I'd better send a truck down to get them. I laughed and thought the station agent was joking when he said to send a truck, but he wasn't, for there were several big heavy boxes with my name, Henry Wilson Merrill, East Hiram, Maine, on them as big as life. And do you know, that stranger had kept his word and sent me whole sets of the most wonderful books on botany that you ever saw. Some had hand-colored plates and genuine leather bindings; some were first editions and some were autographed. I never had dreamed there were such books in the world. And to think that they were all mine—I haven't got over the wonder of it yet and I don't suppose I ever will."

Mr. Merrill mentioned the pleasure it had given him to be asked to write the article for the *American Fern Journal,* to speak at club meetings, and to join some of the scientific societies of his state. But the thing that counted most was that he had found a mental world in which he could dwell contentedly all his life no matter what material misfortunes might come to him.

Charles Hoff of Kennebunkport was an old-time carriage builder who, when that trade tapered off, took up blacksmithing, which he is practicing at the present time. Although he suffered a broken back at seventy-one, he did not become discouraged. No longer able to do any heavy work, he makes light pieces on his forge. He made the handrails to the entrance of the public library and many fireplace furnishings for people in the neighborhood. But the effort of which he is most proud is the mechanism for the town's hook-and-ladder truck which he "worked out" in such a way that one lever controls all the other levers on the truck.

Among the capable blacksmiths of Maine whose work deserves description that space will not permit are: Clarence Howard, a fine craftsman and proprietor of The Iron Shop at Blue Hill; Everett Snowman at West Sedgwick; Frank Judkins at Stonington, known as the "fiddling blacksmith and forge philosopher"; Clyde Turner of Isle au Haut; and finally, not a practicing blacksmith, but one of the most skillful workers at the forge, whose designs of household articles are among the best, Carroll T. Berry, the painter of Wiscasset.

BLACKSMITHS OF NEW HAMPSHIRE

Milton Wend of Mont Vernon, a skillful ironworker, is coming to be known more and more as the blacksmith-author. He became interested in writing and put many of his experiences and observations of country living into a book entitled *How to Live in the Country Without Farming*. In the days of the early craftsmen's fairs of the League of New Hampshire Arts and Crafts Mr. Wend was often a demonstrator. He has made a wide variety of objects but has found it more satisfactory to limit himself to a few of the best.

Converse P. Trufant of Francestown still works in ornamental iron but has long since given up horseshoeing. He has an ancient shop more than a century and a half old in the Monadnock section of New Hampshire; one of his prized possessions, and a comfort on winter days, is an old-fashioned country store stove. Only once in many years has he failed the neighbors and summer visitors who depend upon him for hand-wrought articles of iron such as hinges, andirons, fire irons, candlesticks, and metal brackets. That was in 1939 when "some fellow from the city" persuaded him to go down to the New York World's Fair, where for a year he ran a blacksmith shop in the World of Tomorrow. This was only an episode, however, and did not materially affect the ironworking business at Francestown.

BLACKSMITHS OF VERMONT

In a little red painted shop built in 1837 in Derby Line on the northern border, Henry Wight has his forge in connection with which he does a considerable amount of ironwork and woodwork for the country around. Bruce McDonald of Morrisville, Lamoille County, has been a blacksmith for thirty years. He combines his business with the selling of antiques and furniture repairing. In the same county Clayton Wright of Randolph has turned from blacksmithing to the making of household objects in iron. Edmund C. Welles, a blacksmith at Stowe, specializes in iron lanterns, latches, hinges, and other household equipment.

BLACKSMITHS OF MASSACHUSETTS

Cornelius M. Kelley of Deerfield, a former carriage maker, turned to light metalwork when his trade played out. For more than forty years he has maintained a forge in Deerfield, where collections in Memorial Hall and others in the area offer suggestions for the metalworker. In addition to fireplace implements and other ornamental iron Mr. Kelley makes exact copies of old lighting fixtures, colonial candlesticks, and wall brackets. One of his specialties is a candleholder on a hinged bracket which, when attached to a door-casing, supphes the means of lighting more than one room.

Howard W. Barrus of Barnstable is known in his community as an "artist in iron." He not only expends great care upon the many tools and implements which he makes for farm and home use, but also takes pleasure in hammering out ornamental pieces. As a wedding gift to his daughter, he made a picture frame, using the tools of the horseshoer's trade as motifs: anvil, fitting hammer, horseshoes, nails, pincers, farrier's knife, buttress, sledge hammer, and hoof parer were all hammered out in miniature and worked into the design.

BLACKSMITHS OF CONNECTICUT

On a country lane in the western part of Connecticut in the township of Bakersville stands an old blacksmith shop with a sign over the door reading: GEORGE W. JONES, BLACKSMITH, OX AND HORSE SHOEING. He is the oldest blacksmith in Connecticut—possibly the oldest practicing blacksmith in New England, and the only one known to the writer who shoes oxen with regularity. These are brought to him usually by truck from Lakeville, Litchfield, Middlebury, and even from towns in Massachusetts. They are driven into the sturdily built stall, put into a strong sling, and lifted off the ground. He places the hoofs of both oxen and horses on strong wooden supports which he devised so that he does not have to bear the weight or feel the strain of sudden movement of nervous animals. Mr. Jones performs all operations from making the shoes to fastening them upon the oxen's feet. The oxshoe is small and delicate compared to a horseshoe and is in two parts so as not to bind the cloven foot. In the old blacksmith shop in Storrowton, Springfield, Massachusetts, is another ox-stall and sling, and undoubtedly, there are some still remaining in the state of Maine.

Mr. Jones recalls the time when he and his father used to shoe from ten to twelve pairs of oxen a day. Then horseshoeing came to be one of the principal features of blacksmithing. When horses became fewer, Blacksmith Jones began to make different objects of use in the way of iron tools and finally ornamental ironwork for fireplaces and other home purposes; he also makes excellent ax and hammer handles, most of them from native hickory.

E. B. Pratt of Essex closed his shop in 1942. It was then the oldest blacksmith or metalworking shop in New England, having been founded in 1678 and operated continuously by five generations of the same family.

Arthur L. Bessett of Suffield has a fine commodious old blacksmith shop where he still makes horseshoes, and shoes a good many horses, but his work is principally in ornamental iron for domestic purposes. Mr. Bessett, who was born in Quebec, learned his trade through an apprenticeship, for which he received $75 a year and boarded himself. He has, however, been in the United States for most of his lifetime and has served the community as a practical rural blacksmith for the past fifty years. He is enthusiastic about the old forms of ironwork characteristic of New England in the early days, which he often reproduces.

One of the youngest blacksmiths in New England is Laurence W. Collins of Farmington, who calls himself "a blacksmith and ironmonger." As a boy, Mr. Collins built his own forge in Littleton, New Hampshire. Later he worked with the League of New Hampshire Arts and Crafts and finally established himself in the old single-room schoolhouse in Farmington, which is ideal for his work. He is a member of the Society of Connecticut Craftsmen and president of a group of handicraft workers. He does not shoe horses, but helps farmers repair various kinds of machines and tools and turns from such occupations to creative work in iron, reproducing favorite old pieces or more often creating a new design for household use.

SILVERSMITHING AND OTHER FORMS OF METALWORK

Turning now to other types of metalwork, the inquirer finds a wide variety of expression. Lighter metals are oftener used by craftsmen in this group but occasionally one is found who also works in iron. Enameling and the use of precious and semiprecious stones are important in this category. The various craftsmen will be referred to under the states where they live and work.

Maine. The silverware of Vincent Gookin of Ogunquit is medieval in spirit, with simple lines, sometimes plain and sometimes ornamented with jewels or with embossed work. His hammering is carefully done and exceedingly pleasant to touch; his finishes are finely executed. He has made a beautiful chalice for a Catholic church in Sanford, and was represented at the Worcester Handicraft Exhibition.

Miss Madeleine Burrage of Wiscasset calls herself "a jeweler in native stone," and with justification, for it was through her extensive study of and love for precious and semiprecious stones that she came to make settings for them. It is the stones of New England, and especially from Maine, to which she has devoted the most care, although

81. A HOMEMADE SUNDIAL

THIS FINE ARMILLARY SPHERE BRONZE SUNDIAL WAS DESIGNED AND MADE BY CARLETON
GOFF OF BARRINGTON, RHODE ISLAND. MRS. GOFF HAS MADE MANY HANDSOME PIECES OF
NEEDLEWORK, AND MR. GOFF OBJECTS OF WOOD AND METAL. PART OF HIS MODEL OF A
VIKING SHIP IS SHOWN IN THE FRONTISPIECE.

Edmund de Beaumont, Worcester Art Museum

82. HANDICRAFTS DERIVED FROM THREE EUROPEAN HOMELANDS

WEAVING BY JOHN REHORKA OF SHUTESBURY, MASSACHUSETTS, BORN IN CZECHOSLOVAKIA; EMBROIDERED SHIRT BY MRS. ROSALIA NAMAKA OF AMHERST, MASSACHUSETTS, BORN IN THE UKRAINE; WOODEN FORK AND SPOONS BY LEMPI MIETTINEN OF BETHEL, VERMONT, A DAUGHTER OF FINNISH PARENTS.

83. BIRDCARVINGS OF A MASSACHUSETTS CRAFTSMAN

John Templeman Coolidge of Milton Carved and Mounted These Two Bird Groups. Upper Center, a Great White Heron Perched on a White Cedar Root Elaborated by Mr. Coolidge; Left, Manchurian Crane; Right, an Asiatic White Crane. . . . Lower, White-fronted Geese, Mounted on Driftwood.

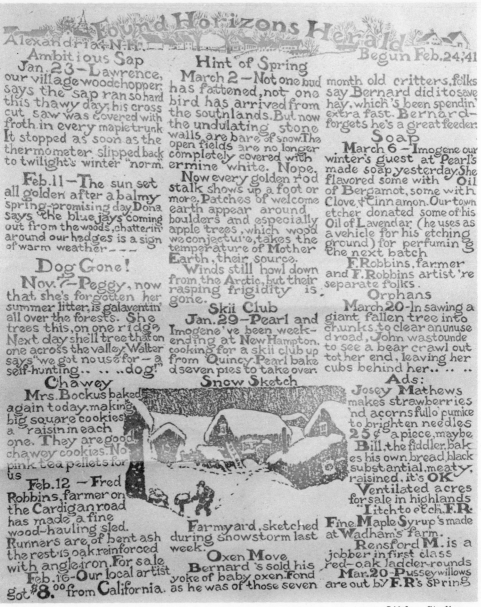

Lifshey Studios

84. A NEWSPAPER MADE FROM ONE BLOCK

Found Horizons Herald WAS WRITTEN, PRINTED, AND ILLUSTRATED BY FREDERICK ROBBINS OF ALEXANDRIA, NEW HAMPSHIRE. THE ENTIRE PAGE WAS CUT FROM A SINGLE LINOLEUM BLOCK AND PRINTED BY HAND ON AN ETCHING PRESS IN HIS ONE-ROOM CABIN AT THE EDGE OF THE VILLAGE.

Lifshey Studios

85. A HANDMADE CRIB QUILT

THE DAHLOV IPCAR FAMILY LIVE ON A LITTLE FARM IN ROBINHOOD, MAINE. MRS.
IPCAR MAKES TOYS, QUILTS, AND CLOTHES FOR HER CHILDREN; THIS QUILT WAS
MADE FOR THE CRIB IN WHICH EACH CHILD HAS HIS TURN AS THE FAMILY GROWS UP.

Edmund de Beaumont

Edmund de Beaumont, School Arts Magazine

86. WOODCARVINGS FROM MAINE AND MASSACHUSETTS

PORTRAIT OF A MAINE CHARACTER WHITTLED BY WAYNE BUXTON OF SEARSPORT; SUBJECT TAKEN FROM AN OLD FAMILY PHOTOGRAPH. . . . THREE BEARS, THE WORK OF MISS CARRIE L. BLAKE OF READING, A MEMBER OF MINUTE-MAN CRAFTS, WHO ON RETIRING FROM TEACHING TOOK UP WOODCARVING.

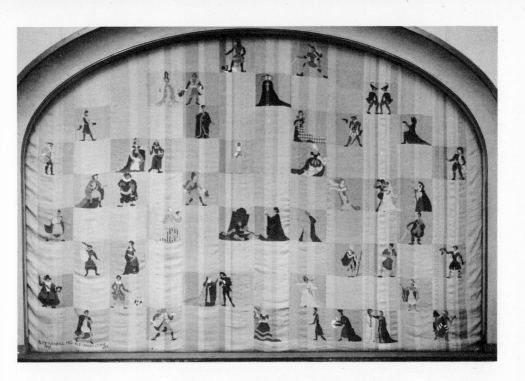

87. A HAND-WOVEN THEATER CURTAIN

THIS BEAUTIFUL CURTAIN, TWENTY-TWO FEET HIGH AND THIRTY FEET WIDE, WAS WOVEN BY MISS ALICE TURNBULL OF HADDAM, CONNECTICUT, FOR THE BAR HARBOR PLAYHOUSE. IT WAS DESIGNED BY ALEXANDER CRANE OF BARNSTABLE, MASSACHUSETTS.

88. MITTENS FROM NEW HAMPSHIRE

Every Year Two Groups in New Hampshire Knit Hundreds of Pairs of Mittens and Other Small Winter Apparel: the League of New Hampshire Arts and Crafts and the Group at Whitefield Whose Products Are Known as Wintersportswear. These Mittens Were Made by the League.

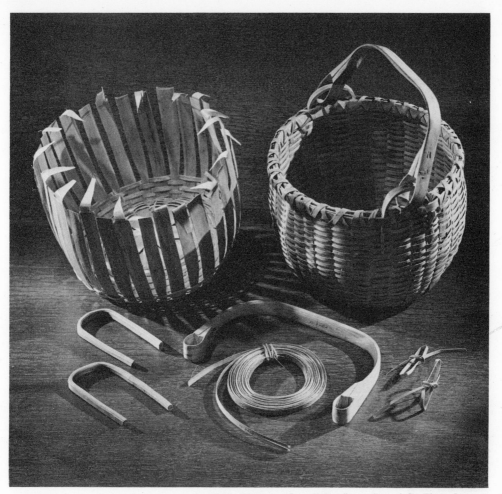

Life Photographer, Fritz Goro, Copyright Time, Inc.

89. THE ANATOMY OF A BASKET

THE MATERIALS IN THESE TWO BASKETS, ONE WITH PARTS UNASSEMBLED, THE OTHER
COMPLETE, WERE PREPARED BY ARTHUR M. SWEETSER OF WATERBURY, VERMONT, TO
SHOW THE CONSTRUCTION AND SUGGEST THE STAGES OF ASH-SPLINT BASKETMAKING.

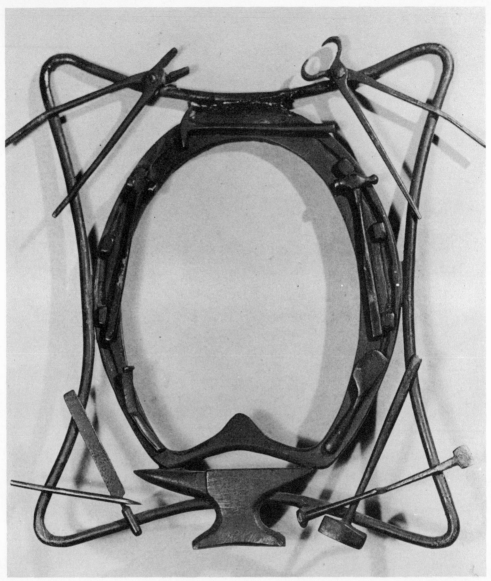

John D. Schiff

90. WORK OF A CAPE COD FARRIER

This Horseshoe Picture Frame Was Made by Howard W. Barrus, a Blacksmith of Barnstable, as a Wedding Gift for His Daughter. An Excellent Example of Craftsmanship in Iron, It Is an Appropriate Family Symbol, for Mr. Barrus' Father Was Also a Farrier.

91. CRAFTSMANSHIP IN HORN, METAL, AND WOOD

J. A. JOHNSON OF WORCESTER, MASSACHUSETTS, MADE THIS REPLICA OF A HISTORIC
SWEDISH DRINKING HORN. . . . WILD DUCK CARVED IN MAHOGANY BY CHARLES CHASE
OF WISCASSET, MAINE. . . . WOODEN ANIMALS BY PHILIP L. MARTIN OF AUBURNDALE,
MASSACHUSETTS.

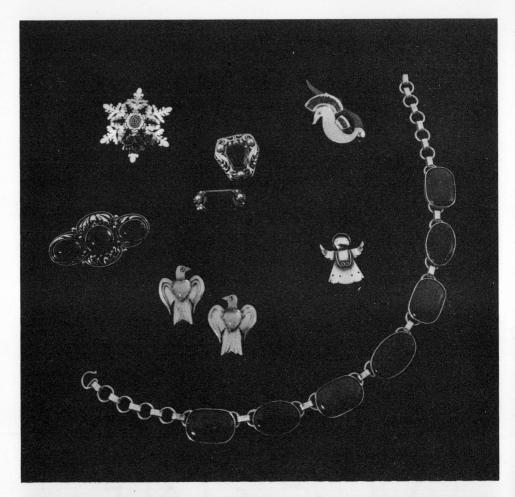

Edmund de Beaumont

92. NEW ENGLAND JEWELRY AND CARVING IN IVORY

ANGEL PIN, MARGARET WHITE, MAINE; SNOWFLAKE, THOMAS GOTSHALL, NEW HAMP-
SHIRE LEAGUE; LARGE BROOCH, HAZEL B. FRENCH, MASSACHUSETTS; PIN, TOURMALINE
AND PEARLS, EDWARD E. OAKES, MASSACHUSETTS; HEXAGONAL BROOCH, FRANK G. HALE,
MASSACHUSETTS; NECKLACE AND SEA HORSE, MADELEINE BURRAGE, MAINE. . . . . CARVING
IN MASTODON IVORY BY PETER PAUL KRSYZEWSKI OF MASSACHUSETTS.

Edmund de Beaumont, School Arts Magazine

93. POTTERY IN NEW HAMPSHIRE

ALL THE PIECES IN THIS GROUP OF POTTERY WERE MADE BY EDWIN AND MARY SCHEIER OF DURHAM. THEY WERE SHOWN AT THE EXHIBITION OF CONTEMPORARY NEW ENGLAND HANDICRAFTS AT WORCESTER, MASSACHUSETTS.

John D. Schiff, School Arts Magazine

94. FOLK CARVING IN MASSACHUSETTS AND MAINE

GEORGE A. GRANT, ONCE DIRECTOR OF NANTUCKET WHALING MUSEUM, CARVED AND PAINTED THIS SIGN FOR THE MUSEUM IN HIS EIGHTY-FIRST YEAR. . . . DELMONT POTTER OF BAR HARBOR HAS WHITTLED THE PRINCIPAL ANIMALS OF MAINE, AND MANY FISHES, FROM NATIVE WOODS.

95. MOSAIC OF MASSACHUSETTS CLAMSHELLS

This Madonna of the Sea Mosaic Was Done by Edward Waldo Forbes, Formerly Director of the Fogg Museum of Art, and His Associates from Tessellae of Quahog Shells, Gathered Mainly from the Shores of the Elizabeth Islands, Off the Coast of Massachusetts.

Tommy Weber, Crossroads of Sport

96. A BIRD FAMILY IN MINIATURE

THIS MINIATURE WOODCARVING OF A WOODCOCK FAMILY BY ALLEN J. KING OF NORTH
SCITUATE, RHODE ISLAND, IS ABOUT AN INCH AND A HALF HIGH.

those from other countries also interest her. Her work is distinguished often for its massiveness, and always for the directness of treatment. One feels that its main purpose is to give the stone the simplest, strongest, and most appropriate setting. Miss Burrage was represented at both the Worcester and the Portland exhibitions.

Mrs. Margaret White of Bangor is both craftsman and teacher. Her carefully executed and delightful miniature designs cut through the silver sheet characterize her work. She uses many patterns, some very spirited; and the simplicity of her technique makes it possible to produce attractive ornaments quite inexpensively.

Maisie S. and William Truitt of the Gray Elf Shop at Hulls Cove are craftsmen in several materials but particularly in the use of copper, which they have worked into such forms as lamp shades, fire screens, and book ends. Because of the shortage of metals during the recent war, they were obliged to turn their attention to other handicrafts. Among these are pottery making, silk-screen painting, and blockprinting. During the summer they devote some of their time to children of families who come for vacations, instructing them in drawing, painting, ceramics, crafts. Miss Constance Howe of Bangor does both metalwork and weaving, and carries her work into the field of recreation. W. J. Leitch, proprietor of the Leitch Artcraft Shop in Fryeburg, works in pewter, copper, silver, and enamel.

New Hampshire. Thousands of people during the annual Craftsman's Fair have seen George Olsson, a native of Sweden, demonstrate the making of jewelry. He learned the jewelry trade in the regular way and became an excellent craftsman; but feeling the increasing pressure that the average employe experiences, as well as the limitation of space, he took up chicken farming near Francestown. He taught jewelry making for the League and trained privately scores of people. This combination of small farming, jewelry making, and teaching, Mr. Olsson said, gives him a full measure of peace and tranquillity.

John G. Herrick of Hillsboro is a fine example of the traditional New England craftsman who has worked with his hands since boyhood. At the age of eighty-three years Mr. Herrick expressed himself in regard to his work as follows: "Having inherited mechanical ability from my ancestors, it was only natural that people should bring all sorts of things to me to be repaired. Violins were one of the items. After repairing violins for a year or more I had a strong desire to try my hand at making one. In 1908 I saw an advertisement of a book on *Violin Making,* and I immediately procured one. Although I have read many books on the subject since that time my first one proved to be the most helpful. During the next ten years I made about sixty violins and repaired many more; also made a few violin bows and one cello. I used some imported wood which many violin makers consider to be the best, but later found that spruce taken from old buildings in New Hampshire for the tops of violins, and curly maple that grew among the hills of New Hampshire for the backs, when aged, was every whit as good as any found in other parts of the world. As I gained experience my violins improved in quality, and I found a ready sale for them until after the first World War."

In recent times Mr. Herrick has worked almost entirely in the reproduction of colonial furniture and metalcraft. Many of the tools that he uses for metalworking and woodworking he has made himself. Probably no craftsman in New England has mastered more crafts or works with greater perfection, whether shaping the smallest bowl in silver or pewter, or building a violin-cello. Occasionally he has made for his own pleasure a ring or some other piece of jewelry, ornamented with native stones cut and polished by himself. In the early days he and Mrs. Herrick were enthusiastic visitors at the annual Craftsman's Fair, where fine examples of Mr. Herrick's work were usually to be seen.

H. L. Herrick is a son of the older craftsman just mentioned. He is a "chip off the same block" and works effectively in both wood and metal. He is also an expert in making chair seats of native rushes, a special skill which he described in the August, 1924, number of *Antiques*.

Maxwell Coulter of Concord does much of his work in his favorite metal, copper. He was represented by a beautiful copper pitcher in the New Hampshire building at the New York World's Fair, and also with pitchers and measuring mugs at the Worcester Exhibition.

New Hampshire has many other metalworkers who deserve mention. Thomas Gotshall, who keeps a general store at Center Sandwich, learned the rudiments of silversmithing in Boston, and has turned out some unusual jewelry; he has also taught some of his neighbors to do metalwork. Miss Helen Chandler, a fine craftsman in jewelry, has made it an outstanding feature at the Manchester Institute of Arts and Sciences. Joseph Holick, who learned metalwork in his native Bohemia, is getting under way as a craftsman in this country and hopes to establish an all-round metal shop at his home in Campton. George G. Howland of Nashua is combining handmade jewelry with metalwork. He has made his own tools and is a very accurate and skillful worker. He demonstrated at the Craftsman's Fair in 1944. Mrs. Maude Leighton, who lives near Temple, is considered one of the best teachers in jewelry making in the state. She attended art school in Boston before she began farming. In her little shop on the farm she has made jewelry for a number of years.

Vermont. The Reverend Ernest I. Rand, pastor of Thetford Center at Union Village, is a metalworker and has also made spoons, salad forks, noggins, and drinking cups of wood. His bowls, candlesticks, sconces, trays, and communion plates of brass and pewter were often made of waste metal during the war years. He has taught his son to work so well in both wood and metal that he thinks him the better craftsman of the two.

Everett Williams of Williamsville is a coppersmith. His particular product is copper measures, which he makes in all sizes from a gill to a gallon. He exhibited some of these at the Worcester Exhibition.

Miss Marion Adams of Northfield learned silversmithing at Goddard College in Plainfield, and earns her living through this work. She makes flower pins, bracelets, buttons, bookmarks, and so forth in many original designs. She also does pewter and copper work.

Massachusetts. Coming into Massachusetts we are confronted with two facts which must be considered in this chapter. First is that the rise of silversmithing and jewelry making to the height that it reached in the first quarter of the present century in New England, out of which has come most of the best work now being done, was largely a development that took place within the Bay State. The second fact is that the extent to which silversmithing and jewelry making are practiced today in Massachusetts has made it impossible to include in this book all the craftsmen so engaged. Therefore the most that can be done is to list a considerable number of them and refer to a few specifically, hoping to suggest the extent of these branches of metalworking and something of their character. In this endeavor it seems logical to give the background of silversmithing and jewelry first.

Early Silversmithing and Jewelry Making

Silversmithing in America began in the first half of the seventeenth century when the first craftsmen came from England. The early flowering of silversmithing, in which Massachusetts had a leading part, took place in the late years of the seventeenth and early years of the eighteenth century when the work of Jeremiah Dummer, John Coney, Edward Winslow, and others set standards in design and workmanship which are the admiration of our silversmiths of today. Around the time of the War for Independence a number of New Englanders, including our distinguished Paul Revere, achieved high places in this aristocratic craft. Later, as individual craftsmen gave way to organized groups and mass production made great strides, silversmithing as an art lost ground steadily for more than a hundred years until the end of the nineteenth century and the beginning of the twentieth.

The manufacturers of silverware in this country had drawn heavily on the designers and craftsmen of Europe to develop this young and growing industry. It was partly from the silver industries of the United States, and partly from trained craftsmen from across the sea, that the Society of Arts and Crafts drew a group of silversmiths that possibly gave the young organization its greatest distinction, and restored to New England something of the traditions and standards for which colonial silversmithing had been famous. We can take, at least, a quick glance over the fifty years since the Society was organized to note briefly some of those who have left an imprint on American culture through silversmithing in New England.

The dean of them all and fondly remembered by many still living was Arthur J. Stone, born in Sheffield, England, in 1847. After an apprenticeship of seven years and a working practice as a designer and chaser for ten years, he came to America in 1884, was employed by a firm in Concord, New Hampshire, and later became superintendent of a silverware company in Gardner, Massachusetts. Encouraged by an exhibition of the Society of Arts and Crafts, he decided to open a shop of his own with the assistance of his young American wife. It has been truly said that the prestige of the Society was "a large factor in the upbuilding of Mr. Stone's reputation, and likewise the fine quality of his work was a cornerstone for the Society's prestige." Mr. Stone's silver was characterized by graceful ornamentation, often inspired by native plants and flowers, and by superb craftsmanship. This high standard is followed today by Mr. Stone's associates and successors. They were well represented in the Worcester Exhibition.

George C. Gebelein, another pioneer of this era, although born in Bavaria, received all his training in the United States. Many know the Williamsburg Communion Set, which he made, and perhaps even more know his famous reproductions of ancient silver. George E. Germer, the son of a Berlin jeweler, came to America in 1893. After nearly twenty years' employment in New York, Boston, and Providence, he set up his shop in Mason, New Hampshire, where his work in ecclesiastical subjects gained recognition for him.

George J. Hunt, born in Liverpool, came to America in 1885. After working in several New York factories, he began as an individual craftsman in Boston, where he did silversmithing, made jewelry, and taught both of these subjects. He also established the now well-known School of the Museum of Fine Arts in Boston.

From Finland came Karl F. Leinonen, and from Malmö, Sweden, F. J. R. Gyllenberg—two craftsmen who were to work together in The Handicraft Shop in Boston. This undertaking was made possible in

1901 by Arthur A. Carey, an early president of the Society of Arts and Crafts. Other workers in the shop were George C. Gebelein; Adolphe Kunkler, a Swiss; C. R. Forssen, Swedish born; Miss Mary C. Knight and Miss Mary Hersey. The workers on the whole produced a sturdy, plain, and, except for fluting, undecorated silver. The Handicraft Shop changed location several times and also auspices, but for many years it furnished shop facilities to craftsmen who worked independently. Mr. Leinonen's son Edwin was for a long time his father's valuable assistant and continues as an active silversmith today; and Alfred H. Swanson was the partner of Mr. Gyllenberg.

An excellent account of these early silversmiths entitled "The Silversmiths of New England," with some illustrations of their work, was written by Henry P. Macomber, and appeared in the *American Magazine of Art* for October, 1932. Many of the facts noted here are based upon Mr. Macomber's article.

Contemporary Silversmiths and Jewelers

We now turn to a few contemporary craftsmen. Edwin M. Gerould of Swampscott is well known throughout the country for his hand-wrought and handspun silver and for his work in copper. Many of his designs are original. He has also made fine copies of early silversmithing, including reproductions of some famous masterpieces.

Mr. and Mrs. Joseph L. Sharrock of Prides Crossing are among the most finished metalworkers in our country. Mr. Sharrock is an experienced teacher as well. One of the silver tea sets shown at the Worcester Exhibition was the work of Mrs. Sharrock and is illustrated here.

George C. Gebelein, already mentioned among the early silversmiths, was also one of the best-known contemporary craftsmen, producing worthy pieces until his death in 1946. He was represented at the Worcester Exhibition by a covered silver cup, a toddy bowl and plate; and in collaboration with George E. Germer, an altar set.

Frank Gardner Hale of Boston and also of Marblehead, who worked mainly in silver and jewelry, was for many years a prominent member of the Society of Arts and Crafts.

James T. Woolley, who spent the last part of his life in Quincy, was a craftsman of wide versatility both as silversmith and jeweler. Like Mr. Gebelein, Mr. Woolley belonged to both the early and the contemporary groups. He learned his craft with the Gorham Company, had bench room with George J. Hunt in the Chestnut Street shop, Boston, sponsored by the Society of Arts and Crafts, and in 1908 set up his own shop. Many of his pieces are excellent adaptations of colonial models. A memorial consisting of a chalice and other altar pieces was executed by Woolley for the chapel at Mercersburg Academy, Pennsylvania, where Calvin Coolidge, Jr., was a student at the time of his death.

Lester H. Vaughan of Taunton has won for pewter a new level of acceptance and has earned for himself the medal of the Society of Arts and Crafts, and the Arthur Heun Prize from the Art Institute of Chicago. The work turned out by Mr. Vaughan and his associates, many objects being shaped by hand while others are cast or spun, is of such importance that it has found its way into museums. Pewter of today is pure black tin hardened with copper and antimony.

William Boogar, Jr., of Provincetown is both a sculptor and metalworker and is very skillful in casting miniature forms, especially birds and small animals. Sea gulls are his favorite product. Mr. Boogar also works in wood, and often combines it with metal. A memorial cross carved by him in wood is shown.

Miss Katharine Pratt of Dedham has been working in metal for thirty years, doing her own designing and carrying out special patterns to order. She makes many objects in silver by hand, including tea sets, bowls, candlesticks, cups, porringers, and so forth. She is a medalist in the Society of Arts and Crafts.

Malcolm Bunker of Harwich likes best to work in copper; his pieces are often of large size. As the first president of Minute-Man Crafts he was a leading spirit in getting his organization thoroughly launched both in production and in the sale of articles. He began his work during the depression of the 1930's, and is always willing to help other craftsmen. Mr. Bunker has recently built a new shop in his home overlooking the sea at Harwich, where visitors have an opportunity to observe processes of metalworking. In a wall of the old house he found a swarm of wild honey bees at work; he removed some of the boards, replaced them with glass, and now the bees put on a special show for Mr. Bunker's customers.

There is a colony of craftsmen on Bearskin Neck in Rockport often visited by travelers in quest of handicrafts. The first contemporary craftsmen to live and work on this crowded point of land running out into the bay are the Whitneys. Their workshop, a picturesque handicraft studio and home with a tiny courtyard adjoining, is the common undertaking of Mr. and Mrs. Lewis Whitney. Mr. Whitney is a self-taught craftsman, a direct and efficient workman with fine feeling for the hard materials with which he has had long experience. Mrs. Whitney is an able assistant in the field of design and the general conduct of the business. Mr. Whitney's preference is for pewter and he has made special tools or dies for a number of decorations. When the war took pewter from the Whitneys, they turned to craft aluminum, copper, and silver, in which they and their now several associates produce a large output.

Examples of Mr. Whitney's more ambitious work are the pewter plaque for the Rockport police and fire station, a figure of Christ in lead for St. Agnes House of the Sisters of St. Ann, also in Rockport, and an altar piece for the Episcopal Church at Ipswich.

Others in the field of handicrafts on Bearskin Neck are Otis and Grace Cook. Mr. Cook has made many local sketches and has etched in pewter scenes around Cape Ann; Mrs. Cook applies enamel to both copper and silver. Wendell Emerson makes silver jewelry, and Peter Koster does furniture decoration.

Connecticut. A. H. Eaton of Collinsville is shown in the illustration repairing an old weathervane. He has long been a careful student of metal accessories in connection with furniture making and has gathered many patterns of furniture hardware, some of the best of which he has reproduced. Mr. Eaton has possibly the largest selection of designs for drawer pulls ever brought together—between two and three thousand patterns—representing about twelve years of work.

Leonard S. Rankin, a craftsman in metal and a pioneer teacher in enameling, with his wife, Myra, a designer and craftsman in both metal and textiles, were strong forces in the development of handicrafts in Connecticut. Mrs. Rankin's work is already familiar to the reader through her designs for the Work Projects Administration. Before coming to Connecticut Mr. Rankin was identified with the New York Society of Craftsmen, and with his teaching experience he was well prepared to take a leading part in establishing the Society of Connecticut Craftsmen, of which he was director and field secretary for ten years. The Rankins selected as the site for their home an old country blacksmith shop on the high banks of a clear running stream not far from the village of Bakersville in the township of New Hartford. They retained in the shop much of its original equipment, including the forge, a sling or harness for shoeing oxen, and other remnants of an earlier day. They built their house on the end of the blacksmith shop, which they so improved that it became an ideal studio for themselves, and their neighbors as well. During a period of ten weeks one summer a group of country women hammered out articles in copper for their own use. Because of farm chores they could not come earlier than nine o'clock in the evening but they stayed until after eleven. Several paid the nominal charge for instruction and materials with farm products and flowers.

An endless experimenter, Mr. Rankin was very much interested in the allied arts. He was one of the first craftsmen to apply enamel extensively to copper and silver. His favorite design for metal or wood was the American eagle, which he worked into many forms, including a brass decoration of bird and stars on the door of the Rankin home, and a copper eagle made for the Guaranty Trust Company building at Worcester. He ran out of material before he finished the latter and, since copper was practically unobtainable at the time, he was obliged to use crumpled scraps from an old fire extinguisher for the eagle's tail feathers. A photograph of Mr. and Mrs. Rankin in their Connecticut shop is shown.

Donn Sheets of New Milford, member of the Society of Connecticut Craftsmen, is one whom the title "artist-craftsman" fits particularly. As a stenciler Mr. Sheets' work, which covers a wide spread in handicrafts, is referred to in Chapter 8, but he is mentioned at this point because he is a craftsman in all the metals—iron, copper, brass, and tin—that contribute to the comfort and beauty of the home. In problems of interior decorating his skills are often supplemented by those of his mother, who is a weaver.

Orazio Curri spent his early years in the village of Alberobello, Italy, where he learned creative ironwork at his father's forge. After an unfortunate business venture in Bridgeport, Mr. Curri started his handicraft shop in the basement of his home, "with an anvil, a hammer, and a heavy mortgage" on the house that he had built for his large family. In a short time he had made other tools and finally established a good business in the making of decorative lamps, candlesticks, gates, andirons, and fire tools; copper and lead garden fountains; church fixtures and chancel equipment.

Because of an old indebtedness he lost his first shop and home in the depression. However, he found another place and with the help of his sons built the business up again, carrying out many fine commissions. In time he retired, and his sons continue to carry on at the Curri Artcraft Shop. An admiring neighbor said: "He was an artist in metal. With a piece of chalk he would make a rough sketch on the large hood of his forge of the piece he intended to form. Then he would begin to hammer, always seeming to have a small boy helping and a larger boy working in another part of the shop. When the need came he would call the older boy to strike with him on the heavy forging. Their hammers were always in tune—the father's and son's striking alternately as the metal gradually took the form of the model roughly sketched on the great copper hood. As the father turned the hot iron the son would hammer down the heavier part of the metal, the father striking the anvil lightly with his hammer to continue the rhythm. Nearby the smaller boy kept the fire going, ready to heat the metal again." Some of the finest ecclesiastical work in Bridgeport was made by Mr. Curri and his sons.

Serge S. Nekrassoff brought to America the skill and traditions of his native Russia, famous for its work in metal. The output of Mr. Nekrassoff's shop at Darien has been largely copper and pewter objects, including some of the most unusual patterns, both medium and large, to be hammered out in New England. This metalwork plant, turning out bowls, trays, candlesticks, and special pieces to order, is largely a family industry in which the son and Mrs. Nekrassoff help with the books. Mr. Nekrassoff does the designing and makes many of their fine copper pieces, but several skillful craftsmen are employed.

On a beautiful stream near rock cliffs on the outskirts of Brookfield, A. J. Tuck has his studio workshop and electroplating plant. Associated with him is his son. His daughter, Mary, makes small objects in metal especially in the form of jewelry. They are well known because of their unusual finish achieved by the electric copper coating, which is applied in Mr. Tuck's shop. Both father and daughter have long been members of the Society of Connecticut Craftsmen.

Among other workers in metal who are members of the Society and who deserve much more space than can be given here are: Mrs. Ned K. Anderson of Braeburn Farm, Sherman, who did work for several years for a New York firm in enameling and painting on jewelry, and now specializes in silver flatware and jewelry of original design; Miss Ruth Wellman of Hamden, an accomplished worker in silver and jewelry, who has conducted shops at East Haven, and Rockport, Massachusetts; Miss Frances Felten of Winsted, a teacher and a craftsman of extraordinary skill and taste, especially in pewter; Miss Nellie Loring of Norwich, an able art teacher and fine craftsman; Evan F. Kullgren of Columbia, president of the Society, and skilled worker both in copper and pewter; Eustace Brothers of Canton Center, who specializes in decorative articles in sheet copper; Mrs. Gladys T. Guerard of Norwalk, who works in both metal and leather, her particular interest being coats-of-arms in both materials; John D. Preu of Newington, an all-round metalworker and jeweler, who makes bowls of hammered copper, brass, silver, and aluminum; Miss Helen A. Haselton of West Hartford, a teacher of wide experience in handicrafts, who in addition to being a puppeteer works in metal, leather, and ceramics; Andrew Pfeiffer of Old Lyme, who makes costume jewelry, small ship models, and other articles to consumer's order.

On watching a lapidarist change rough mineral specimens into objects of beauty, A. L. Taylor of Waterbury was interested to the point of getting himself a stone-grinding equipment and began cutting New England minerals into forms for mounting. But he soon felt that his hobby was not complete until he learned enough of jewelry making to be able to mount appropriately the stones he had cut and polished. Now in his spare time he takes satisfaction in discovering the possibilities of a rough stone and carrying it through to an appropriate setting.

Rhode Island. William E. Brigham of Providence is one of the best-known and most productive metal craftsmen in New England. His connection with other handicrafts was noted in Chapters 5 and 8. He is a jeweler and metalworker who has produced many objects of fine design. An outstanding example of Mr. Brigham's jewelry at the Worcester Exhibition was The Argosy, a beautiful and imaginative ship of Sicilian amber, rubies, pearls, emeralds, and enamel. An altar set by him is illustrated.

ENAMELING ON METAL

Although a number of jewelers mentioned elsewhere apply enamel to copper, silver, or gold, and the work of some enamelers has already been mentioned, it is a handicraft so well represented in New England that the name of a few who specialize in it should be included here.

Among pioneers in this beautiful craft one thinks perhaps first of the Luther sisters of Providence. Miss Mabel W. Luther, long associated with the Rhode Island School of Design, was well represented by her unusually attractive enamels in the Worcester Exhibition. As an early experimenter in enameling on copper and silver she originated and carried out countless examples of this technique and is distinguished for her use of pure color. The application of rich enamels to simple forms of copper brings out the maximum color and texture of this remarkable medium. Miss Jessie Luther is also an experienced craftsman in the same field.

The early work of Mr. and Mrs. Leonard S. Rankin has been mentioned and with it should be included the attractive enameling now being done by Mrs. Rankin. Possibly the most widely known in New England and among the most gifted designers and craftsmen in our country is Karl Drerup of Campton, New Hampshire, whose enameled tiles received the grand prize at the National Ceramic Exhibition in Syracuse, New York, a few years ago. Mrs. Louise Moulton, one of the most talented and sensitive teachers in the New Hampshire League, is an experienced and very successful designer and craftsman in this medium. Mrs. G. F. Hay, a teacher in Northampton, does unusual work in designing and executing enamels on both flat and curved surfaces. Mrs. Waldemar Raemisch of Providence, Rhode Island, was well represented at the Worcester Handicraft show by her enamel dish, New England Farm, and an enameled panel, Malaga; Miss Florence Whitehead of Wellesley, Massachusetts, also exhibited a few of her choice pieces of enameling.

GEM-CUTTING OR LAPIDARY WORK

Examples of gem-cutting or lapidary work are quite frequent throughout New England. Percy C. Leggett of Gorham, New Hampshire, whose recent death deprived the League of New Hampshire Arts and Crafts of one of its most devoted members, did gem-cutting and made jewelry. He also cut and polished many less valuable minerals and rocks. Some of his cut stones he mounted and sold through the League, or from his own shop, and some he supplied to the League's jewelry workers. Many of his polished mineral specimens went to collectors. He worked in both silver and gold and conducted classes in silversmithing. Mr. Leggett made his own equipment for faceting gems; the equipment he could buy for this type of work he found unsatisfactory and not very durable. Mrs. Leggett, who also makes jewelry, is a weaver.

In his own shop at Freeport, Maine, is a lapidarist of unusual ability, I. S. Skillin, who has a remarkable collection of native minerals. No one else has taken the great variety of granites, slate, marble, and other hard stones of Maine and made them into such interesting forms—spheres, cylinders, vases, bowls, cubes, and sometimes simple sculptured shapes as frogs, fish, and abstracts. We have been told in Chapter 4 how Mr. Skillin owes his interest in handicrafts to the great depression which separated him entirely from his former occupation and influenced him to start life anew.

Dr. James C. Clement, a resident of Bangor, spends as much time as possible in the summer at Seal Harbor, where he manages the Seaside Hotel, but gives far more of his attention, so his friends say, to studying local geology and to the cutting of stones.

A very interesting experiment in Maine minerals was that carried out by the famous photographer and artist, Vivian Akers of Norway, who had a lens for special types of photographing ground from native amber-hued crystal. Mr. Akers was seeking a lens which would permit fast exposures, and he decided that the crystals of citrine quartz from a nearby mica mine would give him what he needed. He found a piece that had come from a ledge near Auburn. The yellow tint of the quartz made it possible for Mr. Akers to photograph without a color filter, and thus his experiment proved satisfactory.

C. B. Hamilton, also of Norway, writes, "The only work I have done in handicrafts for some time is lapidary. I have cut cabochon gems [unfaceted] for local trade and a few for other collectors for about ten years. I have cut over 400 stones for a man in Massachusetts."

Stanley Perham of West Paris has a mineral store and deals extensively in natural Maine gems and in pendants, bracelets, ear bobs, rings, and so forth. He also prepared cabochon cuttings for craft workers.

Mrs. Mary S. Shaub of Northampton, Massachusetts, exhibited native stones and her own lapidary work at the handicraft fairs there in 1943 and 1944. Her husband is a geologist at Smith College, and Mrs. Shaub has use of the laboratory. She specializes in stones of Massachusetts and has also worked with clamshells, which she has cut and polished.

JEWELS FROM OLD GLASS

Mrs. Hazel B. French of Sandwich, Massachusetts, has made beautiful rings, chains, pendants, bracelets, and other objects of personal ornament by using fragments of old Sandwich glass gathered from the long buried refuse of the famous old factory near her home on Cape Cod Bay. In the *Independent Woman* for July, 1931, Lavinia Walsh wrote of Mrs. French as follows: "As a child she roved about the countryside, sometimes afoot, more often on her pony; and sometimes she rowed a boat in the streams and marsh creeks, or wandered along the beaches or among the dunes. She hoarded shells and seaweeds . . . and bits of broken glass, for one of her various haunts . . . was the fast decaying ruins of the now art-glorified Deming Jarves plant in Sandwich."

Later Hazel Blake went to the School of the Museum of Fine Arts in Boston, specializing in design under such teachers as C. Howard Walker and Huger Elliott, and to the School of Metallurgy there for instruction in the art of jewelry making from George J. Hunt. After her marriage, continues the article, came the sequel to her childhood wanderings in old cellars of the glass factory: "The Sandwich 'golden ruby,' 'sapphire,' 'opalescent,' 'emerald,' 'amethyst,' and 'jade' represented glass of such clearness and beauty that experts contended it was without an equal in the history of the art. Gleams of these colors from a heap of cullet in the old factory yard chanced to draw Mrs. French's attention one day as she was walking about the ruins, and the thought came— 'If this glass could stand the test of the lapidary's wheel, perhaps it could give me the language of color I need to express my themes in metal designing.'"

When she sent carefully selected examples to a lapidarist, the report was so gratifying that she began to use the fragments with confidence. The jewelry that resulted from Mrs. French's experiments and her skill as a designer is as unique as it is beautiful. The imaginative element in her art is reflected in the names of some of her creations— "the frog pond," "fish under water," "a whaling vessel," "the red currant," and in her many patterns of land, sea, and sky. These pieces are souvenirs of Cape Cod in the best meaning of that word.

CHAPTER 15

NAUTICAL HANDICRAFTS

THE title of this chapter seems to describe the subject matter well, although "marine" or "maritime" would also be fitting words which may be used interchangeably here. Handicrafts of the sea and seacoast include, for our purpose, things made by hand which reflect the life, the work, the culture of both sea and shore—among them ship models, nautical instruments, net-weaving, scrimshaw, knots and braiding, ropework, and shell work. Some driftwood objects are included here, but when driftwood is used as a base for carving and whittling it is usually referred to in Chapter 10.

There is no better branch of nautical handicrafts with which to begin than the making of ship models, and it can be said that there is no other region in the United States where so wide a variety of ship models is made as in New England. There was a time when every ocean- or river-going vessel built in New England was first visualized in the form of a model, sometimes a complete model, but quite often a half hull. Each shipyard and shipbuilding plant would have a model made of the proposed new vessel, always to exact scale whatever the size, and frequently evidencing fine skill and patient craftsmanship. It was common practice to have this hand model mounted and preserved in glass cases or on the walls of the shipyard office. Now in the shipyards such methods of modelmaking have been generally abandoned, in favor of blueprints, although there were instances in New England in connection with the building of vessels for World War II where the old practice was continued. This chapter will not deal so much with architectural models prepared as a preliminary to the building of ships, but rather with the building to scale of small models which preserve the principal characteristics and often the great beauty of ships that have already sailed the sea.

SHIP MODELMAKING

Maine. Robert L. Smallidge of Northeast Harbor is one of the best all-round craftsmen in the New England states. Earlier reference to his work has been made in Chapter 3. His complete ship models, of which he has made a number, are representative of some of his finest craftsmanship. Probably his best-known work is *The Alice Mandel* of New Bedford, an exact-to-scale model of the whaler which used to ply Pacific waters and which was wrecked on the shoals of Pirate Island in the China Sea in 1851. This important piece, shown at the Worcester Handicraft Exhibition, was illustrated in the catalogue; it also appeared in *The* [London] *Studio*, special number on *American Arts*, June, 1944. Mr. Smallidge also makes beautiful half-models of small ships mounted on plaques for wall decoration in which the sails are carved from wood; one of his favorite subjects being the little sloop, *Friendship*, a type which once plied along the coast of Maine.

Captain Otis Candage of South Blue Hill, a ship modelmaker of wide reputation, is referred to at some length in both the Maine Guide series published by the Work Projects Administration and in *Assignment Down East*, by Henry Buxton. We quote from the latter:

> An expert craftsman is this former sea captain whose crippled legs will never again permit him to tread the quarterdeck of schooner or brig. But his capable hands, which have kept firm grip on plunging helm in many a storm, have developed an artistry which transforms blocks of wood into miniature seacraft, clean and speedy of line, and accurate to the last detail in masts, spars, and complicated rigging. . . . The Captain has made more than a hundred square riggers and more than two hundred little schooners and sloops. . . .
> "The happiest moments of my life," said the Captain as he fitted a tiny block to a spar, "were when I was sailing to some foreign port with fair winds under a full spread of canvas. The greatest comfort I now get in life is to make these little boats and imagine them loaded with cargoes and sailing the oceans of the world . . ."

Frederick W. Snow, no longer living, was one of the fine modelmakers of New England. Mrs. Snow has a number of his ships in their home at Kennebunkport, including a sloop of war, *Washington* of 1812, a privateer, and other vessels all beautifully executed. James F. Marden of Frankfort, a former mate on square-riggers, has made a large number of ship models, the best known, perhaps, being one of *Lightning*, which he completed in two years of work.

There are many skillful ship modelmakers in Maine who deserve mention. Among them is Chester Decker of Islesboro, who spends much of his spare time on small pieces of handmade furniture and cabinetwork. He has made models of *Sovereign of the Sea*, and *The Great Republic*. W. C. Leavitt is a modelmaker who worked in government shipyards during World War II. The Reverend Carl F. Hall on

Swans Island, the local minister of the Maine Seacoast Mission, and his wife are both interested in handicrafts. Mr. Hall had completed a model of the *Queen Mary* at the time of the writer's visit to the Island.

Massachusetts. John G. Howard, Jr., of Barnstable was in the Navy when inquiries were made about his work. His father replied: "My son started making boat models in school and continued for a number of years thereafter. A few years ago certain of his customers (he is in the business of renting out, fitting, and storing small boats) requested him to make models of their boats. He made a few half-models and quite a number of whole models on orders. The unique thing about his models is the wooden sails which were carved out of solid pieces and have to be very well done to give the proper effect."

Edward Piel of Bradford builds models which are usually made to sell at a price, are built on a production basis, and are marketed commercially. However, Mr. Piel has also built some very fine individual models, one of which was displayed in the Haverhill Public Library.

The Island Workshop of Vineyard Haven, Martha's Vineyard, has standardized its attractive product. Under the direction of Donald and Luther van Ryper, the once small workshop, which started as a hobby, has come to be one of the town's important industries, making models of many ocean-going ships and some that sail America's great inland lakes.

A feature which distinguishes van Ryper models is that they are waterline boats; that is, all parts of the model that show correspond to the parts of the ship above water. Whenever a new type is developed, the first model to be completed is retained in the shop to serve as a perfect guide for all future orders for the same subject. The models have precision and are the result of trained and skilled workmanship. They are beautifully painted and are comparatively inexpensive. A pamphlet published by the Island Workshop makes this interesting comment:

> Machines can accomplish some things but the excellence of the completed work, the perfection of line, color and smooth finish are the products of working knowledge, patience, and deft hands. The crew of workmen, including many hands, was trained in the construction of models in the workroom of this water-front building at the head of Vineyard Haven Harbor; they have come from many occupations, fishermen, shipyard workers, taxi drivers, cabinet makers, writers, lawyers, artists, apprentices; are schooled individually in the intricate processes of constructing these miniature

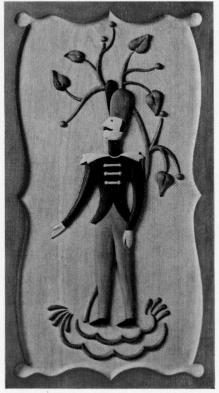

A SOLDIER AND HIS SWEETHEART

THIS LOW RELIEF WOODCARVING IS A SYMBOL OF THE CRAFTS PROJECT OF THE
CONNECTICUT WORK PROJECTS ADMINISTRATION, WHICH MAINTAINED A HIGH STANDARD
OF DESIGN AND CRAFTSMANSHIP IN ITS MANY HANDICRAFT PROGRAMS.

vessels; . . . the common denominator of all hands is a love for ships and the sea.

Mrs. Mary Curtis Cobb of Osterville is noteworthy as one of the few women ship modelmakers of New England. She is the proprietor of Cape Cod Miniature Productions, which is also the outgrowth of a hobby. "We started in the bar," said Mrs. Cobb, "then spread to parts of the house, and will soon need more room because our friends, ever growing in number, have shown an increasing interest in miniature scale models of actual ships." Small in size, the models are reasonable in price, making it possible for many to buy them.

Captain Charlton Smith of Marblehead was an old-time boatbuilder and for many years had a fully equipped carpenter shop on Front Street where he made small ship models for sale. His shop was called The Home of the Brutal Beast.

In New Bedford is a family of three generations of ship model-builders. The middle generation is represented by J. A. DesChenes, Jr., a member of the staff of the Whaling Museum on Johnny Cake Hill, where some of his ship models are shown. He has made more than twenty models, including clippers, whaling barks, sloops, frigates, brigs, and whaling schooners. Mr. DesChenes' father, J. A. DesChenes, taught his son the rudiments of ship modelbuilding and helped him on the hulls of some of his early ships. He has also made small models of boats which he afterward constructed in full size. Among these were a sixteen-foot single-step speedboat, an eighteen-foot sailing sloop, and a twenty-foot runabout speedboat. The youngest DesChenes, J. A., 3d, has been modeling since he was nine. In addition to getting his hand in on some undertakings of his father and his grandfather, he has on his own built trains, ships, amphibians, jeeps, trucks, and very many types of airplanes—Grummans, Avengers, Bearcats, Hellcats, B-25's, B-29's, Flying Fortresses, and one of his latest models, a forty-inch wingspan of a twin-motored Cessna.

A. H. Sjorland of Manchester-by-the-Sea makes ship models of all kinds and teaches ship modeling and other marine handicrafts. He writes: "I was brought from Sweden when I was only seven years old. Manual training was always my hobby and I have made boats all my life. In 1910 I established my modelmaking classes and have continued ever since except during World Wars I and II."

Captain Peter Heinrich Ness of Leydon Street, East Boston, has a large shop finely equipped for modelmaking, where his son, John, and daughter, Margaret, help him on most of his ship models, the latter doing the painting and much of the fine carving. Captain Ness who

has long loved the sea started his modelmaking in a closet of his house
and it took him years of study and planning to realize his present
ideal situation. He is self-taught and testifies that some of his best help
has come from old sailors who knew many things about the construction and sailing of ships not found in books on the subject. Among his
fine models on which all the family have done some work are the
Fredericus Quartus, a Danish warship of 1670; the *Santa Maria*,
Columbus' flagship; and among more recent vessels the *Great Republic*
built entirely of teakwood and fitted with brass by Donald McKay in
East Boston, not far from where the present ship model shop of
Captain Ness now stands.

On Nantucket Island are at least two ship modelmakers who must
be mentioned here: Nikita Carpenko, a citizen of Nantucket from
Russia's Ukraine, whose father was a colonel in the Czar's army, and
Charles Sayle, a native American. Mr. Carpenko's models usually run
from ten to forty inches in length and are constructed from French
pear, cherry, or some other very old wood. One of his models was in
President Roosevelt's collection. *The New Yorker*, writing of him May
31, 1941, said: "Nikita Carpenko, a handsome and temperamental
Russian who lives all year round on Nantucket . . . makes ship models
of the period *circa* 1750 to 1850. He's quite generally accepted as the
foremost ship modeller of this day. . . . It takes from three to six
months for him to make one of his models; his total output for any year
has never exceeded two large ships or five small ones."

Mr. Carpenko is enthusiastic about his neighbor craftsmen on Nantucket Island and, on the day of the writer's visit, spoke with especial
appreciation of Charles Sayle, then in war service.

Mr. Sayle is not a native of Nantucket, but after serving as a seaman
for a number of years he decided to settle on the island because he
"liked the place." A small neat cottage which serves as his living
quarters and workshop is pleasantly decorated with sea relics. His
models are excellent in workmanship and are built from blueprints
with every detail authentic. Mr. Sayle made his first boat model when
he was ten years old and went to sea at fourteen. For four years he
was with fishing boats out of Gloucester. He has built a number of
boats, the *Argonaut* being the last, done with a friend at Nantucket;
Mr. Sayle painted the stern board and the quarterboard decorations
for this boat.

On one visit the writer made to Mr. Sayle's workshop he was completing the miniature hull of the *Lagoda*, a great model which is in
the Whaling Museum at New Bedford. The original hull of the *Lagoda*
had been covered with large sheets of copper. Mr. Sayle had made

several hundred of these sheets to exact scale, seven thirty-seconds of an inch wide and about three-quarters of an inch long, and was fastening them on the hull with copper nails considerably smaller than a small pin. It had taken him thirty-five hours to make sixteen thousand of these nails, but the finished job would be the truest miniature reproduction of the famous ship hull that anyone had ever made. Mr. Sayle likes whales next to ships and makes large weathervanes of his favorite, the sperm whale, and miniature carvings in ebony and black ivory.

Wallace Long, director of the Whaling Museum at Nantucket, has already been mentioned in Chapter 3 because of his superior cabinet-work. He also fits into this chapter for he loves the sea, has made many journeys, and among his handicrafts are numbered many quarter-boards made for the Museum and on order.

Among the most beautiful gallery installations which the writer recalls in New England is the Ship Room in the Addison Gallery of American Art at Phillips Academy, Andover, Massachusetts. The director, Bartlett H. Hayes, Jr., is preparing a monograph on this choice collection of twenty-three models, uniform in scale of one-quarter of an inch to the foot, all representing a cross-section of the history of American shipping during the era of the sail.

Vermont. Although Vermont is the one New England state without a seacoast, there are ship modelmakers there who "follow the sea." W. H. Patno of Graniteville was one of these. Mr. Patno was compression engineer for a large local quarry, and in his workshop in the compressor building made more than fifty models of different vessels. His most ambitious achievement was his model of *The Constitution,* popularly called *Old Ironsides.* The model took three years of his spare time to make, stood five and one-half feet high by eight feet long, and all the wood used came from the old ship itself when it was reconditioned. Mr. Patno also made a model of the granite quarry where he was employed, in which the elaborate machines and rolling stock were operated by small motors, giving a clear picture of a quarry in operation. This model was first worked out in wood by A. St. Onge, also of Graniteville.

Connecticut. Asa Goddard of New London is both a machinist and a ship modelmaker. In addition to original models Mr. Goddard has repaired many ship models for others in his finely equipped machine shop. He is a student of ship lore, an authority on architectural styles, and a skillful woodcarver.

G. E. Reynolds of Saybrook combines ship modelmaking with the designing and construction of nautical instruments. He has made a case full of fine navigating instruments, mostly from very old designs and largely of wood specially selected for the purpose.

The student of ship models will find awaiting him in New England an amazing number of ship model collections, especially of American ships. All that can be done here to suggest this wealth of fascinating research and information, coupled with many excellent examples of this fine miniature art, is to list the names of some of the organizations in New England which have outstanding collections of ship models. These have been gratefully selected from a compilation by Carl C. Cutler, secretary of the Marine Historical Association, Inc., of Mystic, Connecticut, and are: Penobscot Marine Museum, Searsport, Maine; Peabody Museum, Salem, Massachusetts; Addison Gallery of American Art, Andover, Massachusetts; Boston Museum of Fine Arts; Boston Marine Museum; Wadsworth Athenaeum, Hartford, Connecticut; Old Dartmouth Historical Society and Whaling Museum, New Bedford, Massachusetts; Massachusetts Institute of Technology, Boston; and the Marine Historical Association, Inc., of Mystic, Connecticut. Of these the last three have also notable collections of scrimshaw.

OTHER MARINE HANDICRAFTS

Netmaking

One of the most ancient of all handicrafts, netmaking, is carried on in New England in three general forms derived from fishnets: (1) the making of nets for fishing purposes; (2) netmaking for general utility, both on sea and land; and (3) netmaking for personal costumes and decorative purposes, a modern adaptation of this age-old handicraft. Still another type of netting, that for bed canopies, and so forth, was discussed in Chapter 6. In New England's fishing villages are men and women who know how to weave nets and many who still repair them, but modern industrial methods have taken most of the netmaking out of the rural home and loft and into the factory. However, there are a considerable number who still make fishing nets for themselves and their neighbors.

When the writer first met him in 1943, Alpheus A. Pendleton of Islesboro, Maine, had just finished a new mackerel net for his neighbor, Maurice L. Decker, the birdcarver. At the time Mr. Pendleton was eighty-seven years of age. Mr. Decker said it was "a very worthy net." An illustration shows Mr. Pendleton working on it, and Mr. Decker, who used it for his daily fishing, is also shown with some of his wooden decoys.

Mr. Pendleton was one of those all-round New England craftsmen whose principal mission seems to be to meet whatever needs arise in their own household and their neighbors'. In his early days Mr. Pendleton was a well driller. Later he made garden tools, stepladders, and wooden needles and meshboards used in the weaving of fishnets. He might well have been designated here as a maker of ship models on the strength of a fine large model he had just completed on the day of the writer's visit of a four-masted schooner, the *James O'Donahue*, which he made "out of his head with no directions or blueprints from any company." He knew this boat from stem to stern, having carried granite on it to help build Brooklyn Bridge and coal on the return trip from New York to Maine. His boat model, accurate as to parts and dimensions, he had made as a birthday present for his son, then in his sixties.

All the fishnets made in the New England states are not for seacoast fishing. Over in Newport, in northern Vermont, Charles J. Garrett makes excellent nets for fresh-water fishing. The frames are made of Vermont hickory and black cherry. "Some folks say there isn't any hickory in Vermont," Mr. Garrett remarked, "but there it is." His little shop where he makes nets, paddles, and other fishing equipment with great perfection hangs over the shore of Lake Memphremagog.

Turning to the second type of netmaking referred to above, that is, nets for general purposes, Mrs. Pyam Hatch, a daughter of Alpheus Pendleton, and her husband, farmers at Darkharbor, Maine, have for years applied themselves to netmaking during the long winter months. Mrs. Hatch also directed for many years the activities of a large and industrious group of persons at and near Darkharbor, whose netting reached the metropolitan markets and brought an income of about $15,000 to the people of the island. They made bags for many uses, among them landing and mackerel nets, fly nets for horses' ears, basketball bags, pool pockets, eel traps, and so forth. Samples of such different types of netting were brought together by Mr. Hatch and shown at the Worcester Handicraft Exhibition. This island industry finally came into conflict with the minimum wage law, and although an effort was made to form a cooperative it would seem, according to the report of the Department of Labor, that relations between the producing group and the selling agent were not materially changed. The law was invoked and production discontinued.

The making of nets for dresses and decorative purposes, the third type to be mentioned, is an interesting adaptation of fishnet.

Perhaps the best-known stylist in this use of fishnet is Mrs. Ada Worthington of North Truro, Massachusetts. From a modest home industry she has developed an extensive business extending to all parts of the country, and among the objects which she makes are turbans, blouses, evening capes, luncheon sets, belts, bags, snoods, curtains, and many other things for which netting is appropriate. She has an extensive, carefully worked out palette of attractive dyes, and has developed a solution containing caustic by which the netting can be given a pliable stiffness, pinched into any form and the form retained.

Among others who make nets for various decorative purposes is Mrs. George Clements of Darkharbor, Maine. Her work includes shopping bags, some of which she makes in color, doing her own dyeing.

Scrimshaw

To "scrimshaw," as defined by Webster, is "to do any neat small mechanical job; specifically to ornament as shells, ivory, etc., by engraving and (often) rubbing ink or pigments into the incised lines." To this list we would append, especially, whales' teeth—the main substance upon which sailors have left their engravings or from which they have shaped their little utilities—and we would also add the swords of the swordfish. These surfaces continue to intrigue deep-sea fishermen, and craftsmen who still do scrimshaw.

The definitions used are clear and comprehensive enough to include the few contemporaneous examples that can be recorded of this nautical folk art, produced in the whaling days by thousands. Many examples of scrimshaw once so widely practiced are still to be seen in the marine museums of New England and in many private collections of the area and elsewhere. More of these souvenirs of an early and glamorous day are to be found in New England than in any other place in the world. There was hardly a household along the coast of New England in the years when whaling was in its great swing without such souvenirs of the sea. These were often very useful and were sometimes beautiful.

Scrimshaw should interest all Americans, at least in many of its forms, because it is considered to be a handicraft peculiar to this country. As we have suggested, its great days were when New England sailors and fishermen led the world in the whaling industry. Then hundreds of men and boys, during long journeys at sea lasting for months and sometimes for years, or when their ships were in harbor, fashioned countless objects from the ivory of the teeth and from the bones of the whale. Such ivory and bones were practically the only materials available on shipboard for handwork, and it was inevitable that sailors and fishermen with little or nothing to do at certain times, should shape things with their hands; as usually happens when people are turned in on themselves.

Our work is, however, concerned with contemporary handicrafts and not much present-day scrimshaw can be recorded. Therefore interest is heightened in the little good work that is done.

Clarence Montigny of the New Bedford Whaling Museum staff recalls the day when whales' teeth were very common in New Bedford Harbor and second-hand dealers would often have barrels of them for sale at a few cents each. Mr. Montigny, practicing the old technique used by hundreds of New England sailors, has decorated whales' teeth with skill and taste.

On a trip which the writer made in the autumn of 1943 on *The Sunbeam,* the boat of the Maine Seacoast Mission, an example of what may rightly be classified as scrimshaw was discovered on Swans Island. Cleveland Trask, who had fished off George's Banks for swordfish, had amused himself by engraving designs on the flat side of the sword of this famous deep-sea fish. His most interesting souvenir was the sword of a fish which he had caught from the seventy-foot schooner, *Hockomack,* and had cleaned and engraved. The simple but attractive plant design had been drawn on the sword by the ship's cook. Mr. Trask followed the design carefully, and after engraving it he filled it up with colored sealing wax which he procured for the purpose.

Mr. Trask explained that in curing the swords, to cleanse them thoroughly of their natural oil, they would be dragged behind the ship for a week or ten days in the salt water until ready to bleach. The swordfish are spirited and dangerous fighters. Those caught from the *Hockomack* ranged in weight from about 200 to 500 pounds. On a fishing trip lasting from twelve to twenty-four days a crew of eight men sometimes caught over forty fish a day.

Mr. Trask would always bring home souvenirs of the sea from his trips and was glad when he caught a dogfish because the strong small pointed fins resembling large cat claws made excellent needles for his victrola. He had picked up on the last trip a tiny starfish with eleven points (the usual starfish has five), and had saved a little pile of sea trinkets to send to an inland friend who reciprocated by sending him funny papers.

Knots and Braiding

This section must begin with the words of New England's best-known and greatest knotmaker, Clifford W. Ashley, who says in his famous *Book of Knots*: "To me the simple act of tying a knot is an adventure in unlimited space. A bit of string affords a dimensional latitude that is unique among the entities. For an uncomplicated strand is a palpable object that, for all practical purposes, possesses one dimension only. If we move a single strand in a plane, interlacing it at will, actual objects of beauty and of utility can result in what is practically two dimensions; and if we choose to direct our strand out of this one plane, another dimension is added which provides opportunity for an excursion that is limited only by the scope of our own imagery and the length of the ropemaker's coil. What can be more wonderful than that?"

Mr. Ashley's drawings, of which there are over seven thousand in his book, greatly simplify knotmaking for the craftsman. To him this fascinating book of 600 pages will be an education in knots, nooses, bends, hitches, hooks, beckets, toggles, lashings, slings, sennits, and miscellaneous holdfasts. Mr. Ashley learned to make knots before he could read, kept on after he had learned to read and to draw, and continued to learn throughout his career as a writer and a painter of the sea.

Various types of knotting and braiding are practiced throughout New England by amateur craftsmen, mainly as home arts though a few make objects for sale. These are handicrafts which are susceptible of much wider practice than they have as yet enjoyed even in this area; they are inexpensive crafts requiring little equipment, a minimum of room, average skill; there is a considerable variety of material for knotmaking and braiding easily available; with the employment of good taste in design and color they should become increasingly popular.

The practical knots, hitches, and joins used by rural people, by fishermen and sailors, are, of course, practiced widely throughout New England. Sometimes a community will have an unusually handy man who likes to show others how to tie exceptional knots and to splice rope. On Swans Island a sailor, who is also the island poet, taught the school children how to tie about fifty practical knots. A collection of these is a part of their school museum. Incidentally the children of this school, under the guidance and with the encouragement of a gifted teacher, Mrs. Gladys M. Muir, have whittled out and painted a complete set of miniature buoys like those employed by the eighteen lobster fishermen who live on the island and fish in surrounding waters.

An old sailor, Lars Phorsen, of Noank, Connecticut, now retired, spends most of his time painting. He has done some very large dramatic seascapes for the Marine Museum at Mystic, Connecticut. His canvases often illustrate whaling as he saw it done and in which he sometimes had a part long ago. Frequently he makes something for his community or for himself reminiscent of his life as a sailor. He has decorated the halls of a local club with fancy ropework, and recently just for the fun of it, he made himself a ditty bag exactly like the one he did years ago at the order of the captain of the first vessel on which he sailed as a lad from Sweden. Mr. Phorsen, who weaves and makes several handicrafts well, fills the days in his little house by the sea with pleasurable work.

Mosaic of Quahog Shells

One of the most interesting and striking uses of native materials in the arts of New England is the quahog shell mosaic made by Edward Waldo Forbes, for many years director of the Fogg Museum of Art at Harvard University, and his associates. An illustration is shown of this mosaic, named by one of Mr. Forbes' fellow workers The Madonna of the Sea, on account of the material used. It measures thirty-two by forty-two and one-half inches.

Mr. Forbes had been stirred by the beauty of the Santa Sophia mosaics when he visited Constantinople (Istanbul) in 1937, at the invitation of Thomas Whittemore, who was uncovering them. In the following spring Mr. Whittemore, came to the Fogg Museum to lecture on his great discoveries, and it occurred to Mr. Forbes that his talks might seem more vital to the students in the techniques of painting if a copy of a fragment of one of these mosaics could be started. So he had an enlarged photograph of the Mother of God mosaic made, and a portion of the background, part of the halo, and some of the mantle covering the head were laid in. Work on the mosaic was intermittent over a period of eight years, and the figure was finally completed in 1946.

Almost all the mosaic has been made with white, gray, lilac, purple, blue, and red fragments of clamshells gathered mainly from the shores of the Elizabeth Islands, three of which are owned by members of the Forbes family—Naushon, Pasque, and Nashawena. A little variety to the color was given by occasionally cementing small pieces of yellow periwinkle shell to the clamshell tessellae. Once when swimming at the Lido in Venice Mr. Forbes found some gray clamshells which he brought home "to make the color more interesting by having a small part of it neutral."

Mr. Forbes spoke with appreciation of those who had worked with him, among them George Holt, now professor at Bennington College, and students who had helped in the early stages; Miss Nanette Henry and Miss Marjorie W. Beal, who were responsible for much of the actual insert of the Madonna's face, and Miss Elizabeth Robinson for setting the tessellae of the child's face.

The beauty of the shining white and blue surfaces of the inside of the clamshells has long been an attraction to Mr. Forbes, and he often wondered what artistic use could be made of them. He thought of wampum, as made by the Indians, but that seemed too slow and tedious for him; finally the mosaic idea grew out of an experiment in setting a few small pieces of clamshell in an artificial stone called coecal. This material is used in a small part of the mosaic; most of the work was done in the time-honored method of pushing the tessellae into the wet plaster. Some of the shells were ground into shape by a cripple, and others by boys who were glad to work for a modest sum.

In the basement of Mr. Forbes' summer home on Naushon is a very simple workshop with a few hand tools and a grinding wheel. Nearby is a sheltering oak, under which he works on sunny days. Here, and at his home in Cambridge, he has cut and filed many fragments of the quahog shells into small forms, from which a bracelet, a necklace of larger pieces, and several cuff links have been formed, the silverwork being done by a professional. On one occasion he had some of the shells successfully engraved by an old craftsman in London. Although most of his work is done at home where equipment is available, sometimes he has carried clamshells and a file around with him to use in the shaping of small pieces, in place of knitting as he often does in odd moments, and when at the seashore his eyes are on the lookout for shells that will serve his purpose.

CHAPTER 16

MISCELLANEOUS HANDICRAFTS

W E NOW come to a group of handicrafts not included specifically in any of the foregoing chapters; they are some of the
more important left-overs, which we will call miscellaneous. It will
be convenient to take them up in alphabetical order, since they are
not especially related to one another. With archery coming first, the
subjects to be treated are bookbinding, candlemaking, clockmaking,
flytying, glass—stained and leaded, leatherwork, mapmaking, nature-
craft, plastics, stone-carving, and weathervanes.

ARCHERY EQUIPMENT

Archery is a popular sport in New England, and several trained
craftsmen, notably in the state of Maine, make bows and arrows and
other articles for their own use. Among these, Clement Downs of
Blanchard is one of the best known. Robert L. Smallidge of Northeast
Harbor has already been mentioned for his skill in this handicraft in
Chapter 3. The same craft interests Henry E. Jordan of East Holden,
who was represented at the Worcester Exhibition. Some of his bows
and arrows appear in the illustration of sports material. These men
sometimes make equipment for others, but there are a number of
amateur archers who provide their own needs as, for instance, Charles
Cole, now a resident of North Monmouth, who makes bows and
arrows, and targets of both native and foreign woods for his summer
camps. Occasionally boys and girls in summer camps are taught to
make their own equipment for this old sport now so pleasantly revived.

Horace E. Coleman, sometimes known as Indian Coleman, lived
all his life not far from Newfane, Vermont, and was a remarkable
arrowhead maker. His particular hobby was the shaping of arrowheads
of many forms from a great variety of materials. In the course of
twenty years he had so perfected his chipping technique, which was
a secret process with him, that he could shape practically any material
to his desire, turning into arrowheads any pieces of glass, porcelain,

or natural flint he could get. In size and shape Mr. Coleman's product was much like the American Indian arrowhead of flint or other stone. "I like a genuine china teacup to work from," said Mr. Coleman, and explained that he had found his first flint arrowpoint when he was seven years old on the shore of a small lake near Auburn, Massachusetts. He used to say that his success in making arrowheads depended very much upon his mood. He put it this way, "If I feel just right I can do anything I'm a mind to."

BOOKBINDING

Of twenty-five individual bookbinders casually discovered in New England twenty were in the states of Massachusetts, Connecticut, and Rhode Island. Space will not allow an adequate description of their work, but brief mention should be made of some of them for the benefit of students of this subject and for the interest that this useful and beautiful art holds in the catalogue of handicrafts.

In the Worcester Exhibition the Harcourt Bindery of Boston displayed the largest number of books. Albert K. Potter and Mrs. Thomas H. West of Providence were each represented; and there was a special group of books by Henry T. Krumin of Boston, a binder of unusual taste who was born in Russia, and his son, Harold A. Krumin, an excellent craftsman who learned to do fine binding from his father.

Among other bookbinders in Massachusetts Mrs. Rosamond B. Loring should be mentioned here for her attractive and consistently good work. It will be remembered that it was through her need for suitable material for book covers and end papers that she developed to a very high level methods for making paste papers, as mentioned more fully in Chapter 8. These practical and attractive papers she has used in her own bindings, and has made them available to other bookbinders.

In Pittsfield Arno Werner has had his own small bindery since 1943. Born in Germany he served, during his youth, an apprenticeship in trades related to bookbinding, but it was in America that he began to do fine binding with Mr. and Mrs. Gerhard Gerlach of New York as teachers. Later he studied with Ignatz Wiemuler at Leipzig, Germany. He also teaches "this fine old craft" and keeps up with all that goes on in the graphic arts. Not many miles from Mr. Werner lives Mrs. Janet Dana Longcope on Cornhill Farm, in Lee, a rural New Englander and an enthusiastic amateur binder. In 1947 she demonstrated for the Lenox Library the processes of bookbinding, and in her new country home is preparing to continue her work because "it helps to get all sorts of glimpses of pages and people's minds. Then the materials—leather is pleasant, so are papers, making them is fun too, all tied up with the beginning of books. And above all, the accurate and beautiful quality of the work itself."

To the women bookbinders of Massachusetts should be added the names of Mrs. John Sawyer of Wakefield, a member of Minute-Man Crafts, and Mrs. Hilda Kalehmaznen of Worcester, a bookbinder born in Finland.

Peter Franck now of Gaylordsville, Connecticut, is possibly the dean of professional hand bookbinders in our country. A native of Germany, he brought to America many years ago excellent preparation in his craft. One of his early positions was with Elbert Hubbard at East Aurora, New York. In recent years Mr. Franck has bound at his home a few fine books in full leather, of which he had done many in the past. *The Book of Common Prayer*, which he designed and bound lately in full calf vellum, is one of five copies printed by Updike on vellum. He also binds soundly and well technical books in half-leather. Of his home in Connecticut he writes, "Mrs. Franck and I selected the place, materials, style, and laid it out in its main features as a home and studio bindery. We were assisted by a young student of architecture, mainly as a consultant. . . . Mrs. Franck, who has been a part-time associate ever since I started my own bindery again in 1930, has contributed greatly to my 'success' if I may call it that. Fine taste and sensitivity for form are natural to her; we have worked out many a problem together. . . . Whatever we do we strive for technical excellence and attractiveness, using the best material obtainable. It is these essentials, to us, which have helped us to carry on through the years. They are the foundation out of which the art of binding grows or should grow."

There are probably more fine women bookbinders in Connecticut than in any other New England state. The first one to be recalled in the early days of this study was Mrs. Juliette Staats, whose summer workshop was in Litchfield. She had finished several full leather bindings, tooled in gold which, for design, color harmony, and craftsmanship would be acclaimed in any exhibition.

Mrs. Caroline Weir Ely of Old Lyme is the daughter of the eminent American painter, J. Alden Weir, who felt that everyone should have a hobby. While his daughter was in school, he encouraged her to try bookbinding. Miss Weir studied with Helen Noyes in New York, where she established her own bindery. Later she studied in Paris, forwarding with Noulhac, tooling with Cuzin, then with Maylander. Mrs. Ely's work is now principally leather binding, with blind or gold tooling or inlay. A photograph of Mrs. Ely in her home bindery is shown.

Living in Old Lyme also, with a small bindery in her home, Miss Fanny Dudley, although not so active as formerly in either teaching or binding, does keep her hand in, and was represented by a copy of *The Suwannee River* in 1946 at the Architectural League, and later by a binding of Emily Dickinson's *Complete Poems* at the Grolier Club in New York. Miss Dudley feels that the amateur binder today has a distinct advantage in technique over earlier craftsmen because he can learn from teachers who have had better training than was possible in the old days.

In Greenwich Mrs. Joseph C. Huntzinger studied with Emily Preston, who was a pupil of Cobden-Sanderson, author of *The Book Beautiful*, who turned from law as a profession to give his life to his chosen handicraft, bookbinding. Mrs. Huntzinger likes to create her own designs through curved and straight tools, rather than use the binders' stamp tools. Mrs. Amy Weil Wertheimer of Silvermine, Connecticut, is, to use her own words, a "book-taught binder." Her great teacher, whom she never saw, was Douglas Cockerell, an Englishman and disciple of Cobden-Sanderson. Mrs. Wertheimer is not alone in her admiration for Cockerell's *Bookbinding and the Care of Books*, for it is generally acclaimed the best book of instruction in our language. She is both a teacher and a craftsman, and an advocate of handicrafts generally. A unique and beautiful example of taste and skill was a portfolio for musical manuscripts presented in 1945 to Quinto Maganini, conductor of the Norwalk Symphony Orchestra, on his birthday. The portfolio was made of red leather and Italian vellum, bearing ancient musical staffs with the fourteenth century system of notation. A suitable inscription was prepared with the names of the orchestra members and the Board of Governors. The portfolio was designed, constructed, lettered, and illuminated by Mrs. Wertheimer.

Three bookbinders may be noted here from Rhode Island: Daniel Gibson Knowlton of Bristol, Mrs. Dorothy Moulton Latham, and Albert K. Potter of Providence. Although Mr. Knowlton comes into this chapter as a bookbinder, other skills would have entitled him to enter at other points, for with materials salvaged from many places in his neighborhood he has built with his own hands in his spare time, in about three years, most of the house and studio workshop in Longfield, where he binds his books. The house is a restored stable which once belonged to his famous uncle, Charles Dana Gibson. The workshop is perhaps as suitable for carrying on his chosen craft as can be found, and few binders have such complete equipment. He is young in both years and experience, having taken up the craft in Washington in 1944, where, soon after he discovered that this was the work for him, he had an opportunity to purchase a complete bookbinding outfit which had recently been imported from France. When he had completed his studio, he brought most of this equipment in his car from Washington to Bristol in four trips. Now he has everything he wants but time to follow his chosen work, and he is managing to get in a good deal of that. He binds with unusual feeling and skill mainly in finely tooled leather.

Mrs. Dorothy Moulton Latham's bookbinding began as a hobby growing out of her love for books. At first she bound books for herself and friends, then when the depression came she began taking work on order and teaching the craft. She has done some notable bindings in full leather; one, *Holy Communion,* a gift to her own Grace Church in Providence, bound in natural niger, an ivory shade, with doublure in red oasis morocco; a family album with coat-of-arms inlaid in colors; and a copy of Robert P. Tristram Coffin's *Crowns and Cottages.* For her later books she made the marbled end papers, marbling being a special craft with her. Perhaps one of Mrs. Latham's greatest satisfactions has come from the binding and repairing of rare and valuable books and priceless broadsides for the John Carter Brown Library and the John Hay Library at Brown University, Providence.

These too brief accounts of the work of a few New England bookbinders must conclude with a reference to the late Albert K. Potter. When Mr. Potter retired at seventy as professor of English in Brown University, he took up bookbinding as a hobby, studying first with Mrs. Latham and later with Mr. and Mrs. Gerlach of New York, practicing mainly on favorite volumes he had collected in his half-century of teaching. It is doubtful if any bookbinder has more evidence of his industry and progress in this age-old art, or of his love of books. On Mr. Potter's library shelves when the writer visited him were more than eighty volumes which he had bound completely, and even more that he had repaired, including sets of Milton, Bacon, and Shakespeare, editions published in the early 1800's, for which he had provided new calfskin backs and labels. His small but ample bindery was in his home; a photograph of Mr. Potter with a background of some of the books bound by him is shown here.

CANDLEMAKING

Among the colonial handicrafts still practiced today is the making of bayberry candles, from the small gray waxy berry that grows in special profusion on Cape Cod. The old custom is still carried on by several country women for their own households; sometimes these candles are sold to supplement income and in some instances a prosperous industry has been built up.

The Colonial Candle Company of Hyannis is an example of a home handicraft begun as a hobby which has developed into an extensive business. Although candlemaking in the homes had almost disappeared, it seemed to Mrs. Walter D. Baker as she viewed the unnumbered acres of bayberries around her that the sweet smelling candles would be acceptable gifts. Her surmise was correct. The cheerful light of candles and their pleasing odor proved so popular that Mrs. Baker soon was selling them in her husband's local store. Bayberry pickers were hired, and extra help crowded the little kitchen; before long, throughout the village of Hyannis, many hands were busy dipping bayberry candles to supply the need. The business grew to such proportions that Mr. Baker sold his store in 1921 and erected a modern candle factory. Increasing popularity was not due to the bayberry candles alone but to Mrs. Baker's idea of producing a hand-dipped candle in solid color clear through, instead of a white candle dipped in color; experiments were made with wax-soluble pigments until the process was perfected.

The Cape Cod Candle Company, also of Hyannis, uses the old hand-dipping method, as well as more modern ways, and makes candles in a variety of shapes and colors. Farther up the Cape at North Truro Mrs. Ada Worthington makes no attempt to produce bayberry candles in quantity, but a continuous demonstration is held during the summer months so that visitors may see just how hand-dipped candles are made. In Maine, Mrs. Barbara Younger of Brunswick has made bayberry candles for about fifteen years.

CLOCKMAKING AND REPAIRING

Clockmaking was a natural field for New England ingenuity. The making and selling of clocks by Eli Terry, Seth Thomas, and others are important chapters in industrial development; they offer fascinating examples of the transformation of village handicrafts into vast business enterprises. Clockmaking has long passed the stage where it can be considered a handicraft, but there are certain remnants of the old trade in which handwork is the dominant feature. We found only one craftsman who made clocks entirely by hand.

When Charles A. Smith of Brattleboro, Vermont, retired from working in a machine shop with which he had long been associated, he

George French

97. A CARVER OF EAGLES AND OTHER BIRDS OF MAINE

THE EAGLES WHICH MAURICE L. DECKER MADE "OUT OF HIS HEAD" RANK HIGH IN THE REALM OF FOLK ARTS. ONCE WHEN A CITY CLIENT OFFERED TO SUPPLY A BLUE-PRINT, THE CARVER SAID, "ALL YOU NEED TO DO IS TO TELL ME THE MEASURE FROM TIP TO TIP AND I'LL DO THE REST."

Doris Day, School Arts Magazine

98. A MASSACHUSETTS ARCHITECT CREATES A FRENCH VILLAGE

ADDISON B. LeBOUTILLIER OF ROCKPORT HAS DESIGNED AND BUILT THIS LITTLE FRENCH DREAM VILLAGE AND MODELED THE INHABITANTS.

99. LACEMAKING IN NEW ENGLAND

Among the Individual Lacemakers of New England No One Has Mastered More Techniques Than Mrs. Teresa A. Pellegrini of Boston. In This Piece of Pillow Lace Mrs. Pellegrini Is Using More Than Five Hundred Bobbins.

Doris Day

100. AN AMATEUR MARBLE-CARVER OF VERMONT

THE FAMILY OF ERNEST H. WEST, AN APPLE GROWER OF DORSET, HAS LONG BEEN
IDENTIFIED WITH THE MARBLE INDUSTRY. MR. WEST IS HOLDING A DOORSTOP, WHICH
HE HAS CARVED FROM NATIVE MARBLE. HE HAS WRITTEN A HISTORY OF THE MARBLE
QUARRIES OF DORSET.

Doris Day

Doris Day

L. M. A. Roy

101. ARTISTS IN WOOD AND SCULPTURING

HARRY HAMMOND, CABINETMAKER, MEMBER OF THE LEAGUE OF NEW HAMPSHIRE ARTS AND CRAFTS. . . . WALTER MANCHESTER OF PLEASANT VALLEY, CONNECTICUT, ONE OF NEW ENGLAND'S OUTSTANDING VIOLIN MAKERS. . . . PAUL SAINT-GAUDENS OF CORNISH, NEW HAMPSHIRE, POTTER AND SCULPTOR.

Doris Day

102. A VERMONT HARNESS AND SADDLE MAKER

George E. Small of Bennington Makes Harness for Racing Horses, Saddles, and
Other Riding Equipment by Hand for Clients Throughout the East; and for
Local Customers, Belts and Special Leather Novelties.

Doris Day

103. VERMONT SCULPTORS AND POTTERS

BOTH MR. AND MRS. SIMON MOSELSIO OF BENNINGTON COLLEGE, VERMONT, ARE SKILLED
SCULPTORS AND POTTERS; THEY MAKE MANY HOUSEHOLD UTENSILS FOR THEIR OWN USE.

Doris Day, School Arts Magazine   *Doris Day*

L. M. A. Roy

104. CRAFTSMEN FROM NEIGHBORING STATES

Edwin Pease, of Warren, New Hampshire, an Expert Braided Rug Designer and Maker. . . . Rome van Ornam of Calais, Vermont, Once a Sign Painter, Raises Toggenburg Goats and Decorates Furniture. . . . Arthur Cunningham of Antrim, New Hampshire, a Pioneer Demonstrator at the Craftsman's Fair, Works in Wood.

105. A BOOKBINDER'S WORKSHOP IN CONNECTICUT

Mrs. Caroline Weir Ely, Daughter of the Eminent Painter, J. Alden Weir,
Who Encouraged Her to Learn a Handicraft. She Selected Bookbinding, Studied
in America and Europe, and Now Works at Her Home in Old Lyme.

106. A YOUNG MODELMAKER IN MASSACHUSETTS

J. A. DesChenes, 3d, of New Bedford Represents the Third Generation of
Modelmakers. At Fifteen This Young Craftsman Had Made Several Ship Models,
a Miniature Train, and Many Airplanes.

Elinor Easton

107. AN EXPERT BOATBUILDER OF MAINE

George R. Stevenson, an Experienced Boatbuilder, Is Finishing a Canoe Paddle in His Shop at Center Lovell.

Ralph M. Arnold

108. DIRECTOR OF THE OLDEST HANDICRAFT SHOP

JOHN HOWARD BENSON IS DIRECTOR OF THE OLDEST HANDICRAFT SHOP IN NEW ENG-
LAND, AND PERHAPS IN THE UNITED STATES. IT WAS ESTABLISHED BY JOHN STEVENS, A
TOMBSTONE CUTTER, IN 1705 AND HAS BEEN OCCUPIED BY CRAFTSMEN CONTINUOUSLY
FOR 243 YEARS.

Charles L. Hanson, Jr.

109. A NORWEGIAN-BORN HAND SPINNER

MRS. ELSE BÖCKMANN OF NEWTONVILLE, MASSACHUSETTS, SPINNING ON THE LOW
WHEEL WHICH SHE BROUGHT FROM NORWAY; IT HAS BEEN USED BY HER FAMILY
FOR TWO HUNDRED YEARS. MRS. BÖCKMANN'S YARN IS "DYED IN THE WOOL" BEFORE
SHE SPINS IT FOR TAPESTRY WEAVING.

Henry Elkan

110. FIRING POTTERY WITHOUT A KILN

RANDOLPH W. JOHNSTON, OF SOUTH DEERFIELD, MASSACHUSETTS, AND THE DEPARTMENT OF ART OF SMITH COLLEGE, IS THE INVENTOR OF A METHOD OF FIRING POTTERY BY PASSING AN ELECTRIC CURRENT THROUGH A WIRE EMBEDDED IN THE CLAY WHEN THE OBJECT IS BUILT.

George French

111. ONE OF MAINE'S BEST-KNOWN WHITTLERS

GILLMAN MCFARLAND OF SOUTH BRISTOL COMES BY HIS INTEREST IN BIRD LIFE AND
BIRD WHITTLING PARTLY THROUGH HIS FATHER, SYLVANUS, WHO WAS A NATURALIST
AND FRIEND OF JOHN BURROUGHS.

James Pickands, II

112. A CONNECTICUT PUPPETEER

MISS HARRIET PEASLEY OF CHESHIRE WITH AN ARMFUL OF PUPPETS, WHICH SHE HAS MADE FOR THE MANY CHILDREN FOR WHOM SHE WORKS IN BOTH THE NORTH AND SOUTH.

decided to have a shop of his own where he could do just as he pleased and make something useful. His clocks were completely handmade of wood, operated by weights. He cut all wheels and gears, and other parts from native maple and birch, put them together, built the cases, and hand-lettered the cardboard faces. He finished about fifty clocks a year of several models, one of which had an inlaid walnut case. A clock made by Mr. Smith was sent to a province in China where timepieces were almost unknown to the natives. He had built it in such a way that a good Chinese craftsman could reproduce it, and if the day comes when the people of that province feel that accurate time-keeping has been a benefit to mankind, they may trace the making of wooden clocks back to the little Vermont shop, and Charles Smith will then be made a saint, or whatever kind of hero the Chinese of that province recognize. A portrait of Mr. Smith in his shop is shown.

He spent most of his annual vacations hunting woodchucks, going up and down the state shooting these "varmints" wherever he found them, as a service to the farmers of Vermont. He was an expert marksman, prepared his own ammunition, and loaded his gun with a shell, which he said was exactly the right content for a Vermont woodchuck. During the years when he kept score the woodchuck population of the Green Mountain state was cut down by over seven thousand. From the tips of the tails of his victims Mr. Smith made neat little "woodchuck brushes" mounted on the ends of maple handles gracefully turned on his small wood lathe. These were useful for painting or for cleaning his clocks.

Reference has been made elsewhere to the use of handicrafts in the Vermont program for handicapped citizens and how that program, under the direction of Mrs. Eugene C. Rhodes, has been extended to persons in remote rural counties. Among these persons should be mentioned Henry C. Smith, who lives not far from Woodstock, Vermont. He is a veteran of World War I who, after his discharge from the Army, suffered an attack of infantile paralysis. Only with the assistance of a special framework to brace him and a movable chair, can he get around his room, but he is able to adjust himself to the frame so that he can carry on the work of repairing clocks and do other odd jobs. At the time of the writer's visit he showed a very attractive old clock that someone had picked up in an auction for ten cents and had brought to him, thinking he might be able to fix it. This he did so successfully that the clock runs for two or three days without losing more than a few seconds' time. The pride that Mr.

Smith took in this achievement and the care with which he watched the operation of his restored clocks are worthy of mention.

FLYTYING AND OTHER FISHING EQUIPMENT

Throughout New England there are fishermen who make part of their own equipment, including fishing flies; some have been so successful in flytying that they have responded to the demand of sportsmen to sell the flies in which they specialize. Among these clever craftsmen there is space for mention of only three or four. Jim Harvey and his daughter Angie of Lakeville, Connecticut, are expert fishermen and among the outstanding flytiers in the New England states. They have a wide market for the many varieties of flies which they make. Two of those originated by Mr. Harvey are the Darting and the Featherweight Minnows.

Dr. Gustav Wilens of Wayland, Massachusetts, is another expert flytier. He is a practicing physician, who finds time for an avocation. He claims to be the originator of the plastic fly, making use of several intricate techniques involving chemistry, physical design, and pattern. Exact imitation of trout brook insects, aquatic and subaquatic forms, is the compelling influence. Colors are created by pigment developed in situ as well as by prismatic effect. Size is closely correlated with symmetry and silhouette. Optical properties are imparted to all materials, particularly feather and hair to produce the adequate degree of translucency. A certain degree of brilliance is added. Silkworm gut is processed with certain salts to produce a tough, wiry, peripheral non-reflecting coating.

The fly is the business end of the tackle. Although proper tackle equipment and presentation are important, it is the fly or nymph which applies the adequate stimulus to produce the proper response. American-made fishing flies are as good as or superior to those that are imported.

Dr. Wilens emphasizes that his technique is a decided step forward and is a definite phase in the history of fly construction. His book, *The Chemistry of Flytying,* is awaited by many with great interest.

Walter Killam of Noank is a painter but also an all-round craftsman. He has built his own studio, and in fact, he and his wife have practically made their very attractive home "by hand." Mr. Killam says that flytying and casting his flies give him the greatest relaxation of anything he does. He is a close student of the insects, which he imitates in his flytying, even watching them hatch in order that he may get a perfect resemblance.

GLASS—LEADED AND STAINED

In the town of Kent, Connecticut, there is to be found at the sign of The Shining Window, "food and rest for the weary," and in connection with this attractive inn is a truly rural studio and workshop where Len Howard makes stained and leaded glass. A beautiful leaded glass composition is in the front door of the inn, and a pane of decorated glass or a small panel carefully leaded and painted adorns an occasional window of the old house.

The inn, conducted by Mrs. Howard, is an old farmhouse that has been restored. Mint and other herbs and flowers grow in the garden, and the touches of deep light in Len Howard's windows and the flowers from Mrs. Howard's garden lend warmth and color to a charming interior. In one of the village high schools not far away is a large window in which Mr. Howard and the architect have cooperated closely with excellent results. The school children interpreted the legends in the window delightfully to the visitor. Examples of Mr. Howard's work are also in St. George's Church in New York; and he has won prizes in national competitions.

Lack of space makes it impossible to name all the New Englanders who do creative work in painted and leaded glass. Among them the light of the late Charles J. Connick will long shine forth in New England. He did so much to advance the handicraft movement and to commend the fine art of stained glass to the average man. He and Wilbur H. Burnham were well represented at the Worcester Exhibition. A small example of stained glass, the work of Miss Ade Bethune of Newport, Rhode Island, a designer and craftsman of distinction in religious arts is shown in the frontispiece. A miniature model of "a stained glass studio with craftsman at work" by K. O. Svendsen of Boston was also shown at Worcester.

Nicola D'Ascenzo's winter studio and workshop is at Philadelphia but he also has one in his home at Rockport, Massachusetts, where much of his work is thought out. Here he has a fine collection of both American and European handicrafts. A friend and neighbor of Mr. D'Ascenzo had a number of old but beautiful cracked and broken Italian dishes which she was about to discard, when this artist asked if he might have them. These fragments he set in cement on the exterior wall of his house on a plane with the wall surface. The design was so charming that seeing it once would make it difficult for anyone ever again to throw away broken pieces of beautiful porcelain or pottery. Decorated lead work, which almost completely covers the inside of the main door of the living room, is another example of the artist's fine taste and craftsmanship.

Among Mr. D'Ascenzo's treasures from his native Italy are fascinating painted carvings taken from Sicilian donkey carts. The decorating of such carts is an ancient craft that has been practiced in Sicily for over nine hundred years and ranks among the highest expressions of folk art on the European continent. This collection is a reminder of how much our own culture may be enriched through an appreciation of the love our immigrant citizens have for the fine folk things of their native lands.

LEATHERWORK

Much of the hand leatherwork done in New England is similar in type to that of Miss Catherine A. Hood of Haddam, Connecticut, who writes, "My leatherwork has been of the simpler sort, link belts, buttonholes, key cases, purses, billfolds, and so forth, with a little stamping and tooling. I have taught children in camps to do cutting, tooling, and lacing for their merit badges in leathercraft."

Miss Hood, who is a member of the Society of Connecticut Craftsmen, suffered an illness which left her totally deaf and so lame that she requires crutches. She has developed a special process of etching Christmas and gift cards from aluminum plates, the press that she uses being operated from a chair. This comparatively new handicraft is described fully by Miss Hood and well illustrated in the *Volta Review* of December, 1940, under the heading "Simplified Etching Craft, Vocation or Avocation." She feels that leatherwork and etching are suitable for handicapped persons who, like herself, cannot stand when working.

Miss Alice Michaels of Seymour, Connecticut, an occupational therapist who has worked in several hospitals, reports leatherwork as being her favorite handicraft. Because so many useful and attractive things can be made of leather in a short time, it is used in scores of summer camps and in countless Boy Scout and Girl Scout troops. Many country women working with extension agents are reported by Miss Ruth McIntire of Massachusetts State College at Amherst to be making fine gloves for their own and family use. Several members of Minute-Man Crafts do leatherwork, among them Dr. Phyllis Abbott of Arlington and Sidney Gadon of Malden. Richard Shepard showed at the Worcester Exhibition a commando knife which he had made and a leather case especially designed for it, and the Reverend Marvin

S. Stocking of Avon, Connecticut, exhibited his leatherwork at the 1947 exhibition of the Society of Connecticut Craftsmen in Hartford.

George E. Small of Bennington, Vermont, is an experienced saddler and a fine harness maker. He was born in Dublin, Ireland. Horse owners along the Atlantic Coast are able to get exactly what they want from his experienced hand. Mr. Small maintains one of the few small shops left in the country, and in addition to his harness and horse gear, he finds time to make leather belts for men and women.

MAPMAKING

The making of decorative maps of picturesque areas seems to be a natural development in the New England environment. Among the mapmakers are the following: Mrs. Grace Dodge of Boothbay Harbor makes Romance Maps of Maine. Luther Phillips did the original coloring of these and has also made maps of Mt. Desert Island and other sections as far as Wiscasset, of the Rangely Lake region, and the White Mountains of New Hampshire. Miss Viola Jaques of Hyannis makes maps of about six different areas along the eastern coast of Massachusetts, called Cape Cod Maps, some of which are colored. James and Ruth Goldie of Rockville, Connecticut, members of the Society of Connecticut Craftsmen, do expert work in gilding both maps and mirrors. Mrs. Ruth Lepper Gardner of South Yarmouth, Maine, makes both large and postcard sized pictorial maps of sections of the Maine Coast; she does her own color separating in connection with the printing of her largest maps.

NATURECRAFT

Mrs. Tressa Nelson of Center Strafford, New Hampshire, has been a demonstrator at the annual Craftsman's Fair from the earliest days of the League. Hers is an unusual handicraft, one which has proved to be both popular and fairly profitable. Mrs. Nelson and her husband, and sometimes the children, gather grasses, burrs, cones from pine, hemlock, cedar and tamarack, witchhazel capsules, everlasting flowers, acorns, and countless wild seeds, seedpods, and other "wood pretties," as the Southern Highlanders say. From these Mrs. Nelson makes pins, earrings, and other articles for personal decoration. When thoroughly seasoned, colored, or otherwise treated, and mounted on wood, they give a charming, old-fashioned miniature bouquet effect. Mrs. Nelson also makes small paper boxes for her products and handprints a legend on each box, noting the New Hampshire plants. Because all of this material can be gathered on the farm or in the neighboring country-side, little expense is involved except for labor. She has become so expert in separating and arranging these nature objects that she can make many of them in a day. Her earnings have made possible college education for two of her children.

Mrs. Nelson has also made a beautiful collection of blueprints of wild flowers native to her home area, and she and Mr. Nelson have developed color photography as a hobby. One of their recent accomplishments has been in recording the history of the mating of the Cecropia moth. In addition to a good photographic record they have fifty-seven cocoons developing for further study.

There are, of course, many people who make Christmas wreaths and other set pieces from the evergreens and winter plants of New England; many have real charm. In the treatment of both wild and cultivated plants and flowers there is much artistry in spraying with special colored powders. The number of these experiments, some of which are related to herb-raising, are too numerous to record here, but it should be noted that they often enable country people to supplement their income, and others to add interest and beauty to their surroundings. One specific experiment with nature material might be noted here. Mr. and Mrs. George Szarvasy, now at East Haddam, were war refugees from Austria, with appreciation for beautiful forms in nature, but with no way to make it count in helping them to earn money, which was their great need. Finally they found in the woods and fields of Connecticut a beautifully formed and slightly veined fungus, wing-shaped and growing on wood, from a small fraction of an inch in width to two or three inches across. They gathered this velvetlike fungus in different sizes, and made them into handsome boutonnieres, some in natural colors, others they dyed. The writer was told that they had found enough outlets to justify them in giving much of their time to this work.

Sitting at her work table before a window, overlooking an open field, with a blossoming fuchsia nearby, and surrounded by the amateur but fascinating bird paintings of her naturalist father, Miss Mary Brooks of West Newbury, Massachusetts, is a symbol of those rare New Englanders who, through a combination of imagination, skill, and perseverance, create new objects of wonder and beauty. Miss Brooks is known to her neighbors and many others for her Fairy Gardens. They are composed of countless little plant forms which this ingenious craftsman finds with her sharp eyes in the fields, in the woods, or along a stream, and with the point of a needle in the end of a match, and some tiny tweezers arranges compositions that are perfect for their naturalness and charming to view. She has learned how to treat these materials so they will last. The final touch in the composition may be a group of little people, a fairy, or a hummingbird too small for the eye alone to see. They are built of fragments which only Miss Brooks knows how to get and are modeled with pins and needles under a magnifying glass; the fairy's wings are from tiny insects, but all in scale with the garden or landscape. These miniature scenes are as beautiful as they are tiny, and they are about as tiny as they can be.

PLASTIC

Plastic is now coming into the realm of handicrafts in New England but most of the work is still in an experimental stage. In Massachusetts John R. Sloane of Lexington sent plastic jewelry to the Worcester Exhibition. Adrian M. Mathers of New Upper Falls has built a machine for enlarging or reducing plastic models, using small burrs in high-speed cutters to get final forms, which he achieves usually in ivory plastic. In Connecticut Mrs. E. J. Scheide of Hartford makes beautiful flowers for personal wear and house decoration, of very thin, flexible, transparent, or colored plastic outlined with light wire. Mr. and Mrs. Irvin Keiningham of Westbrook, Connecticut, do internal carving in plastic; that is, they carve beautiful flowers, which they dye and make into brooches, earrings, and numerous other articles including lamps. The trade name under which they market their flower forms is Plasti-Flora.

GRANITE, SLATE, MARBLE-CARVING

Maine and Vermont are rich in marble, granite, and slate, with the latter ranking second among the states in the Union in the production of these minerals. Granite is the chief stone quarried in New Hampshire; it is used mainly for building and monumental work. In 1934 the quarries of New England furnished the greater part of the output of granite in the United States.

The people of Monson, Maine, are largely of Welsh and Swedish extraction. The town is a slate center in the heart of local quarries, the product of which is used mainly for roofing; in Monson almost all the houses have slate roofs. The slate is treated with an oil finish, which makes it more intensely black and causes it to hold its color permanently.

Ira Bishop of Monson has made a number of small objects of slate including book ends, paperweights, and other ornamental objects. He is skillful at lettering and has made many name plates, usually filling in the inscriptions with gold leaf. He also uses yellow, red, blue, or other well-selected colors which harmonize with the dark slate; these are less expensive than gold leaf and are very attractive.

It seems strange that with so much marble, especially in Vermont, so few amateurs have carved or otherwise decorated it. It is pleasant, however, to record one instance, which might well be emulated by others of the areas where this beautiful and easily worked material is abundantly available. Ernest H. West of Dorset is of an old Vermont family whose members have been associated with the marble quarries of the Green Mountains for many years. Just for his own pleasure, or as gifts to neighbors, Mr. West has done some carving in low relief with very pleasant results. One of his marble doorstops is illustrated in the portrait study of him.

Mr. West farms and raises fine Vermont apples; he manages to get time to serve as president of the local art club, and has written a fascinating history of the marble quarries of Dorset. The latter is an authentic account of the rise, development, and decline of the once famous industry, with many facts concerning the use of the beautiful marble of the region in different parts of the United States. This manuscript with photographic illustration is filed in the local library. Mrs. West is a member of the West Roaders knitting group mentioned in Chapter 6.

Tombstones

There are, of course, in New England many marble and stonecutters, especially makers of tombstones, who deserve recording which is not possible here; but the writer recalls two who must serve as symbols for the others, and who happily represent what might be called the poles of the tombstone cutters' art. One of the craftsmen chosen is Virgil Flood of Norway, Maine; the other, John Howard Benson of Newport, Rhode Island, who is the most creative and gifted stone-carver whom the writer knows. He has already been referred to in Chapter 8, and too briefly, as a calligrapher who makes many of his tools and follows the best traditions of this very personal art, which he teaches in the Rhode Island School of Design, at Providence. It is, however, as a designer and a carver in stone that he is best known. His preferences in material are the slate, granite, and marble of New England, and nothing responds more pleasantly to his chisel than the black slate of Maine.

Mr. Benson is distinguished also for the craftsmen he gathers about him at Newport, and the fact that he and they occupy the same shop which John Stevens, a stonecutter and tombstone maker, established on this spot in 1705. This is the oldest shop in New England, and probably in the United States, that has been continuously occupied by craftsmen for such a long period of years; and what is much to our point here, it seems certain that at no period in its existence have the occupants turned out work of such fine quality. A memorial in marble designed and carved by Mr. Benson is shown; also portraits of Mr. Flood and Mr. Benson at work.

WEATHERVANES

Weathervanes have been mentioned in Chapter 3 and in Chapter 14. They are characteristic of New England architecture and the landscape, and anyone who knows this area will have his own collection of remembered weathervanes seen on church steeples, courthouse cupolas, barn gables, market places, and the roofs of private workshops and houses. Probably more than half of those he may have seen in a day's journey are homemade.

When a New Englander sets about making a weathervane for himself, it is likely to be something special. It may be very simple, just a shaft serving to show the direction of the wind, but it will be carefully designed even if the metal came from oil cans. If the traveler can get near enough to examine it in detail, he is quite sure to find individuality and ingenuity registered somewhere in the design, the construction, or the restrained decoration. It is well for the observer to remember, as the craftsman must, that a weathervane, whatever it may be in the way of design, must be built to meet the elements, generally for years to come. No one ever makes a weathervane for a single season.

In riding along in the neighborhood of Kennebunkport and inland to Sanford, Maine, the weathervanes sighted within an hour or so included fish, spy-glasses, a horse and buggy, trotting horses, arrows, ships, roosters, sheep, dogs, and finally in Sanford itself, atop the public library, a large well-designed figure of a hand weaver at a loom. A weathervane is usually seen in silhouette, sometimes from a considerable distance so that materials and workmanship cannot often be observed and enjoyed. But the writer recalls a visit to an antique dealer in Litchfield, Connecticut, who preferred to collect these fascinating examples of handicraft rather than to sell them. Here, mounted on their metal supports and planted around the lawn, was a veritable garden of weathervanes—a remarkably fine collection, most of them of metal but some of wood, the best being fifty to a hundred years old.

The weathervane is a part of our heritage from Europe, and in New England some of the earliest ones were copied from old English models. What is believed to be the oldest American vane in existence is, however, probably original in design and in concept. It is a fish made of hard wood and studded with large copper-head nails; it once stood on the roof of Paul Revere's copper shop at Canton, Massachusetts, and is now in the Paul Revere House collection in Boston. It possibly served as both weathervane and shop sign.

The most famous of all early American weathervanes is Deacon Shem Drowne's metal grasshopper, placed atop old Faneuil Hall by its creator in 1749. It was repaired once by Drowne's son after the Boston earthquake in 1755, and later by various others because of damage resulting from severe storms and accidents. To this day it commands a perfect grasshopper's-eye view of Dock Square, "and still looks as if it could jump with the best of its kind." Various reasons are given for the choice of the grasshopper for the famous old hall, but without going into this matter here it may be noted that the grasshopper is thought to be an exact copy of the vane on top of the Royal Exchange in London. Shem Drowne seems to have been the first regular weathervane maker of whom we have record in New England.

Our theme, however, is contemporary handicrafts, and space must therefore be given for a short description of at least one modern weathervane, a unique creation recently completed by Bruce Rogers for his home at New Fairfield, Connecticut. This weathervane features a singing cuckoo and a windmill. It is an unusual piece of craftsmanship done with that skill, precision, and pleasant persistence which characterize so much of Mr. Rogers' work in the field of typography and book design. Through all the years that he has given to fine printing Mr. Rogers has found time to "putter" around indoors and out, creating many delightful water colors of English and American scenes and landscapes, making some excellent ship models, at least one figurehead, a bust of Conrad for the sailing vessel *Joseph Conrad*, and other inventions familiar to those who know him best.

Perhaps this cuckoo weathervane suggests, as well as anything, Mr. Rogers' ever active mind, skillful hand, and sense of humor in the creation of the varied things that interest him. He has a great fondness for windmills; he always wanted to live in one. He likes English cuckoos, too, and it was natural enough for him to combine a windmill and a cuckoo in a weathervane; this combination was not only natural but necessary to achieve the results desired. He began his creative problem by taking his cuckoo clock apart to see how it worked, and how it would contribute to his plan for a weathervane which would combine the essential elements of the two—the song of the cuckoo and the revolutions of the windmill—in one. The greatest single problem was the construction of a cuckoo that would sing, and sing not too often or too infrequently, but with pleasant regularity, and when it sang would raise its tail. Now that this has been achieved there are many witnesses to the fact that this goes on during spring, summer, and autumn months; Mr. Rogers takes the bird and mill indoors for the winter.

It took a long time by the trial and error method to construct a bird with the desired qualifications, and even when this was done, the cuckoo was unable to raise its voice or its tail until the essential mechanism was built and installed within the tower of the windmill. Concealed from view inside the tower is the soundbox for the cuckoo's voice, as well as the mechanism for its gestures. It was all worked out by a series of cams operated by shafts, gears, and pinions from an old clock. An old Ford steering-wheel forms the track on which the mill revolves, and the lid of a coffee tin makes the perch for the cuckoo and holds the sails in the wind. So the cuckoo sings on every eleventh turn of the windmill, and the timing is not in the creator's hands, but rather in the velocity of the breeze. The photograph, shown on another page, was taken when the cuckoo and the mill were at ease.

Part III

SIGNIFICANT INFLUENCES IN THE HANDICRAFT MOVEMENT

CHAPTER 17

SOCIETY OF ARTS AND CRAFTS

THE Society of Arts and Crafts of Boston was for more than a quarter of a century one of the greatest influences in our country for spreading "the gospel of Beauty combined with Usefulness." In New England, and to a considerable extent throughout the nation, it continues to be a strong factor in the handicraft movement, and includes in its membership some of the best craftsmen in the country.

As we noted in Chapter 2, it was the exhibition idea which made the connection between the arts and crafts movement in old England and its expression in New England, resulting in the organization of the Society of Arts and Crafts.

The plea of the young printer, Henry Lewis Johnson, for the establishment here of handicraft exhibitions similar to those held in England and France resulted in his being appointed to carry out plans for the first such exhibit to be held on this continent, in 1897. The members of the committee who made the decision are given because all who are interested in handicrafts owe a great deal to these far-sighted persons. The list is taken from a short history of the Society by May R. Spain, published in 1924 to mark the twenty-fifth anniversary of its founding, which was celebrated in 1922. Free use of Mrs. Spain's material has been made because it is believed that the booklet would itself be available to comparatively few readers.

The members of the organizing committee for the 1897 exhibition were:

General Charles G. Loring, chairman of the trustees of the Museum of Fine Arts; Dr. William Sturgis Bigelow and Denman W. Ross, trustees of the Museum; Ross Turner, the painter; Charles A. Cummings, president of the Boston Society of Architects; R. Clipston Sturgis of the Boston Architectural Club; C. Howard Walker, who had founded the Museum School of Design; A. W. Longfellow, Jr., Sylvester Baxter, then art critic for the Boston Transcript.

281

The prospectus bore the names of the following persons, both men and women, who believed in the importance of this movement:

J. B. Millet, Thomas P. Smith, James Richard Carter, Robert Treat Paine, Jr., Mrs. Henry Whitman, C. H. Blackall, William T. Sedgwick, Curtis Guild, Jr., Robert D. Andrews, Arthur Astor Carey, H. Langford Warren, Mrs. J. Montgomery Sears, Mrs. Richard Morris Hunt, Mrs. Samuel D. Warren, Holker Abbott, Sears Gallagher, E. H. Clement, Rev. E. A. Horton, J. W. Phinney, Will Bradley, Edwin D. Mead, Mrs. Charles S. Sargent, Warren F. Kellogg, F. W. Chandler, H. W. Hartwell, Bertram Grosvenor Goodhue, S. N. D. North, and Samuel B. Capon. . . .

There were some 400 exhibits—many, of course, comprising several articles—by over 100 exhibitors, at least half of whom were women. The more noteworthy included the very valuable collection of jewelry by George Marcus of New York; wrought iron work by Eugene Kulinski and Co., and William H. Jackson and Co.; decorative bookbindings and stained glass by Mrs. Henry Whitman; fine hand wrought silver by Barton P. Jenks, George P. Kendrick, the Gorham Mfg. Co. and L. S. Ipsen; book covers, bookplates and illustrations by Miss Amy M. Sacker; embroidery by Mrs. J. Montgomery Sears, St. Margaret's School, Miss Olive Long and Mrs. D. D. Addison; pen and ink designs by Theodore Brown Hopgood, Jr., and Harry Goodhue; the "Altar Book," with type, initials and borders designed by Bertram Grosvenor Goodhue, pottery designed by Joseph Linden Smith and Charles E. Mills, and executed by Hugh C. Robertson of the Dedham Pottery; a set of fire irons designed by A. W. Longfellow, Jr.; wood carvings by I. Kirchmayer; designs for stained glass by John and Bancel LaFarge; and designs for carpets by William Morris, "to whom this and all the arts and crafts exhibitions owe their existence more than to any other man."

THE SOCIETY ORGANIZED

The success of the exhibition seemed to justify a permanent organization, and on June 28, 1897, the Society of Arts and Crafts was duly incorporated, its purpose as stated in its constitution being "to develop and encourage higher standards in the handicrafts."

[The] twenty-four people signing the articles of agreement . . . were: Charles Eliot Norton, Arthur Astor Carey, C. Howard Walker, A. W. Longfellow, Jr., Morris Gray, Henry Lewis Johnson, H. Langford Warren, Denman W. Ross, Robert D. Andrews, Ralph Adams Cram, Bertram Grosvenor Goodhue, Barton P. Jenks, D. B. Updike, Hugh Cairns, Mrs. D. D. Addison, Mrs. J. Montgomery

Sears, Mrs. Henry Whitman, John Evans, I. Kirchmayer, George P. Kendrick, George R. Shaw, J. T. Coolidge, Jr., Samuel D. Warren and George Edward Barton.

At the first meeting held October 13, 1897, Professor Charles Eliot Norton was elected president, and Arthur Astor Carey, Mrs. Henry Whitman and John Evans, vice-presidents. Morris Gray was the first treasurer, and George Edward Barton, clerk. . . .

The aims of the Society were summed up by Professor Norton in the following words: "The Society of Arts and Crafts is incorporated for the purpose of promoting artistic work in all branches of handicraft. It hopes to bring designers and workmen into mutually helpful relations, and to encourage workmen to execute designs of their own. It endeavors to stimulate in workmen an appreciation of the dignity and value of good design; to counteract the popular impatience of Law and Form, and the desire for over-ornamentation and specious originality. It will insist upon the necessity of sobriety and restraint, of ordered arrangement, of due regard for the relation between the form of an object and its use, and of harmony and fitness in the decoration put upon it."

When Professor Norton resigned as president of the Society, Arthur Astor Carey succeeded him. Early in 1899 the advisability of omitting an exhibition was considered unless the Society could be guaranteed against financial loss. President Carey announced that "a friend had been found who would make good any deficit that might be incurred." The same friend came to the Society's rescue periodically during Mr. Carey's presidency, thus giving an opportunity for progress which would not have been possible under other circumstances. Accordingly the exhibition of 1899 was directed by Mr. Johnson with Professor H. Langford Warren as chairman. "It was continued for three weeks, even being kept open on Sunday at the nominal charge of ten cents for admission in order to reach the people for whom it was primarily intended."

There were about three thousand entries in the 1899 exhibition, including work in jewelry, metals, woodcarving, modeling, printing, bookbinding, engraving, pottery, stained glass, wall hangings in gilded leather, lace by Italian women of North Boston, embroidery from the Society of Blue and White Needlework.

CHRONOLOGY

A few significant facts given in chronological order will serve to acquaint the reader at this point with the Society's growth, as well as its continuing importance in the present handicraft movement.

In the course of its fifty years the Society of Arts and Crafts has occupied several headquarters in Boston with exhibition and salesroom facilities of various kinds. In December, 1900, the first salesroom was opened in the old Twentieth Century Club Building on Somerset Street and Ashburton Place. Sales for the first year were $4,000. By 1904 they had increased to $14,000. The Society was then occupying quarters at 9 Park Street. When a large increase of business in 1905 put sales at $37,000, the Society achieved financial independence. A year later the remaining part of the street floor of Ticknor House was taken over. Between 1909 and 1920 sales increased until they reached $152,000 in the latter year. As would be expected, sales fell off appreciably at the end of the 1920's.

The Society has had a distinguished list of presidents, a complete list of whom follows:

1897-1899 Charles Eliot Norton
1899-1903 Arthur Astor Carey
1903-1917 H. Langford Warren
1917-1920 R. Clipston Sturgis
1920-1921 John Endicott Peabody
1922-1925 C. Howard Walker
1925-1928 William T. Aldrich

1928-1930 William L. Mowll
1930-1933 C. Howard Walker
1933-1935 J. Templeman Coolidge, Jr.
1935-1939 Charles J. Connick
1939-1946 Charles Ewing
1946-   Mrs. John S. Ames

Frederic Allen Whiting, who had become secretary and treasurer of the Society in 1900, organized and managed the first salesroom, and directed the activities of the Society until April, 1911. The Jury of Standards, appointed about the time of the opening of the salesroom, was an institution to which the Society has always attributed much of its success and growth.

The members of the first jury were: J. Templeman Coolidge, Jr., Mrs. J. Montgomery Sears, Mrs. Henry Whitman, Mrs. Hartley Dennett, R. Clipston Sturgis, Professor H. Langford Warren, Laurin H. Martin, Henry Hunt Clark, A. W. Longfellow, Jr., Denman W. Ross, C. Howard Walker, Nils J. Kjellstrom, and George R. Shaw.

There have been changes in membership from the 24 charter members of 1897: In its first year the Society grew to 71; by 1907, its tenth anniversary, membership had reached 700, and its executive officers had begun to give much time to the development of other handicraft groups throughout the country. In 1922 the Society had nearly 1,100 members; today, under the more strict rules indicated below, there are approximately 700.

Four classes of craftsmanship are recognized: junior, craftsman, master craftsman, and medalist. Associate membership consists of persons who are not producing craftsmen, but are interested in supporting the craft movement. The Council, established in 1898, is composed equally of craftsmen and associate members.

By action of the Jury, increasingly high standards of selection have been instituted in recent years. The Society felt that craftsmen had reached the point where such a policy could be enacted. This has inevitably reduced the numbers of acceptable craftsmen and of work approved, and it has caused some reduction in sales. However, growth is measured in different ways and this policy may be placed in the category of a calculated risk.

From 1913, when the custom of awarding a medal for excellence in craftsmanship and service was instituted, until 1948 only sixty-three medals have been conferred, never to more than three craftsmen in any single year. Below is given a complete list of medalists arranged chronologically:

Arthur J. Stone, silversmith; I. Kirchmayer, woodcarver; Henry C. Mercer, potter; Frank L. Koralewsky, ironworker; Mrs. Josephine H. Shaw, jeweler; Mary Crease Sears, bookbinder; Margaret Rogers, jeweler; Mrs. Adelaide Alsop Robineau, potter; Frank Gardner Hale, jeweler; James T. Woolley, silversmith; Mr. and Mrs. L. B. Dixon, jewelers; Elizabeth E. Copeland, enameler; Herbert A. Taylor, silversmith; Bertrand H. Wentworth, photographer; Karl F. Leinonen, silversmith; Douglas Donaldson, metalworker; Walfred Thulin, woodcarver; Sister Magdalen, illuminator.

George C. Gebelein, silversmith; Samuel Yellin, ironworker; Charles J. Connick, stained glass designer; T. M. Cleland, designer and printer; Lester H. Vaughan, metalworker; E. Crosby Doughty, photographer; Winifred M. Crawford, illuminator; Charles F. Binns, potter; Edward E. Oakes, jeweler; Francis O. Libby, photographer; Emile Bernat, tapestry weaver; Ellsworth Woodward, potter; Henry Lewis Johnson, printer; Lydia Bush-Brown, batik dyer and designer; Raymond E. Hanson, photographer.

Arthur E. Baggs, potter; Ernest Watson, blockprinter; Beatrix Holmes, illuminator; D. B. Updike, printer; George E. Germer, silversmith; Mrs. Gertrude S. Bassett, illuminator; Herbert Turner, photographer; Mrs. Louise Chrimes, needleworker; C. Howard Walker, designer, adviser; Joseph G. Reynolds, stained glass designer; F. J. R. Gyllenberg, silversmith; W. J. Phillips, blockprinter; John Templeman Coolidge, Jr., president of Arts and Crafts Society, 1933.

John G. Wiggins, woodcarver; Amy M. Sacker, art teacher; Charles Feurer, decorator; Katharine Pratt, silversmith; Mrs. Grace Corbett Reed, weaver; Edward M. Billings, chaser of silver; Charles W. Brown, spoon maker; William E. Brigham, jeweler; Charles

Ewing, distinguished service; Mrs. Marion Y. Greene, decorator; Marion L. Fosdick, potter; Mildred Watkins, enameler; Mrs. Foster Stearns, needleworker; Porter Blanchard, silversmith; Humphrey J. Emery, distinguished service; Charles D. Maginnis, architect; Mrs. Orin E. Skinner, service in design and technique.

The rare service of C. Howard Walker as critic for the Jury of Standards is one of the great chapters in the history of the Arts and Crafts Society. His death in 1935 brought an outpouring of appreciative comments from many sources, which were used in a memorial issue of the Society's *Bulletin*. His distinguished activities as an architect, city planner, educator, artist, and critic were of national importance, and Boston knew him as one of her "most caustic critics and most affectionate defenders." J. Templeman Coolidge, Jr., who succeeded him as president of the Society, said, "Everything about Howdy was big—his brain, his knowledge, his imagination, and his heart." Of his service on the Jury, "which soon made him its authorized spokesman," Mrs. Robert B. Stone, a member of the Council wrote as follows: "Vigorous, caustic, and fearless in denouncing sham, he was cooperative and kindly toward earnest effort both in his criticism and encouragement. . . . His vividness, his energy and genial presence were a never-failing inspiration. . . . One can hardly estimate the number of those who have been heartened to further effort by . . . his helpful leadership." That a man of such eminence should give mind and heart to the guidance of craftsmen was at once a tribute to his breadth of understanding and to the importance of handicrafts.

THE SOCIETY'S MONTHLY MAGAZINE

The Society's monthly publication, *Handicraft*, which first appeared in April, 1902, was of great interest and benefit to craftsmen, especially to those who could not visit the shop or attend meetings. This booklet combined typographical elements of modesty and beauty as refreshing today as when it was first printed. A note appearing in the first issue read: *"Handicraft* is intended as a means of increasing clearness of thought and community of sentiment among the followers of the Arts and Crafts movement, to offer an opportunity for public discussion of the artistic and economic problems involved, and to be a constant and definite reminder of the strong and wholesome principles which must necessarily underlie permanent success in genuine handicraft. Its aim is to uphold standards of work and taste, and to discuss questions from the point of view of practical good sense."

Some of the subjects discussed in *Handicraft* during its first year were: Aesthetics and Ethics, by Mary Ware Dennett; Style in the Composition of Type, by D. B. Updike; Lace-Making in Boston, by Sylvester Baxter; Art Enamels and Enamelling, by Samuel Bridge Dean; The Present Aspect of American Art from the Point of View of an Illustrator, by Howard Pyle; The Movement for Village Industries, by Sylvester Baxter; Byways Among Craftsmen, by Elizabeth B. Stone; The Qualities of Carving, by H. Langford Warren; The Arts and Crafts: A Diagnosis, by Dr. Denman W. Ross; Indian Handicrafts, by George Wharton James. Each issue contained a one-page editorial, and a favorite quotation was printed on the back cover.

LASTING INFLUENCE OF THE PIONEERS

It is scarcely possible for craftsmen of the present day fully to realize their obligation to the pioneer thinkers and workers who by banding together devoted themselves to the practical problems involved in the creation of objects of beauty by hand. They were largely responsible for a great advance in taste, and for laying the foundation of a handicraft movement which has affected the lives of countless persons throughout our nation.

In line with its broad educational policy the Society voted to send Mr. Whiting to represent it at the Louisiana Purchase Exposition in St. Louis in 1904; the Society's exhibits there in the Division of Applied Arts numbered 477 objects out of a total of 863 shown. Craftsmen from the Society won twenty-seven of the forty-nine medals awarded. Mr. Whiting was in charge of all the applied arts exhibits; he also served on the International Jury of Award. Three of the six United States members of this body belonged to the Society of Arts and Crafts. Mr. and Mrs. Whiting received medals in recognition of their splendid service. The Exposition did much to advance the influence of the Society as a leader in the arts and crafts movement, and craftsmen throughout the country made application for membership.

In 1904 the Society suffered a great loss in the death of Mrs. Henry Whitman, one of its charter members who was also a vice-president and member of the Jury. She was a master craftsman, whose stained glass and designs for book covers and bookbindings had been shown in the 1897 exhibit. A memorial exhibition of her work was held in the spring of 1905.

In 1917 the Society suffered another heavy loss in the sudden death of its president, Professor H. Langford Warren.

INTERESTING EVENTS

The new quarters at 9 Park Street, into which the Society moved in 1904, provided an excellent gallery for display purposes and two exhibitions were planned for the autumn of 1904. The first one was held during the sessions of the Episcopal General Convention, and showed a variety of work designed for church service and decoration. The second exhibition was of modern printing, which included work by the four men who received the only awards made for printing at the St. Louis Exposition: Bruce Rogers, who had received the grand prize; D. B. Updike, who had been awarded the gold medal; and Clark Conwell and Frederic W. Goudy, each of whom had won a bronze medal.

The tenth anniversary of the Society of Arts and Crafts was marked in February, 1907, by an exhibition held in Copley Hall, which attracted international attention and received wide comment by art critics and editors. Professor Warren was chairman of the Exhibition Committee which awarded commendation to twenty-five members and mention to thirty-five. In this exhibition as in others, the Society carried out the rule it had adopted when organized in 1897: to give credit to the individual craftsman or designer for work done whether it was exhibited by him or by his employer. In addition to work by members, exhibits were admitted from affiliated organizations for the anniversary exhibition.

Organization of National League of Handicraft Societies

It was in 1907 during the tenth anniversary celebration that the various arts and crafts societies outside of Boston met in conference with the Boston Society on its invitation and established the National League of Handicraft Societies. Professor Warren was elected president; Mr. Whiting served as secretary and treasurer. An announcement sent out soon after the conference described the purpose of the League as follows: "To bring together the various societies who are working for the same general purpose; to provide a small traveling exhibit which could serve as a set of standards; to provide traveling libraries of technical handbooks and of photographs; to arrange in cooperation with local societies, large exhibitions in various centers; to revive *Handicraft* as an organ of the League; to arrange courses of lectures through cooperation so that the various societies can secure the leading lecturers at a minimum cost."

The constituent societies of the League, numbering originally

twenty-four and later augmented to thirty-three, including the Boston
Society, were as follows:

Colorado: Arts-Crafts Society, Denver
Connecticut: Arts and Crafts Club, Hartford; Art-Crafts Society,
Wallingford
Illinois: Chicago Society of Arts and Crafts; Bradley Arts and Crafts
Club, Peoria; Society of Arts and Crafts, Rockford
Indiana: Arts and Crafts League, Evansville
Maine: Portland Society of Arts and Crafts
Maryland: Handicraft Club of Baltimore
Massachusetts: Whittier Home Association of Arts and Crafts,
Amesbury; Society of Arts and Crafts, Boston; Society of Deerfield
Industries; Arts and Crafts Society, Haverhill; Hingham Society
of Arts and Crafts; Melrose Society of Arts and Crafts; Norwell
Society of Arts and Crafts; Wayland Society of Arts and Crafts
Michigan: Society of Arts and Crafts, Detroit
Minnesota: Handicraft Guild, Minneapolis; Society of Arts and
Crafts, Minneapolis
Missouri: Arts and Crafts Society, Kansas City; Society of Applied
Arts, St. Louis
Montana: Society of Arts and Crafts, Deer Lodge; Helena Society
of Arts and Crafts
New Hampshire: Handicraft Workers of Peterboro
New Jersey: Arts and Crafts Society of New Jersey, East Orange
New York: National Society of Craftsmen, New York City
North Carolina: Arts and Handicrafts Guild, Greensboro
Ohio: William Morris Society, Columbus
Oregon: Portland Arts and Crafts Society
Pennsylvania: Arts and Crafts Guild, Philadelphia
Rhode Island: Handicraft Club, Providence
South Carolina: Handicraft Guild, Charleston

As a result of the organization of the League, two traveling libraries
of books in the arts and crafts were circulated throughout the country
and a reference library was maintained at the main offices of the
Society in Boston for League members. The magazine, *Handicraft*,
was revived under League auspices and was published at The Dyke
Mill, Montague, Massachusetts, for several years with Mr. Whiting as
editor. Carl Purington Rollins was assistant editor and designed its
format.

In spite of the recession of 1907, an educational program was advanced by the Society of Arts and Crafts which gave renewed vitality
to the movement. A number of lectures were arranged under the
auspices of the Library Committee, and the Metal Workers' Guild was

organized. This was followed in 1908 by the organization of the Wood Workers' Guild, and shortly after came the St. Dunstan's Guild for workers in ecclesiastical arts. By 1909 the Society had again become self-supporting; its educational movements were developing appreciation of things beautiful throughout the land, and producing craftsmen found marketing opportunities through the Society and the League. The principle of the Society was to require just enough in the way of commissions to cover the expenses of their sales. This cooperative arrangement for both craftsman and supporter formed a strong basis for steady growth.

As the Society of Arts and Crafts was growing and realizing the hopes of its founders, the countrywide organization was also getting well under way. The National League of Handicraft Societies in 1911 held its annual meeting at the Museum of Fine Arts in Boston, by invitation of the Museum's trustees, and the Society of Arts and Crafts arranged a special exhibition at the Museum for the occasion. Professor Warren and Mr. Whiting had piloted the League to a point where it was strong enough to relieve them of this responsibility and elect other officers. Huger Elliott was elected president of the League and its headquarters were moved to Providence, Rhode Island.

In the following year Mr. Whiting accepted the invitation of the John Herron Art Institute of Indianapolis to become director of its Museum; a year later he was made director of the Cleveland Museum of Art. In 1930 Mr. Whiting became president of the American Federation of Arts at Washington, and one of his able curators, William M. Milliken, succeeded him as director of the Cleveland Museum. Mr. Whiting and Mr. Milliken were responsible for the first local exhibition, held in 1919, showing the handicrafts of our foreign-born citizens. The Cleveland Museum holds annually a notable handicraft exhibition, the work of local craftsmen.

After Mr. Whiting's resignation as director of the Society of Arts and Crafts, responsibility for the work fell for a time upon Mrs. C. S. Ropes, who had assisted him so efficiently, and Judge Frederick P. Cabot, chairman of the salesroom committee. In the autumn of 1912 Henry P. Macomber became director, and Mrs. Ropes assumed full responsibility for sales. Mr. Macomber visited many craftsmen and their organizations throughout the country and thus helped them maintain a close cooperative relationship with the Boston Society.

Later Exhibitions

The exhibition of April, 1913, proved to be especially significant because of the high quality of the entries—fine wrought-iron objects by Frederick Krasser, porcelain and pottery by Mrs. A. A. Robineau, lacquered furniture by Miss B. E. Colman, woodcarvings by I. Kirchmayer, stained glass by Charles J. Connick—and also because it was held at the Museum of Fine Arts in Boston.

Although the Society did not exhibit as a group at the Panama-Pacific Exposition in San Francisco in 1915, it was represented officially by Mr. Macomber, who also served on the International Jury of Award, and individual members of the Society from parts of the country received awards:

Grand Prizes: for pottery, Mrs. A. A. Robineau; for bookbinding, Mrs. L. Averill Howland. Medals of Honor: for miniatures, Miss Laura C. Hills; for pottery, the Fulper Pottery. Gold Medals: for stained glass, Charles J. Connick; for ironwork, Frank L. Koralewsky; for decorated china, Miss Maud M. Mason; for oil paintings, Giovanni B. Troccoli. Silver Medals: for water colors, Mrs. Elizabeth S. G. Elliott; for oil paintings and water colors, H. D. Murphy; for oil paintings, Philip Little. Bronze Medals: for wood engraving, Miss Elizabeth Colwell and Arthur W. Dow; for enamel work, Miss Elizabeth E. Copeland. Mr. Macomber was also awarded a bronze medal for his services.

During this same year the Art Institute at Chicago in its annual exhibition of Applied Arts conferred prizes upon three members of the Society: Arthur E. Baggs for the best exhibit of pottery; George E. Germer for the best original design in silverware; and Mrs. Clara S. Grierson for the best exhibit of textiles.

Early in 1920 an exhibition was held in Boston of Modern British Arts and Crafts, which had been assembled by Miss Helen Plumb of the Detroit Arts and Crafts Society, and which gave much pleasure to the American group. A few years prior to this, C. R. Ashbee, president of the London Guild of Handicrafts, had lectured on William Morris, with whom Ashbee had been closely associated. During all the period of its growth the Society's rooms have been in constant use for exhibitions, meetings, and lectures.

The 1920's were fateful years for the Society. Its twenty-fifth anniversary was marked by the publication of Mrs. Spain's history, and by the part the Society played in arranging a traveling exhibition of handicrafts which, under the auspices of the American Federation of Arts, circulated from 1922 to 1923. Mr. Macomber headed a special committee in charge of this enterprise and C. Howard Walker was a member of the Jury, serving with Frederic Allen Whiting and Bertram Grosvenor Goodhue. The exhibit demonstrated the progress that had taken place in design and craftsmanship since the first exhibition of the Society in 1897.

During the Boston Tercentenary in 1930, the Society was invited to exhibit at the Museum of Fine Arts.

New York Shop Established

In 1924 a large membership and a considerable surplus influenced the Society to take the step, which had long been contemplated, of establishing a New York salesroom at 7 West Fifty-sixth Street—later moved to Madison Avenue—under the direct supervision of Mrs. C. H. Busck and shortly thereafter of Miss Elizabeth Lyman. A committee consisting of Mr. Macomber, George J. Hunt, Henry Hunt Clark, and George C. Greener acted with Mr. Walker in making the arrangements. The new move, while of definite benefit to member craftsmen, proved in the long run to be a serious drain upon the Boston Society. The sales would have been considered high for any city except New York, where expenses soon outran profits. New Yorkers, the shop management thought, appeared to expect orders to be completed the day after they were placed. In any event, it became necessary to close the shop after about four years.

The New York venture had not been separately incorporated, and the burden of its failure fell upon the Boston Society. The surplus of about $20,000, which the Society had accumulated in Boston, was wiped out and an additional debt of the same amount was incurred. That the Society was able to work its way through these difficulties without sacrificing the high standard of craftsmanship it had always maintained, is a remarkable tribute to its leadership and to the loyalty of its member craftsmen, who frequently agreed to postponement of payments. To add to its problems, sales in 1929 began to recede.

Shortly after the close of the New York shop, Mr. Macomber, who had served the Society as its executive officer for sixteen years, left to accept a position at Cranbrook. Grant H. Code was elected director in his stead, a position which he held until the election of Joseph Loud in the spring of 1930.

Recent Years

In June, 1930, Humphrey J. Emery, the present director of the Society, was elected secretary-treasurer. The officers at that time were: C. Howard Walker, president; J. Templeman Coolidge, Jr., and Mrs. Henry Lyman, vice-presidents. Mr. Emery came in at a time when the Society was in serious financial condition and sales were diminishing. The most drastic economies were undertaken, and in the course of three years the expenses of operation were reduced by 60 per cent. It was difficult to maintain the service to which members were accustomed, but a loyal and well-trained staff succeeded in doing so.

By the end of 1932 sales had begun to show a change for the better. Gradually the Society was able to resume its program of education and production. Three special exhibits were held in 1933, and two were sent on tour. The important decision to move to 32 Newbury Street was announced to eight thousand customers and friends in a beautifully printed broadside. Mr. Coolidge, recognizing Mr. Emery's part in improving the Society's condition, remarked at a meeting in 1934, held in the new quarters, that "but for him the Boston Society of Arts and Crafts could not be assembled here tonight." The move to new quarters was based on the careful reasoning that business was moving to the western part of the city, and that at this time leases were available at reasonable rates. Events fully justified the decision.

In 1934 the Society exhibited twenty-eight water colors of descendants of Maximilian the Great by C. Howard Walker. Shortly thereafter the Society collected an Exhibition of Contemporary Craft Work to be judged by a jury independent of its own membership. It comprised: William T. Aldrich, a former president, William Emerson, dean of the Architectural School of the Massachusetts Institute of Technology, and Frank L. Allen of the Massachusetts School of Art. The awards were: first, Charles Harder; second, Katharine Alden; and third, John P. Petterson.

During the next three years the Society was called upon to aid representatives of the churches of Greater Boston by providing exhibitions of ecclesiastical work to be shown during their annual convention. There were at the time several craftsmen especially well fitted to meet the demands of this exhibition. In 1937 members of the Society took part in the International Exposition in Paris through a collection of handicrafts assembled by Horace H. F. Jayne.

In 1938 the Society accepted an invitation to participate in the Fiftieth Exhibition of the Arts and Crafts Exhibition Society of London. In 1943 a committee of the Society selected from the Contemporary Handicrafts Exhibition, sponsored by the Worcester Art Museum, a collection of handicrafts which was shown in Boston.

In the summer of 1946 the Society was obliged to find a new home. This need naturally took precedence over any other matters; even the plans of the Society to celebrate its fiftieth anniversary. When new quarters had been found at 145 Newbury Street, the question of marking the Society's anniversary was again considered. Previous exhibitions of the kind contemplated had been held either at the

Museum of Fine Arts or in halls suitable for the purpose. The Society's officers, however, were eager to bring the Fiftieth Anniversary Exhibition to the attention of a public that knew but little about contemporary American craft work. Since the greatest human traffic exists in the downtown department store area, it seemed logical to turn in this direction for an exhibition gallery. Conferences with Lee W. Court, display manager of the William Filene's Sons Company, resulted in the Company's generously offering the use of show windows on three streets surrounding the store.

The Exhibition was arranged for a period of two weeks beginning at Easter time. The first three windows set forth the past, present, and future work of the Society. The past was represented by objects which had been previously shown in the early exhibitions of 1897 and 1899. The second window showed characteristic work of the period when the Society was at 9 Park Street. The third window covered the most modern work exhibited by the Society. The remaining windows represented contemporary craft work.

An artist and a craftsman himself, Mr. Court saw in the Exhibition an opportunity for the store to help interpret to the people of New England a part of their heritage of contemporary life and culture of the region. Statements were sent to about a hundred newspapers, calling attention to the participation of local craftsmen. Although no sales were made by the store, an information center was maintained there from which prospective purchasers were directed to the Society's headquarters. Of the thousands of people who saw the Exhibition from the street, many of them before and after working hours, several hundred made inquiries regarding opportunities to become craftsmen. The example of interest and cooperation in the handicraft movement set by Filene's has been followed by stores in other cities.

The direct responsibility for the Exhibition was assumed by Miss Louisa Dresser, former acting director of the Worcester Art Museum, to whose skill, taste, tact, and good management Mr. Emery and Mr. Court attest.

CHAPTER 18

THE LEAGUE OF NEW HAMPSHIRE
ARTS AND CRAFTS

DURING one of the war years a visitor at the Craftsman's Fair of the League of New Hampshire Arts and Crafts overheard two members express disappointment that the exhibition was not up to standard. To the visitor the wonder was that the fair was held at all, for pressure was then strong for dropping everything not directly helpful to the war effort. But to many persons handicrafts were considered essential; they enabled those who could not work in war industries to work at home, and they contributed indirectly to the morale of New England. When in 1942 the decision was made by the craftsmen themselves to try out the fair at Plymouth, it was an experiment rather than a commitment for any future war year. As a craftsman born in Sweden put it, "Ve all pitch in and see how ve cum out." So with only a handful of craftsmen and with many volunteers, but no chairman, "it cum out so vell" that another fair was held at Manchester in 1943. By that time the case for continuity was settled.

New Hampshire, as the reader may remember, was the first state in the Union to develop and with legislative support maintain a thorough-going handicraft service for its citizens: the fairs, held in various parts of the state, are milestones in the progress of the League of New Hampshire Arts and Crafts.

SANDWICH HOME INDUSTRIES

The acorn from which the League itself has grown was planted in the village of Center Sandwich in 1925 when a committee from the Sandwich Historical Society, under the chairmanship of Mrs. J. Randolph Coolidge, held an exhibition of one hundred old and new hooked rugs, all of which had been made in the town of Sandwich. So much interest was created by this event that the "Rug Committee" was asked to see if it could find a place where other homemade handicrafts might be exhibited and sold. Center Sandwich was then a village of only about seven hundred inhabitants, among whom the tradition still survived of several crafts, such as spinning, weaving, candle dipping, furniture and basketmaking, rugmaking, and others. There was still a "Basket Street," so named because of the many baskets made in the area years ago. In talking with the women of the village Mrs. Coolidge found some who had been taught one or another of these skills by their parents and who would have liked to see the old handicrafts revived. Mrs. Coolidge felt strongly that whatever was undertaken must be a community affair—done by the townspeople themselves because they wanted it and were willing to work for it.

Following the successful rug exhibit the Committee found a small vacant store which it rented for $12 a month. With this went the use of a tiny house adjoining. Here, by serving afternoon tea, the rent for the store could be earned. Later, tearoom and salesroom were housed together in a small but picturesque building given to the Committee rent free. The next problem was how to get the stock of things to sell.

Mrs. Coolidge, at this writer's urgent request, has recorded some of the practical steps taken: "We began with the blacksmith, and took him andirons and tongs and fire forks to copy; we went to the one basketmaker in town who still made market and clothesbaskets of split ash, and started him on making baskets of many sizes and new shapes; we got the rugmakers to copy some of the old and much better designs of their grandmothers. When we discovered a very big old loom in someone's attic, a summer visitor in Sandwich harnessed it and volunteered to demonstrate and teach weaving in our shop on certain afternoons each week. As far as I know, Deerfield, Massachusetts, and Cape Cod were the only places where weaving was then being revived. It created great interest and people came from miles away to see it. Soon a great variety of hand-woven table covers and mats, scarfs, and woven rugs began to appear in our shop. Next we had to find the purchasers: We advertised in the papers; my husband, an architect, made attractive posters which were put up in shops of nearby towns. Fortunately it was a time when people had leisure in which to choose what they would do, and there were not many distractions or amusements up in the country. We toiled faithfully during the four months of that first summer and we sold $1,000 worth of crafts made in Sandwich, all of the money received from sales going to the makers. Our tearoom paid the rent and also for wrapping paper, string, and left us with $50 in the bank for the next year. It was hard at first to get really good work; most of our contributors had never seen fine things done by other people. It took a long time to get them to appreciate what good design and perfect workmanship was. For that reason we didn't start with teachers and 'standards' and juries."

The Committee was encouraged by the growing interest and even enthusiasm shown to carry on a second year. A 15 per cent commission was now charged, which was paid to a young woman who took charge of the shop each afternoon. More people produced, better work was done, and sales were doubled. In the third year a Christmas sale was held in Concord, and again sales increased by $1,000. "We were happily learning to work together," said Mrs. Coolidge, "and we were becoming proud of our 'Sandwich Home Industries'—there was something really interesting going on in the town!"

The following year, the hard-working Committee who had faithfully scrubbed floors, hung burlap over dilapidated wallpaper, served food and acted as saleswomen, were able to have a Simmons College graduate take over the tearoom, giving Sandwich Home Industries a small percentage of the intake. Luncheons and dinners were served and so many persons came that the Committee still had to help in serving meals. By the summer of 1928, $5,000 worth of articles, all made in Sandwich, was sold.

In the fourth year of Sandwich Home Industries the late Governor John G. Winant of New Hampshire was invited to speak at the County Fair, held annually and attended by thousands. The Committee served lunch to the Governor and his Council. The women felt repaid for the effort expended because the visit stimulated sales and gave the enterprise wide publicity. Later, perhaps as a result of his first-hand view of the Sandwich undertaking, Governor Winant appointed a Commission of Arts and Crafts to organize similar work in other towns.

"Our Committee," said Mrs. Coolidge, "was kept very busy during our fourth season. Many letters had to be answered; people were asking how we had started, for they wanted to organize in their own towns; we had to find sources of supplies of different kinds; our wool came from a flock of sheep owned in the neighborhood and some of the townspeople dyed it with vegetable dyes. These hanks of yarn in their lovely pastel colors went like wildfire. We worked hard to supply the demand; it became a 'specialty' with us. Our little building was bought and restored as a memorial to Mr. Coolidge with money raised by his fellow-townspeople and added to by his family and friends. The work of planning and over-seeing the restoration of the building was given by his former partner. Here again was an instance of that volunteer spirit with which our work had been carried on from the beginning. We in the town were *working together* for our shop, learning to make better designs with better colors and to have the patience to take time for careful workmanship. More than all, we were learning the joy of appreciating beautiful things, of creating them, and of working together for a cause."

COOPERATION WITH THE WOLFEBORO COMMITTEE

While the Sandwich Home Industries were thus developing, the Rotary Club of Wolfeboro, New Hampshire, not knowing at that time what was going on in Center Sandwich, was sponsoring a group of adult craftsmen in various handicrafts, especially metalwork. In the successive winters of 1928-1929 and 1929-1930, classes were formed under volunteer instructors, and in the summer of 1929 an exhibition of work was held. The notice of the exhibition read in part: "During the past few months there has been conducted in Wolfeboro an experiment, the results of which are interesting and possibly important. Realizing the desirability of having some type of employment available to those who have idle time during the winter months, the Wolfeboro Rotary Club has conducted classes in various hand crafts. We have reason to believe that there are in Wolfeboro many who are capable of doing most excellent work in this field."

The notice was signed by the Community Service Committee, Wolfeboro Rotary Club: H. H. Hart, A. Cooper Ballentine, E. H. Trickey, E. B. Rich, and R. F. Thurrell. The group realized that the high standard of craftsmanship which was essential could only be had by better instruction, and a small committee concentrated on ways and means to bring this about.

On Sunday, February 3, 1929, the following news item appeared in a paper published at Center Sandwich: "A compliment was paid the Sandwich Home Industries recently. A party of three men and one woman motored to Sandwich Center from Wolfeboro and interrogated Mrs. Louise Moulton concerning the management and minute details of the industry."

Mrs. Moulton was the shop manager. The "three men" were A. Cooper Ballentine, Harry T. Merritt, and Allan Evans; and the "one woman" was Miss Laura I. Mattoon. It was the thought of the committee from Wolfeboro that the two communities might combine forces to obtain assistance for their work from either the State University Extension Service or the State Board of Education. Mr. Ballentine was deeply interested in the administration of summer camps for young people, and was a strong advocate of creative handicrafts in developing character as well as skills. With Mrs. Coolidge as chairman and Mr. Ballentine as secretary-treasurer a cooperative committee was

John D. Schiff

113. ROMULUS AND REMUS OF ANCIENT ROME

FRANCISCO PEVIRI OF SOUTH FRAMINGHAM, MASSACHUSETTS, A BLIND CARVER, PICTURES IN WOOD SCULPTURE PERSONS AND EPISODES OF FABLE AND HISTORY. HIS CHRIST ON THE CROSS HANGS IN THE NEIGHBORHOOD CHURCH AT SOUTH ORLEANS ON CAPE COD.

Horydczak

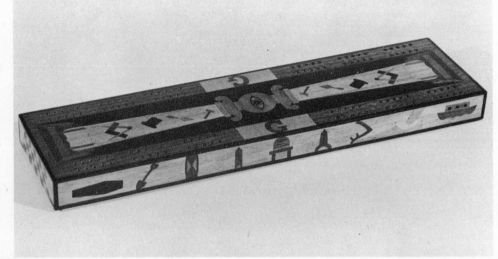

John D. Schiff

114. WHITTLING FROM NEW HAMPSHIRE, INTARSIA FROM MAINE

OMAR MARCOUX OF CONCORD HAS WHITTLED OUT MORE THAN EIGHTY BREEDS OF
AMERICAN DOGS. THESE ARE SOME THAT WERE SHOWN AT THE NATIONAL RURAL ARTS
EXHIBITION IN WASHINGTON, D. C. . . . THE CRIBBAGE BOARD IS A GOOD EXAMPLE OF
INTARSIA, OR WOOD INLAY, BY EDSON W. FLETCHER OF SEARSPORT.

115. A MEMORIAL CROSS OF WOOD

This Cross in Memory of the American Marine Painter, Frederick Waugh of Provincetown, Was Designed and Carved by His Fellow Artist and Townsman, William Boogar, Jr.

This text is a slightly expanded version of a let=
ter written on July 21 1937 to a friend who wanted
to know how one went about designing a typeface.

DEAR RR: *The way I work at present*
is to draw an alphabet 10 times 12 point size, with a
pen or brush, the letters carefully finished. I start with
the lower-case, and let its characters settle the style of
the capitals. Ten times twelve point is a convenient
size to work; and I have a dimishing glass that re=
duces the letters to something like 12 point size when
I put the drawing on the floor and squint at it through
the glass held belt high. This gives a rough idea of what
the reduction does to curves and things.

Having got a start on what I want by this means
I turn the drawing over to G. and he puts a few of the
characters through — possibly lower-case h and p. He
makes his large pattern drawings (64 times 12 point)
cuts, casts and proves the trial characters; and sends
me his large drawings, my 10 times drawings, & proofs
on smooth and rough paper.

By looking at all these for two or three days I get
an idea of how to go forward — or, if the result is a dud,
how to start over again. From the large pattern-sheets
I can see just how details behave when they get down
to size, and can change the weights of serifs, thin lines,

db

10 times 12 point

116. WORK OF A FINE CALLIGRAPHER
A PAGE FROM A HAND-WRITTEN LETTER BY WILLIAM A. DWIGGINS TO RUDOLPH RUZICKA
TELLING HIM HOW HE WORKS AT LETTER MAKING.

Edmund de Beaumont

Edmund de Beaumont

117. VARIOUS NEW ENGLAND HANDICRAFTS

MINIATURE FURNITURE BY W. B. DOUGLASS OF DUNSTABLE, MASSACHUSETTS, AN AUTHENTIC REPRODUCTION OF A ROOM IN HEBRON, NEW HAMPSHIRE. .... VICTORY GARDEN RUG DESIGNED AND HOOKED BY MRS. MOLLY NYE TOBEY OF BARRINGTON, RHODE ISLAND. ... HANDMADE BASKETS FROM DIFFERENT PARTS OF NEW ENGLAND.

Shades of Currier and Ives! What buttonballs! Such barns with corn crib and yard, with white horns tossing over the wall! What a clamor of geese! Then Spencer's Creek and the nearby woods! He who has seen the Spencer place has seen New England.

44

118. CALLIGRAPHER, HAND PRINTER, ILLUSTRATOR

CHARLES D. HUBBARD OF GUILFORD, CONNECTICUT, PRINTED EVERY PAGE BY HAND AND ILLUSTRATED TWO BEAUTIFUL BOOKS: *Old Guilford* AND *An Old New England Village*. THIS IS A PAGE FROM *Old Guilford*.

Ralph M. Arnold

119. MARBLE CARVED BY A RHODE ISLAND CRAFTSMAN

THIS MEMORIAL IN VERMONT MARBLE WAS DESIGNED AND CARVED BY JOHN HOWARD
BENSON OF NEWPORT, CALLIGRAPHER, LETTERER, AND STONECUTTER.

Lifshey Studios

120. PRODUCTS OF ONE VERMONT FAMILY

THESE HANDICRAFTS AND FARM PRODUCTS ARE SOME OF THE ITEMS MADE AND PREPARED BY THE SEVEN MEMBERS OF THE CARPENTER FAMILY FOR THEIR SHOP AT BRATTLEBORO.

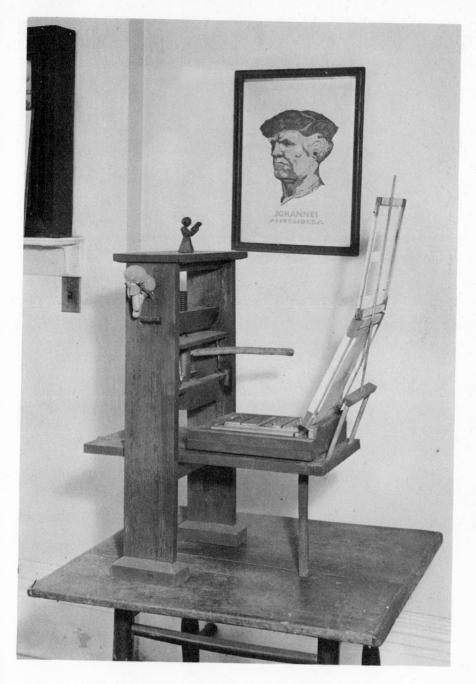

121. MODEL OF GUTENBERG'S PRINTING PRESS

The Original Press on Which Johannes Gutenberg First Printed from Movable
Type Has Long Since Vanished, but Careful Research and a Practical Knowledge
of Printing Have Helped Carl Purington Rollins, Printer Emeritus to Yale
University, Design and Construct This Facsimile.

E. R. Coburn

122. GRANDSIRE WHITTLING

For Generations Character Dolls Have Been Made in New England, and the Handicraft Revival Has Developed New Ones in Every State. This Strawberry Patch Doll Was Made by Mrs. Ralph F. Flather of Meredith, New Hampshire.

Edmund de Beaumont

123. SKILLS IN WOOD, WOOL, AND METAL

COFFEE TABLE BY HUGO LINNELL; CURTAINS BY MRS. LINNELL; RUG BY MRS. WILLIAM
E. BRIGHAM, ALL OF VILLA HANDICRAFTS, PROVIDENCE, RHODE ISLAND. COFFEE SET
OF PEWTER BY LEWIS WHITNEY OF ROCKPORT, MASSACHUSETTS.

Mariners' Museum, Newport News, Virginia

124. A BEAUTIFUL SHIP MODEL

THERE ARE PROBABLY MORE SHIP MODELMAKERS IN NEW ENGLAND THAN IN ANY OTHER AREA OF OUR COUNTRY. THIS MODEL IS AS FINE AS ANY TO BE FOUND IN THESE STATES. IT IS THE *Bangalore* MADE BY CARROLL R. SAWYER OF MANCHESTER, NEW HAMPSHIRE.

Mariners' Museum, Newport News, Virginia

125. A MASTER SHIP MODELMAKER

CARROLL R. SAWYER, MASTER SHIP MODELBUILDER IN HIS "SHIPYARD" AT MANCHESTER, NEW HAMPSHIRE.

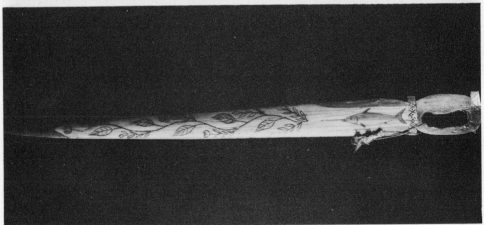

Clemens Kalischer

126. SCRIMSHAW IN MASSACHUSETTS AND MAINE

THE EAGLE'S HEAD WAS CARVED FROM A WHALE'S TOOTH BY WILLIAM PERRY OF NEW
BEDFORD. . . . THE SWORDFISH ENGRAVING BELONGS TO CLEVELAND TRASK OF SWANS
ISLAND, MAINE, WHO CURED THE SWORD. AFTER THE DESIGN WAS ETCHED MR. TRASK
FILLED IT WITH RED, BLUE, AND GREEN SEALING WAX.

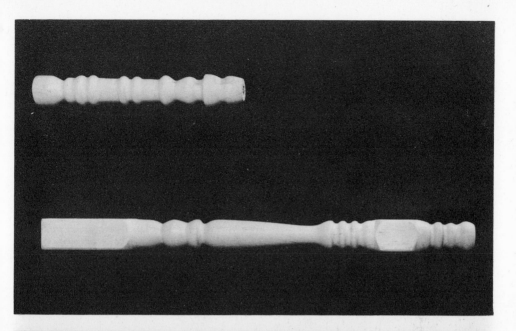

Lifshey Studios

127. WOODTURNING IN CONNECTICUT

THE TWO UPPER TURNINGS WERE DONE AT OLD FARMS CONVALESCENT HOSPITAL,
AVON, BY A G.I. WHO HAD LOST HIS HANDS AND SIGHT IN BOTH EYES. . . . THE BOXES
WERE TURNED BY ALVAN L. DAVIS OF WATERBURY, WHO BRINGS OUT THE CHARACTER
OF THE NATIVE WOODS, SOMETIMES LEAVING THE BARK ON THE COMPLETED WORK.

Life Photographer, Fritz Goro, Copyright Time, Inc.

128. SOUVENIR OF THE STATE OF MAINE

MAURICE DAY AND FAMILY OF DAMARISCOTTA SENT THIS GROUP OF CHICADEES, THE
STATE BIRD OF MAINE, TO THE WORCESTER EXHIBITION OF CONTEMPORARY NEW ENG-
LAND HANDICRAFTS AS AN EXAMPLE OF THEIR CRAFTSMANSHIP.

formed for the purpose of promoting a handicraft movement. Although probably no one realized it at the time, this was in fact the first co-operative step toward what was ultimately to become the League of New Hampshire Arts and Crafts.

The joint committee became active immediately, and at the next meeting it was decided that Mrs. Coolidge should see Governor Winant and apprise him of what had been done and of the committee's hopes. Mr. Ballentine proposed three steps: (1) an approach to the State University Extension Service; (2) consultation with outstanding leaders in the field of arts and crafts; and (3) a statewide plan for training craftsmen. Accordingly, President Edward Morgan Lewis of the University of New Hampshire was visited, and the committee invited Royal B. Farnum of the Rhode Island School of Design and Allen Eaton of Russell Sage Foundation to act as its advisers in work-ing out a statewide plan of training and organization.

Mr. Winant, who had been again chosen governor in November, 1930, said in his second inaugural address in January, 1931: "The rural sections of New Hampshire provide good farming land and should continue to return income to the industrious and intelligent farmer. The winters, however, are long and rigorous. If some inventive mind could establish winter industries which would provide the people on our hills and in our valleys with small craft industries during the winter, it would add appreciably to the happiness of their lives and to the total yearly income."

APPOINTMENT OF COMMISSION OF NEW HAMPSHIRE ARTS AND CRAFTS

The Governor referred later in his address to Mrs. Coolidge and to the experiment with the Sandwich Home Industries, and in May, 1931, he appointed a "Commission of New Hampshire Arts and Crafts to develop in New Hampshire substantial hand crafts as home indus-tries that will reflect the highest standards of craftsmanship. To provide in New Hampshire the best kind of manual and industrial art training at low cost, especially for developing the home industries plan."

The seven members named to the Commission were: Mrs. J. Randolph Coolidge, chairman; A. Cooper Ballentine of Wolfeboro, secretary-treasurer; Miss Margaret Whipple, a craftsman of Bristol; Philip W. Ayres of Franconia, the first forester of the New Hampshire Society for the Protection of Forests; Colonel William A. Barron of Crawford Notch; Dean George W. Case of the University of New

Hampshire; and James N. Pringle, state commissioner of education. Governor Winant had in a special fund the sum of $500 which he made available to the Commission for a preliminary study to determine the extent of New Hampshire's resources in materials and workers, both active and potential. He expressed the hope that the Commission's plans would be supported by legislative appropriations.

First Meeting of the Commission

The Commission lost no time in getting down to work, holding its first meeting on May 28, 1931, in Concord. It was agreed that handicraft industries, as well as home crafts, should be stressed and that care should be taken not to stimulate more interest among individuals and groups than could be sustained by good instruction and by marketing opportunities.

A committee was appointed to study the question of markets and of commissions to be charged, another to make a survey of existing manual arts training schools and courses with a view to understanding New Hampshire's special training needs, and to compile a bibliography of manual arts and of handicraft books and reference materials. Under the direction of Dean Case a survey had been made by George W. Rugg of handicrafts in the Southern Highlands. The study was to be continued in the eastern United States, particularly in New England, and would be available to the Commission.

A "Steering Committee" was asked to formulate some fundamental matters of policy as a guide to the Commission, first in its surveys, and later in its recommendations to craftsmen, so that there would be a clear understanding of "what is meant by superior craftsmanship and salable work worthy of the approval of the New Hampshire Commission." The Commission also proposed to learn of appropriate handicrafts that were at the time beyond competition with the machine and would allow a reasonable margin of profit. The suggestion was made thus early that a New Hampshire Handicraft Guild be organized and that a stamp of approval be placed upon work accepted by its jury and deemed of good quality.

Other Early Meetings

In the course of the second, third, and fourth meetings of the Commission, the last-named held on August 17 at Crawford Notch, the need was stressed by Dean Case for a director, who should be expert in design, and for qualified field workers in manual arts to carry on extension classes, possibly from Durham and Manchester. Mrs. Coolidge advocated an over-all survey or Three Committee Plan, to include (1) a Steering Committee, Colonel Barron, chairman, (2) a Committee on Art and Handicraft Education, Dean Case, chairman, (3) a Committee on Centers, Mrs. Coolidge, chairman. Dean Case and Mr. Ballentine were charged with the responsibility of outlining the scope of the Commission's work. The word "League" began to be used; agreement was general as to the need for expert service in establishing standards, but salary for a director posed a serious problem. Mrs. Coolidge developed further her concept of a Committee on Centers, which should study methods of approach to a community, list places to be developed, plan for cooperation with other organizations, and finally organize the centers, "carrying our plan of the New Hampshire Handicraft League to them." The Committee on Education would be asked to provide the teachers. The purpose was strong among all the members to push vigorously both the survey and the search for a director, as well as to formulate the Commission's plan of organization to be presented to the Governor. Miss Jessie Doe and Miss Elizabeth Sawyer were suggested by Mrs. Coolidge as her assistants in organizing communities. Miss Doe, a trustee of the University of New Hampshire, became a member of the League's first council and a strong champion of its program.

Definite and practical ideas were being expressed by all the members of the Commission. Mr. Ayres, who foresaw clearly the importance of what the Commission was doing for the state, felt that it should not be in a position where a change of administration could cut short its work and its support. However, the whole question of funds was a difficult one: the legislature would not meet for two years and the Commission planned to have much under way before then.

At the fourth meeting of the group Mr. Ballentine presented the report on the proposed scope of activities, a summary of which follows:

> The Commission would be the controlling body with flexible committees under which an independent league of craftsmen would evolve, with a bulletin or some sort of circular letter, and its own jury and standards; there would be a director and field workers, as outlined by Mr. Farnum . . . possibly becoming a nucleus around which would be developed this arts and crafts school which we have in the back of our minds for the future. The Commission would undertake (1) surveys which would proceed in collaboration with the director and should include a study of existing crafts in and out of the state; (2) a study of proved and helpful instruction methods; and (3) a study of the social and educational values derived from its work. These activities, besides leading ultimately to the establishment of the school of design and handicrafts, would also be the

center for our home industries and our educational development for children and adults.

Mrs. Coolidge developed these ideas still further and stressed the procedure for organizing committees:

> In the first place, my idea is that we should form a New Hampshire Handicraft League which should outlive the Governor's term and perhaps the Commission itself. It should have an art director, teachers, and able advisers, and should work quite independently of any other organization. Besides the teaching of high standards of design and workmanship, there is so much more involved in our future work in these small towns . . . I think that our aims should be to teach them [the townspeople] to *work together*, and this, I know by experience, takes patience, tact, and understanding. This cannot be taught wholly by men, for it is the women who need the help and the sort of help that women can best give. It seems to me important to have field workers work through the handicraft organizations in each town and not approach individual workers unless asked to do so by the town organization. . . . It is important for our League to help the towns to organize work together and to learn to manage their own work. Then our teachers will be gratefully received. . . . Of course there may be towns that do not care to organize. In this case there may be individuals who want lessons and help which we can give them.

It was moved by Mr. Ayres that Mr. Ballentine's report on scope be accepted, and it was also proposed that Mrs. Coolidge should take up with Mr. Farnum the finding of a suitable director. Thus the pattern was set for a handicraft league under the direction of the Commission but independent of other organizations and institutions. When Mr. Farnum later proposed the name of Frank Staples as director Mrs. Coolidge, acting for the Commission, was able to engage him promptly. Mr. Staples began work September 15, 1931, as executive assistant, a title soon changed to full director. Miss Barbara Farnum was engaged as his assistant. Mr. Ballentine was chosen as comptroller of the Commission's funds. The Commission was not waiting for events but was making them: in the course of about four months it had hammered out a working plan; had engaged expert help in the courageous belief that funds would be forthcoming; it had under way a survey of the state's small industries and had made a preliminary report to the Governor, which was at once approved. The speed and efficiency with which these things had been accomplished were largely due to the singleness of purpose with which the Commission worked and to the explicit contribution made by each of its members.

Governor Winant informed the Commission that he would recommend to the legislature an appropriation of $5,000 to support the work provided the League of New Hampshire Arts and Crafts (for by now this name had been decided upon) would raise a like amount. In the end he appropriated $5,000 for the first year from his official funds because the legislature would not convene until 1933. The balance was met by gifts from Mrs. Coolidge, Mrs. Andrew Carnegie, and others eager to see the work established.

Two main considerations now confronted the Commission: (1) the organization of workers who should compose the League and (2) the problem of financing its work. Interest shifted from the activities of the Commission to the activities of the Commission's new child, the League.

THE LEAGUE ORGANIZED

When the League of New Hampshire Arts and Crafts met in the State House of Concord on October 20, 1931, to organize, less than five months after the first meeting of the Commission, there came into being the first arts and crafts service to be established by the authority of any state. While the interest and activity of the Commission has never waned and its influence and direction has been ever sustaining, it is the organization of the craftsmen themselves and the development of their work through the League which has caught the imagination of the citizens of New Hampshire and of the general public in ways that we shall briefly record.

Considerable color, as well as authentic information about the earliest activities of the League, is to be found in a letter written by Miss Barbara Farnum, now Mrs. Dwight McCracken, to her father, Royal B. Farnum:

Frank [Mr. Staples] had a few samples from Sandwich to start with. With these he went around to twenty or thirty towns and interested women through the Woman's Clubs, Granges, or by getting one particular person interested.

Miss Whipple of Bristol who had some leisure time and is an expert needleworker organized the first group of people there. Selling outlets were set up in each group—wherever possible—a home in one place, a store, or part of a store in others. Some groups which were remote or couldn't get a place for selling goods brought their work to Concord to the office (then in Frank's home), and it was distributed to groups where there were shops.

As the groups developed under a local chairman, with Frank as the only organizer, instructor, censor, etc., several problems arose. A certain standard had to be met gradually, and articles eventually had to pass the approval of a committee. More selling points were essential, so the Concord shop was rented as a place where all groups could send their things. A system of tagging and bookkeeping had to be worked out for each group and for everything sent outside the main groups through Concord. A "trademark" type of shop sign was made for all shops.

At first a 10% commission was retained by the shops for correspondence and wrapping paper and other incidentals, and the rest was returned to the worker. Then a 20% commission was found necessary.

Instruction was very urgent from the start, as so much of the work first submitted was well done but horribly "old fashioned." . . . As soon as we could offer instruction . . . refusal was made easier.

Weaving and needlework and woodcarving were the first things taught. Then metalwork. Miss Doe soon got going on pottery in Dover as it used to be done long ago. Dover has natural clay. When I left they were finding local semi-precious stones to use. An instructor became available, more and more men joined up—woodcarvers, metalworkers, potters . . . basketmakers, chair caners, carpenters, and so forth.

For the first year and a half Frank was the only expressman, and with only a two-door Ford. Toward the end of that time his trips were endless and his car bristled like a porcupine. It was not a simple matter (and still isn't) to list all the goods, pack them in, unpack them, and distribute them. His office or car was the warehouse and sometimes there would be a path only a foot wide from the door of the office to the desk.

As the League went into its third summer plans were made for a big exhibition of the handicrafts from all the groups. Volunteer workers set up shops so they could make things while the visitors watched. It was a very successful affair, and the first real thing to create statewide and even nationwide interest. It is now an annual event.

The "big exhibition of the handicrafts from all the groups" was the first of what came to be known as the craftsmen's fairs, and will be briefly described presently.

Early Meetings of the League

The first annual meeting of the League of New Hampshire Arts and Crafts was held in the Senate Chamber of the State House at Concord, October 20, 1932. The director's report of the first year's activity showed a League membership of 886. Of these, 842 members belonged to twenty-two groups. There were two founder members, Sandwich and Wolfeboro. The League had been incorporated. Besides instruction in the crafts mentioned by Miss Farnum, original designs numbering one hundred had been sent out and two hundred patterns redesigned. Equipment and supplies had been secured, and information compiled regarding books. Ten shops had been established.

By the time of the second annual meeting, October 19, 1933, membership had grown from 886 to 1,452. Sales had risen over 50 per cent and the number of League shops had almost doubled. The average selling price had also increased, articles priced at $2.50 as contrasted with those of $1.00 making a much better showing. Instruction was now given to fifteen groups in nine crafts. Needlework was the most prevalent, with twelve groups engaging in it. There had been some exhibitions, and the director in the course of traveling over 14,000 miles had filled nineteen speaking engagements. The success of the League had inspired handicraft activities in Brandon, Proctorville, and Bethel, Vermont; Wiscasset, and Ellsworth, Maine; and in several towns in New York State. The New Hampshire State Library through Miss Thelma Brackett, librarian, had offered a book service to the League. Twenty-three producing centers reported and more and better instruction was planned.

This book service proved to be more than its name would indicate, for Miss Brackett visited publishers and second-hand stores to bring together publications bearing on all the crafts, especially books and portfolios rich in illustration. Not only were the books available at Concord, but the librarian arranged to get them to meetings of League members. At the craftsmen's fairs there was always a fine selection of books, often accompanied by an exhibition of objects, where they furnished inspiration for many a design for knitting, weaving, woodcarving, or metalwork. As a result of this research, Miss Brackett herself learned weaving and other crafts and did some excellent suitings. The State Library is adding continuously to its collection of books on arts and crafts under the leadership of Mrs. Mildred McKay, now state librarian.

In his opening address of welcome at the second annual meeting Colonel Barron paid a tribute to Mrs. Coolidge, who was unable to attend because of illness, and to the craftsmen members of the League when he said, "It is your work that has stamped the New Hampshire League of Arts and Crafts as an outstanding recognized success."

Mr. Farnum spoke as an adviser specially experienced in art matters:

"The craftsman must have complete understanding of the union of tool processes and of materials used. He must know the emotions and the psychological reactions which result in the people who see the craftsman's work. Design is the exaltation of an idea; color is the emotional fulfillment of the idea, and ideas are what outsiders expect to find, ideas derived from the New Hampshire people individually—not copies."

Other short addresses were made by Thomas Dreier of the New Hampshire Development Commission, Commissioner James N. Pringle, Leibert Howard Weir, and Miss Jessie Doe.

STRUCTURE AND ADMINISTRATION OF THE LEAGUE

The Commission as we have seen is the body representing the state. It is directly responsible to the legislature, from which it derives authority to function and from which comes the major part of its support. The League as a whole is responsible only to the Commission and not to any other state department or organization. This wise political invention ensures to the League maximum freedom in its government and growth. The commissioners, together with the League's council and officers, had courageously regarded the League not as a temporary experiment, but as a new and permanent educational, economic, and social invention of great democratic importance.

Officers

The first president of the League, Mrs. J. Randolph Coolidge, served until October, 1941, when she resigned and was succeeded by Dean Robert C. Strong of Dartmouth College, who was unanimously elected. Mrs. Coolidge is now the honorary president of the League. Dean Strong was serving as president at the time of his death in June, 1946. In his cordial and sincere spirit he honored the old tradition of helpfulness to other groups and organizations that prevailed in the League. His successor, H. Leslie Smith, who had served as vice-president of the League, was elected in 1946 and resigned in 1947. Edward Y. Blewett, vice-president, was acting president until September, 1947, when he was elected president. A. Cooper Ballentine, the first secretary and treasurer, continues as secretary, and Arthur E. Bean is treasurer. Names of the members of the Council serving from 1932 to 1947 are listed as a roll of honor. Council members are elected every two years by the League and serve with the Executive Committee of the Commission.

Council Members Serving the League of
New Hampshire Arts and Crafts, 1932-1947

Original Members	*Later Members*	*Later Members*
Mrs. J. Randolph Coolidge	Thomas Dreier	Dean Robert C. Strong
Miss Jessie Doe	Mrs. Foster Stearns	Dean Edward Y. Blewett
A. Cooper Ballentine	Mrs. Josephine Hamp Gardner Emmons	Prof. George Thomas
Dean George W. Case	Mrs. W. H. Weston	Arthur E. Bean
James N. Pringle	Edgar C. Hirst	Percy C. Leggett
Col. William A. Barron	Mrs. Stacey L. Hanson	Karl Drerup
Miss Margaret Whipple	Mrs. Edward S. Willis	Howard E. Swain
Philip W. Ayres	Mrs. R. Gilman Lunt	Robb Sagendorph
Edgar H. Hunter	Dr. Lloyd Young	Mrs. John D. Jameson
	William Leroy Young	Miss Thelma Brackett
	Mrs. Robert P. Booth	Dr. Edgar Fuller
	H. Leslie Smith	Laurence I. Duncan
	Willard Rand	

Directors

Through its Council the League has selected four directors, each of whom has made his special contribution. Frank Staples set the pattern, as the commissioners hoped he would, before the idea of a League had fully crystallized and that pattern has been in the main followed through the years. With the support of a loyal and energetic Commission he charted a new and independent course in adult education which has been looked upon with deep interest in New England and far beyond its borders. After serving the League for five years, Mr. Staples became arts and crafts specialist in the National Recreation Association with headquarters in New York though his work takes him to all parts of the country.

The Council then chose Edgar Keen, whose ability and record as a woodcarver have been noted in Chapter 10, to direct the work. His appreciation of design and his high ability as a craftsman were a great encouragement to those striving to uphold standards in the League. He was especially helpful to untrained woodworkers, as well as other craftsmen.

In August, 1938, David R. Campbell succeeded Mr. Keen, serving until 1942, when he was granted leave to enter the Navy, and resuming the office at the end of the war.

For the period of Mr. Campbell's absence, Alon Bement was appointed acting director. Mr. Bement had been on the teaching faculty

of Columbia University and had served as executive director of the
Art Center in New York. Work with the League of New Hampshire
Arts and Crafts was his first experience with a largely rural organization, but he acted with thoughtfulness and patience over a trying
period during which he successfully carried through two annual craftsmen's fairs. Mr. Campbell returned in season to arrange for the fair
held at Wolfeboro in 1945, and was serving as director when this
record was made.

David Campbell's experience in teaching and in the practice of architecture and interior decoration had given him unusual familiarity
with many handicrafts. From the first he gave much encouragement to
original work, making every member's problem his own problem. His
enthusiasm for the League's service not only increased the number
who enlisted as pupils but raised their standards; he built up the
teaching staff to new points of efficiency. Largely through him some
very fine craftsmen have come to New Hampshire to live permanently.
In the spirit of the Commission he has been generous in cooperating
with people outside the state of New Hampshire, serving on the direc-
torate of the American Craftsmen's Cooperative Council, Inc., and
visiting as opportunity would allow craftsmen of other states and of
Canada.

Teachers, Working Centers, and Instruction

Gradually a teaching staff has been built up until at present more
than thirty persons have conducted classes under the League's auspices. Among the earlier teachers were: embroidery, Mrs. Louise
Chrimes, Miss Elizabeth Loring, Miss Elizabeth Christophe; weaving,
Mrs. Jean M. Hodgson, Miss Ruth Hallin; pottery, Miss Helen M. John-
son; woodcarving, Edgar Keen, Leo Malm; metalwork, Andrew Nicoll,
Wayne Griffin. Among those serving more recently have been: rug-
hooking, Mrs. Clara Jane Brown, Mrs. Frank Bush, Mrs. Oscar Carlson,
Mrs. Louise Cummings, Miss Claire F. Ingalls, Mrs. Madeline Wells;
stenciling, Mrs. Arthur Chivers, Miss Louise Deering, Mrs. Adele E.
Ells, Mrs. Elizabeth Gordon, Miss Clara Jones; woodcarving, Hans
Brustle; jewelry, Percy C. Leggett, Mrs. Maude Leighton, George
Olsson, Mrs. Hartley Slater, Miss Laura Young; needlework and enam-
eling, Mrs. Louise Moulton, Miss Florence Nesmith; weaving, Mrs.
Martha Watson.

The regular teachers go to any community where a class is formed.
Thus instruction has been given at least once, and often several times,
in New Hampshire working centers in every county of the state.

Volunteers

Along with the Commission, the director, his teaching staff, and the cooperating craftsmen, equal credit must be given to volunteers throughout New Hampshire who from the beginning have had a major part in making the League work. It is they who have recruited classes and have made initial and practical connection between each community and the central office. Nearly every League shop in the state has been started by volunteers and even now most of the sales force are contributing their time. At first even managers of shops were volunteers, but later it became imperative to provide in most cases some compensation. Many volunteers come year after year to do their part at the craftsmen's fairs which could not succeed without them. Practically all of the local help at the fairs is also given free; the only official recognition of the service of these volunteers is an award designed in their honor by Frederick Robbins.

No account of the League could be given without a tribute to the work of the office staff which has been outstanding in loyalty and efficiency.

Membership

When this record was made, the number of members had increased to over fifteen hundred, most of whom produce some form of handicraft. There are several special groups who meet and work to advance the standards in their respective fields; such as the Saffron and Indigo Society, and the mineralogists, gem-cutters, weavers, rug-hookers, jewelers, and so forth.

Finances

In the League's second year the legislature met and appropriated $5,000 for its work for each of two years. From then on the appropriation has been $10,000 for each year except for two war years when it was $7,500. The League is able to use the appropriations provided by the Smith-Hughes Vocational Education Act and the George-Deen Act[1] to help finance their educational program.

Functions and Activities

The purpose of the League and the law that supports it is to give citizens of New Hampshire an opportunity to produce objects of usefulness and beauty for their own use or for sale. The League is therefore interested in both the educational and the economic aspects of

[1] The George-Deen Act has now been superseded by the George-Barden Act.

handicrafts, and these and other values are well blended in its administration. Although only a small number of persons are able to support themselves entirely by their handicrafts, hundreds of New Hampshire citizens are able to supplement their incomes and enrich their living through hand skills. Besides offering instructions, the League helps to secure materials at low cost and provides a market for the craftsmen's wares. Most of the sales are made in the League's shops distributed throughout the state.

Marketing Centers

The earlier policy of establishing marketing centers in many places —at one time there were twenty in the state—has been abandoned in favor of fewer and larger shops; at this writing, there are shops in each of the following towns: Bristol, Center Sandwich, Concord, Franconia Notch, Hancock, Keene, Meredith, North Conway, and Wolfeboro. Each shop, besides specializing in the best product of its own area, carries a fair representation of handicrafts produced elsewhere.

The total of League sales from handicrafts has increased steadily, beginning in 1932 with $8,000 and reaching in 1946 nearly $79,000. In only two instances in these fifteen years—1939 and 1942—have the totals receded from those of previous years. To date more than half a million dollars in receipts from sales has been distributed to the craftsmen of the state.

Craftsmen's Fairs

In 1934 when the League was approximately three years old an exhibition and sale was held at Crawford Notch. Exhibits and demonstrators excited so much interest on this occasion that an arts and crafts exhibition was proposed for the following year. Thus the pattern was established and since 1934 fairs have been held in the following New Hampshire communities: 1935, Hancock, Mrs. Foster Stearns, chairman; 1936, Rye Beach, Miss Jessie Doe, chairman; 1937, Laconia, Mrs. R. Gilman Lunt, chairman; 1938, Whitefield, Mrs. Joseph Coolidge, chairman; 1939, Durham, Mrs. W. H. Weston, chairman; 1940, Plymouth, Mrs. Edward S. Willis, chairman; 1941, Hanover, Mrs. Eileen McDaniel, chairman; 1942, Plymouth, no chairman; 1943, Manchester, Mrs. Alma Hamilton, chairman; 1944, Portsmouth, Mrs. Hartley Slater, chairman; 1945, Wolfeboro, Mrs. Harry Heslor, chairman. In 1946 at Franconia Notch there was no chairman. At this fair sales amounted to $11,330, thus establishing a new record.

Almost every part of New Hampshire has thus had an opportunity to share in a cooperative enterprise which focuses economic, educational, and social interests. The Craftsman's Fair is the culminating event of the League's year, during the preceding winter of which most of the products have been prepared. It is also the beginning of another League year, for at the Fair new ideas are engendered, plans for handicrafts made, and promises exchanged among friends to meet again wherever in New Hampshire the Craftsman's Fair is to be held. It brings hundreds of craftsmen from a wide area, not alone League members, and attracts visitors from many states and a few from other countries. All in all, it is the most important annual handicraft event to take place in the United States.

The first fair at Crawford Notch lingers in the memory of all who attended. Colonel Barron of the Commission offered the use of a big empty carriage house for exhibition and sales purposes, and the grounds adjacent to his hotel—a perfect setting for a "country fair." The University of New Hampshire through its Extension Service arranged a daily pageant during the week in which the fair was open. Mrs. Coolidge recalls that on the first afternoon a flock of sheep wandered over the lawn accompanied by shepherd and sheep dog; other sheep meanwhile were being sheared.

"The second afternoon," said Mrs. Coolidge, "Sandwich gave a demonstration of spinning, ending with dyeing of the yarn with vegetable dyes. The women taking part were dressed in picturesque old-fashioned costumes. They had brought their children, likewise in old-fashioned dresses, pantalettes and all, who played on teeter boards or jumped rope while their mothers were busy. As a background the great hanks of yarn, dyed in lovely pastel colors, were hung on tall stands. The third afternoon the Wolfeboro group showed weaving done on a huge loom with a weaving dance performed by girls from Camp Kehonka. The final pageant was an exhibition of woven coverlets of various colors. Some sixteen or eighteen were shown in procession, each one held by four women. These pageants were very simply and casually done, but they brought together an enthusiastic audience."

Relations with Other Organizations and Areas

From its beginning the League has been marked for its generous and hospitable spirit. Visitors from other states or countries are always welcome at the central office and scores of letters from those who cannot visit New Hampshire are answered with care and consideration.

As soon as Maine and Vermont began to plan an arts and crafts service, the League gave every encouragement and assistance. In June, 1937, it called together a small group which met at Wolfeboro for the purpose of considering the possibility of a national handicraft organization and the benefits that might result. Representatives came from the Southern Highlands and elsewhere from the area of the Atlantic states —the first gathering of people in recent years to express interest in a national handicraft movement and the first considerable number of New Englanders to discuss together their mutual handicraft problems. An extended "return visit" to the Southern Highlands was made that summer by Mrs. Coolidge and Miss Doe which helped to bring two important handicraft areas into closer cooperation.

When in 1937 the director of the Department of Arts and Social Work of Russell Sage Foundation responded to the invitation of the United States Department of Agriculture to direct a national Rural Arts Exhibition, leaders from New England and Southern Highland areas were well prepared to help the undertaking. New Hampshire sent an important exhibit, and Mrs. Coolidge and Miss Doe went to Washington and gave invaluable service during the entire exhibition period.

A second handicraft conference, called by the University of New Hampshire on the occasion of its seventy-fifth anniversary in 1941, did much to promote the idea of a New England handicraft federation. An unpretentious exhibit of products brought by representatives of various groups gave substance to the conference. The League of New Hampshire Arts and Crafts was one of the three state-sponsored handicraft services then active to attend, Maine and Vermont being the other two.

Newsletters and Bulletins

Intermittently during the past fifteen years a newsletter or bulletin has been a part of the service of the organization to its members. This account is greatly indebted to the League's house organ for many of the facts recorded here. Mimeographed issues began in April, 1932, with a circulation of 370 copies, and ran through four numbers, ending in October when circulation had increased to 797. Among the items in the early issues were short articles on design with rough pen drawings, references to good books for craftsmen, a short report on group activities, names of new members and groups, listing of motifs for design to be found in nature, information on marketing, and a note on "Dover Has a Pottery Kiln," the first one in the League.

The need for some "sheet of communication" piled up until May, 1934, when the first number of the League of New Hampshire Arts and Crafts *Bulletin* was issued, this time in printed form. For eight years without a break, from 1934 to the March-April issue of 1942, in all seventy-three issues, this fine record of the League was edited by Mrs. Foster Stearns, one of the early members of the League's Council. The *Bulletin* made a unique contribution to the handicraft movement in New England.

This publication was succeeded by a renewal of the old *Newsletter*, somewhat changed in content but mimeographed as formerly, and is still in use. The change was due in a measure to curtailments caused by the war, and to the need for centralization. Mr. Campbell is editor of the *Newsletter*.

In concluding this chapter we may add a word on the fundamental principles underlying the work of the League. First of all, it has aimed to help New Hampshire people to help themselves. In attaining that aim, it has not striven to make the League notable for perfect handicraft products by trained and distinguished craftsmen. Such craftsmen have been welcomed with enthusiasm for their own sake and for the influence they exert, but primarily the League has tried to encourage the average craftsman to reach high standards of production through work diligently pursued.

There has been no expectation of seeing many members of the League become entirely self-supporting through handicrafts alone but mainly of helping them supplement other earnings while experiencing at the same time the joy of creative activity. In thus helping its members to make salable products, the League has never sought for mass production or for sales outlets through commercial channels.

New Hampshire's League of Arts and Crafts has been from the first a democratic undertaking bringing together men and women from every walk of life in an enterprise reflecting their common effort and their common pride in such measure of achievement in the arts, especially the handicrafts, as they have been able to attain.

CHAPTER 19

OTHER NEW ENGLAND GROUPS AND THE COUNTRYWIDE MOVEMENT

M*AINE*. The Pine Tree State was the second to develop a handicraft program supported with tax funds. Initiated in 1939, under the name Maine Crafts, it was carried on by the State Department of Education in cooperation with the Maine Development Commission. Although the program was discontinued in 1942, when its director, Ralph W. Haskell, went into war work, many of the projects that had been started or encouraged by the state service continued to prosper.

An independent craftsman's organization, older than the state undertaking, was the Maine Craft Guild, with headquarters at Orono, the home of the University of Maine. The Extension Service, under Director Arthur L. Deering, was active and interested especially in handicrafts throughout the rural areas, and Mrs. Rena Bowles was engaged by the University as a specialist to encourage the work throughout the state. Mrs. Bowles discovered a considerable number of craftsmen in Maine who favored a cooperative organization; working with the Extension Service they organized the Maine Craft Guild. Its first president was the painter, Carroll T. Berry, who is now president of the Maine Seacoast Craftsmen.

During the summer of 1947 the Maine Craft Guild was reorganized and its name changed to Association of Maine Craftsmen, with Miss Adelaide Pearson, chairman; Basil B. White, director; and Mrs. Paul Cobb, treasurer. Maine Industries, started several years ago on the highway near Saco, has become the largest outlet for handicrafts in the state. It is now privately directed by Mr. and Mrs. Basil B. White, and each year it has seen an increase in its sales. There are also several other craft groups in Maine producing and marketing independently. An informal survey made by the Maine Craft Guild a few years ago showed well over a thousand craftsmen in the state. An annual Buyers Fair is held at the University of Maine during the late summer or fall.

In November, 1947, the Portland Society of Arts held its first Exhibition of Maine Crafts and Decorative Arts at the L.D.M. Sweat Memorial Art Museum. In variety of work and in quality of design and craftsmanship, this was the finest exhibition of handicrafts ever held in Maine. An important feature was the Esther Stevens Brazer Memorial Exhibition of Stencils and Decorative Arts. It was of special interest because Portland was the birthplace of Mrs. Brazer, who did more to revive the old craft of stenciling than anyone else in our country. The entire exhibition was sponsored by a statewide committee with Alexander Bower, director of the Museum, as chairman. The principal credit for discovering the handicraft resources of Maine and in bringing them together in this excellent exhibition was accorded to Miss Mildred Burrage of Wiscasset, the executive officer of the group.

New Hampshire. As shown in the preceding chapter, statewide service to handicraft workers in New Hampshire has been given continuously by the League of New Hampshire Arts and Crafts since 1931. Mention should be made of a recently organized group closely affiliated with the League, the Sharon Arts Center, in the town of Sharon, six miles south of Peterborough on Route 123. The Center, incorporated in 1946 as a non-profit organization, was founded by Mr. and Mrs. William Leroy Young, to provide training the year round in the fine arts and handicrafts, for those interested in serious study, either as a hobby or as a means of obtaining supplementary income. Belief that a well-equipped center for such training would be welcomed by the neighbors has been fully justified; the membership of the Center now numbers 296 earnest pupils ranging from ten to eighty-odd years of age, and in experience from beginners to professional people. The pupils come from twenty-five towns, some of them thirty and fifty miles away.

The original properties of the Center, beginning its work in January, 1947, were the old Laws House, owned by the Society for the Preservation of New England Antiquities, and the adjacent barn remodeled into the Craft House; other buildings have since been provided. The charming old farmhouse is the office for the Center and the home of the year-round director, Miss Emily A. Day, who states that among the advantages of the Sharon Arts Center are: excellent teachers with thorough equipment, including tools to meet the needs of pupils; facilities for making coffee and serving light refreshments; discussions, or the working out of special problems, and programs; and regular sales of pupils' approved work. Courses are given in weaving, metalcraft, jewelry, rugcraft, ceramics, stenciling, decoration and furniture refinishing, photography, dressmaking, art, and design. The Center was visited by over 3,000 persons in 1948, and a nine-day sale in August returned $3,600 to the craftsmen.

Vermont. Many individual craftsmen in Vermont had developed their skills and found outlets for their work in characteristically independent fashion, even before handicraft leaders persuaded the legislature in 1941 to pass an act to establish an arts and crafts advisory commission within the State Department of Education. Under this act the Vermont Arts and Crafts Service was inaugurated and has since had continuous financial support. The Arts and Crafts Advisory Commission consists of Carroll L. Coburn, chairman; Mrs. Mildred C. Hayden, secretary; Ralph E. Noble, state commissioner of education; Harold A. Dwinell, director of markets, State Department of Agriculture; and John E. Nelson, state director of vocational education. Mrs. Rebecca Gallagher Williams was appointed the first director of the Service in 1941. After four years, during which the state policy was carefully developed and visits paid to over nine hundred craftsmen, largely in rural areas, Mrs. Williams resigned and was succeeded by Miss Ruth W. Coburn. Mrs. Nellie G. Streeter has been an invaluable assistant to both directors.

Vermont's Arts and Crafts Service is based primarily on a part-time program for adults, with limited provision for the training of children through classes conducted by accredited craft teachers. An information center is maintained in the offices at Montpelier, where data about craftsmen, sources of equipment and supplies, lists of sales outlets in the state, and dates of special events taking place in the interest of arts and crafts are available to workers. A bulletin of information is issued from time to time and circulated among craftsmen. Exhibitions and craft fairs have been held. A revolving fund has been established from which loans may be made to workers for materials and equipment under the terms agreed upon by the Arts and Crafts Advisory Commission. Vermont has long since passed the experimental stage in its encouragement of handicrafts, and future support for an expanding program would seem a safe prediction.

Two Vermont selling outlets may be mentioned: One is the Three Green Doors at Stowe, and the other, the Vermont Products Stores, which operate in both Vermont and Massachusetts. One summer when Mr. and Mrs. Cecil C. Lange were motoring in Vermont, it occurred to them that there should be an "all Vermont shop," where the various handicrafts produced in the state could be marketed. The idea took definite form about 1940, when they established the Three Green Doors as a year-round shop. There products of scores of Vermont craftsmen have been sold, largely to tourists.

Early in the war period, when the government urged Vermont farmers to increase their production of potatoes, Gerald Newell was one who followed the suggestion. When autumn came, he was apprehensive that buyers would not call for potatoes in his section. He arranged for a truck and took the long drive into Massachusetts with part of his own crop, picking up some other rural products on the way. While driving along, he realized that many farmers in rural Vermont could not afford either to buy or hire a truck. When he got to Amherst, where he sold his potatoes, he talked with his sister there about the possibility of opening a store as an outlet for Vermont products. The idea appealed to her and shortly afterward they opened a store in Amherst, later one in Wellesley, and another in Northampton. They also opened a store in Warren, Vermont. Mr. Newell has bought products in practically every town in Vermont and marketed them through these stores, which handle nothing but Vermont products. Included among those served are scores of remotely situated craftsmen who would have no other way of getting their products to town.

Among the forty-eight states in the nation, New Hampshire and Vermont are the only ones now receiving support for handicrafts by direct appropriations of their legislatures; both are giving their citizens a type of service, especially in rural districts, which is increasingly important. But each of the other states in New England is conscious of the importance of hand production and in different ways is advancing the interests of handicrafts.

Preceding the Vermont Arts and Crafts Service, and largely responsible for it, was the organization in 1938 of the Vermont Handicraft Guild with Mrs. Marjorie Johnson (now Mrs. Harold E. Townsend) of Plainfield as president; Mrs. Leon Gay of Cavendish, vice-president; Miss Mabel C. Holcomb of Isle La Motte, recording secretary; Mrs. Lois Greer of Montpelier, corresponding secretary; and Mrs. Maude Whitcomb of Springfield as treasurer. The first Board of Directors included Mrs. Dorothy Canfield Fisher of Arlington; Mrs. Lois Greer, Montpelier; Joseph Winterbotham, Burlington; Mrs. H. A. Mayforth, Barre; Miss Alice Blanchard, Montpelier; Raymond Austin, Weston; Mrs. Dora Walker, Rutland; Mrs. Harold Marsh, Swanton; Mrs. Ruth Mould, Johnson; Simon Moselsio, Bennington; Mrs. C. Curry, Hyde Park; Mrs. A. W. Gottlieb, Stowe; E. R. Beveridge, Johnson; Miss Marjorie Luce, Burlington; Mrs. Carl Cushing, Bethel; Ralph E. Flanders, Springfield; Miss Flora Coutts, Newport; Mrs. Laura

Ferrin, Stowe; Mrs. Stickney Brounlea, Bethel, and Mrs. David Dube, Brattleboro.

This group sponsored the first important and comprehensive exhibition of Vermont handicrafts ever brought together at Montpelier. Mrs. Townsend and other officers and members of the Guild were leaders in working out the plans for the Vermont Arts and Crafts Service and have been active supporters and contributors to its development.

On January 14, 1947, the Annual Award of Merit of the American Association for State and Local History was given to the Community Club of Weston, Vermont, "for the rescue of an ancient tavern from destruction; for its restoration as a historic house museum of exceptional merit; for the establishment of a guild of old-time crafts and industries, with attendant attraction of native craftsmen of unusual skill and talent; together with other activities for the revival of the economic and social life of the town through stimulation of pride and interest in its historical heritage." This citation places the handicrafts of Weston, in the perspective which Raymond Taylor, president of the Community Club, and Vrest Orton, secretary and treasurer of the Vermont Guild of Old-time Crafts and Industries, like to have them regarded by the public.

Fortunately the Vermont Historical Society has published a booklet, *Weston, Vermont,* which includes a description of "The Weston Revival, One Hundred Years Later," by Mr. Orton. Also described are the Vermont Guild of Old-time Crafts and Industries and the main features of Weston, now known far and wide for its philosophy of life and work, and its old-time and modern products, the making of which engages about one-fourth the town's population of about 500 people. Judge Louis G. Whitcomb of Springfield, is chairman of the Guild's Board of Trustees, F. W. Shepardson of Burlington, vice-chairman, and Vrest Orton of Weston, has been secretary and treasurer since 1939.

Massachusetts. In Massachusetts toward the close of the last century and even before the Society of Arts and Crafts was organized in Boston, small groups of craftsmen were meeting, some associated with a community movement, such as the Society of Deerfield Industries, and some independently, but all forming a kind of network. Although the names of these pioneer groups and craftsmen may not all be remembered, the influence of their work and their ideals is a continuing force. Some were members of the National League of Handicraft Societies, which was largely fostered by the Boston Society of Arts and Crafts. After the National League disbanded, there was no coordinating agency in the state for several years. The gap was finally filled in a measure by the series of Craftsmen at Work exhibitions, organized by the Women's Educational and Industrial Union in the late 1920's, which led to the organization of the Federation of Massachusetts Handicraft Guilds.

In 1943 a bill, introduced in the state assembly by Representative Barrus of Hampshire County, to provide legislative support for a handicraft service was defeated. A resolution, however, was passed providing for a commission to study the situation and recommend a program to the state legislature. Although the commission failed to make a recommendation, it undertook to assist the handicraft organizations of the state in the formulation of a plan. A division of opinion developed on the question of state support, but meanwhile plans for a statewide organization were promoted, which resulted in the formation of the Association of Handicraft Groups of Massachusetts.

It is estimated that there are today about twenty handicraft groups in Massachusetts, probably the largest number of units in any state. These are variously organized but have promoted their work in the usual way by exhibitions, demonstrations, and sales. Early in 1945 the Association of Handicraft Groups was formally organized, with Mrs. Leo Lavien of the Worcester Guild of Artists and Craftsmen, chairman; Miss Edith W. Fisher of Boston, secretary; Humphrey J. Emery, treasurer. Miss Louisa Dresser of the staff of the Worcester Art Museum is chairman of the Educational Committee; Mrs. William H. Hubbard of West Boylston is chairman of the Marketing Committee; and Thornton C. Hall of Minute-Man Crafts is chairman of the Bulletin Committee. The Association meets regularly and has developed a program in accordance with its purpose of giving stimulation and encouragement to the handicraft movement. There are approximately thirteen hundred craftsmen belonging to the affiliated societies.

Although differences of opinion still exist concerning the desirable policy for the state, it is generally agreed that there is a positive gain in having a statewide cooperating organization. The proponents of state support believe that the Association will be of great help should a governmental program be developed. They are strong in their conviction that large numbers of people who need and deserve such a service, especially in rural areas, cannot be reached by an organization depending upon volunteer help and without adequate funds for an intensive statewide program. The Association is working meanwhile with the State Department of Education in holding conferences and institutes. Classes in handicrafts under the Vocational Division of the Department are being organized, and in some rural areas the extension service of the State College at Amherst is doing effective work. Miss

Ruth McIntire, extension specialist in recreation, has cooperated closely with the Association of Handicraft Groups.

Connecticut. Untiring efforts by a number of individuals led in 1936 to the founding of the Society of Connecticut Craftsmen, established "to encourage the creation of handmade products in Connecticut and to assist in finding markets for them." A rough estimate at the time indicated that one hundred persons might be found who could qualify for membership; by 1939 the number of members had reached 245, of whom 109 were active craftsmen. Exhibitions, demonstrations of work techniques, and selling booths at public gatherings have aided in keeping the objectives of the Society before the public.

W. S. Dakin, who served the Society as secretary-treasurer, gives this list of early workers: Elmer Thienes, the Society's first president, Paul Donchian, James Goodwin, Mrs. Harold Holcombe, Miss Vera McCracken. Leonard S. Rankin and Alexander Crane each served terms as secretary, and Mrs. Alberta Pfeiffer organized an active group in the area south of Middletown and has given her time also to management of the sales shop in Hadlyme.

The activity of the Society declined during the war period, when many of its members were called into war service or essential industry. Since 1945 progress has been made toward building up a strong membership again. The Society has lately given special heed to a program of rehabilitation for veterans. Courses have been carried on in a well-equipped workshop in Vinal Regional Technical Institute at Middletown, under the direction of Kenneth Lundy of the State Department of Education. Evan F. Kullgren is president of the Society.

In October, 1947, a noteworthy exhibition of Connecticut handicrafts was held at the G. Fox and Company department store in Hartford. Although the Society of Connecticut Craftsmen was the principal organization represented and the program was largely determined by its members under the direction of Mr. Kullgren and Mr. Dakin, a few craftsmen not enrolled in the Society were represented. Much of the credit for the inception of the plan of the exhibition and for its success was due to Mrs. Margaret Kapteyn of Farmington. By her untiring efforts, she had not only discovered a great many craftsmen but developed cooperation between them and selling outlets in Connecticut. The Fox Company lent generous support to the exhibition.

Rhode Island. In Rhode Island the absence of state sponsorship for advancing a program of arts and crafts has been offset, in a measure, by a voluntary group which has been active for over forty years and has extended its membership to all sections of the state. The Handicraft Club of Providence was organized by ten women in October, 1904, to promote "the teaching, practicing, and encouraging of all kinds of artistic handicraft work."

One of the features of the Club's history was the restoring of several old houses for its occupancy. In 1925 the old Beckwith House, built in 1827, was purchased for a permanent home. The Club has had a membership for several years of about four hundred. Mrs. Roger W. Cooke is president, and Mrs. Philip Batchelder is in charge of classes. Only the most experienced teachers in a wide range of handicrafts are engaged, exhibitions are held annually, and a shop is maintained at the clubhouse as an outlet for the products of workers. In proportion to its area, Rhode Island has a goodly number of craftsmen. The Rhode Island School of Design, which is responsible for the training of some of the most distinguished craftsmen in our country, has greatly enriched the culture of this state.

THE COUNTRYWIDE HANDICRAFT MOVEMENT

The full strength of the handicraft movement in New England is not to be measured entirely in the records of the six northeastern states, because New England is not a remote and isolated area of the United States but an integral part of it, influencing other sections of the country and being influenced by them. A useful forecast of the handicrafts in New England must therefore be made in the light of signs throughout the country. We cannot go far into the national situation here, but we can note a few elements in it which give added significance to what has already been recorded about New England.

Revival in the Southern Highlands

Curiously enough, as the careful student of the history of handicrafts will note, the launching of the arts and crafts movement in New England by a national exhibition and the organization of the Boston Society took place at about the same time that Miss Frances L. Goodrich, who was born in New England, was striving to find ways to encourage the people in the mountains of North Carolina to weave coverlets, make baskets, and carry on other handicrafts as their forebears had done. At that time also, across the mountains in Kentucky, the young president of Berea College, William Goodell Frost, unaware of what was being done in North Carolina, was accepting handspun and hand-woven coverlets in payment for the tuition of students from the mountain homes of Tennessee, Kentucky, and Georgia, where money was almost unknown. President Frost, on one of his fund-raising trips to New England, carried a few of these mountain coverlets and sold them to the women of Boston, some of whom recognized in them patterns their great-grandmothers wove a hundred years earlier.

Miss Goodrich in *Mountain Homespun,* published in 1931, tells much of her experience in North Carolina. The story of the revival of handicrafts in the Southern Highlands is told by the writer in *Handicrafts of the Southern Highlands,* published in 1937.

There is no record to suggest that anyone, at that time, saw a connection between the arts and crafts movement in New England and the obscure efforts of missionaries and teachers in the Southern Highlands to revive the homely arts of mountain people. The New England movement both in its ideals and products was clear, sophisticated, and elegant compared to the homely philosophy and primitive products of the isolated and impoverished people of the southern mountains. These seemed about as different in ideals as two efforts in the same country could be, and yet after twenty or thirty years people began to sense their relationship. Without attempting to estimate the relative force of these two influences upon the present handicraft movement, we can assert that the indebtedness of the movement to the Southern Highlands is conspicuous and real. This region represents a unique continuity of handicraft practices in America, a continuity that reaches back to the hand industries of the colonies. There the thread has never been broken, but has been tended by unknown mountain people whose ways of working and whose products were, and to a degree still are, much like those common to all communities along the eastern seaboard at the time of the War for Independence.

The revival of handicrafts in the Highlands in time grew to large proportions, becoming a source of study for New Englanders who were thinking of the many persons, especially in rural areas of the Northeast, that might be benefited by handicrafts and small home industries. Visitors to the Highlands today learn that the little salesroom in Asheville, North Carolina, Allanstand Cottage Industries, started by Miss Goodrich, and the Fireside Industries, inaugurated by President Frost and his associates at Berea College, have been followed by scores of shops where mountain handicrafts can be purchased. The cooperating organizations which represent the Southern Highland workers maintain two year-round outlets for their products, that just mentioned at Asheville, and one at Rockefeller Center, New York, and three summer shops; one at Norris, another at Norris Dam, Tennessee, and a third at Great Meadows, Shenandoah National Park, Virginia.

National Rural Arts Exhibition

One of the most significant countrywide influences upon the handicraft movement, especially in revealing new sources of handmade things, was the Rural Arts Exhibition, which as reported earlier took place in the Administration Building of the United States Department of Agriculture in the winter of 1937. This was the first national event of its kind ever held in our country, and much of importance to craftsmen everywhere has flowed from it. The occasion for the Exhibition was the celebration of the seventy-fifth anniversary of the establishment of this department of the national government, the authorization for which was a bill signed by President Lincoln in 1862. The idea of an exhibition of the arts of our rural people, meaning chiefly handicrafts, was made possible by the cooperation of government and private agencies, including the Department of Agriculture, Department of the Interior, Work Projects Administration, Farm Security Administration, National Youth Administration, Russell Sage Foundation, American Federation of Arts, Southern Highland Handicraft Guild, League of New Hampshire Arts and Crafts, and the Society of Connecticut Craftsmen, as well as a large number of individuals. The Exhibition with its representations from every state and territory in the Union made a profound impression on the visiting public, including President Franklin D. Roosevelt. It was followed by a study of rural arts by the Extension Service of the Department of Agriculture; and later an illustrated bulletin, *Rural Handicrafts in the United States,* by Allen Eaton and Lucinda Crile, was published, in which the Exhibition is described. On the basis of its findings, the Extension Service is strengthening and building up its handicraft program throughout the country.

Some National and Regional Groups

Craftsmen's organizations in different parts of the nation constitute yet another major influence. Brought together by common ideals and objectives, craftsmen form into practical groups, sometimes determined by geographical lines, such as the Pennsylvania Guild of Craftsmen; sometimes by the interests of a common craft, as the Weavers Guild of America, which includes members from all parts of the country, or the Puppeteers of America, which also is national in scope. There are, of course, almost numberless groups, large and small, representing special communities or special purposes. Occasionally like-minded persons will band together to form a smaller handicraft group within a parent organization, such as the modelmakers within the Circus Fans of America. Among these are some of the most enthusiastic and skillful craftsmen in our country. If these greatly varying organizations were brought together under one head, they would make an extensive and impressive array of handicraft workers.

FACTORS INFLUENCING ALL CRAFTSMEN

It is certain that the greatest number of craftsmen in our country are not affiliated with special groups either local or national but are in their own ways, often in their own homes, carrying on one or more handicrafts. Whether working within organized groups or alone, all these craftsmen are affected by at least three general considerations which are discussed briefly here: selling outlets, training courses, and the influence of art museums.

Selling Outlets

Reference has been made earlier to selling places for handicrafts in New England and to the great expansion of selling outlets of the Southern Highlanders in recent years. Many individual craftsmen and groups of craftsmen have market outlets. The many shops established throughout the country have become pillars of the handicraft movement.

America House in New York must be mentioned especially because of its size and importance as a new and successful national market place for the work of hundreds of craftsmen. It was established in 1940 by the American Craftsmen's Cooperative Council, Inc., of which Mrs. Vanderbilt Webb is president, as a retail and wholesale selling outlet for the work of American craftsmen. It has come to be a strong and helpful factor in the movement because its president and other officers and governing board are interested in all that affects standards of craftsmanship and welfare of workers. The Council publishes a magazine, *Craft Horizons,* four times a year. It works closely with the American Craftsmen's Educational Council, which, in addition to staging exhibitions and maintaining a library, cooperates in the management of the School for American Craftsmen, now part of the Liberal Arts College of Alfred University in Alfred, New York.

Training Courses

The many schools, centers, and institutes where handicrafts are now taught constitute another strong factor in the handicraft movement outside as well as within New England. In the area of education hardly a group of organized craftsmen ignores its responsibility for upholding and improving standards by means of training, and among the larger and more important groups training courses are an outstanding feature. Public departments of education and private organizations are not only offering handicraft courses to adults, but in many instances they are preparing children to practice handicrafts. What is equally important in a democratic society, they are exposing young people in less formal ways to the fascinations and advantages of hand production, so that it is reasonable to believe that each new generation will better understand what a wealth of opportunity for happy, useful, and often profitable employment is opening in the handicraft field.

Influence of Art Museums

A favorable influence on the handicraft movement is the increasing attention now given handicrafts by art galleries and art museums. Several of those in New England have already come into the text of this study, but two special events that put handicraft workers in debt to the Worcester Art Museum should be recorded here. One was the fine Exhibition of Modern British Crafts, sent to the United States and Canada by the British Council in the war year of 1942, which was brought to New England by this museum. The other was the Exhibition of Contemporary New England Handicrafts, already familiar to readers of this study, which was held there in 1943. The careful installation of exhibits, the excellent catalogue issued at a popular price, and the program carried out under the supervision of Max W. Sullivan and Miss Louisa Dresser made the latter exhibition outstanding and resulted in many requests from other parts of the country for advice and cooperation concerning similar events.

SOCIETY'S INTEREST IN HANDICRAFTS

In addition to the values that handicrafts have for the individual maker and for the user, the public as a whole has a stake in them. Society is interested in the conservation and encouragement of hand skills, in the democratization of the arts, in the contribution that handicrafts make to local and national culture. But over and above these are certain objective values in handicrafts with which society as a whole is specially concerned. Foremost is the question of their use in communities which are poor in resources and at times of unemployment. We have had a limited experience in dealing with handicrafts on a large scale in our country. Something was learned during the depression of the 1930's but has perhaps been too quickly forgotten, primarily because of our persistent belief that economic dislocation is a temporary thing and that prosperity will always be just around the corner. As the great depression continued, the government found itself involved in handicrafts to an extent never before experienced and with results of vital significance. These results have never been adequately recorded, although enough is known about them to present some idea of the vital part that handicraft projects played in the national emergency and of their almost unlimited potentialities for the future.

The records show that there were under direct governmental control through the WPA about three thousand handicraft projects. Many were probably never heard of outside their respective communities, but others were nationally recognized.

These projects, several of which have been mentioned in this study, employed thousands of persons and developed products that found use in many public institutions. Some of them registered new high points in design and craftsmanship. There were expressions in every form of the graphic arts; in the general field of visual arts there were mural and small paintings, sculpture, decorations of great variety, and particularly the extraordinarily fine recordings of our great heritage in this field of visual arts known as the Index of American Design, which was mentioned in Chapter 2.

An extensive handicraft undertaking of a utilitarian nature, begun in 1940 and continued into the war years, was the Hand-Made Mattress Project. It deserves special consideration because it demonstrated three facts of great importance, namely, that American people generally are eager to use their hands in any constructive work; that by and large they acquire hand skills readily; and that there are numberless families, not eligible for public assistance, whose only equipment for working is their hands. This project was initiated and carried out under the direction of the Extension Service of the United States Department of Agriculture, in cooperation with the Agricultural Adjustment Administration and the Agricultural Marketing Service.

Through a period of two years, ending in June, 1942, over 4,134,000 mattresses and 1,371,000 cotton comforters were made under the supervision of county home demonstration agents in organized community work centers. Rural people who could not afford to buy these articles in the regular market were able, through governmental help, to make them with their own hands. As Grover B. Hill, then Assistant Secretary of Agriculture, expressed it, this cooperation made it possible to turn a farm surplus into a national blessing. A number of social by-products came out of the mattress-making program. One was that the family unit was taken into consideration; always the husband and wife, and often children, were invited to learn the process of making mattresses together. Another important feature was that so many needy families who had never before come in touch with the Extension Service were aided in a very practical and immediate manner.

Another project illustrates the social and economic gains to be had through timely governmental aid to an underprivileged local group.

This was the West Fairlee weaving project. In 1939 Mrs. Marjorie Taylor, director of the Farm Security Administration in Vermont, together with the farm and home demonstration agents, began to work out plans for a group of about forty rural families whose farms provided only the barest subsistence and who had little opportunity to earn any cash income. Technical and financial help was extended to improve the farms, and careful thought was given to developing supplementary earning power for the neighborhood. As a result of community meetings and discussions, it was decided to build looms through the cooperation of the woodworking center in Rutland, the material for the looms to be paid for by the group. About 75 per cent of the cost of the project was to be borne by FSA. A well-lighted building, formerly a blacksmith shop, was found in West Fairlee, and the Homemakers Weaving Guild was established.

About nine of the forty families participated in the venture. They cleaned the shop, contributed a stove and fuel, and accepted responsibility for the rent of the building, which soon became a social as well as a work center. Mrs. Hubert Fowle, a well-qualified instructor, provided by the State Department of Education, taught the families to weave. In due time an exhibit of rugs and other articles was put on display, and greatly to the pride and satisfaction of the weavers fifty-two persons turned out to view the work. A good standard of craftsmanship was maintained. Some of the weavers made excellent rag carpets for their homes. A woman who previously had undertaken to make nothing of an artistic nature wove a beautiful scarf of her own design in red and black. A mother of eight children arose before five and walked six miles to attend. As the enthusiasm of this woman would indicate, the center, with its opportunities and associations, meant everything in the economic recovery and the morale of these country people.

Public interest and handicrafts meet again in the area of small business, the encouragement of which has become so important in our present economy. This study disclosed instances in which a home-craft was developed into a going business through an ingenious craftsman's industry, skill, and management. There would be many more such instances if timely aid were available to workers. The point to be stressed is the disproportion between outlay required and social gain achieved, for comparatively small expenditure of time or money would often free the craftsman to go ahead on his own. For many the need is a market outlet, for others it is guidance in good design, the suitable use of material, or improvement in craftsmanship. Often the bottleneck is of a less objective nature; the craftsman may need only an expression of appreciation and encouragement from someone in whose experience and taste he can feel confidence. Public support is particularly justified when it asks at every step in its program, Will this help the craftsman to help himself?

Of all governmental efforts, state or federal, to promote handicrafts, it may be said that, valuable as many of them proved to be in concrete results, they were even more powerful as symbols of a great and new conviction in American life, the conviction that an economic depression need not rob our people of their skills of hand and mind. For the first time in our history, people during the 1930's were not condemned for being out of work. The writer believes that it is to the eternal credit of President Roosevelt that he made an effort to provide work that people could do, work that would as far as possible use their skills, and work that in spite of the small compensation that could be paid would give them a sense of dignity as individuals and worth as citizens of a government in crisis. He knew what a distraught craftsman meant when he said, "Let me do something, anything, my hands have gone dead."

In times of crisis men and women will do almost anything to approach an American standard of living, but to have a job that satisfies is normally the desire of millions of hearts. Probably many do not achieve it; in numberless instances, however, the frustration of working at uncongenial tasks has been modified or even banished by the pursuit of a handicraft, either as an absorbing hobby or as a vocation.

Part IV

VALUES OF HANDICRAFTS

CHAPTER 20

HANDICRAFTS IN THERAPY

A STUDY of contemporary handicrafts in any area of the United States could not overlook their increasing importance in the field of therapy. Within about thirty years a new profession has come of age in our country, the profession of occupational therapy, which is grounded in the scientific correlation of hand and mind for curative purposes in physical and mental illness. It is fully accredited by and operating under the auspices of the American Medical Association.

This new profession has had its main development in the United States, and New England was a pioneer in experiments to prove the curative value of handicrafts long before the principles of occupational therapy had gained general recognition. The oldest of all the schools of occupational therapy now operating in our country was established in Boston, and today every New England state is making some contribution to the use of handicrafts in the field of both curative and prophylactic medicine. No area of the United States is finding more ways to build bridges over which the patient may cross from his place of treatment in hospital or sanitarium to the community which is to be his permanent home.

THE FUNCTION OF OCCUPATIONAL THERAPY

In foregoing chapters reference has been made frequently to the therapeutic value of handicrafts along with their other values, which it has been the main purpose of this book to bring out. If the occupational therapist is continuously conscious of these several values, she will be able to understand more fully the satisfaction and the inspiration which may come to her patient through the development of a skill and in the making of some favorite object with his hands. It is the function of the prescribing physician to discover the need of the patient for some activity or handicraft which may be beneficial to his patient, but it is the responsibility of the occupational therapist often to discover, or to help the physician or the patient discover, the type of handicraft, the kind of design, the colors, and the compelling motive which give the patient the largest measure of satisfaction in his handwork and which often result in benefits far beyond the exercise of a muscle or the mental activity induced.

The occupational therapist who does most for her patient and for the doctor follows scrupulously the direction of the physician, but has ever in mind the relation of the treatment to the whole life and interest of the patient. Therefore the better the therapist knows the all-round values or benefits that may come from handicraft activities, the more she can contribute to her patient's early recovery and, as often happens, to the establishment of a new and vital life interest for him.

It should not, of course, be understood that handicrafts are cures for all difficulties. In many cases they are very important, sometimes indispensable; in others they may only contribute to the physical and mental health goal. But the tremendous advance of the use of handicrafts in civic and military hospitals, in homes and other areas in recent years, and their recorded results are the strongest evidence of the permanent place which this form of correlation of hand and mind has attained in both preventive and curative medicine.

No one has spoken more clearly and convincingly on the use of handicrafts in therapy than Everett S. Elwood, formerly president of the American Occupational Therapy Association, who has said:

Occupational therapy is any activity, mental or physical, prescribed by a physician for its remedial value. It is recognized by the medical profession as one of the most valuable adjuncts of medicine in the treatment of many types of illness and of many types of injury.

The objects sought by this form of treatment are to arouse interest, courage, and confidence; to exercise mind and body by healthy activity to overcome disability; and to re-establish capacity for industrial and social usefulness.

Physically, its function is to increase muscle strength and joint motion as well as to improve general bodily health.

Mentally, its function is to supply as nearly as possible normal activity through avocational projects, and prevocational studies and training.

Spiritually, its function is to restore confidence in self, hope of future accomplishment, and to rekindle the fires of ambition and courage.

The patient who is injured in body or mind or broken in spirit may be restored to full strength and capacity for successful accomplishment through occupational therapy by the use of some or many of the varied forms of arts and crafts.

Hundreds of cases have cleared through our civic hospitals and sanitariums; but even more numerous, for a given period of time, are the cases of men and women in our military hospitals who have found in the correlation of hand and mind, in the shaping of useful and beautiful things, deep satisfaction and their way back toward normal life. Often the acquirement of a new skill has opened windows of wonder and beauty and fascination hitherto unknown.

In contemplating this form of treatment one of the most important considerations is the fact that the practice of hand skills leads so often to an increased love of beauty in the arts of man, as well as in the world of nature, and the influence of beauty has always been a vital factor in the lives of people whether civilized or savage. Dr. Alexis Carrel in his remarkable book, *Man, the Unknown,* says:

Esthetic sense exists in the most primitive human beings as in the most civilized. It even survives the disappearance of intelligence. . . . The creation of forms, or of series of sounds, capable of awakening an esthetic emotion, is an elementary need of our nature. . . . Esthetic activity manifests itself in both the creation and the contemplation of beauty.

EARLY DEVELOPMENTS

The first clear call to those who were to help in forming the new profession of occupational therapy came toward the end of World War I in 1917 when General John J. Pershing, Commander of the Armies of the United States, cabled from France to Washington requesting several hundred young women to serve in the overseas hospitals "to counteract idleness and build morale by giving instruction in crafts to wounded and otherwise incapacitated soldiers." General Gorgas, Surgeon General of the Army, upon receiving General Pershing's request consulted Colonel E. G. Brackett of Boston, who had been a friend of some of the pioneers in handicraft therapy in New England. Colonel Brackett suggested the following names as the basis for a committee to organize a program of training to meet General Pershing's need: Dr. Herbert J. Hall, Dr. E. E. Southard, Dr. Walter E. Fernald, Dr. William H. Smith, Dr. John D. Adams, and Arthur L. Williston; later the names of Mrs. Joel Goldthwaite, Miss Minnie Brackett, and Mrs. Horace Morrison were added. This committee set up a school in Boston "for training Reconstruction Aides in Occupational Therapy"; it became the Boston School of Occupational Therapy and the Committee its first board of Trustees. Miss Sarah M. Lake served as dean. Mrs. John A. Greene is the present director of the School.

The need at that time was so urgent that the Army advocated an eight weeks' course; the trustees of the School believed twelve weeks should be the minimum, and the Army agreed. The curriculum included training in the simple crafts and a few lectures on hospital service. The requirements for candidates was "a suitable personality, emotional stability, good health, and a minimum age of twenty-five. They were also expected to have a background in arts, crafts, or an allied field." One hundred and twenty-three young women finished the course and each served in either army or navy hospitals in the United States or abroad. Within twelve months peace came, and the School closed.

However, occupational therapy had proved its worth in the work done for soldiers, and an increasing demand for trained therapists in civilian hospitals caused the School to be reopened, with the same board of trustees, in the fall of 1919 to train therapists for civilian needs. Miss Lake was not able to return, and Mrs. Greene persuaded Miss Ruth Wigglesworth, later Mrs. Theodore T. Whitney, to join her in the executive directorship of the School. In 1921 the Boston School of Occupational Therapy was incorporated with Mrs. Greene as director, and plans were laid for a firm and permanent foundation. The Lloyd School (of handicrafts) offered to share its building at 7 Harcourt street with the Boston School and the latter accepted the invitation to move into what is its present home.

The story of how the School was kept going and a strong curriculum and training program developed would include mention of gifts from loyal supporters, low salaries accepted by teachers, rummage sales, benefits, drives, and, since 1928, the Boston Morning Musicals, which still bring the best source of income from benefits. Theoretical courses at the School became more advanced, the therapist was no longer exclusively concerned with what could be accomplished psychologically by craft work but had added functional treatments to her list of accomplishments. The course of study was lengthened to two years in 1928, and her tools were no longer crafts alone but any activity that might fulfill her patient's need.[1]

PRESENT USES OF OCCUPATIONAL THERAPY

Occupational therapy is now a thoroughly accredited and highly respected profession with many more demands for graduates than

[1] The information in this section as well as other information on early developments in occupational therapy was brought together by Ruth A. Robinson, president of the Alumnae Association of the Boston School of Occupational Therapy, for its twenty-fifth anniversary in 1943.

can be filled. A director of occupational therapy is now a member of the staff of the Surgeon General of the Army; approximately seven hundred hospitals in the United States are now staffed with occupational therapists; and since the beginning of World War II the number of schools of occupational therapy has increased from five to twenty-five.

Industry has already opened a new and what promises to be a large field for therapy service in connection with accident insurance and general rehabilitation. Here again a New England organization has taken the lead. The Liberty Mutual Rehabilitation Center in Boston was founded to assist the medical profession in restoring injured industrial workers to maximum usefulness. At this rehabilitation center the most modern facilities approved by the medical profession are in use. Physical, occupational, and recreational therapy "combined under medical direction and guided by trained therapists . . . is sending men and women injured in industrial accidents back to their jobs, their work capacity rebuilt and their ambition and spirit revived." This organization has provided excellent workshops where patients have a wide choice of work in handicrafts. Here is an experiment in rehabilitation which is opening a new door of service to the occupational therapist; it carries into the field of industrial rehabilitation an extensive use of handicrafts.

To the military and industrial factors which have strengthened the profession of occupational therapy, and have drawn upon the skills of doctors and nurses, must be added the work of the Arts and Skills Corps of the American National Red Cross, and the hundreds of volunteer craftsmen, who, during World War II, brought to our hospitals facilities such as these institutions had never known before. In all this service New England has made a fine and inspiring record.

A REMARKABLE ILLUSTRATION

The writer must omit because of space limitations the scores of instances with which he is familiar in New England where handicrafts have served the purposes so ably set forth by Everett Ellwood above; but he would share with the reader a single case, one of the most remarkable instances of handicrafts in therapy of which he knows.

Passing through the workshops of the Old Farms Convalescent Hospital at Avon, Connecticut, about the close of World War II, the writer's eye caught sight of some woodturning unusual in its pattern and very carefully executed. He asked if the craftsman who had done the work was around. "Sure," someone replied. "It's Jim, he is in the next room turning. You ought to know him."

In the next room Jim was absorbed in turning out a leg for a small table and around his lathe sighted men were watching with admiration and astonishment. Here a tall youth from the armed forces who had survived an explosion was doing what seemed impossible. He had been blinded by the blast and both his hands blown off, but he was turning wood with much skill and feeling.

A kind of harness had been attached to the stumps of his forearms, and hooks with pincer-like attachments had been supplied by which he could pick up, hold or drop his turning chisel. While turning he held his chisel with the hooks and the end of the wooden handle rested against his abdomen. In this way he felt the chisel against the revolving stock of wood and regulated the pressure of the cutting edge and the thickness of his shaving. To get the final form desired he stopped the lathe and felt the piece being turned with his lips or his nose.

Jim's story is too long for this space, but after months of wondering what he could do, a teacher told him that he thought he might learn to turn wood, and Jim, remembering seeing his uncle do it long ago, said, "Let me try." This led to other forms of woodworking and before he had left Avon he made several useful objects "with his hands" for the folks down home. The story is told here because towering above his remarkable physical achievement was the triumph of his spirit, and a matchless pride in the skill he had developed.

When the writer said, "Jim what you do is so wonderful that it will encourage every one who ever learns of it," his reply was, "You think it is wonderful, but only I know what it has done for me."

When asked if he would do a simple turning for the writer, Jim said he would gladly. Within a few days it came with a note saying, "I wanted to do your piece all myself, so I went to the pile of wood, picked out my stick, put it into the lathe, turned it, and no other hand has touched it." A recent letter from Jim tells of progress on the new house he is helping to build in the country of his home state, Louisiana.

CHAPTER 21

SUMMARY AND CONCLUSION

"Yea, the work of our hands establish thou it."

IN THE foregoing pages we have traced a little of man's progress in the work of his hands from primitive life to civilization as we know it today. We have seen him improve the forms and add the elements of decoration to the tools of his ascent. We have found that multitudes of objects thus evolved are treasured all over the world in public museums and private collections because of their fine craftsmanship, their attributes of beauty, and their service to the race.

Through these products of man's invention, skill, and artistry we are related proudly to the past, and, in a way, we share in the creative work which men are doing with their hands everywhere. But it is not the distant past with which we have been mainly concerned in this study; our chief emphasis has been on the character and achievements of contemporary craftsmen of one small area of our land, New England. Many of them are unknown outside their home communities yet they symbolize that unique power which has won for man the highest place as a manipulative animal—the power to shape and reshape his environment.

Our interest therefore lies not only in the things which man makes with his hands, but quite as much with what the making of these things means to him, and through him to society. Inquiry into these questions leads us, as citizens, to ask: Are there good reasons why we should favor handicraft production as a part of American economy and culture today; and if so, what are we doing and what can we do to contribute to the handicraft movement?

TWO TYPES OF HANDICRAFT

It has become clear in this book that a handicraft product is one in which the final form or character of the object is determined by the human hand. There are roughly two general divisions of handicrafts—

one, those made entirely by hand, including the preparation of all materials and sometimes even the shaping of the tools required; and two, those which in their early stages may be formed by machines but which are finished by the hand and given the unmistakable character of handwork. When Hiram Corliss, the New Hampshire basketmaker, used to go into the woods, study his black ash tree before he felled it, cut it into eight-foot lengths, and pound out the annual layers which he shaped into splints and wove into baskets, he gave an almost perfect example of the first-named class. After the tree had been felled and the log cut to length, the tools he used were homemade knives and a homemade hickory maul. The woodcarving by Edgar Keen, also of New Hampshire, of an altar for a church, bears the unmistakable stamp of creative craftsmanship, although the mahogany tree, felled by unknown workmen in a forest of South America and brought in the log to a North American mill where it was sawed into planks, was, up to the time that it came into the carver's hands, partly a product of machine processes. In both instances the hand, guided by the mind, produced in the end an object of handicraft.

CRITERIA FOR JUDGMENT

In New England and throughout our country methods of production have evolved in which the average object of utility is a very impersonal thing, to be judged almost entirely by its usefulness to or its acceptance by the consumer. How the object is produced is of little consequence to most of us. A more understanding way to judge a product would be to evaluate it first for itself, that is, how it conforms to the need and taste of the consumer, which is the usual way of judging, and then to inquire what the making of it has meant to the craftsman. The buying public has made only slight advance in this direction, and has far to go. But at least a minority today will not deliberately buy the product of a sweatshop. Such buyers consider it desirable to know, by union label or otherwise, that the purchase has not come into their hands by way of severe hazard or detriment to other human beings. But quite beyond this fundamental requirement of safety and well-being lies an area in which the worker may know relaxation and joy in his work. In this area handicrafts should be given much more consideration than they now have, for undoubtedly they possess creative and constructive values that are not generally recognized.

In many minds handicrafts suffer and the handicraft movement is impeded by an underestimation of the values intrinsic in handwork. There are also certain general prejudices against hand production;

to overcome these in a measure has been part of the motive prompting this book.

SOME MISCONCEPTIONS ABOUT HANDICRAFTS

One of the commonest of these misconceptions is the notion that handicrafts belong to the past, that to produce by hand is a step backward because the machine is now paramount and is leading us, through mass production, into an era of abundance in which everyone may have the essentials of life.

Almost all that we are is of the past, and there is nothing more tragic than the loss of what has once proved its value to the race. The present handicraft movement is bent on recapturing some of the priceless values of the past which modern civilization has almost taken from us. When a man can make an object of use or beauty or interest by hand which he could not possess otherwise, or when through the mastery of a skill which he may have thought was beyond him, he finds an outlet for his creative energies, possibly earning part of the money upon which the health or happiness of himself or his family depends, that cannot be counted a step backward. Such a man is having one of the most rewarding of experiences, and hundreds of such instances in New England have been noted in this book.

Furthermore, we are as yet far from having attained an economy of abundance; the most we can claim is that we have some of the elements that would make such an economy possible. To reach such an era of plenty gigantic production alone is not enough; distribution is essential, and the sustained purchasing power of the masses upon which distribution is based. For these the prospect is not very bright at this writing. Moreover few would contend that the amount of current or prospective handicraft production will ever interfere with the progress of the new order. Even if the era of abundance is ushered in, the personal need of recapturing values inherent in handicrafts will be as urgent as it is today.

Another argument sometimes made against handicrafts is that few persons are able to support themselves from handwork alone; therefore the handworker should go into industry or some field where he can make a full living. There are countless persons throughout the country who depend always upon more than one job to meet their living expenses. The chief economic claim for a handicraft is that it provides the supplementary income so often needed by persons who can earn a decent living only if they can find work in their own communities or can carry on even in their homes. We have several million families in that situation in normal times. Nobody would discourage small farming, gardening, or fishing because these activities may not yield a full livelihood; a handicraft often serves in just the same way. We shall have more to say presently on the economic value of handicrafts.

Finally, the too common objection is made that handicrafts are fads hardly worth the attention, much less the support, of government or public. State programs to encourage handicraft production have been referred to in other chapters; they furnish the best answer to this prejudice.

POSITIVE VALUES IN HANDICRAFTS

The arguments for handicrafts as a vital part of our economy and culture appear even more forceful when we think of the positive values involved. The pursuit of a handicraft is so largely an individual experience that the satisfactions derived from it vary with every craftsman. Yet there are certain returns, or values, that run through all forms of work where hand and mind are coordinated in the shaping of objects. We have found that the direct satisfactions may include social, educational, recreational, therapeutic, aesthetic, and ethical values. The indirect value is the economic return.

Indirect or Economic Value

Living as craftsmen do in the midst of a capitalistic society, it is the economic value more than any other upon which the modern handicraft movement depends. It is the ways in which handicrafts help people to make a living that encourage most persons to work at them and induce legislators to vote money for their support. Earnings from handicrafts we have called the "indirect value" because they, rather than the objects made, are the means of satisfying needs. It has already been said that the economic value need not deprive the worker of any of the other values. Indeed, they are often all combined in the work of a single craftsman.

The full economic or money value of handicrafts produced in the United States each year can only be approximately stated. We know that it runs into thousands of dollars, but few figures are recorded. Records are not available of the quantity or the value of things which people make for their own and their family's use, although one of the largest segments of handicraft production falls into this category. We can, however, frequently observe the things that people make for themselves which they could not have purchased, and also note how they spend the income from handicraft sales. Also to be noted, for rural people especially, is that they can barter their products.

The uses made of earnings from handicrafts tell the story of their economic significance. We have found instances of their expenditure for such things as more and better food; medical and dental services and the "new" teeth that old people have needed for years; eyeglasses; shoes and clothes "good enough for the kids to wear to school and to church"; a fishing boat, a washing machine, a new roof or a second-hand car; books for home reading; a high-school or college education; wallpaper to brighten up an old room; paying off the mortgage, or an installment on a new place; weaving lessons; a pair of Angora rabbits; in short, for any or all the things that people of small income need and long for in order to improve their social and living conditions. If the economic returns from handicrafts represented their only value, they would fully justify themselves.

2. Direct or Intrinsic Values

Among the satisfactions to the worker in handicrafts which are called the direct, intrinsic, or subjective values, the following are conspicuous.

a *Social Value.* The social value derives from the learning of a skill or the making or marketing of an object which extends the social horizon of a craftsman through congenial contacts with others. Teaching and learning are usually processes with a high social content. Often it promotes still further communication through conversation or correspondence. Villages and small towns frequently feel a community pride in a good local carpenter or other skilled workmen. "There's no man in the state who could make you a better bobsled," someone will say, or "She can knit anything, and even spin the yarn for it." The craftsman comes to know the high regard in which he is held; he has an added sense of security because of his acknowledged proficiency in a certain type of work. There is a social gain of real importance to the one whose abilities evoke it, and incidentally to those who in any way participate in it. As we advance toward a better civilization, society will put a higher value on those things which help its members to experience the satisfaction of being prized in family and community.

In rural settings where cultural opportunities are comparatively few and where openings for personal achievement are often limited, a handicraft may partly compensate for some opportunity missed. A quiltmaker whose work was the pride of her neighbors said, "Quilts kind of filled in for the disappointment of not going to school to learn to be an artist."

Educational Value. Handicrafts have a basic educational value to the one who makes them for the reason stated so adequately by former President Eliot of Harvard who said in his book, *Education for Efficiency,* "Accurate work with carpenter's tools, or lathe, or hammer and anvil, or violin, or piano, or pencil, or crayon, or camel's-hair brush, trains well the same nerves and ganglia with which we do what is ordinarily called thinking." When young people have been able to earn their way through high school or college by practicing a handicraft, their progress educationally may be due as much to gains made in learning by doing as to the mental discipline of academic study. Throughout the United States are thousands of persons making models by hand, faithfully reproducing in miniature stationary engines, locomotives, ships, or planes driven by power of various kinds. No one understands better than do these learners-by-doing the advances that have come to our modern world through the application of natural forces and of mechanical principles to industry and transportation.

In addition to learning by doing, there is a special place for handicrafts in adult education because of the invitation to explore which the use of tools, materials, and processes extends to the inquiring mind. An example is a little group of mountain women in North Carolina who began to study the crafts of spinning and weaving which they were following as a means of increasing their meager earnings. They soon made excursions into the fields of geography, history, sociology, science, and art in their quest for facts and lore concerning these ancient home arts, and in so doing found interests which lifted their daily work to a high and important plane. As one of the women observed, "It appears like if you knew all there is to know about spinning and weaving you would know about all there is to know about everything." By inquiry they had become conscious of that perhaps most needed of all qualities in education, the sense of relatedness.

Recreational Value. The recreational value of handicrafts is universally recognized and would be eloquently stressed if a single clear voice could speak for the thousands of craftsmen throughout the United States who make things "just for the fun of it."

While the recreational value in the achievements of craftsmen is always high, it rarely is the prime value for New England craftsmen. It must, however, have played its part when Mrs. Leon Grant of Chelsea, Vermont, recorded in her patchwork quilt the scenes and events of the past fifty years which have interested her most in her neighborhood; or when Clifford W. Ashley, painter and writer of Dartmouth, Massachusetts, learned to tie hundreds of sailor and cowboy knots, many of which his children have learned from him. And the writer has received from the same town a printed and signed pass good for one year on any train, passenger or freight, of the elaborate miniature Padanaram Seaboard Railroad which Charles P. Golding, a lieutenant commander in the Navy, has built in the basement of his home. Women of the Maine Seacoast Missionary Society recorded many of the plants and flowers and animals of the islands along the coast in the designs of their hooked rugs "for the great pleasure of it."

Aesthetic Value. The aesthetic sense, that is, the sense of beauty, as Dr. Alexis Carrel has pointed out so persuasively in his book, *Man, the Unknown,* exists in the most primitive human being as in the most civilized. It evokes a subjective experience, whether measured in terms of the creation or the contemplation of beauty; and one of the high compensations which comes to him who shapes materials into objects of use and beauty with his hands is his participation in the double experience of creating and enjoying. As Dr. Carrel says, "Beauty is an inexhaustible source of happiness for those who discover its abode."

Beauty sometimes has its abode in places overlooked by most of us. The fine toolmaker, for instance, whose work is concerned with the delicate parts of a precision instrument may find in his metal spinning or turning and hand shaping something of the aesthetic satisfaction that an artist finds in painting or in sculpture. No one can shape any material into useful form without experiencing some degree of aesthetic feeling, and he who persists in trying to make things better than they need be for utility alone is in the true sense an artist. What he does may not appeal especially to me, but that is not the main consideration; I may have no familiarity with his subject or interest in it, but the man himself who works the material, changing its shape and its appearance until it conforms to his idea of what it should be, is having a true aesthetic experience. For such experience every handicraft affords some opportunity because form and color and texture, which are basic elements in the enjoyment of beauty, are always present in anything the handworker produces.

Perhaps the joyful quality which is part of the aesthetic experience, and a gift to all creative craftsmen, has never been more charmingly expressed than by Aunt Sal Creech of Pine Mountain, Kentucky, weaver of coverlets, whom the writer quotes in his *Handicrafts of the Southern Highlands.* "Weaving, hit's the purtiest work I ever done. It's settin' and trompin' the treadles and watchin' the blossoms come out and smile at ye in the kiverlet."

Therapeutic Value. Of the therapeutic value of handicrafts we have proof in the recent activities of Army and Navy hospitals which mark the greatest use thus far of the curative principle of occupational therapy. In Chapter 20 this value of handicrafts has been briefly considered; throughout the book many instances have been recorded.

Ethical Value. Finally there is the ethical value of honest purposeful work of which too much can never be said. This was understood and eloquently expressed by Uncle William Creech, Aunt Sal's husband, who deeded his land to Pine Mountain Settlement School, to be so used "as long as the Constitution of the United States stands." Uncle William said, "Hit's better for folkses characters to larn 'em to do things with their hands." Many other educators agree with this Kentucky pioneer and have spoken convincingly of the relation of careful, painstaking work with the hands to moral development. As one old New England craftsman said, after trying out work in several factories and settling down at last to his silversmithing, "I feel like a different man now—like I have religion."

When a craftsman finds himself at home and at peace in his own shop with his own tools, working upon a desired object from its inception to its final form and doing it as well as he is able, his work has a truly ethical value, and there is a permanent quality to the ethic when the result is a completed object carefully shaped by hand for human service. What is often called pride in craftsmanship is one way of expressing a sense of responsibility for work well done; it is an expression of integrity; hence a worthy piece of furniture or a finely made dress may be a symbol of sound ethical qualities in the craftsman. In *Our Present Discontents* William Ralph Inge spoke truly in saying, "Nobody is bored when he is trying to make something that is beautiful, or to discover something that is true."

Blended Values or Compensations. There are areas where all these values blend and where it serves no purpose to distinguish among them. When a handicraft restores to the workman his tools of production, the economic value of the restoration may be no greater than the social or possibly the ethical value. One of the evils of factory production is that it takes the tools and materials from the worker and determines for him what he shall make, when, and how. Even when factories are running full blast the workers' participation in the choice of the processes of production is slight, and when mills are shut down or move away, which has happened often in New England, the worker may be left without personal resources or opportunity for achievement.

For many persons the lack of conscious participation in constructive work, entirely apart from the loss of wages, is an intolerable deprivation. One is reminded of the mountain boy who left a good factory job on the production line and went back to his modest shop in the Southern Highlands because he felt he must work where, as he put it, "I can see what I'm a-doing." Many New Englanders have felt this urge and have established small enterprises where they are able to achieve results, each in a field of his own choice and often following out some special aptitude. To express oneself through an aptitude is at least a high privilege, sometimes a spiritual necessity. And just as we say someone has a green thumb for gardening, so others have a special flair for working with certain materials or by certain processes and shaping some object for the use of man.

Extensive equipment for handicrafts is often unnecessary, for given the hand, the essential tool, and the material, the created object will emerge. Someone suggested to an amateur woodcarver, whose facilities for work consisted of a pocketknife, a piece of sandpaper, and a kitchen table, that power tools would greatly increase his output. "Yes," said the carver, "I would get out more work, but," earnestly patting his old knife, "here is the pleasure."

Some craftsmen feel with special poignancy the sense of relatedness which we have spoken of as so important a factor in education. Gretchen Warren in *Art, Nature, Education* has recently stressed the significance of such a connective of thought relating "near to distant, distant to near, principles to actions, visible to invisible, matter to spirit, and there is no part of human life but should be commanded by it."

The craftsman feels this relatedness through his work, his tools, and his materials. These things tie him to the earliest efforts of man to shape useful things. The tools he uses and the ways in which the craftsman works today are in direct line with the earliest artifacts found on the continents of Asia, Africa, Europe, and the Americas: until a very recent yesterday, all objects of use and beauty were made by hand. And just as the sense of relationship reaches back into past ages of time, so it cuts across the world of today to other countries, especially to those such as India and China which still maintain predominantly handicraft cultures, and creates bonds of understanding and sympathy.

Through the materials he uses, the craftsman finds himself related in a more intimate sense than does the machine worker to the vast and precious storehouse of nature. He comes to "feel" his material, for he must know its qualities; if it be wood his mental reach extends back into the forest whence his tree came and to a knowledge of other trees and plants and perhaps to a consciousness of the endless avenues connecting him with the world of nature. All this does not confuse him, it soothes him, for he is able to identify himself with nature's multiplicity; it is separation from the sources of life that breeds confusion.

The craftsman, more than the average man, is likely to appreciate the comforts that surround him if he sees them as having slowly evolved from earlier simpler forms arrived at by skills practiced sometimes near, sometimes far, in time and space. There is no better way to understand the house one lives in than to learn to cut a stone, rive a board, strike holes in a slate shingle, mix a batch of mortar, and spread it evenly on top of a layer of bricks which one has learned to make. The hand spinner and weaver will get more satisfaction out of mill-made cloth because he knows the processes, and the maker of hooked rugs will feel a thrill of excitement when he discovers that much the same technique was used by the Copts in the first centuries of the Christian era, and that examples of early hooking are among the great textile treasures of our art museums.

Not the least of the satisfactions to the craftsman, indeed, it is often the greatest of all, is the way in which his work relates him to the arts and through the arts to life itself. William Morris' definition of art as the expression of man's joy in his work admits with hospitality all the handicrafts. Life is dignified whenever anything is done well, and as the work of the well-doers in the various handicrafts comes to be accepted into the magic circle of the arts, a distinct advance is made in democratic culture because such an acceptance gives countless workers a chance to participate; if democracy means one thing more than another, it means participation.

There are hundreds of persons who find creative expression in handicrafts to one who finds it in painting, sculpture, or architecture in the fine arts sense. We must not draw lines separating and dividing artists into classes according to the kind of things they make. It is not the thing which is done that makes an object of art; it is the way in which it is done. It may be a painting on canvas, a sculpture in bronze, or a cathedral in stone; but it may also be a printed book, a beautifully handwritten letter, a tiny angel carved out of pine for a homemade crèche, or a sitting room in a fisherman's cottage with a hand-braided rug on the floor, a fire on the hearth, and a geranium in the window.

Handicrafts, more than any other branch of artistic expression, are helping to bring to the people of New England the enjoyment of creating and contemplating beautiful things. Emerson's voice is heard again as he says, "Beauty must come back to the useful arts and the distinction between the fine and the useful arts be forgotten." It was the American painter, Robert Henri, who in *The Art Spirit*, expressed

POTTERY IN NATIVE GLAZES AND ENAMELING

Rowantrees Pottery, a Village Industry of Blue Hill, Maine, Made These Glazes from Minerals Native to the Community. . . . The Enamel Plate, with Snowflake Motifs, Was Designed and Made by Karl Drerup, a Member of the New Hampshire League.

so perfectly the democracy of the arts when he said, "Art when really understood is the province of every human being. . . . He does not have to be a painter or a sculptor to be an artist. He can work in any medium. He simply has to find the gain in the work itself, not outside of it." Increasing numbers in New England are finding that "gain" in handicrafts.

Henri's definition of art

Values to the User

Not the least important social dividend of things made by hand is their meaning to the user. The handicraft movement has brought within the reach of hundreds of thousands of people a great variety of articles of interest, beauty, and worth which would never otherwise have been available, and persons are now building up small collections of our native handicrafts who never before thought of themselves as interested in the arts. For their owners these objects, most of them inexpensive, often open the door to a permanent concern for the other arts of America. When one includes within one's concept of the arts the things of everyday life, the choice things, one becomes more sensitive to beauty wherever found; the old things take on new meaning, antiques come to have special interest and charm, for most of them were handmade; and a natural next step is an appreciation of the folk arts and the artifacts of other peoples. From a love of these one finds oneself the inheritor of all the arts of all time.

The small stream of hand products representative of places and people in different parts of our country, especially of rural America, is constantly increasing and improving. Much inventiveness, much searching for suitable design, and real devotion of good craftsmanship have gone into the whittling, pottery, weaving, baskets, needlework, hand-printed textiles, and other handicrafts that are being made and distributed throughout the United States.

These objects are far more important to the people who own and use them than we often realize. They are not just things, impersonal possessions with no meaning to the owner save the utilitarian ends they serve; they are symbols of the people who made them, and places they came from, the homes and communities which they reflect. A carving of a farm animal from the John C. Campbell Folk School in North Carolina is a symbol of a place where farm and school are one, where art and nature meet, where teaching and learning are intertwined, and where "I sing behind the plow" expresses the philosophy that runs through life and work in that community. A piece of pottery or of fine needlework or a snow crystal pin in silver purchased at a Craftsman's Fair in New Hampshire is not only a souvenir of a time and a place but a symbol of the cooperative spirit in that state.

Such symbols, whether they originate in New England, in the Southern Highlands, on the Great Plains, in the Pacific Coast states, or in other fascinating regions of our country, reflect folkways, bring city and country dwellers into closer touch, and interpret the people of different areas to one another. In *The Condition of Man* Lewis Mumford calls "the ability to create symbols and to respond to symbols . . . an essential difference between the world of brutes and the world of men."

Our people are now earnestly concerned with the contribution of handicrafts to both local and national culture. We are coming to realize that culture is not only what a people's leaders think and say and do, but what people in general think and say and do. To believe that everyone in our democracy counts and to encourage each to make his best contribution is to give special significance to handicrafts because here is by far the largest field of artistic expression in the visual arts, and here countless persons throughout America, hitherto unknown, are making modest, skillful, original, and often beautiful things which reflect their mental world and the elements of their environment.

The United States has boundless handicraft potentialities through its geographical situation, its unlimited natural resources, its diversity of climate—which gives us a vast range of flora and fauna—its natural scenery, unsurpassed for variety and grandeur, and above all its people, who bring to America the skills and traditions of nearly every homeland in the world.

Our native arts and crafts begin with the American Indian whose record in combining utility with beauty is one of the finest in human history. Over 10 per cent of our population are Negroes whose hand skills, too generally unrecognized, may yet be encouraged into a unique contribution possibly comparable to their great gift in music. Other elements in our population stem directly or indirectly from some Old World homeland. We are just beginning to know that in our small number of citizens and resident aliens from Asia are some of the most skillful and artistic craftsmen to be found in our country. All this wealth is ours for the caring. Let us cherish our people and their gifts. Let us welcome every form of art that will add to our store of beauty, for through beauty comes happiness and better understanding, not only for each of us and among ourselves, but between our own and other peoples—perhaps the greatest need and surely the highest privilege ahead of us today.

May we of the West accept the philosophy of the East which holds that "the artist is not a special kind of man, but every man is a special kind of artist." And just as we would encourage every man to make his contribution to the good and to the true, so we would have him make it to the beautiful as we press forward toward a civilization in which, as Morris Gray once said, "those who bring beauty to the heart of man shall yet stand the peer of those who bring knowledge to the mind."

INDEX

Abbe Museum, 62, 63
Abbott, Mr. and Mrs. Charles E., 51, 156
Abbott, Holker, 282
Abbott, Dr. Phyllis, 270
Abbott, Mrs. Sherman, 123
Abnákee Rugs (Albee), 119
Adams, Frank, 183
Adams, Dr. John D., 333
Adams, Marion, 237
Addison, Mrs. D. D., 282
Addison Gallery of American Art, 110, 253, 254
Adrian, Michael, 226
Agriculture, among the Indians, 5f. *See also* United States Department of Agriculture
Akers, Vivian, 245f
Albee, Helen R., 119
Alden, John, 7, 8, 162
Alden, Katharine, 162, 293
Alden, Priscilla, 162
Aldrich, William T., 284, 293
Alfred University, 324
Ali Baba, 222
Alice in Wonderland: wooden cutouts, 207; puppets, 217
Allanstand Cottage Industries, Asheville, N. C., 322
Allen, Frank L., 293
Allen, Ruby G., 140
Allen, Sam, 178
Altman, B. & Co., 120
Aluminum, work of craftsmen in, 241, 270
Amberger, Fritz L., 140f
America House, 213, 324
American Angora Wool Spinning Assn., 67
American Assn. for State and Local History, 318
American Craftsmen's Cooperative Council, Inc., 308, 324
American Craftsmen's Educational Council, 324
American Federation of Arts, 16, 17, 87, 290, 291, 323

American Fern Journal, The, 229, 231
American Forests, 229
American Institute of Architects, 164
American Institute of Graphic Arts, 149
American Magazine of Art, 239
American Medical Assn., 331
American Needlework (Harbeson), 110, 191
American National Red Cross, 71, 103, 104; Arts and Skills Corps of, 20, 335
American Revolution, 10, 322
Ames, Azel, 7n
Ames, Henrietta H., 122, 202
Ames, John S., 284
Anderson, Mrs. C. E., 128, 147
Anderson, Clifford G., 29
Anderson, Henry, 29
Anderson, Mrs. Ned K., 243
Andrews, Edward Deming, 57
Andrews, Faith, 57
Andrews, Robert D., 282
Angora rabbits: for fur and yarn, 73ff, 89, 105; blending other furs with that of, 75; spinning wool from, 76f; dye applied to fur of, 136. *See also* Rabbits
Animal Rescue League of Boston, 226, 227
Animals, domestic: role of, 5; as supplying fibers for spinning, 72f. *See also* Rabbits; Sheep
Animals for You to Make (Martin), 207
Anne, The, 9
Antiques, 236
Archery equipment, 29, 261f
Architectural Club, Boston, 281
Architecture: of the homes of the Pilgrim Fathers, 7; origin of New England, 9f; influence of New England, 19
Argonaut, The, 252
Arms, Katherine F., 145
Armstrong, Margaret, 88f
Aroostook Museum, 28
Arsenault, Norman E., 165

351

This Book

BEING OF NEW ENGLAND, IT SEEMED
fitting to use in its making as many creative and material elements
of the region as was practical. Therefore the types used in the printing were by New England designers: The text pages were set in
Caledonia type designed by W. A. Dwiggins of Hingham, Massachusetts; the chapter headings, in Fairfield by Rudolph Ruzicka of
Concord, Massachusetts; the title page is set in Centaur designed
by Bruce Rogers of Danbury, Connecticut; the dedication page was
composed by William Dana Orcutt of Boston in his Laurentian
type; and the page of quotations set by George F. Trenholm, of
Boston, in Cornell type designed by him.

The photographs of craftsmen at work & most of the objects,
were taken by New England photographers, the largest number, by
Doris Day of Connecticut, and George French of Maine; the illustrations were made and printed in offset, by Murray Printing Co.,
Wakefield, Massachusetts; the paper used throughout the volume is
Warren's Olde Style, manufactured by S. D. Warren Co., of Boston;
and the book is bound in a cloth made by Interlaken Mills at Fisk-
ville, Rhode Island.

This Colophon was designed by W. A. Dwiggins. It is set in his
Electra type and headed with his calligraphy.

Set in Linotype Caledonia
Format by A. W. Rushmore
Manufactured by The Haddon Craftsmen
Published by HARPER & BROTHERS, *New York*

5325

Eaton, Allen Hendershott, 1878-.

Handicrafts of New England.